**THE OFFICIAL BLUE BOOK®**

HANDBOOK OF

# UNITED STATES COINS

## R.S. YEOMAN

EDITOR

## KENNETH BRESSETT

69th Edition
2012
Illustrated Catalog and Prices Dealers
Pay for Coins—1616 to Date

Containing Mint records and wholesale prices for U.S. coins from 1616 to the present time, including colonials, regular issues, commemoratives, territorials, gold, bullion coins, Proof sets, and Mint sets. Information on collecting coins—how coins are produced—mints and mintmarks—grading of coins—location of mintmarks—preserving coins—starting a collection—history of mints—and interesting descriptions of all U.S. copper, nickel, silver, and gold coins. Illustrated.

Handbook of United States Coins™
THE OFFICIAL BLUE BOOK OF UNITED STATES COINS™

THE OFFICIAL BLUE BOOK and OFFICIAL BLUE BOOK OF UNITED
STATES COINS are trademarks of Whitman Publishing, LLC.

WCG™ • OCG™

# Whitman
## Publishing, LLC
PUBLISHING SINCE 1934

www.whitman**books**.com

Printed in the United States of America.

The WCG™ pricing grid used throughout this publication is patent pending.

© 2011 Whitman Publishing, LLC
3101 Clairmont Road • Suite G • Atlanta GA 30329

OCG™ Collecting Guide                                    Whitman®

Whitman Publishing, LLC, does not deal in coins; the values shown here are not offers to sell or buy but are included only as general information. Descriptions of coins are based on the most accurate data available, but could contain beliefs that may change with further research or discoveries. Correspondence regarding this book may be sent to the publisher at the address above.

Scan the QR code at left or visit us at
www.whitman**books**.com for a complete
listing of numismatic reference books,
supplies, and storage products.

# INTRODUCTION

# PRE-FEDERAL ISSUES

# FEDERAL ISSUES

# BULLION

# OTHER ISSUES

# APPENDICES

# INDEX

# CONTRIBUTORS TO THE SIXTY-NINTH EDITION

*Editor: Kenneth Bressett. Special Consultants: Philip Bressett and Jeff Garrett.*
Whitman Publishing extends its thanks to these members of the coin-buying community who have contributed pricing for this year's *Handbook of United States Coins.* Their data were compiled and then reviewed by editor Kenneth Bressett and consultants Phil Bressett and Jeff Garrett. This process ensures input from a broad range of dealers and auctioneers from across the country—experts who buy, sell, and trade coins every day and know the market inside and out.

| | | | |
|---|---|---|---|
| Mark Albarian | Dennis M. Gillio | Steve Ivy | Joel Rettew Jr. |
| Jeff Ambio | Ira M. Goldberg | Donald H. Kagin | Greg Rohan |
| J.H. Cline | Lawrence Goldberg | Bradley S. Karoleff | Maurice Rosen |
| Gary Cohen | J.R. Grellman | Julian M. Leidman | Gerald R. Scherer Jr. |
| Stephen M. Cohen | Steven Hayden | Denis W. Loring | David M. Sundman |
| Sheridan Downey | Gene L. Henry | Robert T. McIntire | Troy Thoreson |
| Chuck Furjanic | John W. Highfill | Michael C. Moline | Ben Todd |
| Jeff Garrett | Jesse Iskowitz | Mike Orlando | Mark S. Yaffe |

**Special credit is due to the following for service in past editions of the Handbook:**

| | | | |
|---|---|---|---|
| Gary Adkins | Tom DeLorey | Kevin Lipton | Leonard R. Saunders |
| David Akers | Silvano DiGenova | Andy Lustig | Mary Sauvain |
| John Albanese | Kenneth Duncan | Dwight N. Manley | Gerald Scherer Jr. |
| Mark Albarian | Steven Ellsworth | David McCarthy | Cherie Schoeps |
| Buddy Alleva | John Feigenbaum | Chris McCawley | Richard Schwary |
| Richard S. Appel | Mike Fuljenz | Harry Miller | James A. Simek |
| Michael Aron | Ronald Gillio | Lee S. Minshull | Craig Smith |
| Richard M. August | Kenneth M. Goldman | Robert Mish | Richard Snow |
| Richard A. Bagg | Ron Guth | Scott P. Mitchell | William J. Spencer |
| Mitchell A. Battino | James Halperin | Paul Montgomery | Lawrence R. Stack |
| Lee J. Bellisario | John Hamrick | Charles Moore | Anthony J. Swiatek |
| Jack Beymer | Ash Harrison | Richard Nachbar | Steve Tanenbaum |
| Mark R. Borckardt | Karl D. Hirtzinger | Chris Napolitano | Anthony Terranova |
| Q. David Bowers | James J. Jelinski | Paul Nugget | Jerry Treglia |
| H. Robert Campbell | A.M. Kagin | John M. Pack | Frank Van Valen |
| Elizabeth W. Coggan | Mike Kliman | William S. Panitch | Fred Weinberg |
| Alan R. Cohen | John J. Kraljevich Jr. | Robert M. Paul | Douglas Winter |
| Steve Contursi | Richard A. Lecce | William P. Paul | David Wnuck |
| Marc Crane | Robert Lecce | Joel Rettew Sr. | |
| Adam Crum | David Leventhal | Robert Rhue | |
| John Dannreuther | Stuart Levine | Tom Rinaldo | |

**Special photo credits are due to the following:**
Douglas F. Bird, Steve Contursi, Bill Fivaz, Ira & Larry Goldberg Coins & Collectibles, Tom Mulvaney, the Museum of the American Numismatic Association, Numismatic Guaranty Corporation of America (NGC), Brent Pogue, Sarasota Rare Coin Gallery, the Smithsonian Institution, Rick Snow, Spectrum, Stack's Bowers Galleries, Superior Galleries, Anthony Swiatek, and the United States Mint.

Since 1942, annually revised editions of the *Official Blue Book of United States Coins*™ have aided thousands of people who have coins to sell or are actively engaged in collecting United States coins. The popular coin-folder method of collecting by date has created ever-changing premium values, based on the supply and demand of each date and mint. Through its panel of contributors, the Blue Book has, over the years, reported these changing values. It also serves as a source of general numismatic information to all levels of interest in the hobby.

The values shown are representative prices paid by dealers for various United States coins. These are averages of prices assembled from many widely separated sources. On some issues slight differences in price among dealers may result from proximity to the various mints or heavily populated centers. Other factors, such as local supply and demand or dealers' stock conditions, may also cause deviations from the prices listed. While many coins bring no premium in circulated grades, they usually bring premium prices in Mint State and Proof. Extremely rare and valuable coins are usually sold at public auction, and prices vary according to current demand.

# *THIS BOOK LISTS PRICES MANY COIN DEALERS WILL PAY.*

*Premium prices are the average amount dealers will pay for coins (according to condition) if required for their stock. This book is not a retail price list.*

## IF YOU HAVE COINS TO SELL

Whitman Publishing, LLC, is not in the rare coin business; however, chances are that the dealer from whom you purchased this book is engaged in the buying and selling of rare coins—contact him first. In the event that you purchased this book from a source other than a numismatic establishment, consult your local telephone directory for the names of coin dealers (they will be found sometimes under the heading of "Stamp and Coin Dealers"). If you live in a city or town that does not have any coin dealers, obtain a copy of one of the trade publications (such as *Coin World* or *Numismatic News*) or check the Internet in order to obtain the names and addresses of many of the country's leading dealers. Information or sample copies may be obtained by writing to the individual publisher.

Current average *retail* valuations of all U.S. coins are listed in Whitman's *A Guide Book of United States Coins*™ by R.S. Yeoman, edited by Kenneth Bressett, Whitman Publishing, LLC, Atlanta, GA ($29.95 Large Print Edition; $19.95 spiralbound hardcover; $16.95 hardcover; $14.95 coilbound).

## HOW TO READ THE CHARTS

A dash in a price column indicates that coins in that grade exist even though there are no current sales or auction records from them. (The dash does *not* necessarily mean that such coins are excessively rare.) Italicized prices indicate unsettled or speculative values. A number of listings of rare coins do not have prices or dashes in certain grades. This indicates that they are not available or not believed to exist in those grades.

Mintages of Proof coins are listed in parentheses.

Italicized mintages are estimates.

*Numismatics* or coin collecting is one of the world's oldest hobbies, dating back several centuries. Coin collecting in America did not develop to any extent until about 1840, as our pioneer forefathers were too busy carving a country out of wilderness to afford the luxury of a hobby. The discontinuance of the large-sized cent in 1857 caused many people to attempt to accumulate a complete set of the pieces while they were still in circulation. One of the first groups of collectors to band together for the study of numismatics was the American Numismatic Society, founded in 1858 and still a dynamic part of the hobby. Lack of an economical method to house a collection held the number of devotees of coin collecting to a few thousand until Whitman Publishing and other manufacturers placed low-priced coin boards and folders on the market in the 1930s. Since that time, the number of Americans collecting coins has increased many-fold.

## THE PRODUCTION OF COINS

To collect coins intelligently it is necessary to have some knowledge of the manner in which they are produced. Coins are made in factories called "mints." The Mint of the United States was established at Philadelphia by a resolution of Congress dated April 2, 1792. The act also provided for the coinage of gold eagles ($10), half eagles, and quarter eagles; silver dollars, half dollars, quarter dollars, dimes (originally spelled "disme"), and half dismes or half dimes; and copper cents and half cents. The first coins struck were one-cent and half-cent pieces, in March of 1793 on a hand-operated press. Most numismatic authorities consider the half disme of 1792 the first United States coinage, quoting the words of George Washington as their authority. Washington, in his annual address, November 6, 1792, said, "There has been a small beginning in the coining of the half dimes, the want of small coins in circulation calling the first attention to them." Though the half disme is considered America's first coinage, it was not the first coinage produced by the Mint; these coins were produced off premises in July of 1792 before the mint was completed. In the new Philadelphia Mint are a number of implements from the original mint, and some coins discovered when the old building was wrecked. These coins included half dismes, and the placard identifying them states that Washington furnished the silver and gave the coined pieces to his friends as souvenirs.

Prior to the adoption of the Constitution, the Continental Congress arranged for the issuance of copper coins under private contract. These are known as the 1787 *Fugio cents* from their design, which shows a sundial and the Latin word "fugio"—"I Fly" or, in connection with the sundial, "Time Flies." The ever-appropriate motto "Mind Your Business" is also on the coin.

In the manufacture of a coin, the first step is die preparation. Dies for early federal coinage were prepared by hand; generally, letters and numbers were added with punches, while portraits and other designs were engraved into the die. Eventually, eagles, Liberty heads, and the like were also added with hubs and punches. After about 1836, many dies were made from masters, which contained all elements except the date and, if applicable, the mintmark. The addition of an element to a master die ensured its consistent placement throughout the life of the die. Today, many design tasks are performed with three-dimensional computer graphics. Mint artists are known as sculptor-engravers, and their work takes place mainly at the Philadelphia Mint. The dies are made of soft steel, which is hardened after the impression is received. The die is then dressed or finished to remove imperfections and make it suitable for coining. A typical die for production coinage can be used to strike hundreds of thousands of pieces. Dies for special issues such as Proofs are replaced more often.

The hand method of cutting dies accounts for the many die varieties of early United States coins. Where the amount of coinage of a given year was large enough to wear out many dies, each new die placed in the coining press created another die variety of that year. The dies being cut by hand, no two were exactly alike in every detail, even though some of the major elements such as the head or wreath, were sunk into the die by individual master punches. Of the cents dated 1794, more than sixty different die varieties have been discovered.

Thousands of dies are now used by the mints of the United States each year, but they are all made from one master die, which is produced in the following manner:

After the design is settled upon, the plaster of paris or wax model is prepared several times the actual size of the coin. When this model is finished an electrotype (an exact duplicate in metal) is made and prepared for the reducing lathe. The reducing lathe is a machine that works on the principle of the pantograph, only in this case the one point traces or follows the form of the model while another much smaller point in the form of a drill cuts away the steel and produces a reduced-size die of the model. The die is finished and details are sharpened or worked over by an engraver with chisel and graver. The master die is used to make duplicates in soft steel which are then hardened and ready for the coining press. To harden dies, they are placed in cast-iron boxes packed with carbon to exclude the air, and when heated to a bright red are cooled suddenly with water.

In the coinage operations the first step is to prepare the metal. Among the alloys that have been used are the following: silver coins, 90% silver and 10% copper; five-cent pieces, 75% copper and 25% nickel; one-cent pieces, 95% copper and 5% zinc. (The 1943 cent consists of steel coated with zinc; and the five-cent piece of 1942–1945 contains 35% silver, 56% copper, and 9% manganese.) Under the Coinage Act of 1965, the composition of dimes, quarters, and half dollars was changed to eliminate or reduce the silver content of these coins. The copper-nickel "clad" dimes, quarters, half dollars, and dollars are composed of an outer layer of copper-nickel (75% copper and 25% nickel) bonded to an inner core of pure copper. The silver clad half dollar and dollar have an outer layer of 80% silver bonded to an inner core of 21% silver, with a total content of 40% silver. Current cents are made from a core of 99.2% zinc, 0.8% copper, with a plating of pure copper. Dollars are composed of a pure copper core with outer layers of manganese-brass.

Alloys are melted in crucibles and poured into molds to form ingots. The ingots are in the form of thin bars and vary in size according to the denomination of the coin. The width is sufficient to allow three or more coins to be cut from the strips.

The ingots are next put through rolling mills to reduce the thickness to required limits. The strips are then fed into cutting presses which cut circular blanks of the approximate size of the finished coin. The blanks are run through annealing furnaces to soften them; next they move through tumbling barrels, rotating cylinders containing cleaning solutions which clean and burnish the metal; and finally into centrifugal drying machines.

The blanks are next fed into a milling machine which produces the raised or upset rim. The blank, now called a *planchet,* is now ready for the coining press.

The planchet is held firmly by a collar, as it is struck under heavy pressure varying from 40 tons for the one-cent pieces and dimes to 170 tons for silver dollars. Upper and lower dies impress the design on both sides of the coin. The pressure is sufficient to produce a raised surface level with that of the milled rim. The collar holding the blank for silver or clad coins is grooved. The pressure forces the metal into the grooves of the collar, producing the "reeding" on the edge of the finished coin.

## HOW A PROOF COIN IS MADE

Selected dies are inspected for perfection and are highly polished and cleaned. They are again wiped clean or polished after every 15 to 25 impressions and are replaced frequently to avoid imperfections from wear. Coinage blanks are polished and cleaned to assure high quality in striking. They are then hand fed into the coinage press one at a time, each blank receiving two blows from the dies to bring up sharp, high-relief details. The coinage operation is done at slow speed. Finished Proofs are individually inspected and are handled by gloves or tongs. They also receive a final inspection by packers before being sonically sealed in special plastic cases.

Certain coins, including Lincoln cents, Buffalo nickels, quarter eagles, half eagles, eagles, and double eagles, between the years 1908 and 1916, were made with Matte Proof (nickel and silver) and Sand Blast and Satin Proof (gold) finishes. These later Proofs have a dull frosted surface which was either applied to the dies, or produced by special treatment after striking.

## MINTS AND MINTMARKS

In addition to the Philadelphia Mint, the U.S. government has from time to time established branch mints in various parts of the country. At present, branch mints operate in Denver, West Point, and San Francisco. Starting in 1968, Proof sets and some of the regular coins were produced at the San Francisco Mint and Assay Office. The Denver Mint has operated since 1906. A mint was operated at New Orleans from 1838 to 1861 and again from 1879 to 1909. Mints were also in service at Carson City, Nevada, from 1870 to 1893; at Charlotte, North Carolina, from 1838 to 1861; at Dahlonega, Georgia, from 1838 to 1861; and at San Francisco since 1854. The U.S. government also operated a mint in the Philippines in the early 1900s.

Coins struck at Philadelphia before 1979 (except 1942 to 1945 five-cent pieces) do not bear a mintmark. Historically the mintmark was used only for branch mints. Recent exceptions include the Lincoln cent and the Kennedy half dollar, which both use the P for Philadelphia. All coins struck after 1967 have the mintmark on the obverse. The letters signifying the various mints are as follows:

C—Charlotte, North Carolina (gold coins only; 1838–1861)
CC—Carson City, Nevada (1870–1893)
D—Dahlonega, Georgia (gold coins only; 1838–1861)
D—Denver, Colorado (1906 to date)
O—New Orleans, Louisiana (1838–1861; 1879–1909)
P—Philadelphia, Pennsylvania (1793 to date; P not used in early years)
S—San Francisco, California (1854 to date)
W—West Point, New York (1984 to date)

The mintmark is of utmost importance to collectors because, historically, coinage of the branch mints has often been much smaller than quantities struck at Philadelphia. Many early coins of the branch mints are very scarce.

## DISTINGUISHING MARKS

The illustrations and explanations in this section will help the collector identify certain well-known varieties.

## Half Cents of 1795–1796 Showing Location of Pole to Cap

The end of the pole lies parallel with the lines of the bust, which is pointed. On some coins, the pole is missing due either to engraver error (while cutting the die) or to an error in "relapping" (when the die is ground to remove wear, clash marks, etc.).

**Pole to Cap**      **No Pole to Cap**

## Stemless Wreath Variety of Half Cents and Large Cents

For this variety, the difference is on the reverse side. Illustrations below show both Stemless and Stems to Wreath types for comparison—stemless wreath found on the 1804, 1805, and 1806 half cents; and on the 1797, 1802, and 1803 large cents.

**Stemless Wreath**      **Stems to Wreath**

## 1864 Bronze Indian Head Cent With "L" on Ribbon

A small "L," the initial of the designer James B. Longacre, was added to the Indian design late in 1864 and was continued through 1909. For coins in less than Fine condition, this small letter will often be worn away. The point of the bust is rounded on the 1864 variety without "L"; the bust is pointed on the

variety with "L." The initial must be visible, however, for the 1864 variety to bring the higher premium. If the coin is turned slightly so that the portrait faces the observer, the highlighted details will usually appear to better advantage.

## Designer Initials, Overstrikes, Die-Doublings, and Date Varieties

*During 1909, initials appeared on the reverse of the Lincoln cent.*
*Starting in 1918, they appear below the shoulder.*

*Prior to 1990, mintmarks for all mints were usually applied directly to working dies at Philadelphia in a hand-punching operation. Occasionally, a die was accidentally marked with one letter on top of another.*

Dies are produced by impressing the raised coin design of a hub into the end of a cylinder of steel. In early years the Mint made use of old dies by repunching the dates on their dies with new numbers. That practice was stopped prior to 1909. Since that time, all overdated coins have been the result of errors that occur when two different-dated hubs have been used in die preparation, and one is impressed over the other by accident.

**1938-D, D Over S**
**Buffalo Nickel**

**1918-S, 8 Over 7**
*A variety of the kind on this quarter dollar is rarely found in coinage of the 20th century.*

**1942, 2 Over 1**
**Mercury Dime**

**Large Date Cent**
**(1960)**

**Small Date Cent**
**(1960)**

**1955, Doubled-Die Obverse**
**Lincoln Cent**

**Large Date Cent**
**(1982)**

**Small Date Cent**
**(1982)**

## CONDITIONS OF COINS
*Essential Elements of the Official ANA Grading System*

**Proof**—A specially made coin distinguished by sharpness of detail and usually with a brilliant, mirrorlike surface. *Proof* refers to the method of manufacture and is not a condition, but normally the term implies nearly perfect condition unless otherwise noted.

**Gem Proof (PF-65)**—Brilliant surfaces with no noticeable blemishes or flaws. A few scattered, barely noticeable marks or hairlines.

**Choice Proof (PF-63)**—Reflective surfaces with only a few blemishes in secondary focal places. No major flaws.

**Proof (PF-60)**—Surface may have several contact marks, hairlines, or light rubs. Luster may be dull and eye appeal lacking.

**Mint State**—The terms *Mint State (MS)* and *Uncirculated (Unc.)* are used interchangeably to describe coins showing no trace of wear. Such coins may vary to some degree because of blemishes, toning, or slight imperfections, as described in the following subdivisions:

**Perfect Uncirculated (MS-70)**—Perfect new condition, showing no trace of wear. The finest quality possible, with no evidence of scratches, handling, or contact with other coins. Very few circulation-issue coins are ever found in this condition.

**Gem Uncirculated (MS-65)**—An above average Uncirculated coin that may be brilliant or lightly toned and that has very few contact marks on the surface or rim. MS-67 through MS-62 indicate slightly higher or lower grades of preservation.

**Choice Uncirculated (MS-63)**—Has some distracting contact marks or blemishes in prime focal areas. Luster may be impaired.

**Uncirculated (MS-60)**—Has no trace of wear but may show a number of contact marks, and surface may be spotted or lack some luster.

**Choice About Uncirculated (AU-55)**—Evidence of friction on high points of design. Most of the mint luster remains.

**About Uncirculated (AU-50)**—Traces of light wear on many of the high points. At least half of the mint luster is still present.

**Choice Extremely Fine (EF-45)**—Light overall wear on highest points. All design details are very sharp. Some of the mint luster is evident.

**Extremely Fine (EF-40)**—Light wear on design throughout, but all features sharp and well defined. Traces of luster may show.

**Choice Very Fine (VF-30)**—Light, even wear on the surface and highest parts of the design. All lettering and major features are sharp.

**Very Fine (VF-20)**—Moderate wear on high points of design. All major details are clear.

**Fine (F-12)**—Moderate to considerable even wear. Entire design is bold with overall pleasing appearance.

**Very Good (VG-8)**—Well worn with main features clear and bold, although rather flat.

**Good (G-4)**—Heavily worn, with design visible but faint in areas. Many details are flat.

**About Good (AG-3)**—Very heavily worn with portions of lettering, date, and legend worn smooth. The date may be barely readable.

*Important:* Damaged coins, such as those that are bent, corroded, scratched, holed, nicked, stained, or mutilated, are worth less than those without defects. Flawless Uncirculated coins are generally worth more than values quoted in this book. Slightly worn coins ("sliders") that have been cleaned and conditioned ("buffed") to simulate Uncirculated luster are worth considerably less than perfect pieces.

Unlike damage inflicted after striking, manufacturing defects do not always lessen values. Examples include colonial coins with planchet flaws and weakly struck designs; early silver and gold with weight-adjustment "file marks" (parallel cuts made prior to striking); and coins with "lint marks" (surface marks due to the presence of dust or other foreign matter during striking).

Brief guides to grading are placed before each major coin type. Grading standards are not scientific and often vary among collectors, dealers, and certification services. For more on grading, consult the *Official ANA Grading Standards for United States Coins*.

## PRESERVING AND CLEANING COINS

Most numismatists will tell you to "never clean a coin" and it is good advice! Cleaning coins almost always reduces their value. Collectors prefer coins in their original condition.

Some effort should be made to protect Uncirculated and Proof coins so they won't need cleaning. Tarnish on a coin is purely a chemical process caused by oxygen in the air acting on the metal, or by chemicals with which the coin comes in contact. One of the most common chemicals causing tarnish is sulphur; most paper, with the exception of specially manufactured "sulphur-free" kinds, contains sulphur due to the sulphuric acid that is used in paper manufacture; therefore do not wrap coins in ordinary paper. Also keep Uncirculated and Proof coins away from rubber bands (a rubber band placed on a silver coin for a few days will eventually produce a black stripe on the coin where the band touched). The utmost in protection is obtained by storing the coin in an airtight box, away from moisture and humidity, and by using holders made of inert materials.

Many coins become marred by careless handling. Always hold the coin by the edge. The accompanying illustration shows the right and wrong way to handle numismatic specimens. It is a breach of numismatic etiquette to handle another collector's coin except by the edge, even if it is not an Uncirculated or Proof piece.

**Right** **Wrong**

## STARTING A COLLECTION

One may start a collection of United States coins with very little expense by systematically assembling the various dates and mintmarks of all the types and denominations that are now in general circulation, using Whitman's many different coin folders and albums, especially those for quarters and dollars with various designs.

With the exception of the price paid for the coin folder, collecting coins received in everyday business transactions entails no expense whatsoever; a Jefferson nickel taken out of circulation, for example, can always be spent for five cents if the occasion arises. Filling an album or two with coins found in circulation is probably the best method of determining whether coin collecting appeals to you. Not everyone can be a successful coin collector. It requires patience, intelligence of a high order, and a certain desire to know the meaning behind a lot of things that at first glance appear meaningless. You may not be cut out to be a collector but you'll never know until you look further into the subject, and if by the time an album or two of coins are collected you have no burning desire to acquire many more different coins, you will probably never be a collector. However, chances are that you will be, because if you have read this far in this book, it shows that you are interested in the subject.

High quality is the goal of every endeavor and coin collecting is no exception. After an album has been filled with circulated specimens, the next step will be to replace them with coins in Uncirculated condition, or perhaps to start collecting an obsolete series; in either case, it will be necessary to purchase some coins from dealers or other collectors. The most logical way to keep abreast of the market, or obtain the addresses of the country's leading dealers, is to subscribe to one or more of the trade publications. These magazines carry advertisements of various dealers listing coins for sale. Moreover, through these sources the beginner may obtain price lists and catalogs from the dealers.

There are several good reference books available at reasonable prices which will be helpful to the collector who wishes to know more about U.S. coins and paper money. R.S. Yeoman's *A Guide Book of United States Coins*™ (the "Red Book") lists retail values of all regular U.S. coins and also lists all coins of the U.S. colonial period and private and territorial gold coins, plus tokens, pattern coins, errors, and other numismatic collectibles.

Most coin, book, and hobby dealers can supply the following titles:

*The Official Red Book®: A Guide Book of United States Coins*™—R.S. Yeoman, edited by Kenneth Bressett

*The Official Red Book®: A Guide Book of United States Coins*™, *Professional Edition*—R.S. Yeoman, edited by Kenneth Bressett

*A Guide Book of Morgan Silver Dollars*—Q. David Bowers

*The Expert's Guide to Collecting and Investing in Rare Coins*—Q. David Bowers

*Coin Collecting: A Beginner's Guide to the World of Coins*—Kenneth Bressett

*History of the United States Mint and Its Coinage*—David W. Lange

*The Official ANA Grading Standards for United States Coins*—Kenneth Bressett, et al.

*A Guide Book of United States Type Coins*—Q. David Bowers

## Join a Coin Club

Beginners should join a "coin club" if they live in a city which has one. Associating with more experienced collectors will be of great benefit. Practically all larger cities have one or more clubs and they are being rapidly organized in smaller towns. Trade publications carry information about coin clubs and events such as coin shows and conventions.

The American Numismatic Association is a national organization that collectors can join. The ANA web site (www.money.org) has a list of member coin clubs throughout the United States. Contact the ANA by mail at 818 North Cascade Avenue, Colorado Springs, CO 80903, or by phone at 800-367-9723.

*Early American coins are rare in conditions better than those listed and are consequently valued much higher.*

# BRITISH NEW WORLD ISSUES

## Sommer Islands (Bermuda)

This coinage, issued around 1616, was the first struck for England's colonies in the New World. The coins were known as "Hogge Money" or "Hoggies."

The pieces were made of copper lightly silvered, in four denominations: shilling, sixpence, threepence, and twopence, indicated by Roman numerals. The hog is the main device and appears on the obverse side of each. SOMMER ISLANDS is inscribed within beaded circles. The reverse shows a full-rigged galleon with the flag of St. George on each of four masts.

Shilling

| | AG | G | VG | F | VF | EF |
|---|---|---|---|---|---|---|
| Twopence | $2,000 | $3,000 | $4,500 | $6,500 | $15,000 | $30,000 |
| Threepence | | | 65,000 | | | |
| Sixpence | 1,750 | 2,750 | 4,000 | 6,500 | 15,000 | 30,000 |
| Shilling | 2,500 | 3,600 | 5,200 | 15,000 | 30,000 | 45,000 |

# Massachusetts

## *"New England" Coinage (1652)*

In 1652 the General Court of Massachusetts ordered the first metallic currency to be struck in the British Americas, the New England silver threepence, sixpence, and shilling. These coins were made from silver bullion procured principally from the West Indies. Joseph Jenks made the punches for the first coins at his Iron Works in Saugus, Massachusetts, close to Boston where the mint was located. John Hull was appointed mintmaster; his assistant was Robert Sanderson.

NE Shilling (1652)

| | G | VG | F | VF | EF |
|---|---|---|---|---|---|
| NE Threepence *(unique)* | | | — | | |
| NE Sixpence *(8 known)* | $20,000 | $40,000 | $50,000 | $125,000 | $150,000 |
| NE Shilling | 25,000 | 45,000 | 70,000 | 150,000 | 180,000 |

### *Willow Tree Coinage (1653–1660)*

The simplicity of the design on the N.E. coins invited counterfeiting and clipping of the edges. Therefore, they were soon replaced by the Willow Tree, Oak Tree, and Pine Tree series. The Willow Tree coins were struck from 1653 to 1660, the Oak Trees 1660 to 1667, and the Pine Trees 1667 to 1682. All of them (with the exception of the Oak Tree twopence) bore the date 1652. Many varieties of all of these coins exist. Values shown are for the most common types.

**Sixpence**

|  | Fair | G | VG | F | VF | EF |
|---|---|---|---|---|---|---|
| 1652 Willow Tree Threepence *(3 known)* .......... |  |  |  | — | — | — |
| 1652 Willow Tree Sixpence *(14 known)* ........... | $6,500 | $15,000 | $20,000 | $40,000 | $90,000 | $150,000 |
| 1652 Willow Tree Shilling ..................... | 8,000 | 17,000 | 25,000 | 50,000 | 110,000 | 175,000 |

### *Oak Tree Coinage (1660–1667)*

**Twopence**

**Threepence**

|  | G | VG | F | VF | EF | AU | Unc. |
|---|---|---|---|---|---|---|---|
| 1662 Oak Tree Twopence ............. | $350 | $500 | $1,500 | $2,750 | $3,750 | $6,000 | $8,500 |
| 1652 Oak Tree Threepence ............ | 350 | 500 | 1,700 | 3,200 | 5,250 | 9,000 | 22,000 |
| 1652 Oak Tree Sixpence .............. | 400 | 700 | 1,800 | 3,750 | 6,500 | 10,000 | 18,000 |
| 1652 Oak Tree Shilling ............... | 450 | 750 | 1,850 | 4,000 | 7,000 | 8,500 | 16,000 |

### *Pine Tree Coinage (1667–1682)*

The first Pine Tree coins were minted on the same size planchets as the Oak Tree pieces. Subsequent issues of the shilling were narrower and thicker, to conform to the size of English coins.

**Shilling, Large Planchet (1667–1674)**          **Shilling, Small Planchet (1675–1682)**

*See next page for chart.*

| | G | VG | F | VF | EF | AU | Unc. |
|---|---|---|---|---|---|---|---|
| 1652 Pine Tree Threepence . . . . . . . . . . . . | $350 | $550 | $1,000 | $2,100 | $3,300 | $5,250 | $10,000 |
| 1652 Pine Tree Sixpence . . . . . . . . . . . . . | 400 | 600 | 1,100 | 2,600 | 3,400 | 6,000 | 11,000 |
| 1652 Pine Tree Shilling, Large Planchet . . . | 450 | 750 | 1,400 | 3,100 | 5,000 | 8,000 | 14,000 |
| 1652 Pine Tree Shilling, Small Planchet . . . | 400 | 650 | 1,200 | 2,750 | 3,700 | 6,000 | 13,000 |

## Maryland
### Lord Baltimore Coinage

In 1659, Cecil Calvert, Lord Baltimore and Lord Proprietor of Maryland, had coinage struck in England for use in Maryland. There were four denominations: shilling, sixpence, fourpence (groat) in silver, and copper penny (denarium). The silver coins have the bust of Lord Baltimore on the obverse, and the Baltimore family arms with the denomination in Roman numerals on the reverse.

Fourpence (groat)                    Lord Baltimore Shilling

| | G | VG | F | VF | EF | AU |
|---|---|---|---|---|---|---|
| Penny copper (9 known) . . . . . . . . . . . . . . . . . . . . . | — | — | $30,000 | $50,000 | — | — |
| Fourpence . . . . . . . . . . . . . . . . . . . . . . . . . . . . . | $850 | $1,700 | 3,500 | 7,500 | $11,000 | $18,000 |
| Sixpence . . . . . . . . . . . . . . . . . . . . . . . . . . . . . | 725 | 1,300 | 2,500 | 5,000 | 7,000 | 9,000 |
| Shilling . . . . . . . . . . . . . . . . . . . . . . . . . . . . . . | 1,000 | 1,700 | 3,500 | 7,000 | 9,000 | 14,000 |

## New Jersey
### St. Patrick or Mark Newby Coinage

Mark Newby, who came to America from Dublin, Ireland, in November 1681, brought copper pieces believed by numismatists to have been struck in England circa 1663 to 1672. These are called St. Patrick coppers. The coin received wide circulation in the New Jersey Province, having been authorized to pass as legal tender by the General Assembly in May 1682. The smaller piece, known as a farthing, was never specifically authorized for circulation in the colonies.

St. Patrick Farthing

| | G | VG | F | VF | EF | AU |
|---|---|---|---|---|---|---|
| St. Patrick "Farthing" . . . . . . . . . . . . . . . . . . . . . . | $90 | $150 | $475 | $1,500 | $3,000 | $7,000 |
| St. Patrick "Halfpenny" . . . . . . . . . . . . . . . . . . . . . | 175 | 400 | 800 | 1,900 | 6,000 | |

**COLONIAL ISSUES**

# COINAGE AUTHORIZED BY BRITISH ROYAL PATENT
## American Plantations Tokens

These tokens struck in nearly pure tin were the first royally authorized coinage for the British colonies in America. They were made under a franchise granted in 1688 to Richard Holt. Restrikes were made circa 1828 from original dies.

| | G | VG | F | VF | EF | AU | Unc. |
|---|---|---|---|---|---|---|---|
| (1688) James II Plantation Token Farthing | | | | | | | |
| 1/24 Part Real . . . . . . . . . . . . . . . . . . . . | $125 | $150 | $300 | $500 | $750 | $1,000 | $2,500 |
| 1/24 Part Real, Restrike . . . . . . . . . . . . . | 60 | 80 | 170 | 250 | 375 | 550 | 950 |

## Coinage of William Wood
### *Rosa Americana Coins*

William Wood, an Englishman, obtained a patent from King George I to make tokens for Ireland and the American colonies. The Rosa Americana pieces were issued in three denominations—halfpenny, penny, and twopence—and were intended for use in America.

Penny

| | VG | F | VF | EF | AU | Unc. |
|---|---|---|---|---|---|---|
| (No date) Twopence, Motto in Ribbon . . . . . . . . . . . . . | $90 | $170 | $375 | $700 | $1,500 | $2,800 |
| 1722 Halfpenny, DEI GRATIA REX UTILE DULCI . . . . . . | 55 | 125 | 210 | 450 | 825 | 1,750 |
| 1722 Penny . . . . . . . . . . . . . . . . . . . . . . . . . . . | 55 | 125 | 210 | 450 | 825 | 1,750 |
| 1722 Twopence . . . . . . . . . . . . . . . . . . . . . . . . . | 80 | 160 | 300 | 550 | 1,000 | 2,200 |

Halfpenny

| | VG | F | VF | EF | AU | Unc. |
|---|---|---|---|---|---|---|
| 1723 Halfpenny . . . . . . . . . . . . . . . . . . . . . . . . | $40 | $100 | $175 | $450 | $900 | $1,775 |

*Entry continued on next page.*                                                    **19**

**Twopence**

|  | VG | F | VF | EF | AU | Unc. |
|---|---|---|---|---|---|---|
| 1723 Penny ............................... | $40 | $110 | $200 | $400 | $650 | $1,400 |
| 1723 Twopence *(illustrated)* ................... | 80 | 130 | 250 | 475 | 850 | 1,500 |

## Wood's Hibernia Coinage

The type intended for Ireland had a seated figure with a harp on the reverse side and the word HIBERNIA. Denominations struck were the halfpenny and the farthing with dates 1722, 1723, and 1724. Although these have no association with the Americas, because of the connection with William Wood many American collectors desire to obtain them.

**1722, Hibernia Halfpenny**     **First Type**     **Second Type**

|  | VG | F | VF | EF | AU | Unc. |
|---|---|---|---|---|---|---|
| 1722 Farthing, second type ................... | $150 | $250 | $600 | $1,100 | $2,000 | $4,500 |
| 1722 Halfpenny (first or second type) ........... | 40 | 55 | 110 | 275 | 420 | 875 |

**1723, Hibernia Farthing**      **1724, Hibernia Halfpenny**

|  | VG | F | VF | EF | AU | Unc. |
|---|---|---|---|---|---|---|
| 1723 Farthing ............................... | $20 | $35 | $80 | $150 | $225 | $425 |
| 1723 Halfpenny ............................... | 20 | 30 | 75 | 140 | 225 | 400 |
| 1724 Farthing ............................... | 40 | 90 | 250 | 400 | 650 | 1,200 |
| 1724 Halfpenny ............................... | 32 | 75 | 170 | 325 | 500 | 950 |

## Virginia Halfpennies

In 1773, coinage of a copper halfpenny was authorized for Virginia by the British Crown. The style is similar to the regular English coinage. These pieces did not arrive in Virginia until 1775, but after then they did circulate on a limited basis. Most examples known today are Uncirculated, by virtue of a hoard of several thousand pieces that came to light in the 19th century and was distributed in numismatic channels.

| | G | VG | F | VF | EF | AU | Unc. |
|---|---|---|---|---|---|---|---|
| 1773 Halfpenny .................... | $10 | $30 | $50 | $125 | $225 | $325 | $575 |

# EARLY AMERICAN AND RELATED TOKENS

## Elephant Tokens

### *London Elephant Tokens*

The London Elephant tokens were struck circa 1672 to 1694. Although they were undated, two examples are known to have been struck over 1672 British halfpennies. Most are struck in copper, but one is made of brass. The legend on this piece, GOD PRESERVE LONDON, is probably just a general plea for divine aid and not a specific reference to the outbreak of plague in 1665 or the great fire of 1666.

These pieces were not struck for the colonies, and probably did not circulate widely in America, although a few may have been carried there by colonists. They are associated with the 1694 Carolina and New England Elephant tokens, through a shared obverse die.

| | VG | F | VF | EF | AU | Unc. |
|---|---|---|---|---|---|---|
| (1694) Halfpenny, GOD PRESERVE LONDON, Thick or Thin Planchet ................... | $160 | $300 | $500 | $900 | $1,300 | $2,000 |

### *Carolina Elephant Tokens*

Although no law is known authorizing coinage for Carolina, very interesting pieces known as Elephant tokens were made with the date 1694. These copper tokens were of halfpenny denomination. The reverse reads GOD PRESERVE CAROLINA AND THE LORDS PROPRIETERS 1694.

The Carolina pieces were probably struck in England and perhaps intended as advertising to heighten interest in the Carolina Plantation.

| | VG | F | VF | EF | AU | Unc. |
|---|---|---|---|---|---|---|
| 1694 CAROLINA . . . . . . . . . . . . . . . . . . . . . . . . . . . . | $2,000 | $3,500 | $6,750 | $10,000 | $15,000 | $30,000 |

### New England Elephant Tokens

Like the Carolina Tokens, the New England Elephant tokens were believed to have been struck in England as promotional pieces to increase interest in the American colonies.

| | F | VF | EF |
|---|---|---|---|
| 1694 NEW ENGLAND . . . . . . . . . . . . . . . . . . . . . . . . . . . . . . . . . . . . . . . . . . . . . . . . . . | $30,000 | $55,000 | $75,000 |

## New Yorke in America Token

Little is known about the origin of this token. The design of a heraldic eagle on a regulated staff with oak leaf finials is identical to the crest found on the arms of William Lovelace, governor of New York, 1668 to 1673. It seems likely that this piece is a token farthing struck by Lovelace for use in New York.

| | VG | F |
|---|---|---|
| (Undated) Brass or Copper . . . . . . . . . . . . . . . . . . . . . . . . . . . . . . . . . . . . . . . . . . . . . . . . | $3,750 | $10,000 |
| (Undated) Pewter . . . . . . . . . . . . . . . . . . . . . . . . . . . . . . . . . . . . . . . . . . . . . . . . . . . . . | — | — |

## Gloucester Tokens

This token appears to have been a private coinage by a merchant of Gloucester (county), Virginia. The only specimens known are struck in brass. The exact origin and use of these pieces are unknown.

| | F |
|---|---|
| 1714 Shilling, brass *(2 known)* .................................................................... | $70,000 |

## Higley or Granby Coppers

The Higley coppers were private issues. All the tokens were made of pure copper. There were seven obverse and four reverse dies. The first issue, in 1737, bore the legend THE VALUE OF THREEPENCE. After a time the quantity exceeded the local demand, and a protest arose against the stated value of the piece. The inscription was changed to VALUE ME AS YOU PLEASE.

| | G | VG | F | VF |
|---|---|---|---|---|
| 1737 THE VALVE OF THREE PENCE, CONNECTICVT, 3 Hammers ........ | $5,000 | $9,000 | $16,000 | $45,000 |
| 1737 THE VALVE OF THREE PENCE, I AM GOOD COPPER, 3 Hammers ..... | 5,500 | 9,500 | 16,000 | 45,000 |
| 1737 VALUE ME AS YOU PLEASE, I AM GOOD COPPER, 3 Hammers ...... | 5,500 | 9,500 | 16,000 | 45,000 |
| (1737) VALUE ME AS YOU PLEASE, J CUT MY WAY THROUGH, Broad Axe .. | 5,500 | 9,500 | 16,000 | 45,000 |
| 1739 VALUE ME AS YOU PLEASE, J CUT MY WAY THROUGH, Broad Axe ... | 6,500 | 11,000 | 20,000 | 70,000 |

## Hibernia–Voce Populi Coins

These coins, struck in the year 1760, were made in Dublin. Although these have no connection with America, they have been listed in numismatic publications in the United States for a long time and are collected by tradition.

Farthing (1760)      Halfpenny (1760)

| | G | VG | F | VF | EF | AU | Unc. |
|---|---|---|---|---|---|---|---|
| 1760 Farthing .................... | $130 | $180 | $300 | $950 | $1,350 | $2,500 | $4,500 |
| 1760 Halfpenny .................... | 40 | 75 | 110 | 170 | 350 | 750 | 1,400 |

## Pitt Tokens

British politician William Pitt is the subject of these pieces, probably intended as commemorative medalets. He was a friend to the interests of America. The so-called halfpenny served as currency during a shortage of regular coinage.

| | VG | F | VF | EF | AU | Unc. |
|---|---|---|---|---|---|---|
| 1766 Farthing | $2,500 | $4,000 | $12,000 | $20,000 | | |
| 1766 Halfpenny | 200 | 400 | 850 | 1,400 | $2,300 | $4,750 |

## Rhode Island Ship Medals

Although this medal has a Dutch inscription, the spelling and design indicate an English or Anglo-American origin. It is believed that this token was struck in England circa 1779–1780 as propaganda to persuade the Dutch to sign the Treaty of Armed Neutrality. Specimens are known in brass, copper, and pewter. As with many colonial issues, modern copies exist.

**1778–1779, Rhode Island Ship Medal**

*Values shown are for brass or copper pieces. Those struck in pewter are rare and valued higher.*

| | VF | EF | AU | Unc. |
|---|---|---|---|---|
| Rhode Island Ship Medal | $500 | $900 | $1,500 | $2,500 |

## John Chalmers Issues

John Chalmers, a silversmith, struck a series of silver tokens at Annapolis in 1783. Certain of the dies were by Thomas Sparrow, who also engraved bank-note plates. As most examples show wear today, these pieces seem to have served well in commerce.

| | VG | F | VF | EF | AU |
|---|---|---|---|---|---|
| 1783 Threepence | $900 | $1,800 | $3,500 | $7,000 | $13,000 |

| | VG | F | VF | EF | AU |
|---|---|---|---|---|---|
| 1783 Sixpence | $1,300 | $3,000 | $6,500 | $12,000 | $18,000 |
| 1783 Shilling | 700 | 1,300 | 2,200 | 5,000 | 9,500 |

## FRENCH NEW WORLD ISSUES

None of the coins of the French regime is strictly American. They were all general issues for the French colonies of the New World. The copper of 1717 to 1722 was authorized by edicts of 1716 and 1721 for use in New France, Louisiana, and the French West Indies.

### Copper Sou or Nine Deniers

| | VG | F | VF | EF |
|---|---|---|---|---|
| 1721-B (Rouen) | $80 | $250 | $700 | $2,000 |
| 1721-H (La Rochelle) | 45 | 100 | 275 | 900 |
| 1722-H | 45 | 100 | 275 | 900 |

### French Colonies in General

Coined for use in the French colonies, these circulated only unofficially in Louisiana, along with other foreign coins and tokens. Most were counterstamped RF (République Française) for use in the West Indies. The mintmark A signifies the Paris Mint.

| | VG | VF | EF | AU |
|---|---|---|---|---|
| 1767 French Colonies, Sou | $45 | $125 | $400 | $900 |
| 1767 French Colonies, Sou, counterstamped RF | 40 | 90 | 200 | 300 |

## SPECULATIVE ISSUES, TOKENS, AND PATTERNS
### Nova Constellatio Coppers

The Nova Constellatio pieces were struck supposedly by order of Gouverneur Morris. Evidence indicates that they were all struck in Birmingham, England, and imported for American circulation as a private business venture.

**1783, CONSTELLATIO, Pointed Rays**

**1783, CONSTELATIO, Blunt Rays**

**1785, CONSTELATIO, Blunt Rays**

**1785, CONSTELLATIO, Pointed Rays**

| | VG | F | VF | EF | AU | Unc. |
|---|---|---|---|---|---|---|
| 1783, CONSTELLATIO, Pointed Rays | $50 | $110 | $250 | $500 | $800 | $1,800 |
| 1783, CONSTELLATIO, Blunt Rays | 55 | 125 | 275 | 650 | 1,850 | 2,500 |
| 1785, CONSTELATIO, Blunt Rays | 55 | 125 | 275 | 700 | 1,500 | 3,000 |
| 1785, CONSTELLATIO, Pointed Rays | 50 | 110 | 250 | 500 | 800 | 1,800 |

### Immune Columbia Pieces

Nearly all of these are very rare. Many if not most seem to be unofficial, including pieces produced at the private Machin's Mills mint in Newburgh, New York.

**1785, Copper, Star Reverse**

**1785, George III Obverse**

| | G | VG | F | VF | EF | AU |
|---|---|---|---|---|---|---|
| 1785 Copper, Star Reverse | | | $8,000 | $14,000 | $19,000 | |
| 1785, George III Obverse | $2,500 | $4,000 | 6,000 | 8,000 | | |

**1787, IMMUNIS COLUMBIA, Eagle Reverse**

| | G | VG | F | VF | EF | AU |
|---|---|---|---|---|---|---|
| 1785, VERMON AUCTORI Obverse, IMMUNE COLUMBIA | $3,200 | $5,500 | $7,500 | $18,000 | | |
| 1787, IMMUNIS COLUMBIA, Eagle Reverse ........ | 150 | 375 | 800 | 2,000 | $3,000 | $4,500 |

## Confederatio Coppers

Some Confederatio coppers may have been patterns, but others seem to have been used in limited numbers for general circulation. This will explain why the die with the CONFEDERATIO legend was combined with other designs such as a bust of George Washington, Libertas et Justitia of 1785, Immunis Columbia of 1786, the New York "Excelsiors," Inimica Tyrannis Americana, and others. In all there were 13 dies struck in 14 combinations. There are two types of the Confederatio reverse. In one instance the stars are contained in a small circle; in the other, larger stars are in a larger circle.

**Typical Obverse**      **Small Circle Reverse**      **Large Circle Reverse**

| | VF |
|---|---|
| 1785, Stars in Small Circle, various obverses ............................................................. | $29,000 |
| 1785, Stars in Large Circle, various obverses ............................................................. | 26,000 |

## Speculative Patterns

**1786, IMMUNIS COLUMBIA**      **Eagle Reverse**      **Shield Reverse**

| | VF | EF |
|---|---|---|
| 1786, IMMUNIS COLUMBIA, Eagle Reverse ................................... | $30,000 | $37,500 |
| 1786, IMMUNIS COLUMBIA, Shield Reverse ................................... | 20,000 | 27,500 |

*Chart continued on next page.*      **27**

|  | VF | EF |
|---|---|---|
| (No date) (1786) Washington Obverse, Shield Reverse | — |  |
| 1786, Eagle Obverse, Shield Reverse | $30,000 |  |
| 1786, Washington Obverse, Eagle Reverse *(2 known)* | — |  |

## COINAGE OF THE STATES
### New Hampshire

New Hampshire was the first of the states to consider the subject of coinage following the Declaration of Independence.

William Moulton was empowered to make a limited quantity of coins of pure copper, authorized by the State House of Representatives in 1776.

|  | VG |
|---|---|
| 1776 New Hampshire Copper | *$20,000* |

### Massachusetts

The coinage of Massachusetts copper cents and half cents in 1787 and 1788 was under the direction of Joshua Witherle. These were the first coins bearing the denomination *cent* as established by Congress. Many varieties exist, the most valuable being that with arrows in the eagle's right talon (on the left side of the coin).

1787 Half Cent                    1787 Cent

1788 Half Cent                    1788 Cent

|  | G | F | VF | EF | AU | Unc. |
|---|---|---|---|---|---|---|
| 1787 Half Cent | $45 | $120 | $300 | $500 | $800 | $1,650 |
| 1787 Cent, Arrows in Right Talon | 4,200 | 10,000 | 25,000 |  |  |  |
| 1787 Cent, Arrows in Left Talon *(illustrated)* | 45 | 120 | 325 | 700 | 1,500 | 2,750 |

| | G | F | VF | EF | AU | Unc. |
|---|---|---|---|---|---|---|
| 1788 Half Cent | $50 | $125 | $300 | $550 | $950 | $1,800 |
| 1788 Cent | 40 | 110 | 275 | 550 | 1,000 | 2,100 |

## Connecticut

Authority for establishing a mint near New Haven was granted by the state to Samuel Bishop, Joseph Hopkins, James Hillhouse, and John Goodrich in 1785. Today, well over 300 different die varieties are known of Connecticut coppers dated from 1785 to 1788. These pieces circulated widely and effectively; most are seen with significant evidence of circulation.

1785, Bust
Facing Right

1785, Bust
Facing Left

1786–1787,
Mailed Bust
Facing Right

1786–1787,
Mailed Bust
Facing Left

1787, Draped
Bust Facing Left

1788, Mailed
Bust Facing Right

*Entry continued on next page.*

**1788, Mailed Bust Facing Left**

**1788, Draped Bust Facing Left**

| | AG | G | VG | F | VF | EF | AU |
|---|---|---|---|---|---|---|---|
| 1785, Bust Facing Right .............. | $12 | $35 | $45 | $95 | $300 | $800 | $1,900 |
| 1785, Bust Facing Left ............... | 30 | 100 | 175 | 300 | 850 | 1,500 | 3,750 |
| 1786, Mailed Bust Facing Right ........ | 15 | 40 | 50 | 100 | 275 | 950 | 1,600 |
| 1786, Mailed Bust Facing Left .......... | 12 | 35 | 45 | 100 | 200 | 550 | 1,400 |
| 1787, Mailed Bust Facing Right ........ | 15 | 42 | 65 | 175 | 475 | 800 | 1,500 |
| 1787, Mailed Bust Facing Left .......... | 10 | 25 | 35 | 75 | 200 | 500 | 1,400 |
| 1787, Draped Bust Facing Left ........ | 10 | 25 | 35 | 75 | 200 | 500 | 1,200 |
| 1788, Mailed Bust Facing Right ........ | 10 | 25 | 50 | 100 | 300 | 700 | 1,400 |
| 1788, Mailed Bust Facing Left .......... | 10 | 25 | 32 | 80 | 210 | 550 | 1,350 |
| 1788, Draped Bust Facing Left ........ | 10 | 25 | 35 | 100 | 250 | 600 | 1,900 |

## New York and Related Issues
### *Brasher Doubloons*

Perhaps the most famous pieces coined before the establishment of the U.S. Mint at Philadelphia were those produced by a well-known goldsmith and jeweler, Ephraim Brasher of New York.

Brasher produced a gold piece weighing about 408 grains, approximately equal in value to a Spanish doubloon (about $15.00 in New York currency).

The punch-mark EB appears in either of two positions as illustrated. This mark is found on some foreign gold coins as well, and probably was so used by Brasher as evidence of his testing of their value. Many modern forgeries exist.

| | EF |
|---|---|
| 1787 New York gold doubloon, EB on Breast ........................................... | $2,000,000 |
| 1787 New York gold doubloon, EB on Wing ............................................ | 1,500,000 |

## *Copper Coinage*

No coinage was authorized by the State of New York following the Revolutionary War, although several propositions were considered. The only coinage laws passed were those regulating coins already in use. Private mints struck several unauthorized coppers.

| | G | VG | F | VF | EF |
|---|---|---|---|---|---|
| 1786, NON VI VIRTUTE VICI ........................... | $2,500 | $4,250 | $8,000 | $17,000 | $26,000 |

| | G | VG | F | VF | EF |
|---|---|---|---|---|---|
| 1787 EXCELSIOR Copper, Eagle on Globe Facing Right ........ | $1,000 | $2,000 | $4,000 | $10,000 | $18,000 |
| 1787 EXCELSIOR Copper, Eagle on Globe Facing Left ......... | 1,000 | 1,800 | 3,500 | 9,000 | 17,000 |

**1787, George Clinton and New York Arms**     **1787, Indian and New York Arms**     **1787, Indian and Eagle on Globe**

| | G | VG | F | VF | EF |
|---|---|---|---|---|---|
| 1787, George Clinton and New York Arms ................. | $4,500 | $8,000 | $14,000 | $27,000 | $75,000 |
| 1787, Indian and New York Arms ...................... | 3,500 | 5,500 | 12,000 | 20,000 | 60,000 |
| 1787, Indian and Eagle on Globe ...................... | 6,000 | 9,000 | 17,500 | 31,000 | 55,000 |

### Nova Eborac Coinage for New York

**1787, NOVA EBORAC Reverse,
Seated Figure Facing Right**

**1787, NOVA EBORAC Reverse,
Seated Figure Facing Left**

| | Fair | G | F | VF | EF | AU |
|---|---|---|---|---|---|---|
| 1787, NOVA EBORAC, Seated Figure Facing Right ... | $30 | $60 | $175 | $500 | $1,200 | $2,100 |
| 1787, NOVA EBORAC, Seated Figure Facing Left .... | 30 | 50 | 150 | 400 | 800 | 1,500 |

## New Jersey

On June 1, 1786, the New Jersey General Assembly granted to Thomas Goadsby, Albion Cox, and Walter Mould authority to coin some three million coppers no later than June 1788, on condition that they delivered to the treasurer of the state "one-tenth part of the full sum they shall strike and coin," in quarterly installments. These coppers were to pass current at 15 to the shilling. Produced in significant quantities, these coins are often seen in the market today and are widely collectible, although certain varieties can be rare and especially valuable.

**Narrow Shield**

**Wide Shield**

| | AG | G | F | VF | EF | AU |
|---|---|---|---|---|---|---|
| 1786, Narrow Shield ........................ | $10 | $25 | $100 | $250 | $550 | $1,000 |
| 1786, Wide Shield ......................... | 12 | 30 | 125 | 300 | 500 | 1,500 |

**Small Planchet**

|                              | AG   | G    | F     | VF    | EF    | AU    |
|------------------------------|------|------|-------|-------|-------|-------|
| 1787, Small Planchet         | $12  | $30  | $100  | $275  | $500  | $900  |
| 1787, Large Planchet         | 15   | 35   | 110   | 300   | 600   | 1,300 |

Fox Before Legend

|                                     | AG   | G    | F     | VF     | EF    | AU     |
|-------------------------------------|------|------|-------|--------|-------|--------|
| 1788, Horse's Head Facing Right     | $12  | $30  | $100  | $300   | $600  | $1,200 |
| 1788, Similar, Fox in Legend        | 30   | 75   | 275   | 900    | 1,900 | 4,500  |
| 1788, Horse's Head Facing Left      | 100  | 200  | 800   | 2,100  | 6,000 | —      |

## Vermont

Reuben Harmon Jr. was granted permission to coin copper pieces beginning July 1, 1785. The franchise was extended for eight years in 1786. However, in 1787 production was shifted to Machin's Mills, Newburgh, New York, in which Harmon had a proprietary interest. Although the Vermont coins were legally issued there, most other products of Machin's Mills were counterfeits, some dies for which were combined with Vermont pieces, creating several illogical pieces below, including the 1785 Immune Columbia and the 1788 Georgivs III Rex.

**1785, IMMUNE COLUMBIA**    **1785–1786, Plow Type**    **1786, Baby Head**

|                                        | AG     | G      | VG     | F      | VF      | EF     |
|----------------------------------------|--------|--------|--------|--------|---------|--------|
| 1785, IMMUNE COLUMBIA                  | $1,900 | $3,200 | $5,500 | $7,500 | $18,000 | —      |
| 1785, Plow Type, VERMONTS              | 100    | 175    | 350    | 600    | 1,500   | $3,000 |
| 1786, Plow Type, VERMONTENSIUM         | 75     | 135    | 260    | 550    | 1,000   | 2,000  |
| 1786, Baby Head                        | 100    | 175    | 300    | 800    | 2,400   | 5,000  |

| | 1786–1787, Bust Left | | 1787, BRITANNIA | | 1787, Bust Right | |
|---|---|---|---|---|---|---|

| | AG | G | VG | F | VF | EF |
|---|---|---|---|---|---|---|
| 1786, Bust Left .......................... | $25 | $85 | $200 | $450 | $1,500 | $2,600 |
| 1787, Bust Left .......................... | 1,000 | 2,500 | 5,500 | 15,000 | 23,000 | — |
| 1787, BRITANNIA ......................... | 12 | 50 | 85 | 160 | 350 | 950 |
| 1787, Bust Right *(several varieties)* ............. | 20 | 70 | 135 | 245 | 600 | 1,500 |

| | 1788, Bust Right | | 1788, GEORGIVS III REX | |
|---|---|---|---|---|

| | AG | G | VG | F | VF | EF |
|---|---|---|---|---|---|---|
| 1788, Bust Right *(several varieties)* ............. | $15 | $60 | $110 | $225 | $450 | $1,000 |
| 1788, GEORGIVS III REX ...................... | 100 | 325 | 600 | 1,400 | 2,800 | 7,000 |

*Note:* This piece should not be confused with the common British halfpence with similar design and reverse legend BRITANNIA.

# PRIVATE TOKENS AFTER CONFEDERATION
## North American Tokens

This piece was struck in Dublin, Ireland. The obverse shows the seated figure of Hibernia facing left. Although dated 1781, it is believed to have been struck early in the next century.

| | VG | F | VF | EF |
|---|---|---|---|---|
| 1781, Copper or brass ............................... | $30 | $75 | $170 | $425 |

## Bar Coppers

The Bar copper is undated and of uncertain origin. It has 13 parallel and unconnected bars on one side. On the other side is the large roman-letter USA monogram. The design was supposedly copied from a Continental Army uniform button.

| | VG | F | VF | EF | AU |
|---|---|---|---|---|---|
| (Undated) (Circa 1785) Bar Copper ..................... | $925 | $1,750 | $3,250 | $5,000 | $7,500 |

## Auctori Plebis Tokens

This token is sometimes included with the coins of Connecticut as it greatly resembles issues of that state. It was struck in England by an unknown maker, possibly for use in America.

| | G | VG | F | VF | EF | AU | Unc. |
|---|---|---|---|---|---|---|---|
| 1787, AUCTORI PLEBIS ............... | $40 | $90 | $150 | $350 | $700 | $1,200 | $3,750 |

## Mott Store Cards

This item has long been considered an early token because of its date (1789). Most scholars believe it was most likely produced circa 1809 as a commemorative of the founding of the Mott Company, and probably served as a business card.

| | VG | F | VF | EF | AU | Unc. |
|---|---|---|---|---|---|---|
| "1789," Mott Token ..................... | $50 | $110 | $200 | $300 | $450 | $800 |

## Standish Barry Threepence

Standish Barry, a Baltimore silversmith, circulated a silver threepence in 1790. The tokens were believed to have been an advertising venture at a time when small change was scarce.

| | VG | F | VF | EF |
|---|---|---|---|---|
| 1790 Threepence | $5,000 | $11,000 | $25,000 | $60,000 |

## Kentucky Tokens

These tokens were struck in England about 1792 to 1794. Each star in the triangle represents a state, identified by its initial letter. These pieces are usually called *Kentucky cents* because the letter K (for Kentucky) happens to be at the top. In the 19th century these were often called *triangle tokens,* from the arrangement of the stars. Values are for the normal issue with plain edge; lettered-edge varieties exist and are scarcer.

| | VG | VF | EF | AU | Unc. |
|---|---|---|---|---|---|
| (1792–1794) Copper, Plain Edge | $50 | $120 | $210 | $350 | $600 |

## Franklin Press Tokens

This piece is an English tradesman's token, but, being associated with Benjamin Franklin, has accordingly been included in American collections.

| | VG | VF | EF | AU | Unc. |
|---|---|---|---|---|---|
| 1794, Franklin Press Token | $60 | $150 | $225 | $375 | $600 |

## Talbot, Allum & Lee Cents

Talbot, Allum & Lee, engaged in the India trade and located in New York, placed a large quantity of English-made coppers in circulation during 1794 and 1795. ONE CENT appears on the 1794 issue.

1794 Cent,
With NEW YORK

1795 Cent

|  | G | VG | VF | EF | AU | Unc. |
|---|---|---|---|---|---|---|
| 1794 Cent, With NEW YORK | $25 | $40 | $150 | $270 | $425 | $850 |
| 1794 Cent, Without NEW YORK | 200 | 300 | 1,500 | 3,000 | 5,000 | 10,000 |
| 1795 Cent | 25 | 40 | 125 | 240 | 300 | 650 |

## WASHINGTON PORTRAIT PIECES

An interesting series of coins and tokens dated from 1783 to 1795 bear the portrait of George Washington. The likenesses in most instances were faithfully reproduced and were designed to honor Washington. Many of these pieces were of English origin and made later than the dates indicate.

1783,
Military Bust

1783,
Draped Bust

|  | F | VF | EF | AU | Unc. |
|---|---|---|---|---|---|
| 1783, Military Bust | $40 | $100 | $200 | $400 | $1,300 |
| 1783, Draped Bust | 45 | 110 | 225 | 425 | 1,200 |

1783, UNITY STATES

|  | VG | F | VF | EF | AU | Unc. |
|---|---|---|---|---|---|---|
| 1783, UNITY STATES | $30 | $60 | $125 | $250 | $425 | $1,250 |

**Undated Double-Head Cent**

| | VG | F | VF | EF | AU | Unc. |
|---|---|---|---|---|---|---|
| (Undated) Double-Head Cent .................. | $30 | $50 | $150 | $250 | $575 | $1,600 |

| Obverse | Large Eagle Reverse | Small Eagle Reverse |
|---|---|---|

| | F | VF | EF | AU | Unc. |
|---|---|---|---|---|---|
| 1791 Cent, Large Eagle (Date on Obverse) ................ | $225 | $300 | $450 | $700 | $1,500 |
| 1791 Cent, Small Eagle (Date on Reverse) ................ | 250 | 325 | 500 | 800 | 1,750 |

| | F | VF | EF | AU |
|---|---|---|---|---|
| 1791 Liverpool Halfpenny, Lettered Edge ...................... | $750 | $1,000 | $2,300 | $3,750 |

| 1792, Eagle With Stars, copper ............................................ | — |
|---|---|
| 1792, Eagle With Stars, silver ............................................. | — |
| 1792, Eagle With Stars, gold *(unique)* ..................................... | — |

**(1792) Undated Cent,**
**WASHINGTON BORN VIRGINIA**

**1792 Cent,**
**WASHINGTON PRESIDENT**

| | VG | F | VF |
|---|---|---|---|
| (1792) Undated Cent, WASHINGTON BORN VIRGINIA, copper | $1,000 | $1,500 | $3,750 |
| 1792 Cent, WASHINGTON PRESIDENT, Plain Edge | 1,500 | 3,750 | 7,000 |

**1792 Getz Pattern**

**1793 Ship Halfpenny**

**1795 Halfpenny, Grate Token**

| | VG | F | VF | EF | AU | Unc. |
|---|---|---|---|---|---|---|
| 1792, Getz Pattern, copper | $4,000 | $7,000 | $14,000 | $25,000 | | |
| 1793 Ship Halfpenny, Lettered Edge | 35 | 110 | 225 | 400 | $650 | $1,750 |
| 1795, Grate Token, Lettered Edge | 50 | 100 | 200 | 425 | 900 | 1,300 |
| 1795, Grate Token, Reeded edge | 30 | 75 | 100 | 225 | 300 | 550 |

|  | F | VF | EF | AU | Unc. |
|---|---|---|---|---|---|
| 1795, LIBERTY AND SECURITY Halfpenny, Plain Edge ........ | $75 | $175 | $400 | $800 | $1,500 |
| 1795, LIBERTY AND SECURITY Halfpenny, Lettered Edge ...... | 65 | 160 | 325 | 650 | 1,700 |
| (1795) Undated, LIBERTY AND SECURITY Penny ............. | 165 | 300 | 450 | 850 | 1,600 |

|  | G | F | VF | EF | AU |
|---|---|---|---|---|---|
| (1795) NORTH WALES Halfpenny ........................ | $60 | $150 | $385 | $850 | $1,500 |

|  | F | VF | EF | AU | Unc. |
|---|---|---|---|---|---|
| SUCCESS Medal, Large, Plain or Reeded Edge ............. | $135 | $275 | $500 | $800 | $1,700 |
| SUCCESS Medal, Small, Plain or Reeded Edge ............. | 150 | 325 | 550 | 850 | 1,800 |

## CONTINENTAL CURRENCY

The Continental Currency pieces probably had some assigned value at their time of issue. The exact nature of their monetary role is uncertain; they might have been experimental, or they might have seen circulation. At any rate, this was the first dollar-sized coin proposed for the United States. They were probably struck in Philadelphia from dies engraved by Elisha Gallaudet. As with many early pieces, modern replicas exist.

| | G | F | VF | EF | AU | Unc. |
|---|---|---|---|---|---|---|
| 1776, CURENCY, pewter *(2 varieties)* | $4,000 | $7,000 | $11,000 | $17,000 | $25,000 | $32,000 |
| 1776, CURENCY, silver *(2 known)* | | 150,000 | | | | |
| 1776, CURRENCY, pewter | 4,000 | 7,000 | 12,000 | 17,500 | 28,000 | 37,500 |
| 1776, CURRENCY, EG FECIT, pewter | 4,000 | 7,000 | 13,000 | 18,500 | 28,000 | 40,000 |

## FUGIO COPPERS

The first coins issued by authority of the United States were the 1787 "Fugio" coppers. The legends have been credited to Benjamin Franklin by many, and the coins, as a consequence, have been referred to as *Franklin cents*.

**1787, With Pointed Rays**

**1787, With Club Rays**

| | VG | F | VF | EF | AU | Unc. |
|---|---|---|---|---|---|---|
| Pointed Rays, STATES UNITED at Side of Circle *(illustrated)* | $150 | $250 | $400 | $800 | $1,100 | $2,100 |
| Pointed Rays, UNITED STATES at Side of Circle | 150 | 250 | 400 | 825 | 1,200 | 2,300 |
| Club Rays, Rounded Ends | 250 | 400 | 1,000 | 2,000 | 3,500 | — |

The half cent was authorized to be coined April 2, 1792. Originally the weight was to have been 132 grains, but this was changed to 104 grains by the Act of January 14, 1793, before coinage commenced. The weight was again changed to 84 grains January 26, 1796, by presidential proclamation in conformity with the Act of March 3, 1795. Coinage was discontinued by the Act of February 21, 1857. All were coined at the Philadelphia Mint.

## LIBERTY CAP (1793–1797)

**AG-3 About Good:** Clear enough to identify.
**G-4 Good:** Outline of bust of Liberty clear, no details. Date readable. Reverse lettering incomplete.
**VG-8 Very Good:** Some hair details. Reverse lettering complete.
**F-12 Fine:** Most of hair detail visible. Leaves worn, but all visible.
**VF-20 Very Fine:** Hair near ear and forehead worn, other areas distinct. Some details in leaves visible.
**EF-40 Extremely Fine:** Light wear on highest parts of head and wreath.
**AU-50 About Uncirculated:** Only a trace of wear on Liberty's face.

**Head Facing Left (1793)**

| | Mintage | AG-3 | G-4 | VG-8 | F-12 | VF-20 | EF-40 | AU-50 |
|---|---|---|---|---|---|---|---|---|
| 1793 . . . . . . . . . . . . . . . . . . . .35,334 | | $900 | $1,650 | $2,800 | $4,200 | $7,200 | $13,250 | $19,000 |

**Head Facing Right (1794–1797)**

| **Pole to Cap** | **Punctuated Date** | **No Pole to Cap** |

| | Mintage | AG-3 | G-4 | VG-8 | F-12 | VF-20 | EF-40 | AU-50 |
|---|---|---|---|---|---|---|---|---|
| 1794 . . . . . . . . . . . . . . . . . . . .81,600 | | $120 | $265 | $350 | $600 | $1,200 | $2,800 | $5,500 |
| 1795, All kinds . . . . . . . . . . . . . .139,690 | | | | | | | | |
|   1795, Lettered Edge, With Pole . . . . . . . | | 80 | 200 | 310 | 525 | 1,200 | 2,600 | 4,500 |
|   1795, Lettered Edge, Punctuated Date . . | | 80 | 200 | 310 | 525 | 1,200 | 2,600 | 4,500 |
|   1795, Plain Edge, Punctuated Date . . . . | | 75 | 160 | 260 | 425 | 1,000 | 2,400 | 3,750 |
|   1795, Plain Edge, No Pole . . . . . . . . . . . | | 75 | 160 | 260 | 425 | 1,000 | 2,400 | 3,750 |
| 1796, With Pole . . . . . . . . . . . . . . .1,390 | | 3,600 | 6,950 | 10,000 | 15,000 | 24,000 | 31,000 | |
| 1796, No Pole . . . . . . . . . . . . . . . . .* | | 7,000 | 15,000 | 20,000 | 32,000 | 50,000 | 75,000 | |

* Included in number above.

**1797, 1 Above 1, Plain Edge**

**1797, Plain Edge**

| | Mintage | AG-3 | G-4 | VG-8 | F-12 | VF-20 | EF-40 | AU-50 |
|---|---|---|---|---|---|---|---|---|
| 1797, All kinds | 127,840 | | | | | | | |
| 1797, 1 Above 1, Plain Edge | | $75 | $210 | $300 | $450 | $900 | $2,000 | $3,250 |
| 1797, Plain Edge | | 90 | 220 | 300 | 600 | 1,000 | 2,100 | 3,500 |
| 1797, Lettered Edge | | 200 | 700 | 1,100 | 2,750 | 6,500 | 14,000 | 32,000 |
| 1797, Gripped Edge | | 3,500 | 13,000 | 27,000 | 35,000 | | | |

## DRAPED BUST (1800–1808)

**AG-3 About Good:** Clear enough to identify.
**G-4 Good:** Outline of bust of Liberty clear, few details, date readable. Reverse lettering worn and incomplete.
**VG-8 Very Good:** Some drapery visible. Date and legends complete.
**F-12 Fine:** Shoulder drapery and hair over brow worn smooth.
**VF-20 Very Fine:** Only slight wear in previously mentioned areas. Slight wear on reverse.
**EF-40 Extremely Fine:** Light wear on highest parts of head and wreath.
**AU-50 About Uncirculated:** Wear slight on hair above forehead.

**1st Reverse** **2nd Reverse**

| | Mintage | AG-3 | G-4 | VG-8 | F-12 | VF-20 | EF-40 | AU-50 |
|---|---|---|---|---|---|---|---|---|
| 1800 | 202,908 | $16 | $35 | $45 | $60 | $150 | $300 | $500 |
| 1802, 2 Over 0 | 20,266 | 130 | 360 | 800 | 1,850 | 5,000 | 13,500 | |
| 1803 | 92,000 | 16 | 35 | 50 | 70 | 160 | 450 | 700 |

**Plain 4** **Crosslet 4** **Stems to Wreath** **Stemless Wreath**

| | Mintage | AG-3 | G-4 | VG-8 | F-12 | VF-20 | EF-40 | AU-50 |
|---|---|---|---|---|---|---|---|---|
| 1804, All kinds | 1,055,312 | | | | | | | |
| 1804, Plain 4, Stems to Wreath | | $18 | $40 | $60 | $95 | $175 | $470 | $1,000 |
| 1804, Plain 4, Stemless Wreath | | 16 | 35 | 45 | 70 | 95 | 160 | 300 |
| 1804, Crosslet 4, Stemless Wreath | | 16 | 35 | 45 | 70 | 95 | 160 | 300 |
| 1804, Crosslet 4, Stems to Wreath | | 16 | 35 | 45 | 70 | 95 | 160 | 300 |

*Entry continued on next page.*

| | 1804, "Spiked Chin" | | Small 5 | | Large 5 | |

| | Mintage | AG-3 | G-4 | VG-8 | F-12 | VF-20 | EF-40 | AU-50 |
|---|---|---|---|---|---|---|---|---|
| 1804, "Spiked Chin" .............* | | $17 | $40 | $50 | $75 | $110 | $200 | $350 |
| 1805, All kinds ..............814,464 | | | | | | | | |
| 1805, Medium 5, Stemless Wreath .... | | 16 | 35 | 45 | 70 | 100 | 160 | 300 |
| 1805, Small 5, Stems to Wreath ...... | | 110 | 375 | 700 | 1,500 | 3,000 | 5,000 | |
| 1805, Large 5, Stems to Wreath ...... | | 16 | 35 | 45 | 70 | 100 | 160 | 300 |

* Included in "1804, All kinds" mintage (previous page).

| Small 6 | | Large 6 | | 1808, 8 Over 7 | | Normal Date | |

| | Mintage | AG-3 | G-4 | VG-8 | F-12 | VF-20 | EF-40 | AU-50 |
|---|---|---|---|---|---|---|---|---|
| 1806, All kinds ..............356,000 | | | | | | | | |
| 1806, Small 6, Stems to Wreath ...... | | $40 | $110 | $185 | $325 | $750 | $1,400 | $3,750 |
| 1806, Small 6, Stemless Wreath ...... | | 16 | 35 | 45 | 55 | 75 | 145 | 290 |
| 1806, Large 6, Stems to Wreath ...... | | 16 | 35 | 45 | 55 | 75 | 145 | 290 |
| 1807 ....................476,000 | | 16 | 35 | 45 | 60 | 100 | 225 | 500 |
| 1808, 8 Over 7 ...................* | | 30 | 70 | 125 | 300 | 700 | 1,750 | 5,000 |
| 1808, Normal Date ..........400,000 | | 16 | 35 | 45 | 60 | 100 | 225 | 500 |

* Included in number below.

## CLASSIC HEAD (1809–1836)

**G-4 Good:** LIBERTY only partly visible on hair band. Lettering, date, and stars worn but visible.
**VG-8 Very Good:** LIBERTY entirely visible on hair band. Lower curls worn.
**F-12 Fine:** Only partial wear on LIBERTY, and hair at top worn in spots.
**VF-20 Very Fine:** Lettering clear-cut. Hair only slightly worn.
**EF-40 Extremely Fine:** Light wear on highest points of hair and leaves.
**AU-50 About Uncirculated:** Sharp hair detail with only a trace of wear on higher points.
**MS-60 Uncirculated:** Typical brown to red surface. No trace of wear.
**MS-63 Choice Uncirculated:** Well-defined color, brown to red. No traces of wear.

| | | 1828, 13 Stars | 1828, 12 Stars |

*Brilliant or red Uncirculated coins are worth more than prices shown. Spotted, cleaned, or discolored pieces are worth less.*

| | Mintage | AG-3 | G-4 | VG-8 | F-12 | VF-20 | EF-40 | AU-50 | MS-60 | MS-63 |
|---|---|---|---|---|---|---|---|---|---|---|
| 1809 .............1,154,572 | | $14 | $25 | $30 | $35 | $55 | $90 | $150 | $325 | $450 |
| 1810 ...............215,000 | | 14 | 25 | 35 | 60 | 110 | 250 | 450 | 950 | 1,500 |
| 1811 ................63,140 | | 50 | 125 | 235 | 450 | 950 | 2,900 | 3,750 | 4,500 | 6,750 |

# HALF CENTS

| | Mintage | G-4 | VG-8 | F-12 | VF-20 | EF-40 | AU-50 | MS-60 | MS-63 | PF-63 |
|---|---|---|---|---|---|---|---|---|---|---|
| 1825 . . . . . . . . . . . . . . .63,000 | | $25 | $30 | $35 | $50 | $90 | $150 | $450 | $750 | |
| 1826 . . . . . . . . . . . . . .234,000 | | 25 | 30 | 35 | 50 | 85 | 125 | 275 | 450 | |
| 1828, 13 Stars . . . . . . . .606,000 | | 23 | 30 | 35 | 45 | 55 | 120 | 190 | 275 | |
| 1828, 12 Stars . . . . . . . . . . . .* | | 24 | 35 | 40 | 50 | 125 | 175 | 650 | 900 | |
| 1829 . . . . . . . . . . . . . .487,000 | | 23 | 30 | 35 | 45 | 65 | 95 | 175 | 325 | |
| 1831 . . . . . . . . . . . . . . . .2,200 | | | | | | | | | | — |
| 1832 . . . . . . . . . . . . . . .51,000 | | 23 | 28 | 32 | 40 | 55 | 95 | 175 | 250 | $2,500 |
| 1833 . . . . . . . . . . . . . .103,000 | | 23 | 28 | 32 | 40 | 55 | 95 | 175 | 250 | 2,500 |
| 1834 . . . . . . . . . . . . . .141,000 | | 23 | 28 | 32 | 40 | 55 | 95 | 175 | 250 | 2,500 |
| 1835 . . . . . . . . . . . . . .398,000 | | 23 | 28 | 32 | 40 | 55 | 95 | 175 | 250 | 2,500 |
| 1836 . . . . . . . . . . . . . . . . . . . . . | | | | | | | | | | 8,000 |

\* Included in number above.

## BRAIDED HAIR (1840–1857)

**VG-8 Very Good:** Beads in hair uniformly distinct. Hair lines visible in spots.
**F-12 Fine:** Hair lines above ear worn. Beads sharp.
**VF-20 Very Fine:** Lowest curl worn; hair otherwise distinct.
**EF-40 Extremely Fine:** Light wear on highest points of hair and on leaves.
**AU-50 About Uncirculated:** Very slight trace of wear on hair above Liberty's ear.
**MS-60 Uncirculated:** No trace of wear. Clear luster.
**MS-63 Choice Uncirculated:** No trace of wear.
**PF-63 Choice Proof:** Nearly perfect; only light blemishes.

*Brilliant or red Uncirculated and Proof coins are worth more than prices shown. Spotted, cleaned, or discolored pieces are worth less.*

| | PF-63 | | PF-63 |
|---|---|---|---|
| 1840, Original . . . . . . . . . . . . . . . . . . . . . . . | $2,700 | 1845, Original . . . . . . . . . . . . . . . . . . . . . . . | $3,500 |
| 1840, Restrike . . . . . . . . . . . . . . . . . . . . . . . | 2,250 | 1845, Restrike . . . . . . . . . . . . . . . . . . . . . . . | 3,250 |
| 1841, Original . . . . . . . . . . . . . . . . . . . . . . . | 2,600 | 1846, Original . . . . . . . . . . . . . . . . . . . . . . . | 3,250 |
| 1841, Restrike . . . . . . . . . . . . . . . . . . . . . . . | 2,500 | 1846, Restrike . . . . . . . . . . . . . . . . . . . . . . . | 2,600 |
| 1842, Original . . . . . . . . . . . . . . . . . . . . . . . | 2,750 | 1847, Original . . . . . . . . . . . . . . . . . . . . . . . | 2,600 |
| 1842, Restrike . . . . . . . . . . . . . . . . . . . . . . . | 2,500 | 1847, Restrike . . . . . . . . . . . . . . . . . . . . . . . | 2,600 |
| 1843, Original . . . . . . . . . . . . . . . . . . . . . . . | 2,500 | 1848, Original . . . . . . . . . . . . . . . . . . . . . . . | 2,600 |
| 1843, Restrike . . . . . . . . . . . . . . . . . . . . . . . | 2,500 | 1848, Restrike . . . . . . . . . . . . . . . . . . . . . . . | 2,600 |
| 1844, Original . . . . . . . . . . . . . . . . . . . . . . . | 3,500 | 1849, Original, Small Date . . . . . . . . . . . . . | 2,900 |
| 1844, Restrike . . . . . . . . . . . . . . . . . . . . . . . | 2,600 | 1849, Restrike, Small Date . . . . . . . . . . . . . | 2,900 |

**Small Date**          **Large Date**

| | Mintage | G-4 | VG-8 | F-12 | VF-20 | EF-40 | AU-50 | MS-60 | MS-63 | PF-63 |
|---|---|---|---|---|---|---|---|---|---|---|
| 1849, Large Date . . . . . . .39,864 | | $17 | $23 | $30 | $40 | $75 | $100 | $225 | $300 | — |
| 1850 . . . . . . . . . . . . . . .39,812 | | 17 | 23 | 30 | 40 | 75 | 100 | 225 | 350 | $4,000 |
| 1851 . . . . . . . . . . . . . .147,672 | | 15 | 20 | 28 | 35 | 50 | 80 | 135 | 250 | 3,000 |
| 1852 . . . . . . . . . . . . . . . . . . . . . | | | | | | | | | | 3,500 |
| 1853 . . . . . . . . . . . . . .129,694 | | 15 | 20 | 28 | 35 | 50 | 80 | 135 | 250 | |
| 1854 . . . . . . . . . . . . . . .55,358 | | 15 | 20 | 28 | 35 | 50 | 80 | 135 | 250 | 3,000 |
| 1855 . . . . . . . . . . . . . . .56,500 | | 15 | 20 | 28 | 35 | 50 | 80 | 135 | 250 | 3,000 |
| 1856 . . . . . . . . . . . . . . .40,430 | | 17 | 22 | 30 | 40 | 60 | 85 | 150 | 275 | 3,000 |
| 1857 . . . . . . . . . . . . . . .35,180 | | 18 | 25 | 45 | 70 | 85 | 130 | 195 | 320 | 3,000 |

Cents and half cents were the first coins struck under the authority of the United States government. Coinage began in 1793 with laws stating that the cent should weigh exactly twice as much as the half cent. Large cents were coined every year from 1793 to 1857 with the exception of 1815, when a lack of copper prevented production. All were coined at the Philadelphia Mint. Varieties listed are those most significant to collectors. Numerous other die varieties may be found, as each of the early dies was individually made.

## FLOWING HAIR (1793)

**AG-3 About Good:** Date and devices clear enough to identify.
**G-4 Good:** Lettering worn but readable. No detail on bust.
**VG-8 Very Good:** Date and lettering distinct, some details of head visible.
**F-12 Fine:** About half of hair and other details visible.
**VF-20 Very Fine:** Ear visible, most details visible.
**EF-40 Extremely Fine:** Wear evident on highest points of hair and back of temple.

### Chain Reverse (1793)

AMERI. Reverse                AMERICA Reverse

| | Mintage | AG-3 | G-4 | VG-8 | F-12 | VF-20 | EF-40 |
|---|---|---|---|---|---|---|---|
| 1793, Chain, All kinds . . . . . . . . . . . . . . . . . | 36,103 | | | | | | |
| 1793, AMERI. in Legend . . . . . . . . . . . . . . . . . . . . | | $1,750 | $4,500 | $9,000 | $15,000 | $25,000 | $45,000 |
| 1793, AMERICA . . . . . . . . . . . . . . . . . . . . . . . . | | 1,300 | 3,500 | 6,750 | 9,500 | 19,000 | 35,000 |

### Wreath Reverse (1793)

Strawberry Leaf Variety

| | Mintage | AG-3 | G-4 | VG-8 | F-12 | VF-20 | EF-40 |
|---|---|---|---|---|---|---|---|
| 1793, Wreath, All kinds . . . . . . . . . . . . . . . . . | 63,353 | | | | | | |
| 1793, Vine and Bars Edge . . . . . . . . . . . . . . . . . . | | $325 | $1,150 | $1,700 | $2,750 | $4,000 | $7,000 |
| 1793, Lettered Edge . . . . . . . . . . . . . . . . . . . . . | | 400 | 1,350 | 1,800 | 3,000 | 4,200 | 8,200 |
| 1793, Strawberry Leaf . . . . . . . . . . . . . | (4 known) | — | — | — | | | |

## LIBERTY CAP (1793–1796)

**1793, Vine and Bars Edge**                **Lettered Edge (1793–1795)**
*Chain and Wreath types only.*                **ONE HUNDRED FOR A DOLLAR**

**Beaded Border (1793)**

**Head of 1793 (1793–1794)**
*Head in high, rounded relief.*

**Head of 1794 (1794)**
*Well-defined hair;*
*hook on lowest curl.*

**Head of 1795 (1794–1796)**
*Head in low relief;*
*no hook on lowest curl.*

| | Mintage | AG-3 | G-4 | VG-8 | F-12 | VF-20 | EF-40 |
|---|---|---|---|---|---|---|---|
| 1793, Liberty Cap | 11,056 | $1,000 | $2,000 | $3,800 | $7,500 | $18,000 | $36,000 |
| 1794, All kinds | 918,521 | | | | | | |
|    1794, "Head of 1793" | | 225 | 700 | 1,400 | 1,800 | 4,250 | 10,000 |
|    1794, "Head of 1794" | | 50 | 125 | 200 | 400 | 800 | 1,750 |
|    1794, "Head of 1795" | | 50 | 125 | 200 | 400 | 800 | 1,750 |
| 1795, Lettered Edge | 37,000 | 50 | 130 | 200 | 400 | 900 | 2,400 |
| 1795, Plain Edge | 501,500 | 35 | 115 | 225 | 350 | 700 | 1,500 |
| 1796, Liberty Cap | 109,825 | 75 | 180 | 275 | 600 | 1,000 | 2,300 |

## DRAPED BUST (1796–1807)

**AG-3 About Good:** Clear enough to identify.
**G-4 Good:** Lettering worn, but clear; date clear. Bust lacking in detail.
**VG-8 Very Good:** Drapery on Liberty partly visible. Less wear in date and lettering.
**F-12 Fine:** Hair over brow smooth; some detail showing in other parts of hair.
**VF-20 Very Fine:** Hair lines slightly worn. Hair over brow better defined.
**EF-40 Extremely Fine:** Hair above forehead and left of eye outlined and detailed. Only slight wear on olive leaves.

**LIHERTY Error**

| | Mintage | AG-3 | G-4 | VG-8 | F-12 | VF-20 | EF-40 |
|---|---|---|---|---|---|---|---|
| 1796, Draped Bust | 363,375 | $40 | $70 | $150 | $300 | $800 | $1,900 |
| 1796, LIHERTY Error | * | 80 | 135 | 325 | 550 | 1,750 | 4,200 |

* Included in number above.

| | With Stems | | Stemless | |
| --- | --- | --- | --- | --- |

Gripped Edge

| | Mintage | AG-3 | G-4 | VG-8 | F-12 | VF-20 | EF-40 |
| --- | --- | --- | --- | --- | --- | --- | --- |
| 1797, All kinds . . . . . . . . . . . . . . . . . . . . . .897,510 | | | | | | | |
| 1797, Gripped Edge, 1796 Reverse . . . . . . . . . . . | | $25 | $65 | $125 | $225 | $425 | $1,550 |
| 1797, Plain Edge, 1796 Reverse . . . . . . . . . . . . . | | 25 | 65 | 125 | 230 | 450 | 1,700 |
| 1797, 1797 Reverse, With Stems . . . . . . . . . . . . . | | 20 | 50 | 100 | 150 | 235 | 825 |
| 1797, 1797 Reverse, Stemless . . . . . . . . . . . . . . | | 25 | 65 | 125 | 250 | 650 | 2,300 |

| 1798, 8 Over 7 | 1799, 9 Over 8 | 1800 Over 1798 | 1800, 80 Over 79 |
| --- | --- | --- | --- |

| | Mintage | AG-3 | G-4 | VG-8 | F-12 | VF-20 | EF-40 |
| --- | --- | --- | --- | --- | --- | --- | --- |
| 1798, All kinds . . . . . . . . . . . . . . . . . . . . . .1,841,745 | | | | | | | |
| 1798, 8 Over 7 . . . . . . . . . . . . . . . . . . . . . . . | | $25 | $65 | $135 | $225 | $800 | $2,700 |
| 1798 . . . . . . . . . . . . . . . . . . . . . . . . . . . . . | | 13 | 35 | 47 | 110 | 225 | 900 |
| 1799, 9 Over 8 . . . . . . . . . . . . . . . . . . . . . . .* | | 700 | 1,400 | 2,500 | 6,000 | 16,500 | |
| 1799, Normal Date . . . . . . . . . . . . . . . . . . . . .* | | 650 | 1,300 | 2,200 | 5,600 | 14,500 | |
| 1800, All kinds . . . . . . . . . . . . . . . . . . . .2,822,175 | | | | | | | |
| 1800, 1800 Over 1798 . . . . . . . . . . . . . . . . . . | | 12 | 28 | 50 | 110 | 350 | 1,400 |
| 1800, 80 Over 79 . . . . . . . . . . . . . . . . . . . . | | 12 | 28 | 50 | 100 | 225 | 1,000 |
| 1800, Normal Date . . . . . . . . . . . . . . . . . . . . | | 12 | 28 | 50 | 100 | 225 | 1,000 |

* Included in "1798, All kinds," mintage.

| Fraction 1/000 | Corrected Fraction | 1801 Reverse, 3 Errors |
| --- | --- | --- |

| | Mintage | AG-3 | G-4 | VG-8 | F-12 | VF-20 | EF-40 |
| --- | --- | --- | --- | --- | --- | --- | --- |
| 1801, All kinds . . . . . . . . . . . . . . . . . . . .1,362,837 | | | | | | | |
| 1801, Normal Reverse . . . . . . . . . . . . . . . . . . | | $11 | $22 | $30 | $75 | $200 | $525 |
| 1801, 3 Errors: 1/000, One Stem, and IINITED . . . . | | 25 | 65 | 120 | 325 | 1,000 | 3,200 |
| 1801, Fraction 1/000 . . . . . . . . . . . . . . . . . . . | | 11 | 27 | 40 | 120 | 225 | 825 |
| 1801, 1/100 Over 1/000 . . . . . . . . . . . . . . . . . | | 12 | 27 | 42 | 125 | 275 | 925 |
| 1802, All kinds . . . . . . . . . . . . . . . . . . . .3,435,100 | | | | | | | |
| 1802, Normal Reverse . . . . . . . . . . . . . . . . . . | | 11 | 24 | 40 | 90 | 175 | 525 |
| 1802, Fraction 1/000 . . . . . . . . . . . . . . . . . . . | | 12 | 30 | 50 | 120 | 250 | 900 |
| 1802, Stemless Wreath . . . . . . . . . . . . . . . . . . | | 11 | 24 | 40 | 90 | 175 | 525 |

| 1803, Small Date, Blunt 1 | 1803, Large Date, Pointed 1 | Small Fraction | Large Fraction |
| --- | --- | --- | --- |

| | Mintage | AG-3 | G-4 | VG-8 | F-12 | VF-20 | EF-40 |
|---|---|---|---|---|---|---|---|
| 1803, All kinds .......................3,131,691 | | | | | | | |
| 1803, Small Date, Small Fraction ............. | $11 | $24 | $40 | $80 | $175 | $525 |
| 1803, Small Date, Large Fraction ............. | 11 | 24 | 40 | 80 | 175 | 525 |
| 1803, Large Date, Small Fraction ............. | 1,000 | 2,300 | 4,000 | 8,250 | 13,500 | |
| 1803, Large Date, Large Fraction ............. | 17 | 33 | 80 | 150 | 425 | 1,400 |
| 1803, 1/100 Over 1/000 ................... | 11 | 27 | 50 | 100 | 225 | 700 |
| 1803, Stemless Wreath ................... | 11 | 27 | 50 | 100 | 225 | 700 |

**Broken Dies**

*All genuine 1804 cents have crosslet 4 in date and a large fraction.*
*The 0 in date is in line with O in OF on reverse.*

| | Mintage | AG-3 | G-4 | VG-8 | F-12 | VF-20 | EF-40 |
|---|---|---|---|---|---|---|---|
| 1804 (a) ..........................96,500 | $350 | $750 | $1,200 | $2,000 | $3,000 | $7,000 |
| 1805 ............................941,116 | 11 | 24 | 40 | 80 | 175 | 500 |
| 1806 ............................348,000 | 11 | 27 | 50 | 95 | 225 | 875 |

a. Values shown are for coins with normal or broken dies.

**Small 1807, 7 Over 6**
**(Blunt 1)**

**Large 1807, 7 Over 6**
**(Pointed 1)**

| | Mintage | AG-3 | G-4 | VG-8 | F-12 | VF-20 | EF-40 |
|---|---|---|---|---|---|---|---|
| 1807, All kinds ......................829,221 | | | | | | | |
| 1807, Small 7 Over 6, Blunt 1 ............... | $410 | $1,200 | $2,200 | $4,500 | $8,200 | $17,000 |
| 1807, Large 7 Over 6 ..................... | 11 | 24 | 35 | 70 | 175 | 550 |
| 1807, Small Fraction ..................... | 11 | 24 | 35 | 70 | 225 | 600 |
| 1807, Large Fraction ..................... | 11 | 24 | 35 | 70 | 200 | 500 |

# CLASSIC HEAD (1808–1814)

**AG-3 About Good:** Details clear enough to identify.

**G-4 Good:** Legends, stars, and date worn, but plain.

**VG-8 Very Good:** LIBERTY all readable. Liberty's ear visible. Details worn but plain.

**F-12 Fine:** Hair on forehead and before ear nearly smooth. Ear and hair under ear sharp.

**VF-20 Very Fine:** Some detail in all hair lines. Slight wear on leaves on reverse.

**EF-40 Extremely Fine:** All hair lines sharp. Very slight wear on high points.

*See next page for chart.*

| | Mintage | AG-3 | G-4 | VG-8 | F-12 | VF-20 | EF-40 |
|---|---|---|---|---|---|---|---|
| 1808 . . . . . . . . . . . . . . . . . . . . . . .1,007,000 | | $13 | $24 | $60 | $150 | $275 | $925 |
| 1809 . . . . . . . . . . . . . . . . . . . . . . . . . .222,867 | | 22 | 50 | 110 | 225 | 650 | 1,800 |

| **1810, 10 Over 09** | **1810, Normal Date** | **1811, Last 1 Over 0** | **1811, Normal Date** |
|---|---|---|---|

| | Mintage | AG-3 | G-4 | VG-8 | F-12 | VF-20 | EF-40 |
|---|---|---|---|---|---|---|---|
| 1810, All kinds . . . . . . . . . . . . . . . . . . . .1,458,500 | | | | | | | |
| 1810, 10 Over 09 . . . . . . . . . . . . . . . . . . . . . . | | $11 | $24 | $45 | $120 | $300 | $750 |
| 1810, Normal Date . . . . . . . . . . . . . . . . . . . . . . | | 11 | 24 | 35 | 120 | 260 | 700 |
| 1811, All kinds . . . . . . . . . . . . . . . . . . . . .218,025 | | | | | | | |
| 1811, Last 1 Over 0 . . . . . . . . . . . . . . . . . . . . . | | 16 | 33 | 60 | 210 | 800 | 2,500 |
| 1811, Normal Date . . . . . . . . . . . . . . . . . . . . . | | 15 | 35 | 70 | 150 | 400 | 850 |
| 1812 . . . . . . . . . . . . . . . . . . . . .1,075,500 | | 11 | 22 | 35 | 110 | 250 | 650 |
| 1813 . . . . . . . . . . . . . . . . . . . . . . . .418,000 | | 13 | 24 | 50 | 125 | 285 | 650 |
| 1814 . . . . . . . . . . . . . . . . . . . . . . . .357,830 | | 11 | 22 | 35 | 110 | 250 | 600 |

## LIBERTY HEAD (1816–1857)

**G-4 Good:** Details on Liberty's head partly visible. Even wear in date and legends.
**VG-8 Very Good:** LIBERTY, date, stars, and legends clear. Part of hair cord visible.
**F-12 Fine:** All hair lines visible. Hair cords uniformly visible.
**VF-20 Very Fine:** Hair cords only slightly worn. Hair lines only partly worn, all well defined.
**EF-40 Extremely Fine:** Both hair cords stand out sharply. All hair lines sharp.
**AU-50 About Uncirculated:** Only traces of wear on hair and highest points on leaves and bow.
**MS-60 Uncirculated:** Typical brown surface. No trace of wear.
**MS-63 Choice Uncirculated:** Some distracting contact marks or blemishes in prime focal areas.
Impaired luster possible.

### Matron Head (1816–1835)

**1817, 13 Stars**                                        **1817, 15 Stars**

*Brilliant or red Uncirculated coins are worth more than prices shown. Spotted, cleaned, or discolored pieces are worth less.*

| | Mintage | G-4 | VG-8 | F-12 | VF-20 | EF-40 | AU-50 | MS-60 | MS-63 |
|---|---|---|---|---|---|---|---|---|---|
| 1816 . . . . . . . . . . . .2,820,982 | | $8 | $11 | $16 | $32 | $70 | $125 | $250 | $375 |
| 1817, 13 Stars . . . .3,948,400 | | 8 | 10 | 14 | 27 | 50 | 100 | 200 | 350 |
| 1817, 15 Stars . . . . . . . . . .* | | 11 | 13 | 16 | 55 | 225 | 350 | 1,100 | — |
| 1818 . . . . . . . . . . . .3,167,000 | | 8 | 10 | 14 | 27 | 50 | 90 | 225 | 325 |

* Included in number above.

1819, 9 Over 8

1820, 20 Over 19

| | Mintage | G-4 | VG-8 | F-12 | VF-20 | EF-40 | AU-50 | MS-60 | MS-63 |
|---|---|---|---|---|---|---|---|---|---|
| 1819 . . . . . . . . . . . .2,671,000 | | $9 | $11 | $15 | $27 | $55 | $125 | $185 | $350 |
| 1819, 9 Over 8 . . . . . . . . . . .* | | 10 | 13 | 18 | 36 | 150 | 175 | 300 | 500 |
| 1820 . . . . . . . . . . . .4,407,550 | | 8 | 10 | 13 | 30 | 60 | 100 | 200 | 350 |
| 1820, 20 Over 19 . . . . . . . . .* | | 10 | 13 | 18 | 45 | 150 | 200 | 500 | 700 |
| 1821 . . . . . . . . . . . . .389,000 | | 16 | 27 | 60 | 185 | 500 | 1,000 | 3,600 | — |
| 1822 . . . . . . . . . . . .2,072,339 | | 9 | 12 | 22 | 50 | 100 | 275 | 475 | 775 |

* Included in number above.

1823, 3 Over 2

1824, 4 Over 2

1826, 6 Over 5

| | Mintage | G-4 | VG-8 | F-12 | VF-20 | EF-40 | AU-50 | MS-60 | MS-63 |
|---|---|---|---|---|---|---|---|---|---|
| 1823, 3 Over 2 . . . . . . . . . . .* | | $27 | $50 | $150 | $300 | $1,000 | $1,900 | $3,400 | — |
| 1823, Normal Date . . . . . . . .* | | 30 | 55 | 175 | 400 | 1,350 | 2,400 | 3,800 | — |
| 1824, 4 Over 2 . . . . . . . . . . .* | | 10 | 18 | 40 | 150 | 550 | 1,200 | 2,500 | $3,750 |
| 1824, Normal Date . .1,262,000 | | 8 | 10 | 16 | 75 | 210 | 350 | 950 | 1,600 |
| 1825 . . . . . . . . . . . .1,461,100 | | 8 | 10 | 16 | 45 | 150 | 250 | 800 | 1,100 |
| 1826, 6 Over 5 . . . . .1,517,425 | | 12 | 17 | 37 | 110 | 425 | 600 | 1,200 | 2,300 |
| 1826, Normal Date . . . . . . . .** | | 8 | 10 | 12 | 45 | 110 | 190 | 400 | 650 |
| 1827 . . . . . . . . . . . .2,357,732 | | 8 | 10 | 12 | 40 | 80 | 150 | 300 | 600 |

* Included in number below. ** Included in number above.

Date Size, Through 1828

Date Size, 1828 and Later

| | Mintage | G-4 | VG-8 | F-12 | VF-20 | EF-40 | AU-50 | MS-60 | MS-63 |
|---|---|---|---|---|---|---|---|---|---|
| 1828, Large Narrow Date . . . . . . . .2,260,624 | | $8 | $10 | $14 | $40 | $70 | $150 | $400 | $650 |
| 1828, Small Wide Date . . . . . . . . . . . . . . . . .* | | 8 | 10 | 16 | 50 | 100 | 200 | 500 | 950 |
| 1829 . . . . . . . . . . . . . . . . . . . . . . .1,414,500 | | 8 | 10 | 13 | 40 | 70 | 110 | 250 | 525 |
| 1830 . . . . . . . . . . . . . . . . . . . . . . .1,711,500 | | 8 | 10 | 13 | 30 | 60 | 100 | 200 | 400 |
| 1831 . . . . . . . . . . . . . . . . . . . . . . .3,359,260 | | 7 | 9 | 12 | 22 | 50 | 100 | 200 | 350 |
| 1832 . . . . . . . . . . . . . . . . . . . . . . .2,362,000 | | 7 | 9 | 12 | 22 | 50 | 80 | 175 | 325 |
| 1833 . . . . . . . . . . . . . . . . . . . . . . .2,739,000 | | 7 | 9 | 12 | 22 | 50 | 80 | 175 | 325 |
| 1834 . . . . . . . . . . . . . . . . . . . . . . .1,855,100 | | 7 | 9 | 12 | 22 | 70 | 100 | 200 | 350 |
| 1835 . . . . . . . . . . . . . . . . . . . . . . .3,878,400 | | 7 | 9 | 12 | 22 | 65 | 90 | 200 | 350 |

* Included in number above.

## Matron Head Modified (1835–1839) and Braided Hair (1837–1857)

**G-4 Good:** Considerably worn. LIBERTY readable.

**VG-8 Very Good:** Hairlines smooth but visible; outline of ear clearly defined.

**F-12 Fine:** Hairlines at top of head and behind ear worn but visible. Braid over brow plain; ear clear.

**VF-20 Very Fine:** All details sharper than for F-12. Only slight wear on hair over brow.

**EF-40 Extremely Fine:** Hair above ear detailed, but slightly worn.

**AU-50 About Uncirculated:** Trace of wear on high points of hair above ear and eye and on highest points on leaves and bow.

**MS-60 Uncirculated:** Typical brown surface. No trace of wear.

**MS-63 Choice Uncirculated:** Some distracting contact marks or blemishes in prime focal areas. Impaired luster possible.

**1839 Over 1836**

*Brilliant or red Uncirculated coins are worth more than prices shown. Cleaned or discolored pieces are worth less.*

| | Mintage | G-4 | VG-8 | F-12 | VF-20 | EF-40 | AU-50 | MS-60 | MS-63 |
|---|---|---|---|---|---|---|---|---|---|
| 1836 | 2,111,000 | $7 | $9 | $12 | $22 | $55 | $85 | $160 | $300 |
| 1837 | 5,558,300 | 7 | 9 | 12 | 22 | 65 | 90 | 160 | 240 |
| 1838 | 6,370,200 | 7 | 9 | 12 | 22 | 30 | 85 | 150 | 220 |
| 1839 | 3,128,661 | 7 | 9 | 12 | 22 | 40 | 80 | 150 | 210 |
| 1839, 1839 Over 1836, Plain Cords | * | 110 | 275 | 550 | 1,250 | 3,500 | 6,500 | — | — |
| 1840 | 2,462,700 | 7 | 9 | 12 | 18 | 40 | 75 | 150 | 275 |
| 1841 | 1,597,367 | 7 | 9 | 12 | 18 | 40 | 75 | 150 | 275 |
| 1842 | 2,383,390 | 7 | 9 | 12 | 18 | 40 | 75 | 150 | 250 |

* Included in number above.

"Head of 1840"
Petite Head (1839–1843)

"Head of 1844"
Mature Head (1843–1857)

**Small Letters**

**Large Letters**

| | Mintage | G-4 | VG-8 | F-12 | VF-20 | EF-40 | AU-50 | MS-60 | MS-63 |
|---|---|---|---|---|---|---|---|---|---|
| 1843, Petite, Small Letters | 2,425,342 | $7 | $9 | $12 | $20 | $30 | $60 | $145 | $185 |
| 1843, Petite, Large Letters | * | 9 | 11 | 20 | 35 | 70 | 125 | 325 | 600 |
| 1843, Mature, Large Letters | * | 8 | 10 | 16 | 25 | 50 | 90 | 160 | 400 |
| 1844, Normal Date | 2,398,752 | 7 | 9 | 12 | 20 | 32 | 65 | 120 | 175 |
| 1844, 44 Over 81 | * | 10 | 13 | 20 | 40 | 110 | 235 | 550 | 1,250 |
| 1845 | 3,894,804 | 7 | 9 | 12 | 20 | 30 | 70 | 125 | 175 |
| 1846 | 4,120,800 | 7 | 9 | 12 | 20 | 30 | 70 | 125 | 175 |
| 1847 | 6,183,669 | 7 | 9 | 12 | 20 | 30 | 70 | 125 | 175 |
| 1847, 7 Over "Small 7" | * | 8 | 11 | 17 | 30 | 65 | 160 | 525 | 1,000 |

* Included in number above.

| | Mintage | G-4 | VG-8 | F-12 | VF-20 | EF-40 | AU-50 | MS-60 | MS-63 |
|---|---|---|---|---|---|---|---|---|---|
| 1848 | 6,415,799 | $7 | $9 | $12 | $18 | $30 | $70 | $110 | $150 |
| 1849 | 4,178,500 | 7 | 9 | 12 | 18 | 30 | 70 | 125 | 190 |
| 1850 | 4,426,844 | 7 | 9 | 12 | 18 | 30 | 70 | 100 | 150 |

**1844, 44 Over 81** | **1851, 51 Over 81** | **1847, 7 Over "Small" 7**

*Brilliant or red Uncirculated coins are worth more than prices shown. Spotted, cleaned, or discolored pieces are worth less.*

| | Mintage | G-4 | VG-8 | F-12 | VF-20 | EF-40 | AU-50 | MS-60 | MS-63 |
|---|---|---|---|---|---|---|---|---|---|
| 1851, Normal Date | 9,889,707 | $7 | $9 | $12 | $18 | $30 | $70 | $100 | $150 |
| 1851, 51 Over 81 | * | 9 | 11 | 18 | 28 | 70 | 110 | 250 | 435 |
| 1852 | 5,063,094 | 7 | 9 | 12 | 18 | 30 | 70 | 100 | 150 |
| 1853 | 6,641,131 | 7 | 9 | 12 | 18 | 30 | 70 | 100 | 150 |
| 1854 | 4,236,156 | 7 | 9 | 12 | 18 | 30 | 70 | 100 | 150 |

* Included in number above.

**1855, Upright 5's** | **1855, Slanting 5's** | **1855, Knob on Ear**

| | Mintage | G-4 | VG-8 | F-12 | VF-20 | EF-40 | AU-50 | MS-60 | MS-63 |
|---|---|---|---|---|---|---|---|---|---|
| 1855, All kinds | 1,574,829 | | | | | | | | |
|   1855, Upright 5's | | $7 | $9 | $12 | $18 | $30 | $70 | $100 | $150 |
|   1855, Slanting 5's | | 7 | 9 | 12 | 18 | 30 | 70 | 115 | 160 |
|   1855, Slanting 5's, Knob on Ear | | 7 | 10 | 14 | 22 | 40 | 90 | 160 | 250 |
| 1856, Upright 5 | 2,690,463 | 7 | 9 | 12 | 18 | 30 | 70 | 100 | 150 |
| 1856, Slanting 5 | * | 7 | 9 | 12 | 18 | 30 | 70 | 100 | 150 |

* Included in number above.

**1857, Large Date** | **1857, Small Date**

| | Mintage | G-4 | VG-8 | F-12 | VF-20 | EF-40 | AU-50 | MS-60 | MS-63 |
|---|---|---|---|---|---|---|---|---|---|
| 1857, Large Date | 333,546 | $16 | $25 | $30 | $35 | $50 | $120 | $200 | $325 |
| 1857, Small Date | * | 17 | 27 | 35 | 40 | 55 | 130 | 220 | 350 |

* Included in number above.

## FLYING EAGLE (1856–1858)

The Act of February 21, 1857, provided for the coinage of the new copper-nickel small cent. The 1856 Flying Eagle cent was not an authorized Mint issue, as the law governing the new-size coin was enacted after the date of issue. It is believed that nearly 1,000 original strikings and 1,500 or more restrikes were made of the 1856. They are properly referred to as *patterns*.

**G-4 Good:** All details worn, but readable.

**VG-8 Very Good:** Details in eagle's feathers and eye evident, but worn.

**F-12 Fine:** Eagle-head details and feather tips sharp.

**VF-20 Very Fine:** Considerable detail visible in feathers in right wing and tail.

**EF-40 Extremely Fine:** Slight wear, all details sharp.

**AU-50 About Uncirculated:** Slight wear on eagle's left wing and breast.

**MS-60 Uncirculated:** No trace of wear. Light blemishes.

**MS-63 Choice Uncirculated:** Some distracting contact marks or blemishes in prime focal areas. Some impairment of luster possible.

**PF-63 Choice Proof:** Nearly perfect.

| 1858, 8 Over 7 | 1856–1858, Large Letters | 1858, Small Letters |

*Brilliant Uncirculated and Proof coins are worth more than prices shown. Spotted, cleaned, or discolored pieces are worth less.*

| | Mintage | G-4 | VG-8 | F-12 | VF-20 | EF-40 | AU-50 | MS-60 | MS-63 | PF-63 |
|---|---|---|---|---|---|---|---|---|---|---|
| 1856 | 2,000 | $4,200 | $4,800 | $5,200 | $6,750 | $8,000 | $9,000 | $11,000 | $13,500 | $13,250 |
| 1857 | 17,450,000 | 13 | 16 | 20 | 28 | 80 | 100 | 200 | 350 | |
| | (485) | | | | | | | | | 4,000 |
| 1858, Large Letters | 24,600,000 | 13 | 16 | 20 | 28 | 80 | 100 | 200 | 350 | |
| | (100) | | | | | | | | | 4,000 |
| 1858, 8 Over 7 | * | | 50 | 110 | 210 | 420 | 725 | 1,900 | 5,000 | |
| 1858, Small Letters | * | 13 | 16 | 20 | 28 | 80 | 100 | 200 | 350 | |
| | (200) | | | | | | | | | 4,000 |

* Included in mintage for 1858, Large Letters.

## INDIAN HEAD (1859–1909)

The small cent was redesigned in 1859, and a representation of Miss Liberty wearing an Indian war bonnet was adopted as the obverse device. The 1859 reverse was also changed to represent a laurel wreath. In 1860 the reverse was modified to display an oak wreath with a small shield at the top. From 1859 into 1864, cents were struck in copper-nickel. In 1864 the composition was changed to bronze, although copper-nickel cents were also struck during that year.

# SMALL CENTS

**G-4 Good:** No LIBERTY visible.
**VG-8 Very Good:** At least some letters of LIBERTY readable on head band.
**F-12 Fine:** LIBERTY mostly visible.
**VF-20 Very Fine:** Slight but even wear on LIBERTY.
**EF-40 Extremely Fine:** LIBERTY sharp. All other details sharp. Only slight wear on ribbon end.
**AU-50 About Uncirculated:** Very slight trace of wear above the ear and the lowest curl of hair.
**MS-60 Uncirculated:** No trace of wear. Light blemishes.
**MS-63 Choice Uncirculated:** Some distracting contact marks or blemishes in prime focal areas. Impaired luster possible.
**PF-63 Choice Proof:** Nearly perfect.

**Without Shield at Top of Wreath (1859 Only)**

**With Shield on Reverse (1860–1909)**

## Variety 1 – Copper-Nickel, Laurel Wreath Reverse (1859)

*Brilliant or red Uncirculated coins are worth more than prices shown. Spotted, cleaned, or discolored pieces are worth less.*

| | Mintage | G-4 | VG-8 | F-12 | VF-20 | EF-40 | AU-50 | MS-60 | MS-63 | PF-63 |
|---|---|---|---|---|---|---|---|---|---|---|
| 1859 . . . . . . . .*(800)* . .36,400,000 | | $7 | $8 | $10 | $27 | $55 | $100 | $135 | $265 | $850 |

## Variety 2 – Copper-Nickel, Oak Wreath With Shield (1860–1864)

| | Mintage | G-4 | VG-8 | F-12 | VF-20 | EF-40 | AU-50 | MS-60 | MS-63 | PF-63 |
|---|---|---|---|---|---|---|---|---|---|---|
| 1860 . . . . . .*(1,000)* . .20,566,000 | | $6.00 | $7 | $8 | $12 | $32 | $65 | $90 | $125 | $550 |
| 1861 . . . . . .*(1,000)* . .10,100,000 | | 11.00 | 13 | 18 | 32 | 65 | 85 | 125 | 150 | 600 |
| 1862 . . . . . . .*(550)* . .28,075,000 | | 5.50 | 6 | 7 | 9 | 22 | 40 | 65 | 100 | 475 |
| 1863 . . . . . . .*(460)* . .49,840,000 | | 5.50 | 6 | 7 | 9 | 22 | 40 | 65 | 100 | 475 |
| 1864 . . . . . . .*(370)* . .13,740,000 | | 8.00 | 10 | 14 | 25 | 38 | 65 | 100 | 140 | 500 |

## Variety 3 – Bronze (1864–1909)

**1864, Indian Head Cent With "L"**

| | Mintage | G-4 | VG-8 | F-12 | VF-20 | EF-40 | AU-50 | MS-60 | MS-63 | PF-63 |
|---|---|---|---|---|---|---|---|---|---|---|
| 1864, All kinds . . . . . .39,233,714 | | | | | | | | | | |
| 1864, No L *(150)* . . . . . . . . . . | | $4 | $6 | $9 | $22 | $32 | $42 | $55 | $85 | $500 |
| 1864, With L *(20)* . . . . . . . . . . | | 27 | 45 | 70 | 100 | 170 | 190 | 225 | 375 | — |
| 1865 . . . . . . . .*(500)* . .35,429,286 | | 4 | 5 | 9 | 12 | 20 | 35 | 50 | 85 | 350 |
| 1866 . . . . . . . .*(725)* . .9,826,500 | | 22 | 25 | 35 | 65 | 100 | 150 | 175 | 275 | 350 |
| 1867 . . . . . . . .*(625)* . .9,821,000 | | 22 | 25 | 35 | 65 | 100 | 150 | 175 | 275 | 350 |
| 1868 . . . . . . . .*(600)* . .10,266,500 | | 22 | 25 | 35 | 65 | 100 | 150 | 175 | 275 | 350 |
| 1869 . . . . . . . .*(600)* . .6,420,000 | | 35 | 40 | 90 | 150 | 225 | 275 | 300 | 450 | 350 |
| 1870 . . . . . .*(1,000)* . .5,275,000 | | 28 | 35 | 85 | 135 | 200 | 275 | 300 | 350 | 350 |
| 1871 . . . . . . . .*(960)* . .3,929,500 | | 35 | 45 | 125 | 185 | 225 | 300 | 365 | 500 | 375 |
| 1872 . . . . . . . .*(950)* . .4,042,000 | | 40 | 60 | 160 | 225 | 300 | 400 | 450 | 650 | 425 |
| 1873 . . . . . .*(1,100)* . .11,676,500 | | 11 | 14 | 24 | 38 | 80 | 100 | 120 | 220 | 275 |
| 1874 . . . . . . . .*(700)* . .14,187,500 | | 9 | 11 | 18 | 30 | 55 | 85 | 110 | 165 | 250 |
| 1875 . . . . . . . .*(700)* . .13,528,000 | | 10 | 14 | 20 | 35 | 50 | 75 | 110 | 165 | 250 |
| 1876 . . . . . .*(1,150)* . .7,944,000 | | 15 | 18 | 20 | 60 | 100 | 145 | 185 | 275 | 250 |
| 1877 . . . . . . . .*(900)* . . .852,500 | | 500 | 725 | 875 | 1,250 | 1,600 | 1,900 | 2,200 | 2,800 | 2,800 |

*Brilliant or red Uncirculated coins are worth more than prices shown. Spotted, cleaned, or discolored pieces are worth less.*

| | Mintage | G-4 | VG-8 | F-12 | VF-20 | EF-40 | AU-50 | MS-60 | MS-63 | PF-63 |
|---|---|---|---|---|---|---|---|---|---|---|
| 1878 .....(2,350) | ....5,797,500 | $14.00 | $18.00 | $25.00 | $65.00 | $100 | $145 | $165 | $250 | $220 |
| 1879 .....(3,200) | ...16,228,000 | 4.00 | 6.00 | 8.00 | 18.00 | 40 | 45 | 50 | 80 | 175 |
| 1880 .....(3,955) | ...38,961,000 | 1.75 | 2.00 | 3.00 | 6.00 | 15 | 25 | 40 | 70 | 140 |
| 1881 .....(3,575) | ...39,208,000 | 1.75 | 2.00 | 3.00 | 5.00 | 10 | 16 | 26 | 37 | 140 |
| 1882 .....(3,100) | ...38,578,000 | 1.75 | 2.00 | 3.00 | 5.00 | 10 | 16 | 26 | 37 | 140 |
| 1883 .....(6,609) | ...45,591,500 | 1.75 | 2.00 | 3.00 | 5.00 | 10 | 16 | 26 | 37 | 140 |
| 1884 .....(3,942) | ...23,257,800 | 2.25 | 2.50 | 3.50 | 6.00 | 14 | 20 | 30 | 60 | 140 |
| 1885 .....(3,790) | ...11,761,594 | 3.00 | 4.00 | 6.00 | 14.00 | 35 | 45 | 60 | 95 | 140 |
| 1886 .....(4,290) | ...17,650,000 | 1.75 | 3.00 | 8.00 | 24.00 | 65 | 85 | 100 | 125 | 150 |
| 1887 .....(2,960) | ...45,223,523 | 1.25 | 1.50 | 1.75 | 2.25 | 8 | 14 | 25 | 35 | 140 |
| 1888 .....(4,582) | ...37,489,832 | 0.85 | 1.10 | 1.80 | 2.75 | 8 | 14 | 25 | 40 | 140 |
| 1889 .....(3,336) | ...48,866,025 | 0.85 | 1.10 | 1.80 | 2.75 | 6 | 12 | 22 | 35 | 140 |
| 1890 .....(2,740) | ...57,180,114 | 0.85 | 1.10 | 1.80 | 2.75 | 6 | 12 | 22 | 35 | 140 |
| 1891 .....(2,350) | ...47,070,000 | 0.85 | 1.10 | 1.80 | 2.75 | 6 | 12 | 22 | 35 | 140 |
| 1892 .....(2,745) | ...37,647,087 | 0.85 | 1.10 | 1.80 | 2.75 | 6 | 12 | 22 | 35 | 140 |
| 1893 .....(2,195) | ...46,640,000 | 0.85 | 1.10 | 1.80 | 2.75 | 6 | 12 | 22 | 35 | 140 |
| 1894 .....(2,632) | ...16,749,500 | 2.00 | 3.00 | 4.75 | 8.50 | 25 | 30 | 40 | 50 | 150 |
| 1895 .....(2,062) | ...38,341,574 | 0.85 | 1.10 | 1.30 | 2.00 | 6 | 11 | 22 | 28 | 140 |
| 1896 .....(1,862) | ...39,055,431 | 0.85 | 1.10 | 1.30 | 2.00 | 6 | 11 | 22 | 28 | 140 |
| 1897 .....(1,938) | ...50,464,392 | 0.85 | 1.10 | 1.30 | 2.00 | 6 | 11 | 22 | 28 | 140 |
| 1898 .....(1,795) | ...49,821,284 | 0.85 | 1.10 | 1.30 | 2.00 | 6 | 11 | 22 | 28 | 140 |
| 1899 .....(2,031) | ...53,598,000 | 0.85 | 1.10 | 1.30 | 2.00 | 6 | 11 | 22 | 28 | 140 |
| 1900 .....(2,262) | ...66,831,502 | 0.80 | 1.00 | 1.10 | 1.50 | 5 | 10 | 18 | 25 | 120 |
| 1901 .....(1,985) | ...79,609,158 | 0.80 | 1.00 | 1.10 | 1.50 | 5 | 10 | 18 | 25 | 120 |
| 1902 .....(2,018) | ...87,374,704 | 0.80 | 1.00 | 1.10 | 1.50 | 5 | 10 | 18 | 25 | 120 |
| 1903 .....(1,790) | ...85,092,703 | 0.80 | 1.00 | 1.10 | 1.50 | 5 | 10 | 18 | 25 | 120 |
| 1904 .....(1,817) | ...61,326,198 | 0.80 | 1.00 | 1.10 | 1.50 | 5 | 10 | 18 | 25 | 120 |
| 1905 .....(2,152) | ...80,717,011 | 0.80 | 1.00 | 1.10 | 1.50 | 5 | 10 | 18 | 25 | 120 |
| 1906 .....(1,725) | ...96,020,530 | 0.80 | 1.00 | 1.10 | 1.50 | 5 | 10 | 18 | 25 | 120 |
| 1907 .....(1,475) | ..108,137,143 | 0.80 | 1.00 | 1.10 | 1.50 | 5 | 10 | 18 | 25 | 120 |

**Location of Mintmark S on Reverse of
Indian Head Cent (1908 and 1909 Only)**

| | Mintage | G-4 | VG-8 | F-12 | VF-20 | EF-40 | AU-50 | MS-60 | MS-63 | PF-63 |
|---|---|---|---|---|---|---|---|---|---|---|
| 1908 .....(1,620) | ...32,326,367 | $0.80 | $1.10 | $1.25 | $1.50 | $5 | $10 | $18 | $25 | $120 |
| 1908S ............. | ...1,115,000 | 40.00 | 50.00 | 55.00 | 65.00 | 95 | 120 | 175 | 210 | |
| 1909 .....(2,175) | ...14,368,470 | 5.00 | 6.00 | 8.00 | 10.00 | 12 | 16 | 25 | 32 | 120 |
| 1909S ............. | ...309,000 | 275.00 | 300.00 | 325.00 | 350.00 | 400 | 450 | 520 | 675 | |

## LINCOLN, WHEAT EARS REVERSE (1909–1958)

Victor D. Brenner designed this cent, which was issued to commemorate the 100th anniversary of Abraham Lincoln's birth. The designer's initials (V.D.B.) appear on the reverse of a limited quantity of cents of 1909. Later in the year they were removed from the dies but restored in 1918 as very small incuse letters beneath the shoulder. The Lincoln type was the first cent to have the motto IN GOD WE TRUST.

**G-4 Good:** Date worn but apparent. Lines in wheat heads missing. Full rims.
**VG-8 Very Good:** Half of lines visible in upper wheat heads.
**F-12 Fine:** Wheat lines worn but visible.
**VF-20 Very Fine:** Lincoln's cheekbone and jawbone worn but separated. No worn spots on wheat heads.
**EF-40 Extremely Fine:** Slight wear. All details sharp.
**AU-50 About Uncirculated:** Slight wear on cheek and jaw and on wheat stalks.
**MS-60 Uncirculated:** No trace of wear. Light blemishes. Brown or red-brown color.
**MS-63 Choice Uncirculated:** No trace of wear. Slight blemishes. Red-brown color.
**MS-65 Gem Uncirculated:** No trace of wear. Barely noticeable blemishes. Nearly full red color.
**PF-63 Choice Proof:** Reflective surfaces with only a few blemishes in secondary focal places. No major flaws.

*Location of mintmark S or D
on obverse of Lincoln cent.*

**Designer's Initials
V.D.B. (1909 Only)**

**No V.D.B.
on Reverse
(1909–1958)**

*Brilliant Uncirculated coins are worth more than prices shown. Spotted, cleaned, or discolored pieces are worth less.*

| | Mintage | G-4 | VG-8 | F-12 | VF-20 | EF-40 | AU-50 | MS-60 | MS-63 | MATTE PF-63 |
|---|---|---|---|---|---|---|---|---|---|---|
| 1909, V.D.B. | | | | | | | | | | |
| .....(1,194) ...27,995,000 | $6.00 | $6.50 | $7.00 | $8.00 | $9.00 | $10.00 | $12.00 | $15 | $1,300 | |
| 1909S ..........484,000 | 450.00 | 500.00 | 550.00 | 725.00 | 825.00 | 975.00 | 1,150.00 | 1,400 | | |
| 1909 .....(2,618) ...72,702,618 | 1.00 | 1.25 | 1.60 | 2.00 | 2.50 | 6.00 | 8.50 | 15 | 225 | |
| 1909S ...........1,825,000 | 50.00 | 60.00 | 70.00 | 95.00 | 150.00 | 165.00 | 200.00 | 235 | | |
| 1910 .....(4,118) ..146,801,218 | 0.07 | 0.10 | 0.15 | 0.30 | 1.00 | 2.50 | 9.00 | 13 | 150 | |
| 1910S .............6,045,000 | 7.50 | 9.00 | 11.00 | 12.00 | 25.00 | 40.00 | 55.00 | 70 | | |
| 1911 .....(1,725) ..101,177,787 | 0.10 | 0.15 | 0.30 | 0.50 | 1.50 | 3.50 | 11.00 | 25 | 175 | |
| 1911D ............12,672,000 | 2.25 | 3.00 | 4.50 | 9.00 | 21.00 | 35.00 | 50.00 | 70 | | |
| 1911S .............4,026,000 | 18.00 | 25.00 | 30.00 | 35.00 | 45.00 | 60.00 | 110.00 | 150 | | |
| 1912 .....(2,172) ...68,153,060 | 0.15 | 0.25 | 0.70 | 2.00 | 2.50 | 8.00 | 17.00 | 25 | 150 | |
| 1912D ............10,411,000 | 2.75 | 3.50 | 4.25 | 10.00 | 25.00 | 40.00 | 75.00 | 120 | | |
| 1912S .............4,431,000 | 11.00 | 13.00 | 15.00 | 18.00 | 35.00 | 47.00 | 90.00 | 125 | | |
| 1913 .....(2,983) ...76,532,352 | 0.15 | 0.20 | 0.50 | 1.50 | 8.00 | 12.00 | 16.00 | 25 | 160 | |
| 1913D ............15,804,000 | 0.75 | 1.00 | 1.50 | 3.50 | 20.00 | 26.00 | 50.00 | 100 | | |
| 1913S .............6,101,000 | 5.50 | 6.75 | 9.00 | 12.00 | 27.00 | 50.00 | 85.00 | 135 | | |
| 1914 .....(1,365) ...75,238,432 | 0.20 | 0.30 | 0.75 | 2.00 | 6.50 | 17.00 | 25.00 | 37 | 180 | |
| 1914D **(a)** ..........1,193,000 | 100.00 | 125.00 | 200.00 | 250.00 | 450.00 | 800.00 | 1,100.00 | 2,000 | | |
| 1914S .............4,137,000 | 11.00 | 14.00 | 16.00 | 19.00 | 40.00 | 90.00 | 175.00 | 260 | | |
| 1915 .....(1,150) ...29,092,120 | 0.40 | 1.00 | 2.00 | 8.00 | 26.00 | 35.00 | 46.00 | 65 | 275 | |
| 1915D ............22,050,000 | 0.50 | 1.00 | 1.50 | 2.25 | 9.00 | 22.00 | 45.00 | 60 | | |
| 1915S .............4,833,000 | 8.00 | 9.00 | 11.00 | 14.00 | 30.00 | 60.00 | 100.00 | 150 | | |
| 1916 .....(1,050) ..131,833,677 | 0.05 | 0.08 | 0.15 | 0.50 | 2.00 | 5.00 | 10.00 | 15 | 450 | |
| 1916D ............35,956,000 | 0.10 | 0.20 | 0.50 | 1.50 | 5.50 | 12.00 | 35.00 | 65 | | |
| 1916S ............22,510,000 | 0.50 | 0.75 | 1.50 | 3.00 | 10.00 | 20.00 | 45.00 | 90 | | |
| 1917 ............196,429,785 | 0.05 | 0.07 | 0.10 | 0.25 | 0.60 | 3.00 | 10.00 | 15 | | |
| 1917D ............55,120,000 | 0.10 | 0.20 | 0.40 | 1.50 | 14.00 | 19.00 | 39.00 | 70 | | |
| 1917S ............32,620,000 | 0.08 | 0.10 | 0.25 | 0.50 | 2.75 | 12.00 | 35.00 | 65 | | |

**a.** Beware of altered date or mintmark. No V.D.B. on shoulder of genuine 1914-D cent.

*Designer's initials placed on Lincoln's shoulder next to rim, starting 1918.*

*Brilliant Uncirculated coins before 1934 are worth more than prices shown. Spotted, cleaned, or discolored pieces are worth less.*

| | Mintage | G-4 | VG-8 | F-12 | VF-20 | EF-40 | AU-50 | MS-60 | MS-63 |
|---|---|---|---|---|---|---|---|---|---|
| 1918 | 288,104,634 | $0.04 | $0.05 | $0.10 | $0.20 | $1.00 | $3.00 | $6.00 | $15.00 |
| 1918D | 47,830,000 | 0.10 | 0.15 | 0.60 | 1.25 | 6.00 | 12.00 | 33.00 | 68.00 |
| 1918S | 34,680,000 | 0.10 | 0.15 | 0.50 | 1.00 | 4.00 | 15.00 | 35.00 | 75.00 |
| 1919 | 392,021,000 | 0.04 | 0.05 | 0.07 | 0.15 | 0.75 | 1.50 | 5.00 | 14.00 |
| 1919D | 57,154,000 | 0.05 | 0.06 | 0.10 | 0.40 | 2.50 | 15.00 | 28.00 | 60.00 |
| 1919S | 139,760,000 | 0.05 | 0.06 | 0.10 | 0.30 | 1.35 | 7.00 | 18.00 | 70.00 |
| 1920 | 310,165,000 | 0.03 | 0.05 | 0.07 | 0.15 | 0.50 | 1.50 | 6.00 | 12.00 |
| 1920D | 49,280,000 | 0.20 | 0.40 | 0.80 | 2.00 | 6.00 | 15.00 | 35.00 | 60.00 |
| 1920S | 46,220,000 | 0.10 | 0.20 | 0.30 | 0.70 | 3.50 | 17.00 | 45.00 | 115.00 |
| 1921 | 39,157,000 | 0.06 | 0.08 | 0.15 | 0.35 | 1.50 | 6.00 | 22.00 | 40.00 |
| 1921S | 15,274,000 | 0.35 | 0.50 | 0.70 | 1.50 | 15.00 | 35.00 | 55.00 | 100.00 |
| 1922D | 7,160,000 | 7.00 | 8.00 | 9.00 | 11.00 | 17.00 | 28.00 | 45.00 | 75.00 |
| 1922, No D (b) | .........* | 325.00 | 385.00 | 575.00 | 700.00 | 1,450.00 | 3,000.00 | 5,000.00 | 16,000.00 |
| 1923 | 74,723,000 | 0.04 | 0.05 | 0.07 | 0.15 | 1.00 | 2.50 | 7.00 | 14.00 |
| 1923S | 8,700,000 | 1.00 | 1.50 | 2.00 | 3.00 | 15.00 | 35.00 | 100.00 | 225.00 |
| 1924 | 75,178,000 | 0.04 | 0.05 | 0.07 | 0.15 | 1.50 | 3.50 | 15.00 | 25.00 |
| 1924D | 2,520,000 | 18.00 | 20.00 | 25.00 | 30.00 | 55.00 | 95.00 | 150.00 | 225.00 |
| 1924S | 11,696,000 | 0.40 | 0.50 | 0.80 | 1.10 | 9.00 | 30.00 | 55.00 | 110.00 |
| 1925 | 139,949,000 | 0.03 | 0.04 | 0.05 | 0.15 | 0.50 | 2.00 | 5.00 | 10.00 |
| 1925D | 22,580,000 | 0.10 | 0.15 | 0.50 | 1.00 | 4.50 | 11.00 | 27.00 | 38.00 |
| 1925S | 26,380,000 | 0.04 | 0.06 | 0.10 | 0.25 | 3.00 | 14.00 | 40.00 | 80.00 |
| 1926 | 157,088,000 | 0.03 | 0.04 | 0.05 | 0.15 | 0.50 | 2.00 | 5.00 | 8.00 |
| 1926D | 28,020,000 | 0.25 | 0.35 | 0.70 | 1.10 | 3.00 | 10.00 | 35.00 | 50.00 |
| 1926S | 4,550,000 | 3.00 | 3.50 | 4.50 | 6.00 | 14.00 | 32.00 | 65.00 | 140.00 |
| 1927 | 144,440,000 | 0.03 | 0.04 | 0.05 | 0.20 | 0.50 | 1.00 | 5.00 | 10.00 |
| 1927D | 27,170,000 | 0.10 | 0.15 | 0.50 | 1.00 | 2.00 | 6.00 | 26.00 | 42.00 |
| 1927S | 14,276,000 | 0.25 | 0.30 | 0.50 | 1.25 | 4.00 | 11.00 | 35.00 | 70.00 |
| 1928 | 134,116,000 | 0.03 | 0.04 | 0.05 | 0.15 | 0.50 | 1.00 | 4.50 | 10.00 |
| 1928D | 31,170,000 | 0.04 | 0.06 | 0.10 | 0.25 | 0.85 | 4.00 | 15.00 | 34.00 |
| 1928S | 17,266,000 | 0.06 | 0.10 | 0.25 | 0.50 | 1.50 | 5.00 | 34.00 | 55.00 |
| 1929 | 185,262,000 | 0.03 | 0.04 | 0.05 | 0.15 | 0.35 | 1.50 | 4.00 | 6.00 |
| 1929D | 41,730,000 | 0.04 | 0.06 | 0.10 | 0.25 | 1.00 | 2.00 | 12.00 | 15.00 |
| 1929S | 50,148,000 | 0.03 | 0.05 | 0.10 | 0.15 | 0.60 | 1.75 | 7.00 | 11.00 |
| 1930 | 157,415,000 | 0.03 | 0.04 | 0.05 | 0.15 | 0.25 | 0.75 | 2.00 | 3.50 |
| 1930D | 40,100,000 | 0.04 | 0.06 | 0.10 | 0.25 | 0.60 | 1.00 | 5.00 | 10.00 |
| 1930S | 24,286,000 | 0.03 | 0.05 | 0.10 | 0.15 | 0.40 | 2.00 | 3.50 | 5.00 |
| 1931 | 19,396,000 | 0.15 | 0.20 | 0.30 | 0.40 | 0.60 | 2.00 | 10.00 | 15.00 |
| 1931D | 4,480,000 | 2.00 | 2.25 | 3.00 | 3.50 | 5.00 | 14.00 | 30.00 | 42.00 |
| 1931S | 866,000 | 50.00 | 60.00 | 65.00 | 75.00 | 80.00 | 85.00 | 90.00 | 100.00 |
| 1932 | 9,062,000 | 0.40 | 0.50 | 0.60 | 1.00 | 1.25 | 3.75 | 10.00 | 13.00 |
| 1932D | 10,500,000 | 0.25 | 0.35 | 0.40 | 0.50 | 1.00 | 3.25 | 10.00 | 15.00 |
| 1933 | 14,360,000 | 0.30 | 0.40 | 0.50 | 0.70 | 1.25 | 3.75 | 10.00 | 15.00 |
| 1933D | 6,200,000 | 1.00 | 1.25 | 1.50 | 2.50 | 4.25 | 7.00 | 13.00 | 16.00 |

* Included in number above. **b.** 1922 cents with a weak or missing mintmark were made from extremely worn dies that originally struck normal 1922-D cents. Three different die pairs were involved; two of them produced "Weak D" coins. One die pair (no. 2, identified by a "strong reverse") is acknowledged as striking "No D" coins. Weak D cents are worth considerably less. Beware of removed mintmark.

| | Mintage | G-4 | VG-8 | F-12 | VF-20 | EF-40 | AU-50 | MS-60 | MS-63 | PF-63 |
|---|---|---|---|---|---|---|---|---|---|---|
| 1934 | 219,080,000 | $0.03 | $0.03 | $0.03 | $0.03 | $0.10 | $1.00 | $3.00 | $4.50 | |
| 1934D | 28,446,000 | 0.04 | 0.06 | 0.08 | 0.15 | 0.50 | 2.00 | 9.00 | 15.00 | |
| 1935 | 245,388,000 | 0.03 | 0.03 | 0.03 | 0.04 | 0.06 | 0.20 | 2.00 | 3.00 | |
| 1935D | 47,000,000 | 0.03 | 0.03 | 0.03 | 0.04 | 0.20 | 0.50 | 3.00 | 4.00 | |
| 1935S | 38,702,000 | 0.03 | 0.04 | 0.04 | 0.04 | 0.12 | 1.25 | 4.00 | 6.00 | |
| 1936 .....(5,569) | 309,632,000 | 0.03 | 0.03 | 0.03 | 0.04 | 0.06 | 0.25 | 1.00 | 3.00 | $85 |
| 1936D | 40,620,000 | 0.03 | 0.03 | 0.03 | 0.04 | 0.08 | 0.20 | 1.00 | 3.00 | |
| 1936S | 29,130,000 | 0.03 | 0.03 | 0.03 | 0.04 | 0.10 | 0.20 | 1.00 | 3.00 | |
| 1937 .....(9,320) | 309,170,000 | 0.02 | 0.03 | 0.03 | 0.03 | 0.05 | 0.20 | 0.50 | 3.00 | 34 |
| 1937D | 50,430,000 | 0.02 | 0.03 | 0.03 | 0.03 | 0.06 | 0.30 | 0.80 | 4.00 | |
| 1937S | 34,500,000 | 0.03 | 0.03 | 0.03 | 0.04 | 0.06 | 0.30 | 0.80 | 4.00 | |
| 1938 ....(14,734) | 156,682,000 | 0.02 | 0.03 | 0.03 | 0.03 | 0.05 | 0.30 | 0.75 | 2.00 | 25 |
| 1938D | 20,010,000 | 0.02 | 0.03 | 0.04 | 0.06 | 0.15 | 0.50 | 1.00 | 5.00 | |
| 1938S | 15,180,000 | 0.06 | 0.08 | 0.10 | 0.12 | 0.15 | 0.30 | 1.00 | 4.00 | |
| 1939 ....(13,520) | 316,466,000 | 0.02 | 0.03 | 0.03 | 0.03 | 0.03 | 0.20 | 0.30 | 2.50 | 23 |
| 1939D | 15,160,000 | 0.06 | 0.08 | 0.10 | 0.12 | 0.15 | 0.35 | 1.00 | 4.00 | |
| 1939S | 52,070,000 | 0.03 | 0.03 | 0.03 | 0.04 | 0.10 | 0.30 | 1.00 | 4.00 | |
| 1940 ....(15,872) | 586,810,000 | 0.02 | 0.03 | 0.03 | 0.03 | 0.03 | 0.20 | 0.30 | 2.00 | 16 |
| 1940D | 81,390,000 | 0.02 | 0.03 | 0.03 | 0.03 | 0.03 | 0.20 | 0.40 | 2.00 | |
| 1940S | 112,940,000 | 0.02 | 0.03 | 0.03 | 0.03 | 0.04 | 0.20 | 0.40 | 2.75 | |
| 1941 ....(21,100) | 887,018,000 | 0.02 | 0.03 | 0.03 | 0.03 | 0.03 | 0.20 | 0.30 | 2.00 | 15 |
| 1941D | 128,700,000 | 0.02 | 0.03 | 0.03 | 0.03 | 0.03 | 0.40 | 0.80 | 3.00 | |
| 1941S | 92,360,000 | 0.02 | 0.03 | 0.03 | 0.03 | 0.04 | 0.35 | 1.00 | 5.00 | |
| 1942 ....(32,600) | 657,796,000 | 0.02 | 0.03 | 0.03 | 0.03 | 0.03 | 0.10 | 0.15 | 1.00 | 15 |
| 1942D | 206,698,000 | 0.02 | 0.03 | 0.03 | 0.03 | 0.03 | 0.10 | 0.15 | 2.00 | |
| 1942S | 85,590,000 | 0.02 | 0.03 | 0.03 | 0.03 | 0.10 | 1.00 | 2.00 | 8.00 | |

## Variety 2 – Zinc-Coated Steel (1943)

| | Mintage | F-12 | VF-20 | EF-40 | MS-60 | MS-63 | MS-65 |
|---|---|---|---|---|---|---|---|
| 1943 | 684,628,670 | $0.05 | $0.10 | $0.15 | $0.70 | $1.25 | $3.00 |
| 1943D | 217,660,000 | 0.05 | 0.10 | 0.15 | 0.90 | 2.00 | 4.50 |
| 1943S | 191,550,000 | 0.06 | 0.12 | 0.20 | 1.20 | 2.75 | 6.25 |

## Variety 1 (Bronze) Resumed (1944–1958)

**1944-D, D Over S**          **1955, Doubled-Die Obverse**

| | Mintage | VF-20 | EF-40 | MS-63 | MS-65 | PF-65 |
|---|---|---|---|---|---|---|
| 1944 | 1,435,400,000 | $0.03 | $0.03 | $0.15 | $0.50 | |
| 1944D | 430,578,000 | 0.03 | 0.03 | 0.20 | 0.50 | |
| 1944D, D Over S | * | 75.00 | 90.00 | 225.00 | 600.00 | |
| 1944S | 282,760,000 | 0.03 | 0.03 | 0.15 | 1.50 | |

* Included in number above.

*Chart continued on next page.*

| | Mintage | VF-20 | EF-40 | MS-63 | MS-65 | PF-65 |
|---|---|---|---|---|---|---|
| 1945 | 1,040,515,000 | $0.03 | $0.03 | $0.20 | $0.50 | |
| 1945D | 266,268,000 | 0.03 | 0.03 | 0.15 | 0.50 | |
| 1945S | 181,770,000 | 0.03 | 0.03 | 0.10 | 2.00 | |
| 1946 | 991,655,000 | 0.03 | 0.03 | 0.10 | 0.50 | |
| 1946D | 315,690,000 | 0.03 | 0.03 | 0.15 | 1.00 | |
| 1946S | 198,100,000 | 0.03 | 0.03 | 0.15 | 1.25 | |
| 1947 | 190,555,000 | 0.03 | 0.03 | 0.25 | 0.50 | |
| 1947D | 194,750,000 | 0.03 | 0.03 | 0.12 | 0.50 | |
| 1947S | 99,000,000 | 0.03 | 0.03 | 0.15 | 1.50 | |
| 1948 | 317,570,000 | 0.03 | 0.03 | 0.15 | 0.50 | |
| 1948D | 172,637,500 | 0.03 | 0.03 | 0.12 | 0.60 | |
| 1948S | 81,735,000 | 0.03 | 0.03 | 0.20 | 1.50 | |
| 1949 | 217,775,000 | 0.03 | 0.03 | 0.30 | 0.75 | |
| 1949D | 153,132,500 | 0.03 | 0.03 | 0.20 | 0.75 | |
| 1949S | 64,290,000 | 0.04 | 0.05 | 0.50 | 2.00 | |
| 1950 | (51,386) 272,635,000 | 0.03 | 0.03 | 0.25 | 0.50 | $30.00 |
| 1950D | 334,950,000 | 0.03 | 0.03 | 0.10 | 0.50 | |
| 1950S | 118,505,000 | 0.03 | 0.03 | 0.25 | 0.80 | |
| 1951 | (57,500) 284,576,000 | 0.03 | 0.03 | 0.25 | 0.80 | 35.00 |
| 1951D | 625,355,000 | 0.03 | 0.03 | 0.10 | 0.50 | |
| 1951S | 136,010,000 | 0.03 | 0.03 | 0.30 | 0.60 | |
| 1952 | (81,980) 186,775,000 | 0.03 | 0.03 | 0.15 | 0.60 | 25.00 |
| 1952D | 746,130,000 | 0.03 | 0.03 | 0.15 | 0.60 | |
| 1952S | 137,800,004 | 0.03 | 0.03 | 0.50 | 1.50 | |
| 1953 | (128,800) 256,755,000 | 0.03 | 0.03 | 0.10 | 0.50 | 25.00 |
| 1953D | 700,515,000 | 0.03 | 0.03 | 0.10 | 0.50 | |
| 1953S | 181,835,000 | 0.03 | 0.04 | 0.12 | 0.50 | |
| 1954 | (233,300) 71,640,050 | 0.03 | 0.06 | 0.10 | 0.50 | 10.00 |
| 1954D | 251,552,500 | 0.03 | 0.03 | 0.05 | 0.30 | |
| 1954S | 96,190,000 | 0.03 | 0.03 | 0.05 | 0.30 | |
| 1955 | (378,200) 330,958,200 | 0.03 | 0.03 | 0.06 | 0.30 | 10.00 |
| 1955, Doubled-Die Obverse | * | 750.00 | 900.00(a) | 1,750.00 | 7,500.00 | |
| 1955D | 563,257,500 | 0.03 | 0.03 | 0.05 | 0.25 | |
| 1955S | 44,610,000 | 0.10 | 0.15 | 0.15 | 0.50 | |
| 1956 | (669,384) 420,745,000 | 0.03 | 0.03 | 0.05 | 0.25 | 1.75 |
| 1956D | 1,098,201,100 | 0.03 | 0.03 | 0.05 | 0.30 | |
| 1957 | (1,247,952) 282,540,000 | 0.03 | 0.03 | 0.05 | 0.30 | 1.75 |
| 1957D | 1,051,342,000 | 0.03 | 0.03 | 0.05 | 0.30 | |
| 1958 | (875,652) 252,525,000 | 0.03 | 0.03 | 0.05 | 0.30 | 2.00 |
| 1958D | 800,953,300 | 0.03 | 0.03 | 0.05 | 0.30 | |

\* Included in number above. **a.** Value for MS-60 Uncirculated is $1,250.

## LINCOLN, MEMORIAL REVERSE (1959–2008)

Small Date      Large Date

| | Mintage | MS-63 | MS-65 | PF-65 |
|---|---|---|---|---|
| 1959 | (1,149,291) 609,715,000 | $0.01 | $0.10 | $1.00 |

| 1969-S, Doubled-Die Obverse | Small Date, Numbers Aligned at Top | Large Date, Low 7 in Date | Enlarged Detail of 1972 Doubled-Die Obverse |

| | Mintage | MS-63 | MS-65 | PF-65 |
|---|---|---|---|---|
| 1959D | 1,279,760,000 | $0.02 | $0.10 | |
| 1960, Lg Dt | 586,405,000 | 0.02 | 0.10 | |
| | (1,691,602) | | | $0.50 |
| 1960, Sm Dt | * | 1.00 | 2.70 | |
| | * | | | 9.50 |
| 1960D, | | | | |
| Lg Dt | 1,580,884,000 | 0.02 | 0.10 | |
| 1960D, Sm Dt | * | 0.02 | 0.10 | |
| 1961 | 753,345,000 | 0.02 | 0.10 | |
| | (3,028,244) | | | 0.50 |
| 1961D | 1,753,266,700 | 0.02 | 0.10 | |
| 1962 | 606,045,000 | 0.02 | 0.10 | |
| | (3,218,019) | | | 0.50 |
| 1962D | 1,793,148,140 | 0.02 | 0.10 | |
| 1963 | 754,110,000 | 0.02 | 0.10 | |
| | (3,075,645) | | | 0.50 |
| 1963D | 1,774,020,400 | 0.02 | 0.10 | |
| 1964 | 2,648,575,000 | 0.02 | 0.10 | |
| | (3,950,762) | | | 0.50 |
| 1964D | 3,799,071,500 | 0.02 | 0.10 | |
| 1965 | 1,497,224,900 | 0.03 | 0.12 | |
| 1966 | 2,188,147,783 | 0.04 | 0.12 | |
| 1967 | 3,048,667,100 | 0.03 | 0.12 | |
| 1968 | 1,707,880,970 | 0.03 | 0.12 | |
| 1968D | 2,886,269,600 | 0.02 | 0.10 | |
| 1968S | 258,270,001 | 0.02 | 0.10 | |
| | (3,041,506) | | | 0.50 |
| 1969 | 1,136,910,000 | 0.05 | 0.20 | |
| 1969D | 4,002,832,200 | 0.03 | 0.10 | |
| 1969S | 544,375,000 | 0.03 | 0.10 | |
| | (2,934,631) | | | 0.50 |
| 1969S, DDO | * | — | — | |
| 1970 | 1,898,315,000 | 0.05 | 0.10 | |
| 1970D | 2,891,438,900 | 0.02 | 0.10 | |
| 1970S, Sm Dt | | | | |
| (High 7) | ** | 20.00 | 30.00 | |
| | ** | | | 35.00 |
| 1970S, Lg Dt | | | | |
| (Low 7) | 690,560,004 | 0.03 | 0.10 | |
| | (2,632,810) | | | 0.25 |

| | Mintage | MS-63 | MS-65 | PF-65 |
|---|---|---|---|---|
| 1971 | 1,919,490,000 | $0.05 | $0.20 | |
| 1971D | 2,911,045,600 | 0.03 | 0.20 | |
| 1971S | 525,133,459 | 0.03 | 0.20 | |
| | (3,220,733) | | | $0.25 |
| 1972, DDO | ** | 190.00 | 300.00 | |
| 1972 | 2,933,255,000 | 0.02 | 0.05 | |
| 1972D | 2,665,071,400 | 0.02 | 0.10 | |
| 1972S | 376,939,108 | 0.02 | 0.10 | |
| | (3,260,996) | | | 0.25 |
| 1973 | 3,728,245,000 | 0.02 | 0.10 | |
| 1973D | 3,549,576,588 | 0.02 | 0.10 | |
| 1973S | 317,177,295 | 0.02 | 0.10 | |
| | (2,760,339) | | | 0.25 |
| 1974 | 4,232,140,523 | 0.02 | 0.10 | |
| 1974D | 4,235,098,000 | 0.02 | 0.10 | |
| 1974S | 409,426,660 | 0.03 | 0.10 | |
| | (2,612,568) | | | 0.25 |
| 1975 | 5,451,476,142 | 0.02 | 0.10 | |
| 1975D | 4,505,275,300 | 0.02 | 0.10 | |
| 1975S | (2,845,450) | | | 1.60 |
| 1976 | 4,674,292,426 | 0.02 | 0.10 | |
| 1976D | 4,221,592,455 | 0.02 | 0.10 | |
| 1976S | (4,149,730) | | | 1.25 |
| 1977 | 4,469,930,000 | 0.02 | 0.10 | |
| 1977D | 4,194,062,300 | 0.02 | 0.10 | |
| 1977S | (3,251,152) | | | 1.00 |
| 1978 | 5,558,605,000 | 0.02 | 0.10 | |
| 1978D | 4,280,233,400 | 0.02 | 0.10 | |
| 1978S | (3,127,781) | | | 1.00 |
| 1979 | 6,018,515,000 | 0.02 | 0.10 | |
| 1979D | 4,139,357,254 | 0.02 | 0.10 | |
| 1979S, Filled S | (3,677,175) | | | 1.75 |
| 1979S, Clear S | * | | | 2.00 |
| 1980 | 7,414,705,000 | 0.02 | 0.10 | |
| 1980D | 5,140,098,660 | 0.02 | 0.10 | |
| 1980S | (3,554,806) | | | 1.00 |
| 1981 | 7,491,750,000 | 0.02 | 0.10 | |
| 1981D | 5,373,235,677 | 0.02 | 0.10 | |
| 1981S, Filled S | (4,063,083) | | | 1.50 |
| 1981S, Clear S | * | | | 18.00 |

* Included in number above. ** Included in number below.

**Large Date**   **Small Date**

| | Mintage | MS-63 | MS-65 | PF-65 |
|---|---|---|---|---|
| 1982, | | | | |
| Lg Dt | 10,712,525,000 | $0.02 | $0.10 | |
| 1982, Sm Dt ..........* | | 0.03 | 0.12 | |

\* Included in number above.

| | Mintage | MS-63 | MS-65 | PF-65 |
|---|---|---|---|---|
| 1982D, | | | | |
| Lg Dt ..6,012,979,368 | | $0.02 | $0.10 | |
| 1982S ........(3,857,479) | | | | $1.60 |

## Copper-Plated Zinc (1982–2008)

**Close AM**   **Wide AM**   *1995, Doubled Die showing strong doubling on word LIBERTY.*

| | Mintage | MS-63 | MS-65 | PF-65 |
|---|---|---|---|---|
| 1982, Lg Dt ..........* | | $0.02 | $0.15 | |
| 1982, Sm Dt ..........* | | 0.02 | 0.20 | |
| 1982D, Lg Dt ..........* | | 0.05 | 0.50 | |
| 1982D, Sm Dt ..........* | | 0.01 | 0.05 | |
| 1983 ......7,752,355,000 | | 0.01 | 0.10 | |
| 1983D ....6,467,199,428 | | 0.01 | 0.10 | |
| 1983S ........(3,279,126) | | 0.01 | 0.05 | $1.10 |
| 1984 ......8,151,079,000 | | 0.01 | 0.05 | |
| 1984, Dbl Ear ..........** | | 50.00 | 100.00 | |
| 1984D ....5,569,238,906 | | 0.01 | 0.10 | |
| 1984S ........(3,065,110) | | | | 1.10 |
| 1985 ......5,648,489,887 | | | 0.05 | |
| 1985D ....5,287,339,926 | | 0.01 | 0.05 | |
| 1985S ........(3,362,821) | | | | 1.25 |
| 1986 ......4,491,395,493 | | 0.01 | 0.06 | |
| 1986D ....4,442,866,698 | | 0.01 | 0.05 | |
| 1986S ........(3,010,497) | | | | 2.00 |
| 1987 ......4,682,466,931 | | 0.01 | 0.05 | |
| 1987D ....4,879,389,514 | | 0.01 | 0.05 | |
| 1987S ........(4,227,728) | | | | 1.10 |
| 1988 ......6,092,810,000 | | 0.01 | 0.05 | |
| 1988D ....5,253,740,443 | | 0.01 | 0.05 | |
| 1988S ........(3,262,948) | | | | 3.25 |
| 1989 ......7,261,535,000 | | 0.01 | 0.05 | |
| 1989D ....5,345,467,111 | | 0.01 | 0.05 | |
| 1989S ........(3,220,194) | | | | 3.00 |
| 1990 ......6,851,765,000 | | 0.01 | 0.05 | |
| 1990D ....4,922,894,533 | | 0.01 | 0.05 | |
| 1990S ........(3,299,559) | | | | 2.00 |
| 1990, Pf, No S ..........** | | | | — |

| | Mintage | MS-63 | MS-65 | PF-65 |
|---|---|---|---|---|
| 1991 ......5,165,940,000 | | $0.01 | $0.05 | |
| 1991D ....4,158,446,076 | | 0.01 | 0.05 | |
| 1991S ........(2,867,787) | | | | $8.00 |
| 1992 ......4,648,905,000 | | 0.01 | 0.05 | |
| 1992, Close AM (a) .....** | | — | — | |
| 1992D ....4,448,673,300 | | 0.01 | 0.05 | |
| 1992D, Close AM (a) ....** | | — | — | |
| 1992S ........(4,176,560) | | | | 1.10 |
| 1993 ......5,684,705,000 | | 0.01 | 0.05 | |
| 1993D ....6,426,650,571 | | 0.01 | 0.05 | |
| 1993S ........(3,394,792) | | | | 2.00 |
| 1994 ......6,500,850,000 | | 0.01 | 0.05 | |
| 1994D ....7,131,765,000 | | 0.01 | 0.05 | |
| 1994S ........(3,269,923) | | | | 2.00 |
| 1995 ......6,411,440,000 | | 0.01 | 0.05 | |
| 1995, DblDie Obv .......** | | 4.00 | 18.00 | |
| 1995D ....7,128,560,000 | | 0.01 | 0.05 | |
| 1995S ........(2,797,481) | | | | 2.00 |
| 1996 ......6,612,465,000 | | 0.01 | 0.05 | |
| 1996, Wide AM (a) ......** | | — | | |
| 1996D ....6,510,795,000 | | 0.01 | 0.05 | |
| 1996S ........(2,525,265) | | | | 1.25 |
| 1997 ......4,622,800,000 | | 0.01 | 0.05 | |
| 1997D ....4,576,555,000 | | 0.01 | 0.05 | |
| 1997S ........(2,796,678) | | | | 2.25 |
| 1998 ......5,032,155,000 | | 0.01 | 0.05 | |
| 1998, Wide AM (a) ......** | | 2.00 | 4.00 | |
| 1998D ....5,225,353,500 | | 0.01 | 0.05 | |
| 1998S ........(2,086,507) | | | | 2.00 |
| 1998S, Close AM (a) ....** | | | | — |

\* Included in previous section's mintages. \*\* Included in number above. **a.** Varieties were made using Proof dies that have a wide space between AM in AMERICA. The letters nearly touch on other Uncirculated cents.

| | Mintage | MS-63 | MS-65 | PF-65 |
|---|---|---|---|---|
| 1999 | 5,237,600,000 | $0.01 | $0.05 | |
| 1999, Wide AM (a) | ** | | — | |
| 1999D | 6,360,065,000 | 0.01 | 0.05 | |
| 1999S | (3,347,966) | | | $2 |
| 1999S, Close AM (a) | ** | | — | |
| 2000 | 5,503,200,000 | 0.01 | 0.05 | |
| 2000, Wide AM (a) | ** | 2.00 | 2.50 | |
| 2000D | 8,774,220,000 | 0.01 | 0.05 | |
| 2000S | (4,047,993) | | | 1 |
| 2001 | 4,959,600,000 | 0.01 | 0.05 | |
| 2001D | 5,374,990,000 | 0.01 | 0.05 | |
| 2001S | (3,184,606) | | | 1 |
| 2002 | 3,260,800,000 | 0.01 | 0.05 | |
| 2002D | 4,028,055,000 | 0.01 | 0.05 | |
| 2002S | (3,211,995) | | | 1 |
| 2003 | 3,300,000,000 | 0.01 | 0.05 | |
| 2003D | 3,548,000,000 | 0.01 | 0.05 | |
| 2003S | (3,298,439) | | | $1.00 |
| 2004 | 3,379,600,000 | $0.01 | $0.05 | |
| 2004D | 3,456,400,000 | 0.01 | 0.05 | |
| 2004S | (2,965,422) | | | 1.00 |
| 2005 | 3,935,600,000 | 0.01 | 0.05 | |
| 2005D | 3,764,450,500 | 0.01 | 0.05 | |
| 2005S | (3,344,679) | | | 1.00 |
| 2006 | 4,290,000,000 | 0.01 | 0.05 | |
| 2006D | 3,944,000,000 | 0.01 | 0.05 | |
| 2006S | (3,054,436) | | | 1.00 |
| 2007 | 3,762,400,000 | 0.01 | 0.05 | |
| 2007D | 3,638,800,000 | 0.01 | 0.05 | |
| 2007S | (2,577,166) | | | 1.00 |
| 2008 | 2,558,800,000 | 0.01 | 0.05 | |
| 2008D | 2,849,600,000 | 0.01 | 0.05 | |
| 2008S | (2,169,561) | | | 1.00 |

** Included in number above. **a.** Varieties were made using Proof dies that have a wide space between AM in AMERICA. The letters nearly touch on other Uncirculated cents.

## LINCOLN, BICENTENNIAL (2009)

One-cent coins issued during 2009 are a unique tribute to President Abraham Lincoln, recognizing the bicentennial of his birth and the 100th anniversary of the first issuance of the Lincoln cent. These coins use four different design themes on the reverse to represent the four major aspects of President Lincoln's life. The obverse of each of these coins carries the traditional portrait of Lincoln that has been in use since 1909.

The special reverse designs, released as quarterly issues throughout 2009, are described as: Birth and Early Childhood in Kentucky (designer, Richard Masters; sculptor, Jim Licaretz); Formative Years in Indiana (designer and sculptor, Charles Vickers); Professional Life in Illinois (designer, Joel Iskowitz; sculptor, Don Everhart); and Presidency in Washington (designer, Susan Gamble; sculptor, Joseph Menna). Those issued for commercial circulation are made of the exact same copper-plated composition used since 1982. Special versions included in collector sets are made of the same metallic composition as was used for the original 1909 cents (95% copper, 5% tin and zinc).

2009 Lincoln cent reverse designs

| | Mintage | MS-63 | MS-65 | PF-65 |
|---|---|---|---|---|
| 2009, Birth and Early Childhood | 284,400,000 | $0.05 | $0.10 | |
| 2009D, Birth and Early Childhood | 350,400,000 | 0.05 | 0.10 | |
| 2009S, Birth and Early Childhood | (2,172,373) | | | $2 |
| 2009, Formative Years | 376,000,000 | 0.05 | 0.10 | |
| 2009D, Formative Years | 363,600,000 | 0.05 | 0.10 | |
| 2009S, Formative Years | (2,172,373) | | | 2 |

*Chart continued on next page.*

| | Mintage | MS-63 | MS-65 | PF-65 |
|---|---|---|---|---|
| 2009, Professional Life | 316,000,000 | $0.05 | $0.10 | |
| 2009D, Professional Life | 336,000,000 | 0.05 | 0.10 | |
| 2009S, Professional Life | (2,172,373) | | | $2 |
| 2009, Presidency | 129,600,000 | 0.05 | 0.10 | |
| 2009D, Presidency | 198,000,000 | 0.05 | 0.10 | |
| 2009S, Presidency | (2,172,373) | | | 2 |

## LINCOLN, SHIELD REVERSE (2010 TO DATE)

At the conclusion of the 2009 Bicentennial One-Cent Program, future one-cent coins feature a reverse that has "an image emblematic of President Lincoln's preservation of the United States of America as a single and united country."

| | Mintage | MS-65 | PF-65 |
|---|---|---|---|
| 2010 | 1,963,630,000 | $0.01 | |
| 2010D | 2,047,200,000 | 0.01 | |
| 2010S | (1,455,015) | | $2 |
| 2011 | | 0.01 | |
| 2011D | | 0.01 | |
| 2011S | | | 2 |

# TWO-CENT PIECE (1864–1873)

The Act of April 22, 1864, which changed the weight and composition of the cent, included a provision for the bronze two-cent piece. The weight was specified as 96 grains, the alloy being the same as for the cent. There are two varieties for the first year of issue, 1864: the Small Motto and the Large Motto. The differences are illustrated in the closeups below.

**1864, Small Motto**

**1864, Large Motto**

On the obverse the D in GOD is narrow on the Large Motto variety. The stem to the leaf shows plainly on the Small Motto variety.

**G-4 Good:** At least part of IN GOD visible.
**VG-8 Very Good:** WE weakly visible.
**F-12 Fine:** Complete motto visible. The word WE weak.
**VF-20 Very Fine:** WE is clear, but not strong.
**EF-40 Extremely Fine:** The word WE bold.
**AU-50 About Uncirculated:** Traces of wear visible on leaf tips, arrow points, and the word WE.
**MS-60 Uncirculated:** No trace of wear. Light blemishes.
**MS-63 Choice Uncirculated:** Some distracting contact marks or blemishes in prime focal areas. Some impairment of luster possible.
**PF-63 Choice Proof:** Reflective surfaces with only a few blemishes in secondary focal places. No major flaws.

Brilliant red choice Uncirculated and Proof coins are worth more than prices shown. Cleaned or discolored pieces are worth less.

| | Mintage | G-4 | VG-8 | F-12 | VF-20 | EF-40 | AU-50 | MS-60 | MS-63 | PF-63 |
|---|---|---|---|---|---|---|---|---|---|---|
| 1864, Small Motto | . . . . . . . . . . . . . . . . .* | $85 | $100 | $140 | $225 | $325 | $400 | $575 | $800 | $10,000 |
| 1864, Large Motto | ..(100+) ..19,847,500 | 8 | 9 | 12 | 16 | 23 | 32 | 55 | 90 | 325 |
| 1865 | . . . . . . . . . . .(500+) ..13,640,000 | 8 | 9 | 12 | 16 | 23 | 32 | 55 | 90 | 275 |
| 1866 | . . . . . . . . . . .(725+) ...3,177,000 | 8 | 9 | 12 | 16 | 23 | 32 | 55 | 90 | 275 |
| 1867 | . . . . . . . . . .(625+) ..2,938,750 | 8 | 9 | 12 | 16 | 23 | 32 | 55 | 90 | 275 |
| 1868 | . . . . . . . . . .(600+) ..2,803,750 | 8 | 9 | 14 | 18 | 25 | 37 | 65 | 110 | 275 |
| 1869 | . . . . . . . . . .(600+) ...1,546,500 | 9 | 10 | 14 | 19 | 32 | 60 | 100 | 110 | 275 |
| 1870 | . . . . . . . . . .(1,000+) ....861,250 | 11 | 13 | 19 | 25 | 45 | 80 | 125 | 150 | 375 |
| 1871 | . . . . . . . . . . .(960+) ....721,250 | 13 | 15 | 22 | 30 | 65 | 90 | 165 | 190 | 400 |
| 1872 | . . . . . . . . . . .(950+) .....65,000 | 150 | 200 | 225 | 275 | 400 | 500 | 650 | 950 | 600 |
| 1873 | . . . . . . . . . .(1,000+) . . . . . . . . . . | | | | | | 700 | | | 1,000 |

\* Included in number below.

# SILVER THREE-CENT PIECES (TRIMES) (1851–1873)

This smallest of United States silver coins was authorized by Congress March 3, 1851. The first three-cent silver pieces had no lines bordering the six-pointed star. From 1854 through 1858 there were two lines, while issues of the last 15 years show only one line. Issues from 1854 through 1873 have an olive sprig over the III and a bundle of three arrows beneath.

**G-4 Good:** Star worn smooth. Legend and date readable.
**VG-8 Very Good:** Outline of shield defined. Legend and date clear.
**F-12 Fine:** Only star points worn smooth.
**VF-20 Very Fine:** Only partial wear on star ridges.
**EF-40 Extremely Fine:** Ridges on star points visible.
**AU-50 About Uncirculated:** Trace of wear visible at each star point. Center of shield possibly weak.
**MS-60 Uncirculated:** No trace of wear. Light blemishes.
**MS-63 Choice Uncirculated:** Some distracting contact marks or blemishes in prime focal areas. Some impairment of luster possible.
**PF-63 Choice Proof:** Reflective surfaces with only a few blemishes in secondary focal places. No major flaws.

*Mintmark location.*

| No Outline Around Star (1851–1853) | Three Outlines to Star, Large Date (1854–1858) | Two Outlines to Star, Small Date (1859–1873) | 1862, 2 Over 1 |
|---|---|---|---|

*Well-struck specimens command higher prices.*

| | Mintage | G-4 | VG-8 | F-12 | VF-20 | EF-40 | AU-50 | MS-60 | MS-63 | PF-63 |
|---|---|---|---|---|---|---|---|---|---|---|
| 1851 | 5,447,400 | $13 | $16 | $18 | $24 | $33 | $70 | $90 | $150 | — |
| 1851O | 720,000 | 16 | 20 | 25 | 47 | 75 | 110 | 180 | 260 | |
| 1852 | 18,663,500 | 13 | 16 | 18 | 24 | 33 | 70 | 85 | 150 | — |
| 1853 | 11,400,000 | 13 | 16 | 18 | 24 | 33 | 70 | 85 | 150 | |
| 1854 | 671,000 | 14 | 17 | 20 | 26 | 55 | 115 | 175 | 325 | $6,500 |
| 1855 | 139,000 | 16 | 28 | 30 | 50 | 100 | 135 | 275 | 450 | 2,200 |
| 1856 | 1,458,000 | 13 | 16 | 20 | 26 | 50 | 100 | 150 | 320 | 1,800 |
| 1857 | 1,042,000 | 13 | 16 | 20 | 26 | 50 | 100 | 150 | 320 | 1,800 |
| 1858 | (210) 1,603,700 | 13 | 16 | 20 | 26 | 50 | 90 | 150 | 320 | 1,200 |
| 1859 | (800) 364,200 | 13 | 16 | 20 | 26 | 35 | 75 | 90 | 175 | 275 |
| 1860 | (1,000) 286,000 | 13 | 16 | 20 | 26 | 35 | 75 | 90 | 175 | 275 |
| 1861 | (1,000) 497,000 | 13 | 16 | 20 | 26 | 35 | 75 | 90 | 175 | 275 |
| 1862, 2/1 | * | 13 | 16 | 20 | 26 | 35 | 90 | 110 | 225 | |
| 1862 | (550) 343,000 | 13 | 16 | 20 | 26 | 35 | 75 | 90 | 175 | 285 |
| 1863 | (460) 21,000 | | | | 150 | 200 | 275 | 350 | 550 | 320 |
| 1864 | (470) 12,000 | | | | 150 | 200 | 275 | 350 | 550 | 310 |

| | Mintage | VF-20 | EF-40 | AU-50 | MS-60 | MS-63 | PF-63 |
|---|---|---|---|---|---|---|---|
| 1865 | (500) 8,000 | $175 | $200 | $300 | $375 | $525 | $315 |
| 1866 | (725) 22,000 | 150 | 175 | 275 | 350 | 500 | 315 |
| 1867 | (625) 4,000 | 175 | 200 | 300 | 375 | 525 | 315 |
| 1868 | (600) 3,500 | 175 | 200 | 300 | 375 | 600 | 315 |
| 1869 | (600) 4,500 | 175 | 200 | 300 | 375 | 500 | 315 |
| 1870 | (1,000) 3,000 | 175 | 200 | 300 | 375 | 500 | 325 |
| 1871 | (960) 3,400 | 175 | 200 | 300 | 375 | 500 | 325 |
| 1872 | (950) 1,000 | 200 | 225 | 300 | 375 | 600 | 350 |
| 1873, Proof only | (600) | | 400 | | | | 700 |

* Included in number below.

# NICKEL THREE-CENT PIECES (1865–1889)

The three-cent pieces struck in nickel composition were designed to replace the silver three-cent coins. Composition is 75% copper and 25% nickel. All were coined at Philadelphia and have plain edges.

**G-4 Good:** Date and legends complete though worn. III smooth.
**VG-8 Very Good:** III half worn. Rims complete.
**VF-20 Very Fine:** Three-quarters of hair details visible.
**EF-40 Extremely Fine:** Slight, even wear.
**AU-50 About Uncirculated:** Slight wear on hair curls, above forehead, and on wreath and numeral III.
**MS-60 Uncirculated:** No trace of wear. Light blemishes.
**MS-63 Choice Uncirculated:** Some distracting contact marks or blemishes in prime focal areas. Some impairment of luster possible.
**PF-63 Choice Proof:** Reflective surfaces with only a few blemishes in secondary focal places. No major flaws.

*Brilliant choice Uncirculated and Proof coins are worth more than prices shown. Spotted, cleaned, or discolored pieces are worth less.*

| | Mintage | G-4 | VG-8 | F-12 | VF-20 | EF-40 | AU-50 | MS-60 | MS-63 | PF-63 |
|---|---|---|---|---|---|---|---|---|---|---|
| 1865 . . . . . . . . .(500+) | 11,382,000 | $7 | $9 | $10 | $12 | $15 | $25 | $50 | $90 | $650 |
| 1866 . . . . . . . . .(725+) | . .4,801,000 | 7 | 9 | 10 | 12 | 15 | 25 | 50 | 90 | 160 |
| 1867 . . . . . . . . .(625+) | . .3,915,000 | 7 | 9 | 10 | 12 | 15 | 25 | 50 | 90 | 160 |
| 1868 . . . . . . . . .(600+) | . .3,252,000 | 7 | 9 | 10 | 12 | 15 | 25 | 50 | 90 | 160 |
| 1869 . . . . . . . . .(600+) | . .1,604,000 | 7 | 9 | 10 | 12 | 15 | 25 | 50 | 90 | 160 |
| 1870 . . . . . . . .(1,000+) | . .1,335,000 | 7 | 9 | 10 | 12 | 15 | 25 | 50 | 90 | 160 |
| 1871 . . . . . . . . .(960+) | . . . .604,000 | 7 | 9 | 10 | 12 | 15 | 25 | 50 | 100 | 160 |
| 1872 . . . . . . . . .(950+) | . . . .862,000 | 7 | 9 | 10 | 12 | 15 | 25 | 50 | 100 | 160 |
| 1873 . . . . . . . .(1,100+) | . . . .390,000 | 7 | 9 | 10 | 12 | 15 | 25 | 50 | 90 | 160 |
| 1874 . . . . . . . . .(700+) | . . . .790,000 | 8 | 10 | 11 | 13 | 17 | 27 | 60 | 110 | 160 |
| 1875 . . . . . . . . .(700+) | . . . .228,000 | 9 | 11 | 12 | 14 | 20 | 32 | 80 | 110 | 160 |
| 1876 . . . . . . . .(1,150+) | . . . .162,000 | 9 | 11 | 12 | 15 | 22 | 38 | 110 | 125 | 175 |
| 1877, Pf only . .(510+) | . . . . . . . . . . | | | | 550 | 600 | | | | 900 |
| 1878, Pf only . .(2,350) | | | | | 250 | 375 | | | | 475 |
| 1879 . . . . . . . .(3,200) | . . . . . .38,000 | 20 | 25 | 30 | 40 | 60 | 75 | 130 | 200 | 200 |
| 1880 . . . . . . .(3,955) | . . . . . .21,000 | 40 | 45 | 50 | 60 | 70 | 85 | 150 | 180 | 200 |
| 1881 . . . . . . . .(3,575) | . . .1,077,000 | 7 | 9 | 10 | 12 | 15 | 25 | 50 | 90 | 160 |
| 1882 . . . . . . . .(3,100) | . . . . . .22,200 | 35 | 45 | 50 | 60 | 80 | 100 | 150 | 200 | 225 |
| 1883 . . . . . . . .(6,609) | . . . . . . .4,000 | 75 | 85 | 100 | 135 | 160 | 180 | 200 | 375 | 235 |
| 1884 . . . . . . . .(3,942) | . . . . . . .1,700 | 155 | 175 | 190 | 250 | 275 | 300 | 400 | 550 | 275 |
| 1885 . . . . . . . .(3,790) | . . . . . . .1,000 | 175 | 200 | 225 | 275 | 325 | 325 | 450 | 550 | 275 |
| 1886, Pf only . .(4,290) | . . . . . . . . . . | | | | 175 | 200 | | | | 250 |
| 1887 . . . . . . . .(2,960) | . . . . . . .5,001 | 120 | 140 | 150 | 160 | 175 | 225 | 250 | 275 | 250 |
| 1887, 7/6 . . . . . . .* | . . . . . . . . . . | | | | 175 | 200 | | | | 275 |
| 1888 . . . . . . . .(4,582) | . . . . . .36,501 | 20 | 23 | 27 | 35 | 45 | 60 | 140 | 175 | 185 |
| 1889 . . . . . . . .(3,436) | . . . . . .18,125 | 35 | 45 | 60 | 75 | 85 | 100 | 150 | 200 | 185 |

* Included in number above.

## SHIELD (1866–1883)

The Shield type nickel was made possible by the Act of May 16, 1866. Its weight was set at 77-16/100 grains with the same composition as the nickel three-cent piece.

**G-4 Good:** All letters in motto readable.

**VG-8 Very Good:** Motto clear and stands out. Rims slightly worn but even. Part of shield lines visible.

**F-12 Fine:** Half of each olive leaf worn smooth.

**EF-40 Extremely Fine:** Slight wear to leaf tips and cross over shield.

**AU-50 About Uncirculated:** Traces of light wear on only the high design points. Half of mint luster present.

**MS-60 Uncirculated:** No trace of wear. Light blemishes.

**MS-63 Choice Uncirculated:** Some distracting blemishes in prime focal areas. Impaired luster possible.

**PF-63 Choice Proof:** Reflective surfaces. Only a few blemishes in secondary focal areas. No major flaws.

**With Rays (1866–1867)**

**Without Rays (1867–1883)**

**Typical Example of
1883, 3 Over 2**
*Other varieties exist.*

*Brilliant choice Uncirculated and Proof coins are worth more than prices shown. Spotted, cleaned, or discolored pieces are worth less.*

| | Mintage | G-4 | VG-8 | F-12 | EF-40 | AU-50 | MS-60 | MS-63 | PF-63 |
|---|---|---|---|---|---|---|---|---|---|
| 1866, Rays | (600+) . .14,742,500 | $13 | $19 | $22 | $85 | $110 | $125 | $200 | $1,250 |
| 1867, Rays | (25+) . . .2,019,000 | 15 | 22 | 27 | 90 | 125 | 225 | 275 | 16,000 |
| 1867, Without Rays | (600+) . .28,890,500 | 9 | 10 | 11 | 20 | 25 | 70 | 120 | 220 |
| 1868 | (600+) . .28,817,000 | 9 | 10 | 11 | 20 | 25 | 70 | 120 | 220 |
| 1869 | (600+) . .16,395,000 | 9 | 10 | 11 | 20 | 25 | 70 | 120 | 220 |
| 1870 | (1,000+) . . .4,806,000 | 9 | 10 | 11 | 20 | 25 | 70 | 120 | 220 |
| 1871 | (960+) . . . .561,000 | 25 | 30 | 50 | 100 | 135 | 180 | 250 | 250 |
| 1872 | (950+) . . .6,036,000 | 10 | 11 | 13 | 24 | 50 | 90 | 125 | 220 |
| 1873, Close 3 | (1,100+) . . . .436,050 | 10 | 11 | 13 | 30 | 55 | 100 | 175 | 220 |
| 1873, Open 3 | . . . .4,113,950 | 9 | 10 | 11 | 25 | 50 | 90 | 125 | |
| 1874 | (700+) . . .3,538,000 | 10 | 11 | 13 | 24 | 50 | 90 | 130 | 220 |
| 1875 | (700+) . . .2,097,000 | 12 | 14 | 20 | 40 | 55 | 100 | 140 | 225 |
| 1876 | (1,150+) . . .2,530,000 | 12 | 14 | 20 | 40 | 55 | 100 | 120 | 220 |
| 1877, Proof only | (510+) . . . . . . . . . . | | | 425 | 900 | | | | 1,350 |
| 1878, Proof only | (2,350) . . . . . . . . . . . | | | 300 | 500 | | | | 950 |
| 1879 | (3,200) . . . . . .25,900 | 180 | 225 | 275 | 325 | 350 | 400 | 475 | 400 |
| 1880 | (3,955) . . . . . .16,000 | 190 | 240 | 290 | 500 | 800 | 1,600 | 2,500 | 450 |
| 1881 | (3,575) . . . . . .68,800 | 125 | 150 | 175 | 250 | 275 | 350 | 450 | 300 |
| 1882 | (3,100) . . .11,472,900 | 8 | 9 | 10 | 19 | 25 | 60 | 100 | 175 |
| 1883 | (5,419) . . . .1,451,500 | 8 | 9 | 10 | 19 | 25 | 65 | 100 | 180 |
| 1883, 3 Over 2 | . . . . . . . . . . . . . . . . . . . . .* | 50 | 110 | 200 | 300 | 400 | 500 | 650 | |

* Included in number above.

## LIBERTY HEAD (1883–1913)

In 1883 the design was changed to the "Liberty head." This type first appeared without the word CENTS on the coin, merely a large letter V. These "CENTS-less" coins were goldplated by fraudsters and passed as $5 pieces. Later in that year the word CENTS was added.

**G-4 Good:** No details in head. LIBERTY obliterated.
**VG-8 Very Good:** Some letters in LIBERTY legible.
**F-12 Fine:** All letters in LIBERTY legible.
**VF-20 Very Fine:** LIBERTY bold, including letter L.
**EF-40 Extremely Fine:** LIBERTY sharp. Corn grains at bottom of wreath visible on reverse.
**AU-50 About Uncirculated:** Traces of light wear on only high points of design. Half of mint luster present.
**MS-60 Uncirculated:** No trace of wear. Contact marks possible. Surface may be spotted, or luster faded.
**MS-63 Choice Uncirculated:** No trace of wear. Light blemishes.
**PF-63 Choice Proof:** Reflective surfaces. Only a few blemishes in secondary focal areas. No major flaws.

**Variety 1, Without CENTS (1883 Only)**   **Variety 2, With CENTS (1883–1913)**   **Mintmark Location**

*Brilliant choice Uncirculated and Proof coins are worth more than prices shown; spotted or cleaned coins, less.*

| | Mintage | G-4 | VG-8 | F-12 | VF-20 | EF-40 | AU-50 | MS-60 | MS-63 | PF-63 |
|---|---|---|---|---|---|---|---|---|---|---|
| 1883, Without CENTS ..(5,219) ...5,474,300 | | $2.35 | $3.00 | $3.25 | $4 | $5 | $6.25 | $18 | $26 | $165 |
| 1883, CENTS (6,783) ..16,026,200 | | 7.00 | 9.00 | 13.00 | 21 | 35 | 45.00 | 75 | 100 | 140 |
| 1884 . . . . . . .(3,942) ..11,270,000 | | 8.00 | 12.00 | 14.00 | 21 | 35 | 50.00 | 100 | 130 | 130 |
| 1885 . . . . . . .(3,790) ...1,472,700 | | 230.00 | 275.00 | 325.00 | 450 | 550 | 750.00 | 1,000 | 1,200 | 700 |
| 1886 . . . . . . .(4,290) ...3,326,000 | | 100.00 | 125.00 | 200.00 | 250 | 310 | 395.00 | 450 | 800 | 375 |
| 1887 . . . . . . .(2,960) ..15,260,692 | | 4.00 | 7.00 | 11.00 | 20 | 40 | 45.00 | 75 | 125 | 150 |
| 1888 . . . . . . .(4,582) ..10,167,901 | | 10.00 | 15.00 | 25.00 | 50 | 65 | 90.00 | 135 | 180 | 150 |
| 1889 . . . . . . .(3,336) ..15,878,025 | | 4.00 | 5.00 | 11.00 | 20 | 35 | 50.00 | 75 | 125 | 140 |
| 1890 . . . . . . .(2,740) ..16,256,532 | | 2.50 | 4.00 | 10.00 | 15 | 25 | 30.00 | 75 | 125 | 140 |
| 1891 . . . . . . .(2,350) ..16,832,000 | | 2.50 | 4.00 | 10.00 | 15 | 25 | 30.00 | 75 | 125 | 140 |
| 1892 . . . . . . .(2,745) ..11,696,897 | | 2.50 | 4.00 | 10.00 | 15 | 25 | 30.00 | 75 | 125 | 140 |
| 1893 . . . . . . .(2,195) ..13,368,000 | | 2.50 | 4.00 | 10.00 | 15 | 30 | 35.00 | 80 | 135 | 140 |
| 1894 . . . . . . .(2,632) ...5,410,500 | | 6.00 | 10.00 | 40.00 | 75 | 115 | 150.00 | 180 | 210 | 140 |
| 1895 . . . . . . .(2,062) ...9,977,822 | | 1.50 | 2.50 | 7.00 | 10 | 25 | 30.00 | 75 | 130 | 140 |
| 1896 . . . . . . .(1,862) ...8,841,058 | | 2.00 | 5.00 | 15.00 | 20 | 35 | 50.00 | 90 | 140 | 140 |
| 1897 . . . . . . .(1,938) ..20,426,797 | | 2.00 | 5.00 | 9.00 | 12 | 22 | 24.00 | 50 | 125 | 140 |
| 1898 . . . . . . .(1,795) ..12,530,292 | | 2.00 | 5.00 | 9.00 | 12 | 22 | 24.00 | 50 | 125 | 140 |
| 1899 . . . . . . .(2,031) ..26,027,000 | | 0.75 | 1.00 | 3.00 | 6 | 14 | 22.00 | 50 | 100 | 140 |
| 1900 . . . . . . .(2,262) ..27,253,733 | | 0.75 | 1.00 | 3.00 | 6 | 14 | 21.00 | 40 | 90 | 135 |
| 1901 . . . . . . .(1,985) ..26,478,228 | | 0.75 | 1.00 | 3.00 | 6 | 14 | 21.00 | 40 | 80 | 135 |
| 1902 . . . . . . .(2,018) ..31,487,561 | | 0.75 | 1.00 | 3.00 | 6 | 14 | 21.00 | 40 | 80 | 135 |
| 1903 . . . . . . .(1,790) ..28,004,935 | | 0.75 | 1.00 | 2.00 | 4 | 12 | 21.00 | 40 | 80 | 135 |
| 1904 . . . . . . .(1,817) ..21,403,167 | | 0.75 | 1.00 | 2.00 | 4 | 12 | 21.00 | 40 | 80 | 135 |
| 1905 . . . . . . .(2,152) ..29,825,124 | | 0.75 | 1.00 | 2.00 | 4 | 12 | 21.00 | 40 | 80 | 135 |
| 1906 . . . . . . .(1,725) ..38,612,000 | | 0.75 | 1.00 | 2.00 | 4 | 12 | 21.00 | 40 | 80 | 135 |
| 1907 . . . . . . .(1,475) ..39,213,325 | | 0.75 | 1.00 | 2.00 | 4 | 12 | 21.00 | 40 | 80 | 135 |
| 1908 . . . . . . .(1,620) ..22,684,557 | | 0.75 | 1.00 | 2.00 | 4 | 12 | 21.00 | 40 | 80 | 135 |

*Chart continued on next page.*

| | Mintage | G-4 | VG-8 | F-12 | VF-20 | EF-40 | AU-50 | MS-60 | MS-63 | PF-63 |
|---|---|---|---|---|---|---|---|---|---|---|
| 1909 . . . . . .(4,763) . .11,585,763 | | $0.75 | $1.00 | $2 | $4 | $12 | $21 | $45 | $95 | $135 |
| 1910 . . . . . .(2,405) . .30,166,948 | | 0.75 | 1.00 | 2 | 4 | 12 | 21 | 40 | 80 | 135 |
| 1911 . . . . . .(1,733) . .39,557,639 | | 0.75 | 1.00 | 2 | 4 | 12 | 21 | 40 | 80 | 135 |
| 1912 . . . . . .(2,145) . .26,234,569 | | 0.75 | 1.00 | 2 | 4 | 12 | 21 | 40 | 80 | 135 |
| 1912D . . . . . . . . . . . .8,474,000 | | 1.00 | 1.50 | 4 | 13 | 35 | 85 | 135 | 160 | |
| 1912S . . . . . . . . . . . . . .238,000 | | 65.00 | 100.00 | 125 | 225 | 425 | 650 | 750 | 950 | |
| 1913 Liberty Head *(5 known)* . . . . . | | | | | | | | | 2,000,000 | |

## INDIAN HEAD OR BUFFALO (1913–1938)

The Buffalo nickel was designed by James E. Fraser, whose initial F is below the date. He modeled the bison after Black Diamond in the New York Central Park Zoo.

**G-4 Good:** Legends and date readable. Buffalo's horn does not show.
**VG-8 Very Good:** Horn worn nearly flat.
**F-12 Fine:** Horn and tail smooth but partially visible. Obverse rim intact.
**VF-20 Very Fine:** Much of horn visible. Indian's cheekbone worn.
**EF-40 Extremely Fine:** Horn lightly worn. Slight wear on Indian's hair ribbon.
**AU-50 About Uncirculated:** Traces of light wear on high points of design. Half of mint luster present.
**MS-60 Uncirculated:** No trace of wear. May have several blemishes.
**MS-63 Choice Uncirculated:** No trace of wear. Light blemishes.
**Matte PF-63 Choice Proof:** Crisp surfaces. Only a few blemishes in secondary focal areas. No major flaws.

### Variety 1 – FIVE CENTS on Raised Ground (1913)

*Brilliant choice Uncirculated coins are worth more than prices shown. Spotted, cleaned, weakly struck, or discolored pieces are worth less.*

| | Mintage | G-4 | VG-8 | F-12 | VF-20 | EF-40 | AU-50 | MS-60 | MS-63 | MATTE PF-63 |
|---|---|---|---|---|---|---|---|---|---|---|
| 1913, Variety 1 . .(1,520) . .30,992,000 | | $4 | $5 | $6 | $8 | $11 | $12 | $21 | $30 | $750 |
| 1913D, Variety 1 . . . . . . . . . .5,337,000 | | 6 | 8 | 10 | 14 | 18 | 23 | 35 | 45 | |
| 1913S, Variety 1 . . . . . . . . . .2,105,000 | | 17 | 22 | 24 | 28 | 40 | 50 | 70 | 90 | |

### Variety 2 – FIVE CENTS in Recess (1913–1938)

| Mintmark Below FIVE CENTS | 1916, Doubled-Die Obverse | 1918-D, 8 Over 7 |
|---|---|---|

| | Mintage | G-4 | VG-8 | F-12 | VF-20 | EF-40 | AU-50 | MS-60 | MS-63 | MATTE PF-63 |
|---|---|---|---|---|---|---|---|---|---|---|
| 1913, Variety 2 . . . . . .29,857,186 | | $4.25 | $5.50 | $6.50 | $7.50 | $11 | $15 | $22 | $32 | |
| . . . . . . . . . . . . . . . .(1,514) | | | | | | | | | | $600 |
| 1913D, Variety 2 . . . . .4,156,000 | | 50.00 | 60.00 | 75.00 | 90.00 | 120 | 140 | 150 | 175 | |
| 1913S, Variety 2 . . . . . .1,209,000 | | 150.00 | 165.00 | 210.00 | 240.00 | 325 | 375 | 500 | 625 | |
| 1914 . . . . . . . . . . . .20,664,463 | | 10.00 | 11.00 | 12.00 | 14.00 | 16 | 22 | 35 | 50 | |
| . . . . . . . . . . . . . . . .(1,275) | | | | | | | | | | 675 |

# NICKEL FIVE-CENT PIECES

Brilliant choice Uncirculated coins are worth more than prices shown. Spotted, cleaned, weakly struck, or discolored pieces are worth less.

| | Mintage | G-4 | VG-8 | F-12 | VF-20 | EF-40 | AU-50 | MS-60 | MS-63 | MATTE PF-63 |
|---|---|---|---|---|---|---|---|---|---|---|
| 1914D | 3,912,000 | $35.00 | $50.00 | $65.00 | $100.00 | $150 | $200 | $235 | $325 | |
| 1914S | 3,470,000 | 12.00 | 14.00 | 18.00 | 35.00 | 50 | 80 | 100 | 240 | |
| 1915 | 20,986,220 | 2.50 | 3.00 | 4.00 | 5.00 | 12 | 30 | 45 | 50 | |
| | (1,050) | | | | | | | | | $700 |
| 1915D | 7,569,000 | 8.00 | 11.00 | 18.00 | 35.00 | 75 | 85 | 140 | 175 | |
| 1915S | 1,505,000 | 19.00 | 25.00 | 40.00 | 72.00 | 150 | 185 | 275 | 425 | |
| 1916 | 63,497,466 | 2.00 | 2.50 | 3.00 | 3.50 | 5 | 10 | 28 | 35 | |
| | (600) | | | | | | | | | 900 |
| 1916, DblDie Obv | * | 1,000.00 | 1,800.00 | 3,600.00 | 5,600.00 | 8,500 | 14,000 | 30,000 | 70,000 | |
| 1916D | 13,333,000 | 6.50 | 10.00 | 11.00 | 22.00 | 45 | 60 | 90 | 135 | |
| 1916S | 11,860,000 | 4.00 | 6.00 | 9.00 | 22.00 | 45 | 65 | 100 | 165 | |
| 1917 | 51,424,019 | 2.00 | 2.50 | 3.00 | 4.00 | 7 | 16 | 30 | 60 | |
| 1917D | 9,910,000 | 7.00 | 12.00 | 18.00 | 42.00 | 75 | 110 | 175 | 375 | |
| 1917S | 4,193,000 | 9.00 | 13.00 | 20.00 | 50.00 | 85 | 135 | 225 | 600 | |
| 1918 | 32,086,314 | 1.50 | 2.00 | 2.50 | 6.00 | 16 | 22 | 60 | 135 | |

* Included in number above.

| | Mintage | G-4 | VG-8 | F-12 | VF-20 | EF-40 | AU-50 | MS-60 | MS-63 |
|---|---|---|---|---|---|---|---|---|---|
| 1918D, 8 Over 7 | ** | $550.00 | $650.00 | $1,300.00 | $2,500.00 | $4,500.00 | $6,000 | $15,000 | $32,000 |
| 1918D | 8,362,000 | 8.00 | 14.00 | 18.00 | 70.00 | 130.00 | 175 | 235 | 600 |
| 1918S | 4,882,000 | 5.00 | 12.00 | 16.00 | 45.00 | 90.00 | 150 | 210 | 1,500 |
| 1919 | 60,868,000 | 0.50 | 0.55 | 0.80 | 2.00 | 7.00 | 15 | 32 | 60 |
| 1919D (a) | 8,006,000 | 6.00 | 10.00 | 30.00 | 70.00 | 130.00 | 160 | 325 | 770 |
| 1919S (a) | 7,521,000 | 4.00 | 8.00 | 17.00 | 60.00 | 130.00 | 160 | 325 | 900 |
| 1920 | 63,093,000 | 0.45 | 0.60 | 1.25 | 2.50 | 6.00 | 15 | 32 | 70 |
| 1920D (a) | 9,418,000 | 3.00 | 6.00 | 12.00 | 65.00 | 150.00 | 175 | 275 | 800 |
| 1920S | 9,689,000 | 1.50 | 4.00 | 10.00 | 50.00 | 120.00 | 150 | 275 | 900 |
| 1921 | 10,663,000 | 0.80 | 2.00 | 3.00 | 10.00 | 25.00 | 35 | 70 | 140 |
| 1921S | 1,557,000 | 32.00 | 55.00 | 90.00 | 300.00 | 465.00 | 550 | 865 | 1,200 |
| 1923 | 35,715,000 | 0.45 | 0.60 | 0.80 | 4.00 | 7.50 | 18 | 32 | 80 |
| 1923S (a) | 6,142,000 | 3.00 | 3.50 | 9.00 | 60.00 | 150.00 | 180 | 235 | 550 |
| 1924 | 21,620,000 | 0.40 | 0.60 | 0.80 | 4.00 | 9.00 | 25 | 40 | 80 |
| 1924D | 5,258,000 | 3.50 | 4.00 | 10.00 | 40.00 | 120.00 | 140 | 190 | 500 |
| 1924S | 1,437,000 | 8.00 | 18.00 | 40.00 | 225.00 | 650.00 | 875 | 1,200 | 2,200 |
| 1925 | 35,565,100 | 0.75 | 1.25 | 2.00 | 4.00 | 8.00 | 16 | 25 | 47 |
| 1925D (a) | 4,450,000 | 4.00 | 5.00 | 18.00 | 45.00 | 85.00 | 125 | 210 | 325 |
| 1925S | 6,256,000 | 2.00 | 5.00 | 10.00 | 50.00 | 90.00 | 125 | 230 | 1,200 |
| 1926 | 44,693,000 | 0.35 | 0.45 | 0.60 | 3.00 | 5.00 | 12 | 22 | 32 |
| 1926D (a) | 5,638,000 | 3.00 | 6.00 | 10.00 | 50.00 | 90.00 | 140 | 160 | 235 |
| 1926S | 970,000 | 9.00 | 16.00 | 40.00 | 235.00 | 450.00 | 1,300 | 2,000 | 4,200 |
| 1927 | 37,981,000 | 0.50 | 0.45 | 0.60 | 1.50 | 6.00 | 10 | 24 | 36 |
| 1927D | 5,730,000 | 0.85 | 2.00 | 2.50 | 15.00 | 40.00 | 55 | 85 | 160 |
| 1927S | 3,430,000 | 0.60 | 0.90 | 1.75 | 18.00 | 45.00 | 75 | 250 | 1,100 |
| 1928 | 23,411,000 | 0.40 | 0.45 | 0.60 | 2.00 | 5.00 | 10 | 22 | 30 |
| 1928D | 6,436,000 | 0.45 | 0.85 | 1.75 | 6.00 | 20.00 | 23 | 28 | 48 |
| 1928S | 6,936,000 | 0.60 | 0.75 | 1.25 | 5.00 | 15.00 | 50 | 125 | 300 |
| 1929 | 36,446,000 | 0.35 | 0.40 | 0.60 | 2.00 | 5.00 | 10 | 16 | 35 |
| 1929D | 8,370,000 | 0.45 | 0.60 | 0.80 | 3.00 | 15.00 | 18 | 32 | 65 |
| 1929S | 7,754,000 | 0.40 | 0.60 | 0.75 | 0.90 | 5.50 | 12 | 25 | 45 |

** Included in number below.  a. Uncirculated pieces with full, sharp details are worth considerably more.

**1937-D, "3-Legged" Variety**

**1938-D, D Over S**

*Brilliant choice Uncirculated coins are worth more than prices shown. Spotted, cleaned, weakly struck, or discolored pieces are worth less.*

| | Mintage | G-4 | VG-8 | F-12 | VF-20 | EF-40 | AU-50 | MS-60 | MS-63 | PF-63 |
|---|---|---|---|---|---|---|---|---|---|---|
| 1930 | 22,849,000 | $0.40 | $0.50 | $0.70 | $0.80 | $5.00 | $11.00 | $16 | $35 | |
| 1930S | 5,435,000 | 0.40 | 0.50 | 0.70 | 0.80 | 6.00 | 15.00 | 25 | 60 | |
| 1931S | 1,200,000 | 7.00 | 8.00 | 8.80 | 9.25 | 15.00 | 25.00 | 28 | 45 | |
| 1934 | 20,213,003 | 0.35 | 0.45 | 0.55 | 0.75 | 3.00 | 9.00 | 16 | 30 | |
| 1934D | 7,480,000 | 0.50 | 0.75 | 1.25 | 3.00 | 9.00 | 21.00 | 35 | 55 | |
| 1935 | 58,264,000 | 0.35 | 0.45 | 0.55 | 0.75 | 1.25 | 4.25 | 10 | 22 | |
| 1935D | 12,092,000 | 0.35 | 0.50 | 1.00 | 3.00 | 6.00 | 19.00 | 30 | 40 | |
| 1935S | 10,300,000 | 0.35 | 0.45 | 0.55 | 0.75 | 2.00 | 7.50 | 15 | 36 | |
| 1936 | (4,420) | 118,997,000 | 0.35 | 0.45 | 0.55 | 0.75 | 1.25 | 4.00 | 10 | 23 | $650 |
| 1936D | 24,814,000 | 0.45 | 0.60 | 0.75 | 0.95 | 1.75 | 4.50 | 16 | 19 | |
| 1936S | 14,930,000 | 0.35 | 0.45 | 0.55 | 0.75 | 1.25 | 4.50 | 11 | 16 | |
| 1937 | (5,769) | 79,480,000 | 0.35 | 0.45 | 0.55 | 0.75 | 1.25 | 2.75 | 13 | 16 | 550 |
| 1937D | 17,826,000 | 0.35 | 0.45 | 0.55 | 0.75 | 1.25 | 4.00 | 11 | 16 | |
| 1937D, 3-Legged | * | 250.00 | 350.00 | 450.00 | 550.00 | 650.00 | 750.00 | 1,250 | 2,800 | |
| 1937S | 5,635,000 | 0.35 | 0.45 | 0.55 | 0.75 | 1.25 | 4.00 | 11 | 20 | |
| 1938D | 7,020,000 | 1.00 | 1.10 | 1.50 | 1.75 | 2.00 | 4.00 | 11 | 15 | |
| 1938D, D Over S | * | 1.00 | 1.25 | 4.00 | 5.00 | 8.00 | 12.00 | 25 | 36 | |

* Included in number above.

## JEFFERSON (1938 TO DATE)

This nickel was originally designed by Felix Schlag. He won an award of $1,000 in a competition with some 390 artists. It established the definite public approval of portrait and pictorial rather than symbolic devices on our coinage. On October 8, 1942, the wartime five-cent piece composed of copper (56%), silver (35%), and manganese (9%) was introduced to eliminate nickel, a critical war material. A larger mintmark was placed above the dome. The letter P (Philadelphia) was used for the first time, indicating the change of alloy. The designer's initials FS were added below the bust starting in 1966. The mintmark position was moved to the obverse starting in 1968.

**VG-8 Very Good:** Second porch pillar from right nearly gone, other three still visible but weak.
**F-12 Fine:** Jefferson's cheekbone worn flat. Hair lines and eyebrow faint. Second pillar weak, especially at bottom.
**VF-20 Very Fine:** Second pillar plain and complete on both sides.
**EF-40 Extremely Fine:** Cheekbone, hair lines, eyebrow slightly worn but well defined. Base of triangle above pillars visible but weak.
**MS-63 Select Uncirculated:** No trace of wear. Slight blemishes.
**MS-65 Choice Uncirculated:** No trace of wear. Barely noticeable blemishes.
**PF-65 Gem Proof:** Brilliant surfaces. No noticeable blemishes or flaws. May have a few barely noticeable marks or hairlines.

**Mintmark Located at Right of Building**

**Mintmark, Starting 1968**

# NICKEL FIVE-CENT PIECES

*Uncirculated pieces with fully struck steps are valued higher.*

| | Mintage | VG-8 | F-12 | VF-20 | EF-40 | MS-63 | MS-65 | PF-65 |
|---|---|---|---|---|---|---|---|---|
| 1938 . . . . . . . .(19,365) . . .19,496,000 | | $0.10 | $0.12 | $0.20 | $0.25 | $1.10 | $5.00 | $50 |
| 1938D . . . . . . . . . . . . . . . . .5,376,000 | | 0.25 | 0.35 | 0.75 | 1.00 | 2.25 | 7.00 | |
| 1938S . . . . . . . . . . . . . . . . .4,105,000 | | 0.40 | 0.60 | 0.85 | 1.50 | 2.75 | 8.00 | |
| 1939 . . . . . . . .(12,535) . .120,615,000 | | 0.08 | 0.10 | 0.12 | 0.25 | 1.00 | 2.00 | 50 |
| 1939D . . . . . . . . . . . . . . . . .3,514,000 | | 1.20 | 1.60 | 2.50 | 4.00 | 35.00 | 50.00 | |
| 1939S . . . . . . . . . . . . . . . . .6,630,000 | | 0.25 | 0.30 | 0.50 | 1.35 | 12.00 | 20.00 | |
| 1940 . . . . . . . .(14,158) . .176,485,000 | | 0.05 | 0.05 | 0.05 | 0.10 | 1.00 | 2.00 | 45 |
| 1940D . . . . . . . . . . . . . . . .43,540,000 | | 0.05 | 0.05 | 0.05 | 0.10 | 1.25 | 3.50 | |
| 1940S . . . . . . . . . . . . . . . .39,690,000 | | 0.05 | 0.05 | 0.05 | 0.10 | 1.25 | 3.50 | |
| 1941 . . . . . . . .(18,720) . .203,265,000 | | 0.05 | 0.05 | 0.05 | 0.10 | 0.50 | 2.00 | 45 |
| 1941D . . . . . . . . . . . . . . . .53,432,000 | | 0.05 | 0.05 | 0.05 | 0.10 | 1.25 | 3.00 | |
| 1941S . . . . . . . . . . . . . . . .43,445,000 | | 0.05 | 0.05 | 0.05 | 0.10 | 1.50 | 3.50 | |
| 1942 . . . . . . . .(29,600) . .49,789,000 | | 0.05 | 0.05 | 0.05 | 0.10 | 1.25 | 4.00 | 45 |
| 1942D . . . . . . . . . . . . . . . .13,938,000 | | 0.10 | 0.15 | 0.25 | 1.00 | 16.00 | 23.00 | |

## Wartime Silver Alloy (1942–1945)

**Mintmark Location**

**1943, 3 Over 2**

| | Mintage | VG-8 | F-12 | VF-20 | EF-40 | MS-63 | MS-65 | PF-65 |
|---|---|---|---|---|---|---|---|---|
| 1942P . . . . . . . .(27,600) . . .57,873,000 | | $1 | $1 | $1 | $1.25 | $4 | $8.00 | $110 |
| 1942S . . . . . . . . . . . . . . . .32,900,000 | | 1 | 1 | 1 | 1.25 | 4 | 9.00 | |
| 1943P, 3 Over 2 . . . . . . . . . . . . . . . . . . . .* | | | 15 | 20 | 38.00 | 130 | 320.00 | |
| 1943P . . . . . . . . . . . . . . . .271,165,000 | | 1 | 1 | 1 | 1.25 | 3 | 6.00 | |
| 1943D . . . . . . . . . . . . . . . .15,294,000 | | 1 | 1 | 1 | 1.25 | 5 | 7.00 | |
| 1943S . . . . . . . . . . . . . . . .104,060,000 | | 1 | 1 | 1 | 1.25 | 3 | 6.00 | |
| 1944P . . . . . . . . . . . . . . . .119,150,000 | | 1 | 1 | 1 | 1.25 | 5 | 8.50 | |
| 1944D . . . . . . . . . . . . . . . .32,309,000 | | 1 | 1 | 1 | 1.25 | 5 | 8.00 | |
| 1944S . . . . . . . . . . . . . . . .21,640,000 | | 1 | 1 | 1 | 1.25 | 4 | 8.00 | |
| 1945P . . . . . . . . . . . . . . . .119,408,100 | | 1 | 1 | 1 | 1.25 | 3 | 8.00 | |
| 1945D . . . . . . . . . . . . . . . .37,158,000 | | 1 | 1 | 1 | 1.25 | 3 | 7.00 | |
| 1945S . . . . . . . . . . . . . . . .58,939,000 | | 1 | 1 | 1 | 1.25 | 3 | 7.00 | |

* Included in number below.

## Prewar Composition, Mintmark Style Resumed (1946–1967)

**1954-S, S Over D**      **1955-D, D Over S**

| | Mintage | VF-20 | EF-40 | MS-63 | MS-65 | PF-65 |
|---|---|---|---|---|---|---|
| 1946 . . . . . . . . . . . . . . . . . . . . . . . . . . . . . . . . . . . .161,116,000 | | $0.05 | $0.05 | $0.60 | $2.50 | |
| 1946D . . . . . . . . . . . . . . . . . . . . . . . . . . . . . . . . . . .45,292,200 | | 0.05 | 0.05 | 0.60 | 2.50 | |
| 1946S . . . . . . . . . . . . . . . . . . . . . . . . . . . . . . . . . . .13,560,000 | | 0.05 | 0.06 | 0.25 | 1.75 | |

*Chart continued on next page.*

| | Mintage | VF-20 | EF-40 | MS-63 | MS-65 | PF-65 |
|---|---|---|---|---|---|---|
| 1947 | 95,000,000 | $0.05 | $0.05 | $0.35 | $1.75 | |
| 1947D | 37,822,000 | 0.05 | 0.05 | 0.35 | 1.75 | |
| 1947S | 24,720,000 | 0.05 | 0.06 | 0.35 | 1.75 | |
| 1948 | 89,348,000 | 0.05 | 0.05 | 0.35 | 1.75 | |
| 1948D | 44,734,000 | 0.05 | 0.06 | 0.50 | 2.00 | |
| 1948S | 11,300,000 | 0.05 | 0.06 | 0.50 | 2.00 | |
| 1949 | 60,652,000 | 0.05 | 0.10 | 2.00 | 3.00 | |
| 1949D | 36,498,000 | 0.05 | 0.05 | 0.50 | 2.00 | |
| 1949D, D Over S | * | 18.00 | 30.00 | 100.00 | 160.00 | |
| 1949S | 9,716,000 | 0.05 | 0.10 | 0.40 | 2.00 | |
| 1950 | (51,386) 9,796,000 | 0.05 | 0.10 | 0.50 | 2.50 | $30.00 |
| 1950D | 2,630,030 | 3.00 | 3.50 | 8.00 | 11.00 | |
| 1951 | (57,500) 28,552,000 | 0.05 | 0.06 | 1.25 | 3.00 | 25.00 |
| 1951D | 20,460,000 | 0.05 | 0.06 | 2.00 | 3.50 | |
| 1951S | 7,776,000 | 0.05 | 0.10 | 0.50 | 2.50 | |
| 1952 | (81,980) 63,988,000 | 0.05 | 0.05 | 0.35 | 1.75 | 18.00 |
| 1952D | 30,638,000 | 0.05 | 0.05 | 2.00 | 3.00 | |
| 1952S | 20,572,000 | 0.05 | 0.05 | 0.55 | 1.50 | |
| 1953 | (128,800) 46,644,000 | 0.05 | 0.05 | 0.10 | 0.35 | 16.00 |
| 1953D | 59,878,600 | 0.05 | 0.05 | 0.10 | 0.35 | |
| 1953S | 19,210,900 | 0.05 | 0.05 | 0.25 | 0.50 | |
| 1954 | (233,300) 47,684,050 | 0.05 | 0.05 | 0.50 | 1.00 | 8.00 |
| 1954D | 117,183,060 | 0.05 | 0.05 | 0.20 | 0.50 | |
| 1954S | 29,384,000 | 0.05 | 0.05 | 0.50 | 1.00 | |
| 1954S, S Over D | * | 2.50 | 5.00 | 18.00 | 35.00 | |
| 1955 | (378,200) 7,888,000 | 0.06 | 0.08 | 0.40 | 0.50 | 6.00 |
| 1955D | 74,464,100 | 0.05 | 0.05 | 0.20 | 0.60 | |
| 1955D, D Over S (a) | * | 3.00 | 5.00 | 23.00 | 40.00 | |
| 1956 | (669,384) 35,216,000 | 0.05 | 0.05 | 0.10 | 0.40 | 1.00 |
| 1956D | 67,222,940 | 0.05 | 0.05 | 0.10 | 0.40 | |
| 1957 | (1,247,952) 38,408,000 | 0.05 | 0.05 | 0.10 | 0.40 | 1.00 |
| 1957D | 136,828,900 | 0.05 | 0.05 | 0.20 | 0.60 | |
| 1958 | (875,652) 17,088,000 | 0.05 | 0.05 | 0.20 | 0.60 | 1.50 |
| 1958D | 168,249,120 | 0.05 | 0.05 | 0.10 | 0.40 | |
| 1959 | (1,149,291) 27,248,000 | 0.05 | 0.05 | 0.10 | 0.20 | 0.75 |
| 1959D | 160,738,240 | 0.05 | 0.05 | 0.10 | 0.20 | |
| 1960 | (1,691,602) 55,416,000 | 0.05 | 0.05 | 0.10 | 0.20 | 0.75 |
| 1960D | 192,582,180 | 0.05 | 0.05 | 0.10 | 0.30 | |
| 1961 | (3,028,144) 73,640,100 | 0.05 | 0.05 | 0.10 | 0.20 | 0.75 |
| 1961D | 229,342,760 | 0.05 | 0.05 | 0.10 | 0.30 | |
| 1962 | (3,218,019) 97,384,000 | 0.05 | 0.05 | 0.10 | 0.20 | 0.75 |
| 1962D | 280,195,720 | 0.05 | 0.05 | 0.10 | 0.25 | |
| 1963 | (3,075,645) 175,776,000 | 0.05 | 0.05 | 0.10 | 0.20 | 0.75 |
| 1963D | 276,829,460 | 0.05 | 0.05 | 0.10 | 0.20 | |
| 1964 | (3,950,762) 1,024,672,000 | 0.05 | 0.05 | 0.10 | 0.20 | 0.75 |
| 1964D | 1,787,297,160 | 0.05 | 0.05 | 0.10 | 0.20 | |
| 1965 | 136,131,380 | 0.05 | 0.05 | 0.10 | 0.20 | |

* Included in number above. **a.** Varieties exist. Values are for the variety illustrated.

## 1966 Through 2003

| | Mintage | MS-63 | MS-65 | PF-65 | | Mintage | MS-63 | MS-65 | PF-65 |
|---|---|---|---|---|---|---|---|---|---|
| 1966 | 156,208,283 | $0.10 | $0.20 | | 1968D | 91,227,880 | $0.10 | $0.20 | |
| 1967 | 107,325,800 | 0.10 | 0.20 | | 1968S | 100,396,004 | 0.10 | 0.20 | |

| | Mintage | MS-63 | MS-65 | PF-65 |
|---|---|---|---|---|
| 1968S, Proof | (3,041,506) | | | $0.75 |
| 1969D | 202,807,500 | $0.10 | $0.20 | |
| 1969S | 120,165,000 | 0.10 | 0.20 | |
| | (2,934,631) | | | 0.75 |
| 1970D | 515,485,380 | 0.10 | 0.20 | |
| 1970S | 238,832,004 | 0.10 | 0.20 | |
| | (2,632,810) | | | 0.75 |
| 1971 | 106,884,000 | 0.25 | 0.50 | |
| 1971D | 316,144,800 | 0.10 | 0.20 | |
| 1971S | (3,220,733) | | | 1.00 |

| | Mintage | MS-65 | PF-65 |
|---|---|---|---|
| 1975 | 181,772,000 | $0.35 | |
| 1975D | 401,875,300 | 0.20 | |
| 1975S | (2,845,450) | | $0.85 |
| 1976 | 367,124,000 | 0.20 | |
| 1976D | 563,964,147 | 0.20 | |
| 1976S | (4,149,730) | | 0.85 |
| 1977 | 585,376,000 | 0.20 | |
| 1977D | 297,313,422 | 0.50 | |
| 1977S | (3,251,152) | | 0.75 |
| 1978 | 391,308,000 | 0.20 | |
| 1978D | 313,092,780 | 0.20 | |
| 1978S | (3,127,781) | | 0.75 |
| 1979 | 463,188,000 | 0.20 | |
| 1979D | 325,867,672 | 0.20 | |
| 1979S, Filled S | (3,677,175) | | 0.75 |
| 1979S, Clear S | * | | 1.00 |
| 1980P | 593,004,000 | 0.20 | |
| 1980D | 502,323,448 | 0.20 | |
| 1980S | (3,554,806) | | 0.75 |
| 1981P | 657,504,000 | 0.20 | |
| 1981D | 364,801,843 | 0.20 | |
| 1981S | (4,063,083) | | 0.85 |
| 1982P | 292,355,000 | 3.00 | |
| 1982D | 373,726,544 | 1.75 | |
| 1982S | (3,857,479) | | 1.00 |
| 1983P | 561,615,000 | 2.00 | |
| 1983D | 536,726,276 | 1.50 | |
| 1983S | (3,279,126) | | 1.00 |
| 1984P | 746,769,000 | 1.25 | |
| 1984D | 517,675,146 | 0.20 | |
| 1984S | (3,065,110) | | 1.50 |
| 1985P | 647,114,962 | 0.25 | |
| 1985D | 459,747,446 | 0.25 | |
| 1985S | (3,362,821) | | 1.25 |
| 1986P | 536,883,483 | 0.25 | |
| 1986D | 361,819,140 | 0.60 | |
| 1986S | (3,010,497) | | 2.75 |
| 1987P | 371,499,481 | 0.20 | |
| 1987D | 410,590,604 | 0.20 | |
| 1987S | (4,227,728) | | 1.00 |

| | Mintage | MS-63 | MS-65 | PF-65 |
|---|---|---|---|---|
| 1972 | 202,036,000 | $0.10 | $0.20 | |
| 1972D | 351,694,600 | 0.10 | 0.20 | |
| 1972S | (3,260,996) | | | $1.00 |
| 1973 | 384,396,000 | 0.10 | 0.20 | |
| 1973D | 261,405,000 | 0.10 | 0.20 | |
| 1973S | (2,760,339) | | | 1.00 |
| 1974 | 601,752,000 | 0.10 | 0.20 | |
| 1974D | 277,373,000 | 0.10 | 0.20 | |
| 1974S | (2,612,568) | | | 1.00 |

| | Mintage | MS-65 | PF-65 |
|---|---|---|---|
| 1988P | 771,360,000 | $0.20 | |
| 1988D | 663,771,652 | 0.20 | |
| 1988S | (3,262,948) | | $2.00 |
| 1989P | 898,812,000 | 0.20 | |
| 1989D | 570,842,474 | 0.20 | |
| 1989S | (3,220,194) | | 1.50 |
| 1990P | 661,636,000 | 0.20 | |
| 1990D | 663,938,503 | 0.20 | |
| 1990S | (3,299,559) | | 1.75 |
| 1991P | 614,104,000 | 0.20 | |
| 1991D | 436,496,678 | 0.20 | |
| 1991S | (2,867,787) | | 2.00 |
| 1992P | 399,552,000 | 1.00 | |
| 1992D | 450,565,113 | 0.20 | |
| 1992S | (4,176,560) | | 1.50 |
| 1993P | 412,076,000 | 0.20 | |
| 1993D | 406,084,135 | 0.20 | |
| 1993S | (3,394,792) | | 1.50 |
| 1994P | 722,160,000 | 0.20 | |
| 1994D | 715,762,110 | 0.20 | |
| 1994S | (3,269,923) | | 1.50 |
| 1995P | 774,156,000 | 0.40 | |
| 1995D | 888,112,000 | 0.20 | |
| 1995S | (2,797,481) | | 2.00 |
| 1996P | 829,332,000 | 0.20 | |
| 1996D | 817,736,000 | 0.20 | |
| 1996S | (2,525,265) | | 1.00 |
| 1997P | 470,972,000 | 0.20 | |
| 1997D | 466,640,000 | 0.20 | |
| 1997S | (2,796,678) | | 1.75 |
| 1998P | 688,272,000 | 0.20 | |
| 1998D | 635,360,000 | 0.20 | |
| 1998S | (2,086,507) | | 1.75 |
| 1999P | 1,212,000,000 | 0.20 | |
| 1999D | 1,066,720,000 | 0.20 | |
| 1999S | (3,347,966) | | 2.00 |
| 2000P | 846,240,000 | 0.20 | |
| 2000D | 1,509,520,000 | 0.20 | |
| 2000S | (4,047,993) | | 1.75 |
| 2001P | 675,704,000 | 0.20 | |

* Included in number above.

*Chart continued on next page.*

| | Mintage | MS-65 | PF-65 |
|---|---|---|---|
| 2001D | 627,680,000 | $0.20 | |
| 2001S | (3,184,606) | | $1.75 |
| 2002P | 539,280,000 | 0.20 | |
| 2002D | 691,200,000 | 0.20 | |

| | Mintage | MS-65 | PF-65 |
|---|---|---|---|
| 2002S | (3,211,995) | | $1.50 |
| 2003P | 441,840,000 | $0.20 | |
| 2003D | 383,040,000 | 0.20 | |
| 2003S | (3,298,439) | | 1.50 |

## "Westward Journey" Nickels

The Westward Journey Nickel Series™ (2004–2006) commemorates the bicentennial of the Louisiana Purchase and the journey of Meriwether Lewis and William Clark to explore that vast territory. **2004**—*Obverse:* traditional portrait of Jefferson. *Reverses:* Louisiana Purchase / Peace Medal reverse, by Mint sculptor Norman E. Nemeth. Keelboat reverse, by Mint sculptor Al Maletsky. **2005**—*Obverse:* new portrait of Jefferson, designed by Joe Fitzgerald after a 1789 marble bust by Jean-Antoine Houdon, and rendered by Mint sculptor Don Everhart. *Reverses:* American Bison reverse, designed by Jamie Franki and produced by Norman E. Nemeth. "Ocean in View" reverse, designed by Joe Fitzgerald and produced by Mint sculptor Donna Weaver. **2006**—*Obverse:* facing portrait of Jefferson, designed by Jamie Franki and sculpted by Donna Weaver. *Reverse:* traditional depiction of Monticello.

**2004 Obverse**

**Peace Medal**

**Keelboat**

**2005 Obverse**

**American Bison**

**Ocean in View**

**2006 Obverse**

**Monticello**
*Design used from 2006 to date.*

| | Mintage | MS-65 | PF-65 |
|---|---|---|---|
| 2004P, Peace Medal | 361,440,000 | $0.25 | |
| 2004D, Peace Medal | 372,000,000 | 0.25 | |
| 2004S, Peace Medal | (2,992,069) | | $1.10 |
| 2004P, Keelboat | 366,720,000 | 0.25 | |
| 2004D, Keelboat | 344,880,000 | 0.25 | |
| 2004S, Keelboat | (2,965,422) | | 1.10 |
| 2005P, American Bison | 448,320,000 | 0.25 | |
| 2005D, American Bison | 487,680,000 | 0.25 | |
| 2005S, American Bison | (3,344,679) | | 1.10 |
| 2005P, Ocean in View | 394,080,000 | 0.25 | |
| 2005D, Ocean in View | 411,120,000 | 0.25 | |
| 2005S, Ocean in View | (3,344,679) | | 1.10 |
| 2006P, Monticello | 693,120,000 | 0.25 | |
| 2006D, Monticello | 809,280,000 | 0.25 | |
| 2006S, Monticello | (3,054,436) | | 1.10 |

| | Mintage | MS-65 | PF-65 |
|---|---|---|---|
| 2007P | 571,680,000 | $0.20 | |
| 2007D | 626,160,000 | 0.20 | |
| 2007S | (2,577,166) | | $1.10 |
| 2008P | 279,840,000 | 0.20 | |
| 2008D | 345,600,000 | 0.20 | |
| 2008S | (2,169,561) | | 1.10 |
| 2009P | 39,840,000 | 0.20 | |
| 2009D | 4,680,000 | 0.20 | |
| 2009S | (2,172,313) | | 1.10 |
| 2010P | 229,920,000 | 0.20 | |
| 2010D | 260,640,000 | 0.20 | |
| 2010S | (1,455,015) | | 1.10 |
| 2011P | | 0.20 | |
| 2011D | | 0.20 | |
| 2011S | | | 1.10 |

The half dime types present the same general characteristics as larger United States silver coins. Authorized by the Act of April 2, 1792, they were not coined until February 1795, although dated 1794. At first the weight was 20.8 grains, and fineness .8924. By the Act of January 18, 1837, the weight was slightly reduced to 20-5/8 grains and the fineness changed to .900. Finally, the weight was reduced to 19.2 grains by the Act of February 21, 1853.

## FLOWING HAIR (1794–1795)

**AG-3 About Good:** Details clear enough to identify.
**G-4 Good:** Eagle, wreath, bust outlined but lack details.
**VG-8 Very Good:** Some details on face. All lettering legible.
**F-12 Fine:** Hair ends visible. Hair at top smooth.
**VF-20 Very Fine:** Hair lines at top visible. Hair about ear defined.
**EF-40 Extremely Fine:** Hair above forehead and at neck well defined but shows some wear.

**AU-50 About Uncirculated:** Slight wear on high waves of hair, near ear and face, and on head and tips of eagle's wings.
**MS-60 Uncirculated:** No trace of wear. Light blemishes.
**MS-63 Choice Uncirculated:** Some distracting marks or blemishes in prime focal areas. Some impairment of luster possible.

*Weakly struck Uncirculated coins are worth less than values shown.*

| | Mintage | AG-3 | G-4 | VG-8 | F-12 | VF-20 | EF-40 | AU-50 | MS-60 | MS-63 |
|---|---|---|---|---|---|---|---|---|---|---|
| 1794 . . . . . . . . . . . . . . .86,416 | | $400 | $750 | $900 | $1,250 | $1,900 | $3,600 | $5,500 | $9,500 | $17,500 |
| 1795 . . . . . . . . . . . . . . . . . . . .* | | 275 | 625 | 725 | 950 | 1,550 | 2,750 | 3,750 | 7,000 | 11,000 |

* Included in number above.

## DRAPED BUST (1796–1805)

**AG-3 About Good:** Details clear enough to identify.
**G-4 Good:** Date, stars, LIBERTY readable. Bust of Liberty outlined, but no details.
**VG-8 Very Good:** Some details visible.
**F-12 Fine:** Hair and drapery lines worn, but visible.
**VF-20 Very Fine:** Only left side of drapery indistinct.
**EF-40 Extremely Fine:** Details visible in all hair lines.
**AU-50 About Uncirculated:** Slight wear on bust, shoulder, and hair; wear on eagle's head and top of wings.
**MS-60 Uncirculated:** No trace of wear. Light blemishes.
**MS-63 Choice Uncirculated:** Some distracting marks or blemishes in prime focal areas. Impaired luster possible.

### Small Eagle Reverse (1796–1797)

| | Mintage | AG-3 | G-4 | VG-8 | F-12 | VF-20 | EF-40 | AU-50 | MS-60 | MS-63 |
|---|---|---|---|---|---|---|---|---|---|---|
| 1796, 6 Over 5 . . . . . . . . .10,230 | | $275 | $600 | $750 | $1,100 | $2,000 | $3,500 | $6,000 | $11,500 | $20,000 |
| 1796 . . . . . . . . . . . . . . . . . . . . .* | | 250 | 500 | 700 | 1,000 | 1,600 | 3,000 | 5,000 | 7,000 | 13,000 |
| 1796, LIBERTY . . . . . . . . . . . . .* | | 250 | 500 | 700 | 1,000 | 1,600 | 3,000 | 5,000 | 7,000 | 15,000 |
| 1797, 15 Stars . . . . . . . . .44,527 | | 250 | 500 | 700 | 1,000 | 1,600 | 3,000 | 5,000 | 7,000 | 12,000 |
| 1797, 16 Stars . . . . . . . . . . . . .* | | 250 | 500 | 700 | 1,000 | 1,600 | 3,000 | 5,000 | 7,000 | 12,000 |
| 1797, 13 Stars . . . . . . . . . . . . .* | | 300 | 600 | 800 | 1,300 | 1,800 | 4,000 | 7,000 | 15,000 | 20,000 |

* Included in number above.

## Heraldic Eagle Reverse (1800–1805)

**1800 LIBEKTY**

| | Mintage | AG-3 | G-4 | VG-8 | F-12 | VF-20 | EF-40 | AU-50 | MS-60 | MS-63 |
|---|---|---|---|---|---|---|---|---|---|---|
| 1800 | 24,000 | $150 | $300 | $450 | $700 | $1,000 | $1,500 | $3,000 | $4,500 | $9,500 |
| 1800, LIBEKTY | 16,000 | 150 | 300 | 450 | 700 | 1,000 | 1,500 | 3,000 | 4,500 | 9,500 |
| 1801 | 27,760 | 150 | 300 | 500 | 800 | 1,100 | 2,000 | 3,500 | 6,000 | 10,500 |
| 1802 | 3,060 | 9,000 | 15,000 | 20,000 | 27,000 | 50,000 | 95,000 | — | — | — |
| 1803 | 37,850 | 175 | 400 | 500 | 850 | 1,150 | 1,750 | 3,750 | 6,200 | 10,500 |
| 1805 | 15,600 | 175 | 400 | 500 | 850 | 1,500 | 3,400 | 8,000 | — | — |

## CAPPED BUST (1829–1837)

**G-4 Good:** Bust of Liberty outlined, no detail. Date and legend legible.
**VG-8 Very Good:** Complete legend and date plain. At least three letters
of LIBERTY on edge of cap show clearly.
**F-12 Fine:** All letters in LIBERTY visible.
**VF-20 Very Fine:** Full rims. Ear and shoulder clasp show plainly.
**EF-40 Extremely Fine:** Ear very distinct; eyebrow and hair well defined.
**AU-50 About Uncirculated:** Traces of light wear on many of the high points. At least half of mint luster
still present.
**MS-60 Uncirculated:** No trace of wear. Light blemishes.
**MS-63 Choice Uncirculated:** No trace of wear. Light blemishes. Attractive mint luster.

| | Mintage | G-4 | VG-8 | F-12 | VF-20 | EF-40 | AU-50 | MS-60 | MS-63 |
|---|---|---|---|---|---|---|---|---|---|
| 1829 | 1,230,000 | $20 | $25 | $30 | $45 | $75 | $110 | $185 | $400 |
| 1830 | 1,240,000 | 20 | 25 | 30 | 45 | 75 | 110 | 185 | 400 |
| 1831 | 1,242,700 | 20 | 25 | 30 | 45 | 75 | 110 | 185 | 400 |
| 1832 | 965,000 | 20 | 25 | 30 | 45 | 75 | 110 | 185 | 400 |
| 1833 | 1,370,000 | 20 | 25 | 30 | 45 | 75 | 110 | 185 | 400 |
| 1834 | 1,480,000 | 20 | 25 | 30 | 45 | 75 | 110 | 185 | 400 |
| 1835 | 2,760,000 | 20 | 25 | 30 | 45 | 75 | 110 | 185 | 400 |
| 1836 | 1,900,000 | 20 | 25 | 30 | 45 | 75 | 110 | 185 | 400 |
| 1837, Small 5c | 871,000 | 24 | 30 | 40 | 75 | 115 | 200 | 475 | 1,000 |
| 1837, Large 5c | * | 20 | 25 | 30 | 45 | 75 | 110 | 185 | 400 |

* Included in number above.

## LIBERTY SEATED (1837–1873)

**G-4 Good:** LIBERTY on shield smooth. Date and letters legible.
**VG-8 Very Good:** At least three letters in LIBERTY visible.
**F-12 Fine:** Entire LIBERTY visible, weak spots.
**VF-20 Very Fine:** Entire LIBERTY strong and even.
**EF-40 Extremely Fine:** LIBERTY and scroll edges distinct.
**AU-50 About Uncirculated:** Traces of light wear on many of the high points. At least half of mint luster
still present.
**MS-60 Uncirculated:** No trace of wear. Light blemishes.
**MS-63 Choice Uncirculated:** No trace of wear. Light blemishes. Attractive mint luster.

## Variety 1 – No Stars on Obverse (1837–1838)

# HALF DIMES

| | Mintage | G-4 | VG-8 | F-12 | VF-20 | EF-40 | AU-50 | MS-60 | MS-63 |
|---|---|---|---|---|---|---|---|---|---|
| 1837 | 1,405,000 | $15 | $20 | $30 | $60 | $100 | $175 | $400 | $500 |
| 18380, No Stars | 70,000 | 35 | 60 | 100 | 210 | 350 | 575 | 900 | 3,500 |

## Variety 2 – Stars on Obverse (1838–1853)

From 1838 through 1859 the mintmark was located above the bow on the reverse. Large, medium, or small mintmark varieties occur for several dates.

| | Mintage | G-4 | VG-8 | F-12 | VF-20 | EF-40 | AU-50 | MS-60 | MS-63 |
|---|---|---|---|---|---|---|---|---|---|
| 1838 | 2,255,000 | $7 | $8 | $12 | $15 | $30 | $65 | $150 | $180 |
| 1839 | 1,069,150 | 7 | 8 | 12 | 15 | 30 | 65 | 150 | 180 |
| 18390 | 1,060,000 | 9 | 11 | 13 | 20 | 35 | 65 | 185 | 800 |
| 1840 | 1,344,085 | 7 | 8 | 11 | 14 | 30 | 65 | 150 | 180 |
| 18400 | 935,000 | 9 | 11 | 13 | 20 | 35 | 85 | 275 | 950 |
| 1841 | 1,150,000 | 7 | 8 | 11 | 14 | 30 | 65 | 100 | 125 |
| 18410 | 815,000 | 8 | 10 | 15 | 20 | 45 | 115 | 325 | 650 |
| 1842 | 815,000 | 7 | 8 | 13 | 16 | 32 | 65 | 90 | 125 |
| 18420 | 350,000 | 13 | 15 | 27 | 75 | 210 | 375 | 525 | 850 |
| 1843 | 1,165,000 | 7 | 8 | 11 | 14 | 30 | 65 | 90 | 130 |
| 1844 | 430,000 | 7 | 8 | 11 | 14 | 30 | 65 | 90 | 130 |
| 18440 | 220,000 | 32 | 45 | 85 | 225 | 485 | 1,450 | 2,400 | 6,000 |
| 1845 | 1,564,000 | 7 | 8 | 11 | 14 | 30 | 65 | 90 | 130 |
| 1846 | 27,000 | 110 | 180 | 300 | 400 | 1,100 | 2,200 | 6,000 | 9,500 |
| 1847 | 1,274,000 | 7 | 8 | 11 | 14 | 30 | 65 | 110 | 220 |
| 1848 | 668,000 | 7 | 8 | 11 | 14 | 30 | 65 | 100 | 130 |
| 18480 | 600,000 | 9 | 11 | 15 | 23 | 45 | 110 | 190 | 270 |
| 1849, 9 Over 6 | * | 10 | 12 | 16 | 23 | 45 | 110 | 200 | 600 |
| 1849, 9 Over 8 | * | 10 | 13 | 25 | 40 | 75 | 125 | 275 | 700 |
| 1849, Normal Date | 1,309,000 | 7 | 8 | 11 | 14 | 30 | 65 | 100 | 200 |
| 18490 | 140,000 | 12 | 17 | 33 | 90 | 200 | 400 | 1,000 | 1,900 |
| 1850 | 955,000 | 7 | 8 | 11 | 15 | 35 | 60 | 90 | 145 |
| 18500 | 690,000 | 8 | 10 | 13 | 21 | 45 | 135 | 325 | 700 |
| 1851 | 781,000 | 7 | 8 | 11 | 15 | 35 | 60 | 90 | 125 |
| 18510 | 860,000 | 8 | 10 | 12 | 18 | 45 | 100 | 225 | 350 |
| 1852 | 1,000,500 | 7 | 8 | 11 | 14 | 28 | 60 | 90 | 125 |
| 18520 | 260,000 | 12 | 17 | 27 | 55 | 110 | 210 | 385 | 900 |
| 1853, No Arrows | 135,000 | 14 | 18 | 27 | 55 | 110 | 175 | 325 | 475 |
| 18530, No Arrows | 160,000 | 80 | 125 | 160 | 300 | 650 | 1,200 | 2,600 | 5,500 |

* Included in number below.

## Variety 3 – Arrows at Date (1853–1855)

As on the dimes, quarters, and halves, arrows were placed at the sides of the date for a short period starting in 1853 to denote the reduction of weight.

| | Mintage | G-4 | VG-8 | F-12 | VF-20 | EF-40 | AU-50 | MS-60 | MS-63 | PF-63 |
|---|---|---|---|---|---|---|---|---|---|---|
| 1853 | 13,210,020 | $7 | $8 | $10 | $14 | $30 | $55 | $110 | $130 | |
| 18530 | 2,200,000 | 8 | 9 | 12 | 19 | 32 | 70 | 135 | 400 | |
| 1854 | 5,740,000 | 7 | 8 | 10 | 14 | 30 | 60 | 110 | 140 | $4,000 |

*Chart continued on next page.*

| | Mintage | G-4 | VG-8 | F-12 | VF-20 | EF-40 | AU-50 | MS-60 | MS-63 | PF-63 |
|---|---|---|---|---|---|---|---|---|---|---|
| 1854O | 1,560,000 | $8 | $9 | $11 | $18 | $30 | $70 | $135 | $350 | |
| 1855 | 1,750,000 | 7 | 8 | 10 | 14 | 30 | 55 | 110 | 130 | $4,000 |
| 1855O | 600,000 | 7 | 10 | 11 | 24 | 80 | 110 | 275 | 485 | |

## Variety 2 Resumed, with Weight Standard of 1853 (1856–1859)

1858 Over Inverted Date

| | Mintage | G-4 | VG-8 | F-12 | VF-20 | EF-40 | AU-50 | MS-60 | MS-63 | PF-63 |
|---|---|---|---|---|---|---|---|---|---|---|
| 1856 | 4,880,000 | $7 | $8 | $9 | $12 | $25 | $50 | $80 | $120 | $2,000 |
| 1856O | 1,100,000 | 7 | 8 | 10 | 20 | 40 | 100 | 210 | 450 | |
| 1857 | 7,280,000 | 7 | 8 | 9 | 12 | 25 | 50 | 80 | 120 | 1,750 |
| 1857O | 1,380,000 | 7 | 8 | 10 | 16 | 30 | 80 | 175 | 210 | |
| 1858 ........(300) | 3,500,000 | 7 | 8 | 9 | 12 | 25 | 50 | 80 | 120 | 750 |
| 1858, Over Inverted Dt ........* | | 15 | 20 | 30 | 50 | 95 | 150 | 300 | 600 | |
| 1858O | 1,660,000 | 7 | 8 | 10 | 18 | 28 | 60 | 125 | 200 | |
| 1859 ........(800) | 340,000 | 8 | 9 | 12 | 20 | 50 | 90 | 130 | 175 | 650 |
| 1859O | 560,000 | 8 | 9 | 12 | 20 | 50 | 90 | 130 | 150 | |

\* Included in number above.

## Variety 4 – Legend on Obverse (1860–1873)

| | Mintage | G-4 | VG-8 | F-12 | VF-20 | EF-40 | AU-50 | MS-60 | MS-63 | PF-63 |
|---|---|---|---|---|---|---|---|---|---|---|
| 1860 ......(1,000) | 799,000 | $7 | $8 | $10 | $12 | $19 | $30 | $75 | $100 | $300 |
| 1860O | 1,060,000 | 7 | 8 | 10 | 12 | 19 | 35 | 100 | 135 | |
| 1861 ......(1,000) | 3,360,000 | 7 | 8 | 10 | 12 | 19 | 30 | 75 | 100 | 300 |
| 1862 ........(550) | 1,492,000 | 9 | 12 | 18 | 20 | 25 | 40 | 110 | 125 | 300 |
| 1863 ........(460) | 18,000 | 60 | 70 | 95 | 125 | 200 | 270 | 300 | 400 | 350 |
| 1863S | 100,000 | 11 | 15 | 18 | 21 | 60 | 160 | 350 | 450 | |
| 1864 ........(470) | 48,000 | 110 | 175 | 210 | 275 | 400 | 500 | 550 | 600 | 350 |
| 1864S | 90,000 | 18 | 20 | 35 | 50 | 110 | 180 | 310 | 700 | |
| 1865 ........(500) | 13,000 | 100 | 125 | 180 | 210 | 275 | 300 | 400 | 600 | 350 |
| 1865S | 120,000 | 11 | 15 | 18 | 22 | 60 | 200 | 450 | 850 | |
| 1866 ........(725) | 10,000 | 100 | 115 | 150 | 200 | 300 | 320 | 375 | 600 | 320 |
| 1866S | 120,000 | 10 | 15 | 18 | 22 | 60 | 180 | 200 | 400 | |
| 1867 ........(625) | 8,000 | 175 | 200 | 250 | 300 | 350 | 400 | 475 | 620 | 350 |
| 1867S | 120,000 | 9 | 13 | 18 | 25 | 60 | 140 | 210 | 500 | |
| 1868 ........(600) | 88,600 | 20 | 25 | 40 | 70 | 120 | 200 | 300 | 400 | 350 |
| 1868S | 280,000 | 7 | 9 | 11 | 13 | 19 | 40 | 125 | 250 | |
| 1869 ........(600) | 208,000 | 7 | 9 | 11 | 13 | 19 | 60 | 120 | 150 | 300 |
| 1869S | 230,000 | 7 | 9 | 11 | 13 | 19 | 50 | 150 | 350 | |
| 1870 ......(1,000) | 535,000 | 7 | 9 | 10 | 11 | 19 | 30 | 70 | 120 | 300 |
| 1870S (unique) ............ | | | | | | | | — | | |
| 1871 ........(960) | 1,873,000 | 7 | 9 | 10 | 11 | 19 | 30 | 70 | 120 | 300 |
| 1871S | 161,000 | 8 | 11 | 15 | 25 | 40 | 75 | 135 | 210 | |
| 1872 ........(950) | 2,947,000 | 7 | 9 | 10 | 11 | 19 | 30 | 70 | 120 | 300 |
| 1872S | 837,000 | 7 | 9 | 10 | 11 | 19 | 30 | 70 | 120 | |
| 1873 ........(600) | 7,126,000 | 7 | 9 | 10 | 11 | 19 | 30 | 70 | 120 | 300 |
| 1873S | 324,000 | 7 | 9 | 10 | 11 | 19 | 30 | 70 | 120 | |

The designs of the dimes, first coined in 1796, follow closely those of the half dimes up through the Liberty Seated type. The dimes in each instance weigh twice as much as the half dimes.

## DRAPED BUST (1796–1807)
### Small Eagle Reverse (1796–1797)

**AG-3 About Good:** Details clear enough to identify.
**G-4 Good:** Date legible. Bust outlined, but no detail.
**VG-8 Very Good:** All but deepest drapery folds worn smooth. Hair lines nearly gone and curls lacking in detail.
**F-12 Fine:** All drapery lines visible. Hair partly worn.
**VF-20 Very Fine:** Only left side of drapery indistinct.
**EF-40 Extremely Fine:** Hair well outlined with details visible.
**AU-50 About Uncirculated:** Traces of light wear on many of the high points. At least half of mint luster still present.
**MS-60 Uncirculated:** No trace of wear. Light blemishes.
**MS-63 Choice Uncirculated:** Some distracting marks or blemishes in prime focal areas. Impaired luster possible.

1797, 16 Stars　　　　　　　1797, 13 Stars

| | Mintage | AG-3 | G-4 | VG-8 | F-12 | VF-20 | EF-40 | AU-50 | MS-60 | MS-63 |
|---|---|---|---|---|---|---|---|---|---|---|
| 1796 . . . . . . . . . . . . . . . .22,135 | | $500 | $1,000 | $1,500 | $2,100 | $3,000 | $5,000 | $7,000 | $10,000 | $16,000 |
| 1797, All kinds . . . . . . . . .25,261 | | | | | | | | | | |
| 1797, 16 Stars . . . . . . . . . . . . | | 500 | 1,100 | 1,700 | 2,300 | 3,250 | 6,000 | 8,000 | 14,000 | 20,000 |
| 1797, 13 Stars . . . . . . . . . . . . . | | 525 | 1,200 | 1,750 | 2,500 | 3,500 | 6,250 | 9,000 | 18,000 | 24,000 |

### Heraldic Eagle Reverse (1798–1807)

| | Mintage | AG-3 | G-4 | VG-8 | F-12 | VF-20 | EF-40 | AU-50 | MS-60 | MS-63 |
|---|---|---|---|---|---|---|---|---|---|---|
| 1798, All kinds . . . . . . . . .27,550 | | | | | | | | | | |
| 1798, 8 Over 7, 16 Stars on Reverse . . . . . . . | | $125 | $275 | $425 | $500 | $800 | $1,250 | $2,100 | $3,200 | $7,250 |
| 1798, 8 Over 7, 13 Stars on Rev . . . . . . . . . . | | 250 | 700 | 1,000 | 1,500 | 2,500 | 3,500 | — | — | |
| 1798 . . . . . . . . . . . . . . . . . . . | | 125 | 225 | 300 | 425 | 650 | 1,100 | 1,600 | 2,700 | 7,000 |
| 1800 . . . . . . . . . . . . . .21,760 | | 125 | 225 | 300 | 425 | 600 | 1,100 | 1,600 | 2,700 | 7,000 |
| 1801 . . . . . . . . . . . . . .34,640 | | 125 | 250 | 300 | 500 | 1,200 | 2,100 | 3,750 | 7,000 | 14,000 |
| 1802 . . . . . . . . . . . . . .10,975 | | 160 | 425 | 550 | 900 | 1,400 | 3,200 | 4,600 | 12,500 | |
| 1803 . . . . . . . . . . . . . .33,040 | | 110 | 225 | 325 | 450 | 700 | 1,800 | 3,700 | 6,500 | |
| 1804 . . . . . . . . . . . . . . .8,265 | | 300 | 600 | 1,200 | 3,000 | 5,000 | 10,000 | 20,000 | — | |
| 1805 . . . . . . . . . . . . . .120,780 | | 100 | 220 | 285 | 400 | 525 | 1,000 | 1,500 | 3,000 | 5,000 |
| 1807 . . . . . . . . . . . . . .165,000 | | 100 | 220 | 285 | 400 | 525 | 950 | 1,300 | 2,800 | 4,750 |

## CAPPED BUST (1809–1837)

**G-4 Good:** Date, letters, and stars discernible. Bust outlined, no details.
**VG-8 Very Good:** Legends and date plain. Some letters in LIBERTY visible.
**F-12 Fine:** Clear LIBERTY. Ear and shoulder clasp visible. Part of rim visible on both sides.
**VF-20 Very Fine:** LIBERTY distinct. Full rim. Ear and clasp plain and distinct.
**EF-40 Extremely Fine:** LIBERTY sharp. Ear distinct. Hair above eye well defined.
**AU-50 About Uncirculated:** Traces of light wear on only the high points of the design. Half of mint luster present.
**MS-60 Uncirculated:** No trace of wear. Light blemishes.
**MS-63 Choice Uncirculated:** Some distracting marks or blemishes in prime focal areas. Impaired luster possible.

### Variety 1 – Wide Border (1809–1828)

| 1823, 3 Over 2 | 1824, 4 Over 2 | 1828, Large Date | 1828, Small Date |

| | Mintage | G-4 | VG-8 | F-12 | VF-20 | EF-40 | AU-50 | MS-60 | MS-63 |
|---|---|---|---|---|---|---|---|---|---|
| 1809 . . . . . . . . . . . . . . . . . . . . . . . . . .51,065 | | $55 | $85 | $150 | $275 | $600 | $900 | $2,000 | $3,000 |
| 1811, 11 Over 09 . . . . . . . . . . . . . . .65,180 | | 40 | 60 | 125 | 225 | 500 | 800 | 1,700 | 2,750 |
| 1814 . . . . . . . . . . . . . . . . . . . .421,500 | | 14 | 17 | 28 | 70 | 200 | 275 | 500 | 1,200 |
| 1820 . . . . . . . . . . . . . . . . . . . .942,587 | | 14 | 17 | 25 | 60 | 200 | 275 | 500 | 1,200 |
| 1821 . . . . . . . . . . . . . . . . . . . .1,186,512 | | 14 | 17 | 25 | 60 | 200 | 275 | 500 | 1,200 |
| 1822 . . . . . . . . . . . . . . . . . . . .100,000 | | 185 | 400 | 700 | 950 | 1,600 | 3,750 | 5,000 | 8,500 |
| 1823, 3 Over 2, All kinds . . . . . . . . . .440,000 | | | | | | | | | |
|    1823, 3 Over 2, Small E's . . . . . . . . . . . . . . | | 14 | 17 | 25 | 60 | 200 | 275 | 550 | 1,100 |
|    1823, 3 Over 2, Large E's . . . . . . . . . . . . . . | | 14 | 17 | 25 | 60 | 200 | 275 | 550 | 1,100 |
| 1824, 4 Over 2 . . . . . . . . . . . . . .510,000 | | 15 | 20 | 40 | 140 | 300 | 600 | 1,000 | 1,800 |
| 1825 . . . . . . . . . . . . . . . . . . . . . .* | | 14 | 17 | 20 | 50 | 175 | 275 | 500 | 1,100 |
| 1827 . . . . . . . . . . . . . . . . . . . .1,215,000 | | 14 | 17 | 20 | 50 | 175 | 275 | 500 | 1,100 |
| 1828, Large Date, Curl Base 2 . . . . . . .125,000 | | 17 | 30 | 50 | 140 | 300 | 600 | 1,000 | 1,800 |

\* Included in number above.

### Variety 2 – Modified Design (1828–1837)

| 1829, Small 10c | 1829, Large 10c | 1830, 30 Over 29 |

| | Mintage | G-4 | VG-8 | F-12 | VF-20 | EF-40 | AU-50 | MS-60 | MS-63 |
|---|---|---|---|---|---|---|---|---|---|
| 1828, Small Date, Square Base 2 . . . . . . . . . .* | | $14 | $18 | $30 | $65 | $200 | $325 | $625 | $1,100 |
| 1829, Small 10c . . . . . . . . . . . . . .770,000 | | 13 | 15 | 18 | 35 | 120 | 180 | 400 | 750 |
| 1829, Medium 10c . . . . . . . . . . . . . . . . . .* | | 13 | 15 | 18 | 35 | 120 | 180 | 350 | 650 |
| 1829, Large 10c . . . . . . . . . . . . . . . . . . .* | | 13 | 16 | 22 | 50 | 135 | 200 | 400 | 675 |
| 1830, 30 Over 29 . . . . . . . . . . . . . .510,000 | | 14 | 25 | 45 | 90 | 250 | 275 | 500 | 1,100 |

\* Included in number above.

|  | Mintage | G-4 | VG-8 | F-12 | VF-20 | EF-40 | AU-50 | MS-60 | MS-63 |
|---|---|---|---|---|---|---|---|---|---|
| 1830, Large 10c ..........* | | $13 | $15 | $18 | $35 | $120 | $180 | $350 | $675 |
| 1830, Small 10c ..........* | | 13 | 15 | 18 | 35 | 120 | 180 | 350 | 675 |
| 1831 .............771,350 | | 13 | 15 | 18 | 35 | 120 | 180 | 350 | 675 |
| 1832 .............522,500 | | 13 | 15 | 18 | 35 | 120 | 180 | 350 | 675 |
| 1833 .............485,000 | | 13 | 15 | 18 | 35 | 120 | 180 | 350 | 675 |
| 1834 .............635,000 | | 13 | 15 | 18 | 35 | 120 | 180 | 350 | 675 |
| 1835 ...........1,410,000 | | 13 | 15 | 18 | 35 | 120 | 180 | 350 | 675 |
| 1836 ...........1,190,000 | | 13 | 15 | 18 | 35 | 120 | 180 | 350 | 675 |
| 1837 .............359,500 | | 13 | 15 | 18 | 35 | 120 | 180 | 350 | 675 |

\* Included in mintage for 1830, 30 Over 29 (previous page).

# LIBERTY SEATED (1837–1891)
## Variety 1 – No Stars on Obverse (1837–1838)

**G-4 Good:** LIBERTY on shield smooth. Date and letters legible.
**F-12 Fine:** LIBERTY visible, weak spots.
**VF-20 Very Fine:** LIBERTY strong and even.
**EF-40 Extremely Fine:** LIBERTY and scroll edges distinct.
**AU-50 About Uncirculated:** Wear on Liberty's shoulder and hair high points.
**MS-60 Uncirculated:** No trace of wear. Light blemishes.
**MS-63 Choice Uncirculated:** Some distracting marks or blemishes in focal areas. Impaired luster possible.

**No Drapery From Elbow**
**No Stars on Obverse**

*Mintmarks on Liberty Seated dimes on reverse, within or below the wreath. Size of mintmark varies on many dates.*

|  | Mintage | G-4 | F-12 | VF-20 | EF-40 | AU-50 | MS-60 | MS-63 |
|---|---|---|---|---|---|---|---|---|
| 1837 ...................682,500 | | $18 | $35 | $125 | $220 | $325 | $600 | $850 |
| 18380 ...................406,034 | | 21 | 60 | 160 | 300 | 550 | 1,300 | 3,000 |

## Variety 2 – Stars on Obverse (1838–1853)

**No Drapery From Elbow, Tilted Shield (1838–1840)**

**1838, Small Stars**        **1838, Large Stars**

**Drapery From Elbow, Upright Shield (1840–1891)**

|  | Mintage | G-4 | F-12 | VF-20 | EF-40 | AU-50 | MS-60 | MS-63 |
|---|---|---|---|---|---|---|---|---|
| 1838, All kinds ..............1,992,500 | | | | | | | | |
| 1838, Small Stars .................. | | $9 | $18 | $35 | $70 | $175 | $400 | $600 |
| 1838, Large Stars ................. | | 8 | 11 | 14 | 40 | 100 | 150 | 350 |
| 1838, Partial Drapery .............. | | 9 | 18 | 35 | 75 | 210 | 425 | 1,000 |
| 1839 ....................1,053,115 | | 8 | 11 | 14 | 40 | 100 | 150 | 350 |
| 18390 ...................1,291,600 | | 9 | 13 | 16 | 45 | 120 | 175 | 500 |
| 1840, No Drapery ............981,500 | | 8 | 11 | 14 | 40 | 100 | 150 | 350 |
| 18400, No Drapery .........1,175,000 | | 9 | 13 | 20 | 50 | 120 | 475 | 950 |
| 1840, Drapery .............377,500 | | 13 | 30 | 55 | 125 | 170 | 425 | 2,200 |

*Chart continued on next page.*

| | Mintage | G-4 | F-12 | VF-20 | EF-40 | AU-50 | MS-60 | MS-63 |
|---|---|---|---|---|---|---|---|---|
| 1841 | 1,622,500 | $8 | $11 | $14 | $20 | $50 | $135 | $250 |
| 1841O | 2,007,500 | 9 | 13 | 15 | 28 | 90 | 425 | 900 |
| 1842 | 1,887,500 | 8 | 11 | 14 | 20 | 50 | 135 | 250 |
| 1842O | 2,020,000 | 9 | 13 | 17 | 100 | 500 | 1,300 | 2,600 |
| 1843 | 1,370,000 | 8 | 11 | 14 | 20 | 50 | 135 | 300 |
| 1843O | 150,000 | 17 | 45 | 110 | 275 | 900 | 2,250 | — |
| 1844 | 72,500 | 100 | 225 | 350 | 600 | 800 | 1,400 | 4,000 |
| 1845 | 1,755,000 | 8 | 11 | 14 | 20 | 50 | 135 | 300 |
| 1845O | 230,000 | 9 | 20 | 80 | 185 | 475 | 1,300 | — |
| 1846 | 31,300 | 32 | 90 | 160 | 475 | 1,000 | 1,900 | 7,000 |
| 1847 | 245,000 | 9 | 16 | 27 | 55 | 120 | 400 | 1,000 |
| 1848 | 451,500 | 8 | 11 | 16 | 35 | 60 | 210 | 400 |
| 1849 | 839,000 | 8 | 11 | 14 | 20 | 50 | 150 | 425 |
| 1849O | 300,000 | 8 | 17 | 50 | 110 | 300 | 1,000 | 2,400 |
| 1850 | 1,931,500 | 8 | 11 | 14 | 20 | 50 | 125 | 300 |
| 1850O | 510,000 | 9 | 13 | 33 | 65 | 150 | 425 | 975 |
| 1851 | 1,026,500 | 8 | 11 | 14 | 20 | 50 | 160 | 325 |
| 1851O | 400,000 | 9 | 17 | 35 | 100 | 175 | 1,000 | 1,400 |
| 1852 | 1,535,500 | 8 | 11 | 14 | 20 | 50 | 150 | 300 |
| 1852O | 430,000 | 10 | 20 | 50 | 100 | 175 | 800 | 1,300 |
| 1853, No Arrows | 95,000 | 22 | 55 | 90 | 150 | 225 | 375 | 400 |

## Variety 3 – Arrows at Date (1853–1855)

| | Mintage | G-4 | F-12 | VF-20 | EF-40 | AU-50 | MS-60 | MS-63 | PF-63 |
|---|---|---|---|---|---|---|---|---|---|
| 1853, With Arrows | 12,078,010 | $7 | $8 | $12 | $22 | $60 | $150 | $300 | |
| 1853O | 1,100,000 | 7 | 8 | 17 | 45 | 120 | 475 | 1,300 | |
| 1854 | 4,470,000 | 7 | 8 | 12 | 22 | 60 | 150 | 300 | $5,250 |
| 1854O | 1,770,000 | 7 | 8 | 13 | 35 | 75 | 285 | 500 | |
| 1855 | 2,075,000 | 7 | 8 | 12 | 22 | 60 | 175 | 400 | 5,250 |

## Variety 2 Resumed, With Weight Standard of Variety 3 (1856–1860)

**Small Date, Arrows Removed (1856–1860)**

| | Mintage | G-4 | F-12 | VF-20 | EF-40 | AU-50 | MS-60 | MS-63 | PF-63 |
|---|---|---|---|---|---|---|---|---|---|
| 1856, All kinds | 5,780,000 | | | | | | | | |
| 1856, Large Date | | $7 | $8 | $11 | $18 | $40 | $140 | $275 | |
| 1856, Small Date | | 7 | 8 | 11 | 18 | 40 | 140 | 275 | $1,800 |
| 1856O | 1,180,000 | 7 | 8 | 11 | 24 | 90 | 300 | 650 | |
| 1856S | 70,000 | 40 | 130 | 225 | 425 | 650 | 1,450 | — | |

| | Mintage | G-4 | F-12 | VF-20 | EF-40 | AU-50 | MS-60 | MS-63 | PF-63 |
|---|---|---|---|---|---|---|---|---|---|
| 1857 . . . . . . . . . . . | 5,580,000 | $7 | $8 | $10 | $18 | $40 | $135 | $275 | $1,800 |
| 1857O . . . . . . . . . . | 1,540,000 | 7 | 8 | 11 | 18 | 70 | 190 | 275 | |
| 1858 . . . . (300+) . . | 1,540,000 | 7 | 8 | 10 | 18 | 40 | 135 | 275 | 900 |
| 1858O . . . . . . . . . | 290,000 | 8 | 15 | 35 | 75 | 125 | 300 | 450 | |
| 1858S . . . . . . . . . | 60,000 | 35 | 90 | 160 | 350 | 650 | 1,450 | | |
| 1859 . . . (800+) . . . | 429,200 | 7 | 8 | 11 | 25 | 50 | 135 | 275 | 700 |
| 1859O . . . . . . . . . | 480,000 | 7 | 9 | 18 | 37 | 100 | 180 | 375 | |
| 1859S . . . . . . . . . | 60,000 | 35 | 110 | 200 | 500 | 900 | 4,250 | | |
| 1860S . . . . . . . . . | 140,000 | 12 | 20 | 50 | 125 | 350 | 950 | 1,800 | |

## Variety 4 – Legend on Obverse (1860–1873)

| | Mintage | G-4 | F-12 | VF-20 | EF-40 | AU-50 | MS-60 | MS-63 | PF-63 |
|---|---|---|---|---|---|---|---|---|---|
| 1860 . . . . . . (1,000) . | 606,000 | $7 | $8 | $10 | $18 | $40 | $135 | $250 | $400 |
| 1860O . . . . . . . . . . | 40,000 | 155 | 350 | 675 | 1,600 | 2,500 | 5,500 | — | |
| 1861 . . . . . . (1,000) | 1,883,000 | 7 | 8 | 10 | 18 | 40 | 100 | 180 | 400 |
| 1861S . . . . . . . . . | 172,500 | 13 | 40 | 80 | 160 | 210 | 600 | 1,800 | |
| 1862 . . . . . . . (550) . | 847,000 | 7 | 8 | 10 | 16 | 25 | 100 | 120 | 350 |
| 1862S . . . . . . . . . | 180,750 | 11 | 21 | 50 | 100 | 125 | 600 | 1,000 | |
| 1863 . . . . . . . (460) . | 14,000 | 100 | 200 | 300 | 350 | 400 | 550 | 600 | 400 |
| 1863S . . . . . . . . . | 157,500 | 11 | 20 | 40 | 70 | 125 | 450 | 1,200 | |
| 1864 . . . . . . . (470) . | 11,000 | 80 | 170 | 210 | 350 | 425 | 550 | 600 | 400 |
| 1864S . . . . . . . . . | 230,000 | 8 | 17 | 32 | 60 | 110 | 500 | 550 | |
| 1865 . . . . . . . (500) . | 10,000 | 75 | 200 | 250 | 310 | 375 | 525 | 600 | 400 |
| 1865S . . . . . . . . . | 175,000 | 8 | 17 | 32 | 100 | 250 | 800 | 1,900 | |
| 1866 . . . . . . . (725) . | 8,000 | 120 | 235 | 375 | 400 | 600 | 700 | 800 | 400 |
| 1866S . . . . . . . . . | 135,000 | 11 | 20 | 40 | 100 | 135 | 550 | 1,100 | |
| 1867 . . . . . . . (625) . | 6,000 | 175 | 275 | 400 | 475 | 550 | 675 | 800 | 450 |
| 1867S . . . . . . . . . | 140,000 | 9 | 20 | 40 | 100 | 220 | 600 | 900 | |
| 1868 . . . . . . . (600) . | 464,000 | 7 | 8 | 16 | 31 | 60 | 175 | 375 | 300 |
| 1868S . . . . . . . . . | 260,000 | 7 | 13 | 30 | 50 | 75 | 185 | 450 | |
| 1869 . . . . . . . (600) . | 256,000 | 7 | 13 | 25 | 40 | 70 | 185 | 400 | 300 |
| 1869S . . . . . . . . . | 450,000 | 7 | 11 | 17 | 35 | 65 | 185 | 375 | |
| 1870 . . . . . . (1,000) . | 470,500 | 7 | 8 | 11 | 18 | 40 | 110 | 200 | 300 |
| 1870S . . . . . . . . . | 50,000 | 100 | 150 | 200 | 280 | 350 | 750 | 1,000 | |
| 1871 . . . . . . . (960) . | 906,750 | 7 | 8 | 11 | 16 | 65 | 140 | 180 | 300 |
| 1871CC . . . . . . . . . | 20,100 | 450 | 1,250 | 2,000 | 4,000 | 8,500 | — | — | |
| 1871S . . . . . . . . . | 320,000 | 7 | 8 | 11 | 15 | 65 | 110 | 200 | |
| 1872 . . . . . . . (950) | 2,395,500 | 7 | 8 | 11 | 13 | 35 | 75 | 110 | 300 |
| 1872CC . . . . . . . . . | 35,480 | 200 | 600 | 1,400 | 2,800 | 7,000 | — | — | |
| 1872S . . . . . . . . . | 190,000 | 10 | 35 | 50 | 95 | 175 | 500 | 1,000 | |
| 1873, Close 3 (1,100) | 1,506,900 | 7 | 8 | 11 | 13 | 30 | 100 | 125 | 300 |
| 1873, Open 3 . . . . . . . | 60,000 | 9 | 20 | 30 | 60 | 90 | 195 | 550 | |
| 1873CC (unique) . . . . . | 12,400 | | | | | | — | | |

### Variety 5 – Arrows at Date (1873–1874)

In 1873, the dime was increased in weight from 2.49 grams to 2.50 grams. Arrows at the date in 1873 and 1874 indicate this change.

| | Mintage | G-4 | F-12 | VF-20 | EF-40 | AU-50 | MS-60 | MS-63 | PF-63 |
|---|---|---|---|---|---|---|---|---|---|
| 1873 . . . . . (800) | . . .2,377,700 | $7 | $11 | $22 | $55 | $120 | $275 | $450 | $700 |
| 1873CC . . . . . . . . . . . . .18,791 | | 400 | 1,400 | 3,200 | 7,500 | 14,000 | — | — | |
| 1873S . . . . . . . . . . . . .455,000 | | 8 | 16 | 28 | 65 | 175 | 450 | 950 | |
| 1874 . . . . . (700) | . . .2,939,300 | 7 | 11 | 22 | 55 | 125 | 285 | 450 | 700 |
| 1874CC . . . . . . . . . . . . .10,817 | | 1,250 | 3,000 | 7,000 | 11,000 | 20,000 | — | — | |
| 1874S . . . . . . . . . . . .240,000 | | 11 | 27 | 45 | 90 | 220 | 400 | 900 | |

## Variety 4 Resumed, With Weight Standard of Variety 5 (1875–1891)

| | Mintage | G-4 | F-12 | VF-20 | EF-40 | AU-50 | MS-60 | MS-63 | PF-63 |
|---|---|---|---|---|---|---|---|---|---|
| 1875 . . . . . (700) | . .10,350,000 | $6 | $7 | $9 | $13 | $30 | $75 | $110 | $250 |
| 1875CC . . . . . . . . .4,645,000 | | 6 | 7 | 10 | 15 | 32 | 125 | 185 | |
| 1875S . . . . . . . . . .9,070,000 | | 6 | 7 | 9 | 13 | 30 | 75 | 110 | |
| 1876 . . . .(1,150) | . .11,450,000 | 6 | 7 | 9 | 13 | 30 | 75 | 110 | 250 |
| 1876CC . . . . . . . . .8,270,000 | | 6 | 7 | 9 | 15 | 32 | 100 | 175 | |
| 1876S . . . . . . . . . .10,420,000 | | 6 | 7 | 9 | 13 | 30 | 75 | 110 | |
| 1877 . . . . . (510) | . . .7,310,000 | 6 | 7 | 9 | 13 | 30 | 75 | 110 | 275 |
| 1877CC . . . . . . . . .7,700,000 | | 6 | 7 | 9 | 13 | 30 | 100 | 160 | |
| 1877S . . . . . . . . . .2,340,000 | | 6 | 7 | 9 | 13 | 30 | 75 | 110 | |
| 1878 . . . . . (800) | . . .1,677,200 | 6 | 7 | 9 | 13 | 30 | 80 | 110 | 250 |
| 1878CC . . . . . . . . . .200,000 | | 20 | 50 | 75 | 150 | 200 | 450 | 700 | |
| 1879 . . . .(1,100) | . . . . .14,000 | 70 | 120 | 180 | 210 | 275 | 325 | 350 | 250 |
| 1880 . . . .(1,355) | . . . .36,000 | 50 | 100 | 125 | 175 | 225 | 275 | 350 | 250 |
| 1881 . . . . . (975) | . . . .24,000 | 50 | 100 | 125 | 175 | 225 | 300 | 350 | 250 |
| 1882 . . . .(1,100) | . . .3,910,000 | 6 | 7 | 9 | 13 | 30 | 75 | 110 | 250 |
| 1883 . . . .(1,039) | . . .7,674,673 | 6 | 7 | 9 | 13 | 30 | 75 | 110 | 250 |
| 1884 . . . . . (875) | . . .3,365,505 | 6 | 7 | 9 | 13 | 30 | 75 | 110 | 250 |
| 1884S . . . . . . . . . .564,969 | | 9 | 13 | 20 | 35 | 110 | 325 | 575 | |
| 1885 . . . . . (930) | . . .2,532,497 | 6 | 7 | 9 | 13 | 30 | 75 | 110 | 250 |
| 1885S . . . . . . . . . . .43,690 | | 150 | 335 | 600 | 1,000 | 2,000 | 2,600 | 4,200 | |
| 1886 . . . . . (886) | . .6,376,684 | 6 | 7 | 9 | 13 | 30 | 75 | 110 | 250 |
| 1886S . . . . . . . . . .206,524 | | 10 | 20 | 30 | 50 | 90 | 275 | 500 | |
| 1887 . . . . . (710) | . .11,283,229 | 6 | 7 | 9 | 13 | 30 | 75 | 110 | 250 |
| 1887S . . . . . . . . . .4,454,450 | | 6 | 7 | 9 | 13 | 30 | 75 | 110 | |
| 1888 . . . . . (832) | . . .5,495,655 | 6 | 7 | 9 | 13 | 30 | 75 | 110 | 250 |
| 1888S . . . . . . . . . .1,720,000 | | 6 | 7 | 9 | 15 | 40 | 120 | 300 | |
| 1889 . . . . . (711) | . . .7,380,000 | 6 | 7 | 9 | 13 | 30 | 75 | 110 | 250 |
| 1889S . . . . . . . . . .972,678 | | 7 | 10 | 20 | 35 | 60 | 200 | 400 | |
| 1890 . . . . . (590) | . . .9,910,951 | 6 | 7 | 9 | 13 | 30 | 75 | 110 | 250 |
| 1890S . . . . . . . . . .1,423,076 | | 7 | 9 | 17 | 30 | 60 | 135 | 275 | |
| 1891 . . . . . (600) | . .15,310,000 | 6 | 7 | 9 | 13 | 30 | 75 | 110 | 275 |
| 1891O . . . . . . . . . .4,540,000 | | 6 | 7 | 9 | 15 | 40 | 110 | 150 | |
| 1891S . . . . . . . . . .3,196,116 | | 6 | 7 | 9 | 13 | 35 | 100 | 125 | |

## BARBER OR LIBERTY HEAD (1892–1916)

This type was designed by Charles E. Barber, chief engraver of the Mint. His initial B is at the truncation of the neck. He also designed the quarters and half dollars of the same period.

**G-4 Good:** Date and letters plain. LIBERTY obliterated.
**VG-8 Very Good:** Some letters visible in LIBERTY.
**F-12 Fine:** Letters in LIBERTY visible, though some weak.
**VF-20 Very Fine:** Letters of LIBERTY evenly plain.
**EF-40 Extremely Fine:** All letters in LIBERTY sharp, distinct. Headband edges distinct.
**AU-50 About Uncirculated:** Slight traces of wear on hair cheekbone and on leaf tips in wreath.
**MS-60 Uncirculated:** No trace of wear. Light blemishes.
**MS-63 Choice Uncirculated:** Some distracting blemishes in prime focal areas. Impaired luster possible.

*Mintmark location is on reverse, below wreath.*

| | Mintage | G-4 | VG-8 | F-12 | VF-20 | EF-40 | AU-50 | MS-60 | MS-63 | PF-63 |
|---|---|---|---|---|---|---|---|---|---|---|
| 1892 . . . . . .(1,245) . .12,120,000 | | $2.50 | $4.00 | $9.00 | $14.00 | $16 | $35 | $80 | $120 | $300 |
| 1892O . . . . . . . . . . . . .3,841,700 | | 5.00 | 7.00 | 15.00 | 24.00 | 35 | 45 | 100 | 175 | |
| 1892S . . . . . . . . . . . . . .990,710 | | 35.00 | 45.00 | 85.00 | 125.00 | 160 | 180 | 240 | 400 | |
| 1893, 3/2 . . . . . . . . . . . . . . .* | | | | | | 120 | 160 | 350 | 1,000 | 525 |
| 1893 . . . . . . .(792) . . .3,339,940 | | 4.00 | 6.00 | 10.00 | 15.00 | 24 | 35 | 100 | 140 | 300 |
| 1893O . . . . . . . . . . . . .1,760,000 | | 15.00 | 25.00 | 65.00 | 80.00 | 90 | 125 | 175 | 350 | |
| 1893S . . . . . . . . . . . . .2,491,401 | | 7.00 | 14.00 | 18.00 | 25.00 | 40 | 75 | 150 | 375 | |
| 1894 . . . . . . .(972) . . .1,330,000 | | 8.00 | 20.00 | 55.00 | 75.00 | 90 | 100 | 175 | 350 | 300 |
| 1894O . . . . . . . . . . . . . .720,000 | | 30.00 | 45.00 | 100.00 | 150.00 | 210 | 360 | 825 | 1,400 | |
| 1894S . . . . . . . . . . . . . . . . .24 | | | | | | | | 600,000 | | |
| 1895 . . . . . . .(880) . . . .690,000 | | 35.00 | 45.00 | 100.00 | 250.00 | 290 | 325 | 400 | 810 | 335 |
| 1895O . . . . . . . . . . . . . .440,000 | | 180.00 | 210.00 | 450.00 | 720.00 | 1,400 | 1,700 | 3,000 | 4,500 | |
| 1895S . . . . . . . . . . . . .1,120,000 | | 20.00 | 30.00 | 75.00 | 100.00 | 125 | 175 | 300 | 625 | |
| 1896 . . . . . . .(762) . . .2,000,000 | | 4.00 | 10.00 | 28.00 | 36.00 | 50 | 60 | 100 | 275 | 300 |
| 1896O . . . . . . . . . . . . . .610,000 | | 35.00 | 75.00 | 160.00 | 200.00 | 280 | 325 | 575 | 1,300 | |
| 1896S . . . . . . . . . . . . . .575,056 | | 40.00 | 70.00 | 150.00 | 200.00 | 275 | 310 | 500 | 825 | |
| 1897 . . . . . . .(731) . .10,868,533 | | 2.00 | 2.10 | 3.00 | 6.00 | 12 | 30 | 70 | 125 | 300 |
| 1897O . . . . . . . . . . . . . .666,000 | | 35.00 | 50.00 | 140.00 | 200.00 | 250 | 325 | 500 | 950 | |
| 1897S . . . . . . . . . . . . .1,342,844 | | 8.00 | 16.00 | 50.00 | 75.00 | 90 | 125 | 250 | 650 | |
| 1898 . . . . . . .(735) . .16,320,000 | | 2.00 | 2.10 | 3.00 | 6.00 | 12 | 30 | 65 | 100 | 300 |
| 1898O . . . . . . . . . . . . .2,130,000 | | 5.00 | 10.00 | 35.00 | 60.00 | 80 | 120 | 275 | 650 | |
| 1898S . . . . . . . . . . . . .1,702,507 | | 2.00 | 5.00 | 16.00 | 25.00 | 40 | 75 | 180 | 600 | |
| 1899 . . . . . . .(846) . .19,580,000 | | 2.00 | 2.10 | 3.00 | 6.00 | 12 | 30 | 65 | 100 | 300 |
| 1899O . . . . . . . . . . . . .2,650,000 | | 4.50 | 6.00 | 35.00 | 45.00 | 70 | 100 | 210 | 575 | |
| 1899S . . . . . . . . . . . . .1,867,493 | | 4.00 | 4.50 | 8.00 | 16.00 | 20 | 55 | 160 | 425 | |
| 1900 . . . . . . .(912) . .17,600,000 | | 2.00 | 2.10 | 3.00 | 6.00 | 12 | 30 | 65 | 100 | 300 |

* Included in number below.

*Chart continued on next page.*

| | Mintage | G-4 | VG-8 | F-12 | VF-20 | EF-40 | AU-50 | MS-60 | MS-63 | PF-63 |
|---|---|---|---|---|---|---|---|---|---|---|
| 1900O | 2,010,000 | $8.00 | $20.00 | $45.00 | $50.00 | $120 | $160 | $320 | $500 | |
| 1900S | 5,168,270 | 2.00 | 2.10 | 5.00 | 7.00 | 13 | 35 | 120 | 220 | |
| 1901 (813) | 18,859,665 | 2.00 | 2.10 | 3.00 | 6.00 | 12 | 32 | 65 | 100 | $300 |
| 1901O | 5,620,000 | 2.00 | 2.25 | 5.00 | 9.00 | 30 | 50 | 250 | 460 | |
| 1901S | 593,022 | 45.00 | 70.00 | 185.00 | 250.00 | 300 | 350 | 635 | 875 | |
| 1902 (777) | 21,380,000 | 2.00 | 2.10 | 2.50 | 4.00 | 12 | 30 | 65 | 100 | 300 |
| 1902O | 4,500,000 | 2.00 | 2.25 | 6.00 | 12.00 | 25 | 50 | 180 | 450 | |
| 1902S | 2,070,000 | 3.00 | 6.00 | 18.00 | 30.00 | 45 | 70 | 180 | 450 | |
| 1903 (755) | 19,500,000 | 2.00 | 2.10 | 2.50 | 4.00 | 12 | 30 | 65 | 100 | 300 |
| 1903O | 8,180,000 | 2.00 | 2.50 | 7.00 | 9.00 | 18 | 35 | 160 | 295 | |
| 1903S | 613,300 | 40.00 | 60.00 | 200.00 | 250.00 | 400 | 500 | 750 | 1,000 | |
| 1904 (670) | 14,600,357 | 2.00 | 2.10 | 2.50 | 4.00 | 12 | 30 | 65 | 90 | 300 |
| 1904S | 800,000 | 20.00 | 35.00 | 75.00 | 100.00 | 150 | 250 | 425 | 850 | |
| 1905 (727) | 14,551,623 | 2.00 | 2.10 | 2.50 | 4.00 | 12 | 30 | 65 | 90 | 300 |
| 1905D | 3,400,000 | 2.00 | 3.00 | 13.00 | 25.00 | 50 | 75 | 150 | 250 | |
| 1905S | 6,855,199 | 2.00 | 2.10 | 4.00 | 7.00 | 18 | 40 | 140 | 200 | |
| 1906 (675) | 19,957,731 | 2.00 | 2.10 | 2.50 | 5.00 | 12 | 30 | 65 | 90 | 300 |
| 1906D | 4,060,000 | 2.00 | 2.10 | 2.50 | 8.00 | 13 | 32 | 95 | 200 | |
| 1906O | 2,610,000 | 3.00 | 5.00 | 20.00 | 35.00 | 45 | 65 | 120 | 175 | |
| 1906S | 3,136,640 | 2.00 | 2.10 | 5.00 | 10.00 | 16 | 50 | 125 | 210 | |
| 1907 (575) | 22,220,000 | 2.00 | 2.10 | 2.50 | 4.00 | 12 | 30 | 65 | 90 | 300 |
| 1907D | 4,080,000 | 2.00 | 2.50 | 5.00 | 8.00 | 18 | 60 | 150 | 475 | |
| 1907O | 5,058,000 | 2.50 | 3.50 | 15.00 | 18.00 | 24 | 45 | 100 | 185 | |
| 1907S | 3,178,470 | 2.00 | 2.50 | 6.00 | 12.00 | 20 | 45 | 200 | 400 | |
| 1908 (545) | 10,600,000 | 2.00 | 2.10 | 2.50 | 4.00 | 12 | 30 | 65 | 90 | 300 |
| 1908D | 7,490,000 | 2.00 | 2.10 | 4.00 | 6.00 | 14 | 35 | 70 | 150 | |
| 1908O | 1,789,000 | 3.00 | 5.00 | 22.00 | 35.00 | 50 | 80 | 150 | 275 | |
| 1908S | 3,220,000 | 2.00 | 3.00 | 6.00 | 8.00 | 16 | 75 | 175 | 350 | |
| 1909 (650) | 10,240,000 | 2.00 | 2.10 | 2.50 | 3.50 | 12 | 30 | 65 | 90 | 300 |
| 1909D | 954,000 | 3.50 | 10.00 | 35.00 | 50.00 | 75 | 100 | 275 | 600 | |
| 1909O | 2,287,000 | 2.00 | 3.00 | 6.00 | 10.00 | 20 | 60 | 120 | 275 | |
| 1909S | 1,000,000 | 3.00 | 8.50 | 40.00 | 50.00 | 90 | 165 | 275 | 650 | |
| 1910 (551) | 11,520,000 | 2.00 | 2.10 | 2.50 | 3.50 | 12 | 30 | 65 | 90 | 300 |
| 1910D | 3,490,000 | 2.00 | 3.00 | 5.00 | 6.00 | 18 | 45 | 125 | 225 | |
| 1910S | 1,240,000 | 2.25 | 4.00 | 21.00 | 34.00 | 60 | 90 | 250 | 370 | |
| 1911 (543) | 18,870,000 | 2.00 | 2.10 | 2.50 | 3.50 | 12 | 30 | 65 | 90 | 300 |
| 1911D | 11,209,000 | 2.00 | 2.10 | 2.50 | 3.50 | 12 | 30 | 65 | 90 | |
| 1911S | 3,520,000 | 2.00 | 3.00 | 8.00 | 8.00 | 16 | 45 | 120 | 220 | |
| 1912 (700) | 19,349,300 | 2.00 | 2.10 | 2.50 | 3.50 | 12 | 30 | 65 | 90 | 300 |
| 1912D | 11,760,000 | 2.00 | 2.10 | 2.50 | 3.50 | 12 | 30 | 65 | 100 | |
| 1912S | 3,420,000 | 2.00 | 3.00 | 5.00 | 8.00 | 16 | 50 | 100 | 165 | |
| 1913 (622) | 19,760,000 | 2.00 | 2.10 | 2.50 | 3.50 | 12 | 30 | 65 | 90 | 300 |
| 1913S | 510,000 | 9.00 | 18.00 | 45.00 | 80.00 | 125 | 175 | 260 | 375 | |
| 1914 (425) | 17,360,230 | 2.00 | 2.10 | 2.50 | 3.50 | 12 | 30 | 65 | 90 | 300 |
| 1914D | 11,908,000 | 2.00 | 2.10 | 2.50 | 3.50 | 12 | 30 | 65 | 90 | |
| 1914S | 2,100,000 | 2.00 | 3.00 | 6.00 | 8.00 | 12 | 30 | 110 | 190 | |
| 1915 (450) | 5,620,000 | 2.00 | 2.10 | 2.50 | 3.50 | 12 | 30 | 65 | 90 | 300 |
| 1915S | 960,000 | 2.25 | 3.00 | 15.00 | 20.00 | 30 | 65 | 140 | 275 | |
| 1916 | 18,490,000 | 2.00 | 2.10 | 2.50 | 3.50 | 12 | 30 | 65 | 90 | |
| 1916S | 5,820,000 | 2.00 | 2.10 | 2.50 | 3.50 | 12 | 30 | 65 | 90 | |

# WINGED LIBERTY HEAD
# OR "MERCURY" (1916–1945)

Although this coin is commonly called the *Mercury* dime, the main device is in fact a representation of Liberty. The wings crowning her cap are intended to symbolize liberty of thought. The designer's monogram AW is at the right of the neck.

**G-4 Good:** Letters and date clear. Lines and bands in fasces obliterated.
**VG-8 Very Good:** Half of sticks discernible in fasces.
**F-12 Fine:** All sticks in fasces defined. Diagonal bands worn nearly flat.
**VF-20 Very Fine:** Diagonal bands definitely visible.
**EF-40 Extremely Fine:** Only slight wear on diagonal bands. Braids and hair before ear clearly visible.
**AU-50 About Uncirculated:** Slight trace of wear. Most mint luster present.
**MS-63 Choice Uncirculated:** No trace of wear. Light blemishes. Attractive mint luster.
**MS-65 Gem Uncirculated:** Only light, scattered marks that are not distracting. Strong luster, good eye appeal.

*Mintmark location is on reverse, left of fasces.*

Uncirculated values shown are for average pieces with minimum blemishes; those with sharp strikes and split horizontal bands on reverse are worth much more.

| | Mintage | G-4 | VG-8 | F-12 | VF-20 | EF-40 | MS-60 | MS-63 | MS-65 |
|---|---|---|---|---|---|---|---|---|---|
| 1916 | 22,180,080 | $2.25 | $2.50 | $3.50 | $4.25 | $5.50 | $18.00 | $24 | $50 |
| 1916D | 264,000 | 500.00 | 800.00 | 1,200.00 | 1,600.00 | 2,750.00 | 8,000.00 | 9,000 | 16,000 |
| 1916S | 10,450,000 | 3.00 | 4.00 | 5.00 | 6.00 | 10.00 | 20.00 | 35 | 125 |
| 1917 | 55,230,000 | 2.00 | 2.00 | 2.25 | 3.00 | 4.00 | 15.00 | 26 | 85 |
| 1917D | 9,402,000 | 2.25 | 3.25 | 5.00 | 8.00 | 22.00 | 65.00 | 180 | 700 |
| 1917S | 27,330,000 | 2.00 | 2.00 | 3.00 | 3.50 | 6.00 | 30.00 | 90 | 250 |
| 1918 | 26,680,000 | 2.00 | 2.00 | 3.00 | 6.00 | 13.00 | 40.00 | 90 | 225 |
| 1918D | 22,674,800 | 2.00 | 2.00 | 3.00 | 6.00 | 12.00 | 55.00 | 120 | 250 |
| 1918S | 19,300,000 | 2.00 | 2.00 | 2.50 | 5.00 | 8.50 | 45.00 | 150 | 375 |
| 1919 | 35,740,000 | 2.00 | 2.00 | 2.25 | 3.00 | 6.00 | 22.00 | 55 | 175 |
| 1919D | 9,939,000 | 2.00 | 2.00 | 4.00 | 10.00 | 20.00 | 110.00 | 250 | 1,000 |
| 1919S | 8,850,000 | 2.00 | 2.00 | 3.00 | 8.00 | 20.00 | 110.00 | 270 | 650 |
| 1920 | 59,030,000 | 2.00 | 2.00 | 2.25 | 3.50 | 5.00 | 27.00 | 35 | 150 |
| 1920D | 19,171,000 | 2.00 | 2.00 | 2.50 | 6.00 | 11.00 | 85.00 | 220 | 450 |
| 1920S | 13,820,000 | 2.00 | 2.00 | 2.50 | 6.00 | 10.00 | 65.00 | 175 | 650 |
| 1921 | 1,230,000 | 30.00 | 40.00 | 80.00 | 175.00 | 300.00 | 650.00 | 900 | 1,700 |
| 1921D | 1,080,000 | 35.00 | 70.00 | 100.00 | 200.00 | 400.00 | 675.00 | 1,000 | 1,750 |
| 1923 | 50,130,000 | 2.00 | 2.00 | 2.25 | 3.00 | 4.00 | 26.00 | 25 | 65 |
| 1923S | 6,440,000 | 2.00 | 2.00 | 4.00 | 8.00 | 32.00 | 80.00 | 220 | 600 |
| 1924 | 24,010,000 | 2.00 | 2.00 | 2.25 | 3.00 | 7.00 | 23.00 | 60 | 120 |
| 1924D | 6,810,000 | 2.00 | 2.00 | 3.50 | 8.00 | 26.00 | 95.00 | 280 | 600 |
| 1924S | 7,120,000 | 2.00 | 2.00 | 3.00 | 5.00 | 24.00 | 90.00 | 290 | 625 |
| 1925 | 25,610,000 | 2.00 | 2.00 | 2.25 | 3.00 | 4.50 | 17.00 | 45 | 125 |
| 1925D | 5,117,000 | 2.50 | 3.25 | 6.00 | 22.00 | 60.00 | 180.00 | 425 | 950 |
| 1925S | 5,850,000 | 2.00 | 2.00 | 3.00 | 7.00 | 30.00 | 90.00 | 275 | 800 |
| 1926 | 32,160,000 | 2.00 | 2.00 | 2.25 | 3.00 | 4.50 | 15.00 | 35 | 130 |
| 1926D | 6,828,000 | 2.00 | 2.00 | 3.00 | 6.00 | 17.00 | 60.00 | 150 | 350 |
| 1926S | 1,520,000 | 4.00 | 6.25 | 12.00 | 32.00 | 140.00 | 600.00 | 850 | 1,800 |
| 1927 | 28,080,000 | 2.00 | 2.00 | 2.25 | 3.00 | 4.00 | 13.00 | 32 | 80 |
| 1927D | 4,812,000 | 2.00 | 2.00 | 3.00 | 12.00 | 35.00 | 110.00 | 225 | 725 |

*Chart continued on next page.*

# DIMES

| | Mintage | G-4 | VG-8 | F-12 | VF-20 | EF-40 | MS-60 | MS-63 | MS-65 |
|---|---|---|---|---|---|---|---|---|---|
| 1927S | 4,770,000 | $2.00 | $2.00 | $2.75 | $4.00 | $15.00 | $120.00 | $275 | $800 |
| 1928 | 19,480,000 | 2.00 | 2.00 | 2.75 | 3.00 | 4.50 | 25.00 | 30 | 70 |
| 1928D | 4,161,000 | 2.00 | 2.00 | 4.00 | 10.00 | 24.00 | 85.00 | 180 | 475 |
| 1928S | 7,400,000 | 2.00 | 2.00 | 2.25 | 2.75 | 8.00 | 35.00 | 160 | 265 |
| 1929 | 25,970,000 | 2.00 | 2.00 | 2.25 | 2.50 | 3.00 | 13.00 | 20 | 40 |
| 1929D | 5,034,000 | 2.00 | 2.00 | 2.25 | 4.00 | 8.00 | 17.00 | 22 | 40 |
| 1929S | 4,730,000 | 2.00 | 2.00 | 2.25 | 2.75 | 5.00 | 18.00 | 25 | 60 |
| 1930 | 6,770,000 | 2.00 | 2.00 | 2.25 | 2.75 | 4.00 | 15.00 | 25 | 60 |
| 1930S | 1,843,000 | 2.00 | 2.00 | 3.00 | 3.80 | 8.00 | 30.00 | 65 | 110 |
| 1931 | 3,150,000 | 2.00 | 2.00 | 2.25 | 3.00 | 5.00 | 20.00 | 40 | 80 |
| 1931D | 1,260,000 | 4.00 | 5.00 | 7.00 | 11.00 | 18.00 | 48.00 | 75 | 140 |
| 1931S | 1,800,000 | 2.50 | 3.00 | 3.50 | 5.00 | 8.50 | 38.00 | 75 | 150 |

| | Mintage | VG-8 | F-12 | VF-20 | EF-40 | MS-60 | MS-63 | MS-65 | PF-63 |
|---|---|---|---|---|---|---|---|---|---|
| 1934 | 24,080,000 | $2.00 | $2.00 | $2.25 | $2.25 | $10.00 | $15 | $25 | |
| 1934D | 6,772,000 | 2.00 | 2.00 | 2.25 | 2.25 | 20.00 | 30 | 45 | |
| 1935 | 58,830,000 | 2.00 | 2.00 | 2.25 | 2.25 | 6.50 | 9 | 18 | |
| 1935D | 10,477,000 | 2.00 | 2.00 | 2.25 | 2.25 | 20.00 | 25 | 50 | |
| 1935S | 15,840,000 | 2.00 | 2.00 | 2.25 | 2.25 | 12.00 | 16 | 25 | |
| 1936 ....(4,130) | 87,500,000 | 2.00 | 2.00 | 2.25 | 2.25 | 5.00 | 12 | 16 | $1,200 |
| 1936D | 16,132,000 | 2.00 | 2.00 | 2.25 | 2.25 | 14.00 | 20 | 30 | |
| 1936S | 9,210,000 | 2.00 | 2.00 | 2.25 | 2.25 | 12.00 | 15 | 22 | |
| 1937 ....(5,756) | 56,860,000 | 2.00 | 2.00 | 2.25 | 2.25 | 4.00 | 9 | 15 | 425 |
| 1937D | 14,146,000 | 2.00 | 2.00 | 2.25 | 2.25 | 14.00 | 16 | 24 | |
| 1937S | 9,740,000 | 2.00 | 2.00 | 2.25 | 2.25 | 12.00 | 15 | 22 | |
| 1938 ....(8,728) | 22,190,000 | 2.00 | 2.00 | 2.25 | 2.25 | 7.00 | 9 | 15 | 250 |
| 1938D | 5,537,000 | 2.00 | 2.00 | 2.25 | 2.25 | 9.00 | 10 | 16 | |
| 1938S | 8,090,000 | 2.00 | 2.00 | 2.25 | 2.25 | 8.00 | 9 | 15 | |
| 1939 ....(9,321) | 67,740,000 | 2.00 | 2.00 | 2.25 | 2.25 | 4.50 | 8 | 15 | 225 |
| 1939D | 24,394,000 | 2.00 | 2.00 | 2.25 | 2.25 | 4.50 | 8 | 16 | |
| 1939S | 10,540,000 | 2.00 | 2.00 | 2.25 | 2.25 | 12.00 | 15 | 25 | |
| 1940 ...(11,827) | 65,350,000 | 2.00 | 2.00 | 2.25 | 2.25 | 4.50 | 7 | 15 | 210 |
| 1940D | 21,198,000 | 2.00 | 2.00 | 2.25 | 2.25 | 4.50 | 9 | 16 | |
| 1940S | 21,560,000 | 2.00 | 2.00 | 2.25 | 2.25 | 4.50 | 8 | 16 | |
| 1941 ...(16,557) | 175,090,000 | 2.00 | 2.00 | 2.25 | 2.25 | 4.50 | 7 | 15 | 200 |
| 1941D | 45,634,000 | 2.00 | 2.00 | 2.25 | 2.25 | 4.50 | 9 | 16 | |
| 1941S | 43,090,000 | 2.00 | 2.00 | 2.25 | 2.25 | 4.50 | 8 | 16 | |
| 1942, 2 Over 1 | * | 275.00 | 375.00 | 400.00 | 500.00 | 1,200.00 | 2,200 | 8,500 | |
| 1942 ...(22,329) | 205,410,000 | 2.00 | 2.00 | 2.25 | 2.25 | 4.50 | 7 | 15 | 200 |
| 1942D, 2 Over 1 | * | 275.00 | 375.00 | 400.00 | 500.00 | 1,200.00 | 2,400 | 4,500 | |
| 1942D | 60,740,000 | 2.00 | 2.00 | 2.25 | 2.25 | 5.50 | 9 | 16 | |
| 1942S | 49,300,000 | 2.00 | 2.00 | 2.25 | 2.25 | 6.50 | 9 | 16 | |
| 1943 | 191,710,000 | 2.00 | 2.00 | 2.25 | 2.25 | 4.50 | 6 | 15 | |
| 1943D | 71,949,000 | 2.00 | 2.00 | 2.25 | 2.25 | 5.50 | 7 | 16 | |
| 1943S | 60,400,000 | 2.00 | 2.00 | 2.25 | 2.25 | 5.50 | 7 | 15 | |
| 1944 | 231,410,000 | 2.00 | 2.00 | 2.25 | 2.25 | 4.50 | 6 | 15 | |
| 1944D | 62,224,000 | 2.00 | 2.00 | 2.25 | 2.25 | 4.50 | 6 | 15 | |
| 1944S | 49,490,000 | 2.00 | 2.00 | 2.25 | 2.25 | 4.50 | 6 | 15 | |
| 1945 | 159,130,000 | 2.00 | 2.00 | 2.25 | 2.25 | 4.50 | 6 | 15 | |
| 1945D | 40,245,000 | 2.00 | 2.00 | 2.00 | 2.25 | 2.25 | 6 | 16 | |
| 1945S | 41,920,000 | 2.00 | 2.00 | 2.25 | 2.25 | 4.50 | 7 | 16 | |
| 1945S, Micro S | * | 2.00 | 2.00 | 2.25 | 2.50 | 9.00 | 15 | 45 | |

* Included in number above.

## ROOSEVELT (1946 TO DATE)

John R. Sinnock (whose initials, JS, are at the truncation of the neck) designed this dime showing a portrait of Franklin D. Roosevelt. The design has heavier lettering and a more modernistic character than preceding types.

**VF-20 Very Fine:** Moderate wear on high points of design. All major details are clear.

**EF-40 Extremely Fine:** All lines of torch, flame, and hair very plain.

**MS-63 Choice Uncirculated:** Some distracting contact marks or blemishes in prime focal areas. Impaired luster possible.

**MS-65 Gem Uncirculated:** Only light, non-distracting scattered marks. Strong luster, good eye appeal.

**PF-65 Gem Proof:** Nearly perfect.

Mintmark on reverse, 1946–1964.

Mintmark on obverse, starting 1968.

### Silver Coinage (1946–1964)

| | Mintage | VF-20 | EF-40 | MS-63 | MS-65 | PF-65 |
|---|---|---|---|---|---|---|
| 1946 | 255,250,000 | $2 | $2 | $2.25 | $6.00 | |
| 1946D | 61,043,500 | 2 | 2 | 3.00 | 7.00 | |
| 1946S | 27,900,000 | 2 | 2 | 4.00 | 10.00 | |
| 1947 | 121,520,000 | 2 | 2 | 3.00 | 6.00 | |
| 1947D | 46,835,000 | 2 | 2 | 3.25 | 6.00 | |
| 1947S | 34,840,000 | 2 | 2 | 3.00 | 6.00 | |
| 1948 | 74,950,000 | 2 | 2 | 3.00 | 6.00 | |
| 1948D | 52,841,000 | 2 | 2 | 3.00 | 6.00 | |
| 1948S | 35,520,000 | 2 | 2 | 2.75 | 6.00 | |
| 1949 | 30,940,000 | 2 | 2 | 12.50 | 16.00 | |
| 1949D | 26,034,000 | 2 | 2 | 5.00 | 9.00 | |
| 1949S | 13,510,000 | 2 | 2 | 20.00 | 25.00 | |
| 1950 | (51,386) ..50,130,114 | 2 | 2 | 6.00 | 7.00 | $25.00 |
| 1950D | 46,803,000 | 2 | 2 | 3.00 | 6.00 | |
| 1950S | 20,440,000 | 2 | 2 | 18.00 | 22.00 | |
| 1951 | (57,500) ..103,880,102 | 2 | 2 | 2.25 | 5.00 | 25.00 |
| 1951D | 56,529,000 | 2 | 2 | 2.25 | 5.00 | |
| 1951S | 31,630,000 | 2 | 2 | 6.00 | 10.00 | |
| 1952 | (81,980) ...99,040,093 | 2 | 2 | 2.25 | 5.00 | 16.00 |
| 1952D | 122,100,000 | 2 | 2 | 2.25 | 3.25 | |
| 1952S | 44,419,500 | 2 | 2 | 4.00 | 6.00 | |
| 1953 | (128,800) ..53,490,120 | 2 | 2 | 4.00 | 6.00 | 14.00 |
| 1953D | 136,433,000 | 2 | 2 | 2.25 | 4.00 | |
| 1953S | 39,180,000 | 2 | 2 | 2.25 | 4.00 | |
| 1954 | (233,300) ..114,010,203 | 2 | 2 | 2.25 | 4.00 | 10.00 |
| 1954D | 106,397,000 | 2 | 2 | 2.25 | 4.00 | |
| 1954S | 22,860,000 | 2 | 2 | 2.25 | 4.00 | |
| 1955 | (378,200) ..12,450,181 | 2 | 2 | 2.25 | 5.00 | 8.00 |
| 1955D | 13,959,000 | 2 | 2 | 2.25 | 4.00 | |
| 1955S | 18,510,000 | 2 | 2 | 2.25 | 4.00 | |
| 1956 | (669,384) ..108,640,000 | 2 | 2 | 2.25 | 4.00 | 2.50 |
| 1956D | 108,015,100 | 2 | 2 | 2.25 | 3.50 | |
| 1957 | (1,247,952) ..160,160,000 | 2 | 2 | 2.25 | 3.50 | 2.50 |

*Chart continued on next page.*

| | Mintage | VF-20 | EF-40 | MS-63 | MS-65 | PF-65 |
|---|---|---|---|---|---|---|
| 1957D | 113,354,330 | $2 | $2 | $2.25 | $3.25 | |
| 1958 | (875,652) . . .31,910,000 | 2 | 2 | 2.25 | 4.00 | $2.50 |
| 1958D | 136,564,600 | 2 | 2 | 2.25 | 4.00 | |
| 1959 | (1,149,291) . . .85,780,000 | 2 | 2 | 2.25 | 3.50 | 2.50 |
| 1959D | 164,919,790 | 2 | 2 | 2.25 | 3.50 | |
| 1960 | (1,691,602) . . .70,390,000 | 2 | 2 | 2.25 | 3.50 | 2.50 |
| 1960D | 200,160,400 | 2 | 2 | 2.25 | 3.00 | |
| 1961 | (3,028,244) . . .93,730,000 | 2 | 2 | 2.25 | 3.00 | 2.50 |
| 1961D | 209,146,550 | 2 | 2 | 2.25 | 3.00 | |
| 1962 | (3,218,019) . . .72,450,000 | 2 | 2 | 2.25 | 3.00 | 2.50 |
| 1962D | 334,948,380 | 2 | 2 | 2.25 | 3.00 | |
| 1963 | (3,075,645) . . .123,650,000 | 2 | 2 | 2.25 | 3.00 | 2.50 |
| 1963D | 421,476,530 | 2 | 2 | 2.25 | 3.00 | |
| 1964 | (3,950,762) . .929,360,000 | 2 | 2 | 2.25 | 3.00 | 2.50 |
| 1964D | 1,357,517,180 | 2 | 2 | 2.25 | 3.00 | |

## Clad Coinage and Silver Proofs (1965 to Date)

| | Mintage | MS-63 | MS-65 | PF-65 |
|---|---|---|---|---|
| 1965 | 1,652,140,570 | $0.15 | $0.75 | |
| 1966 | 1,382,734,540 | 0.15 | 0.65 | |
| 1967 | 2,244,007,320 | 0.15 | 0.50 | |
| 1968 | 424,470,400 | 0.15 | 0.50 | |
| 1968D | 480,748,280 | 0.15 | 0.50 | |
| 1968S | (3,041,506) | | | $0.50 |
| 1969 | 145,790,000 | 0.25 | 0.90 | |
| 1969D | 563,323,870 | 0.15 | 0.25 | |
| 1969S | (2,394,631) | | | 0.50 |
| 1970 | 345,570,000 | 0.15 | 0.25 | |
| 1970D | 754,942,100 | 0.15 | 0.25 | |
| 1970S | (2,632,810) | | | 0.50 |
| 1971 | 162,690,000 | 0.18 | 0.30 | |
| 1971D | 377,914,240 | 0.16 | 0.20 | |
| 1971S | (3,220,733) | | | 0.50 |
| 1972 | 431,540,000 | 0.15 | 0.25 | |
| 1972D | 330,290,000 | 0.15 | 0.25 | |
| 1972S | (3,260,996) | | | 0.50 |
| 1973 | 315,670,000 | 0.15 | 0.25 | |
| 1973D | 455,032,426 | 0.15 | 0.25 | |
| 1973S | (2,760,339) | | | 0.50 |
| 1974 | 470,248,000 | 0.15 | 0.25 | |
| 1974D | 571,083,000 | 0.15 | 0.25 | |
| 1974S | (2,612,568) | | | 0.50 |
| 1975 | 585,673,900 | 0.15 | 0.25 | |
| 1975D | 313,705,300 | 0.15 | 0.25 | |
| 1975S | (2,845,450) | | | 0.70 |
| 1976 | 568,760,000 | 1.50 | 0.25 | |
| 1976D | 695,222,774 | | 0.15 | |
| 1976S | (4,149,730) | | | 0.70 |
| 1977 | 796,930,000 | 0.15 | 0.25 | |
| 1977D | 376,607,228 | 0.15 | 0.25 | |

| | Mintage | MS-63 | MS-65 | PF-65 |
|---|---|---|---|---|
| 1977S | (3,251,152) | | | $0.50 |
| 1978 | 663,980,000 | | $0.15 | |
| 1978D | 282,847,540 | | 0.15 | |
| 1978S | (3,127,781) | | | 0.40 |
| 1979 | 315,440,000 | $0.15 | 0.25 | |
| 1979D | 390,921,184 | 0.15 | 0.25 | |
| 1979S, Filled S | (3,677,175) | | | 0.50 |
| 1979S, Clear S | . . . . . . . . . .* | | | 1.40 |
| 1980P | 735,170,000 | 0.15 | 0.25 | |
| 1980D | 719,354,321 | 0.15 | 0.25 | |
| 1980S | (3,554,806) | | | 0.40 |
| 1981P | 676,650,000 | 0.15 | 0.25 | |
| 1981D | 712,284,143 | 0.15 | 0.25 | |
| 1981S | (4,063,083) | | | 0.40 |
| 1982, No Mmk | | 90.00 | 225.00 | |
| 1982P | 519,475,000 | 1.50 | 2.25 | |
| 1982D | 542,713,584 | 0.60 | 1.10 | |
| 1982S | (3,857,479) | | | 0.70 |
| 1983P | 647,025,000 | 1.25 | 2.75 | |
| 1983D | 730,129,224 | 0.35 | 0.65 | |
| 1983S | (3,279,126) | | | 0.50 |
| 1984P | 856,669,000 | 0.15 | 0.30 | |
| 1984D | 704,803,976 | 0.20 | 0.50 | |
| 1984S | (3,065,110) | | | 0.70 |
| 1985P | 705,200,962 | 0.15 | 0.25 | |
| 1985D | 587,979,970 | 0.15 | 0.25 | |
| 1985S | (3,362,821) | | | 0.50 |
| 1986P | 682,649,693 | 0.25 | 0.35 | |
| 1986D | 473,326,970 | 0.25 | 0.35 | |
| 1986S | (3,010,497) | | | 1.25 |
| 1987P | 762,709,481 | 0.15 | 0.35 | |
| 1987D | 653,203,402 | 0.15 | 0.35 | |

* Included in number above.

| | Mintage | MS-63 | MS-65 | PF-65 |
|---|---|---|---|---|
| 1987S | (4,227,728) | | | $1.20 |
| 1988P | 1,030,550,000 | $0.12 | $0.20 | |
| 1988D | 962,385,489 | 0.12 | 0.20 | |
| 1988S | (3,262,948) | | | 1.00 |
| 1989P | 1,298,400,000 | 0.10 | 0.20 | |
| 1989D | 896,535,597 | 0.10 | 0.20 | |
| 1989S | (3,220,194) | | | 1.50 |
| 1990P | 1,034,340,000 | 0.10 | 0.20 | |
| 1990D | 839,995,824 | 0.10 | 0.20 | |
| 1990S | (3,299,559) | | | 0.75 |
| 1991P | 927,220,000 | 0.10 | 0.20 | |
| 1991D | 601,241,114 | 0.12 | 0.20 | |
| 1991S | (2,867,787) | | | 1.20 |
| 1992P | 593,500,000 | 0.10 | 0.15 | |
| 1992D | 616,273,932 | 0.10 | 0.15 | |
| 1992S | (2,858,981) | | | 2.00 |
| 1992S, Silver | (1,317,579) | | | 3.00 |
| 1993P | 766,180,000 | 0.10 | 0.15 | |
| 1993D | 750,110,166 | 0.10 | 0.15 | |
| 1993S | (2,633,439) | | | 2.00 |
| 1993S, Silver | (761,353) | | | 3.00 |
| 1994P | 1,189,000,000 | 0.10 | 0.15 | |
| 1994D | 1,303,268,110 | 0.10 | 0.15 | |
| 1994S | (2,484,594) | | | 2.00 |
| 1994S, Silver | (785,329) | | | 3.00 |
| 1995P | 1,125,500,000 | 0.10 | 0.20 | |
| 1995D | 1,274,890,000 | 0.15 | 0.25 | |
| 1995S | (2,117,496) | | | 6.00 |
| 1995S, Silver | (679,985) | | | 9.00 |
| 1996P | 1,421,163,000 | 0.10 | 0.20 | |
| 1996D | 1,400,300,000 | 0.10 | 0.20 | |
| 1996W | 1,457,000 | 6.00 | 10.00 | |
| 1996S | (1,750,244) | | | 1.00 |
| 1996S, Silver | (775,021) | | | 3.00 |
| 1997P | 991,640,000 | 0.10 | 0.15 | |
| 1997D | 979,810,000 | 0.10 | 0.15 | |
| 1997S | (2,055,000) | | | 3.50 |
| 1997S, Silver | (741,678) | | | 10.00 |
| 1998P | 1,163,000,000 | 0.10 | 0.15 | |
| 1998D | 1,172,250,000 | 0.10 | 0.15 | |
| 1998S | (2,086,507) | | | 2.00 |
| 1998S, Silver | (878,792) | | | 3.00 |
| 1999P | 2,164,000,000 | 0.10 | 0.15 | |
| 1999D | 1,397,750,000 | 0.10 | 0.15 | |
| 1999S | (2,543,401) | | | 1.00 |
| 1999S, Silver | (804,565) | | | 3.50 |
| 2000P | 1,842,500,000 | 0.10 | 0.15 | |
| 2000D | 1,818,700,000 | 0.10 | 0.15 | |
| 2000S | (3,082,572) | | | 1.00 |
| 2000S, Silver | (965,421) | | | 2.25 |
| 2001P | 1,369,590,000 | 0.10 | 0.15 | |
| 2001D | 1,412,800,000 | 0.10 | 0.15 | |
| 2001S | (2,294,909) | | | 0.50 |
| 2001S, Silver | (889,697) | | | 2.25 |
| 2002P | 1,187,500,000 | 0.10 | 0.15 | |
| 2002D | 1,379,500,000 | 0.10 | 0.15 | |
| 2002S | (2,319,766) | | | 0.75 |
| 2002S, Silver | (892,229) | | | 3.00 |
| 2003P | 1,085,500,000 | 0.10 | 0.15 | |
| 2003D | 986,500,000 | 0.10 | 0.15 | |
| 2003S | (2,172,684) | | | 0.50 |
| 2003S, Silver | (1,125,755) | | | 2.50 |
| 2004P | 1,328,000,000 | 0.10 | 0.15 | |
| 2004D | 1,159,500,000 | 0.10 | 0.15 | |
| 2004S | (1,789,488) | | | 0.60 |
| 2004S, Silver | (1,175,934) | | | 2.50 |
| 2005P | 1,412,000,000 | 0.10 | 0.15 | |
| 2005D | 1,423,500,000 | 0.10 | 0.15 | |
| 2005S | (2,275,000) | | | 0.60 |
| 2005S, Silver | (1,069,679) | | | 2.50 |
| 2006P | 1,381,000,000 | 0.10 | 0.15 | |
| 2006D | 1,447,000,000 | 0.10 | 0.15 | |
| 2006S | (2,000,428) | | | 0.60 |
| 2006S, Silver | (1,054,008) | | | 2.50 |
| 2007P | 1,047,500,000 | 0.10 | 0.15 | |
| 2007D | 1,042,000,000 | 0.10 | 0.15 | |
| 2007S | (1,702,116) | | | 0.50 |
| 2007S, Silver | (875,050) | | | 2.50 |
| 2008P | 391,000,000 | 0.10 | 0.15 | |
| 2008D | 624,500,000 | 0.10 | 0.15 | |
| 2008S | (1,405,674) | | | 0.50 |
| 2008S, Silver | 763,887 | | | 2.50 |
| 2009P | 96,500,000 | 0.10 | 0.15 | |
| 2009D | 49,500,000 | 0.10 | 0.15 | |
| 2009S | (1,477,967) | | | 0.50 |
| 2009S, Silver | (694,406) | | | 2.25 |
| 2010P | 557,000,000 | 0.10 | 0.15 | |
| 2010D | 562,000,000 | 0.10 | 0.15 | |
| 2010S | | | | 0.50 |
| 2010S, Silver | | | | 2.25 |
| 2011P | | 0.10 | 0.15 | |
| 2011D | | 0.10 | 0.15 | |
| 2011S | | | | 0.50 |
| 2011S, Silver | | | | 2.25 |

## LIBERTY SEATED (1875–1878)

The twenty-cent piece was a short-lived coin authorized by the Act of March 3, 1875. The edge of the coin is plain. Most of the 1876-CC coins were melted at the Mint and never released. The mintmark is on the reverse below the eagle.

**G-4 Good:** LIBERTY on shield obliterated. Letters and date legible.

**VG-8 Very Good:** One or two letters in LIBERTY barely visible. Other details bold.

**F-12 Fine:** Some letters of LIBERTY possibly visible.

**VF-20 Very Fine:** LIBERTY readable, but partly weak.

**EF-40 Extremely Fine:** LIBERTY mostly sharp. Only slight wear on high points of coin.

**AU-50 About Uncirculated:** Slight trace of wear on breast, head, and knees.

**MS-60 Uncirculated:** No trace of wear. Light blemishes.

**MS-63 Choice Uncirculated:** Some distracting blemishes in prime focal areas. Some impairment of luster possible.

**PF-63 Choice Proof:** Reflective surfaces with only a few blemishes in secondary focal places. No major flaws.

| | Mintage | G-4 | VG-8 | F-12 | VF-20 | EF-40 | AU-50 | MS-60 | MS-63 | PF-63 |
|---|---|---|---|---|---|---|---|---|---|---|
| 1875 . . . . . . . .(2,790) . . . .36,910 | | $80 | $100 | $125 | $185 | $235 | $270 | $425 | $725 | $1,300 |
| 1875CC . . . . . . . . . . . .133,290 | | 160 | 185 | 250 | 275 | 450 | 500 | 900 | 1,750 | |
| 1875S . . . . . . . . . . . . .1,155,000 | | 52 | 57 | 65 | 85 | 125 | 155 | 275 | 600 | |
| 1876 . . . . . . . .(1,260) . . . .14,640 | | 90 | 125 | 150 | 200 | 250 | 300 | 450 | 750 | 1,350 |
| 1876CC . . . . . . . . . . . . .10,000 | | | | | | | | 80,000 | | |
| 1877 . . . . . . . .(350) . . . . . . . . | | | | | 1,000 | 1,200 | | | | 2,200 |
| 1878 . . . . . . . .(600) . . . . . . . . | | | | | 900 | 1,000 | | | | 1,800 |

Authorized in 1792, this denomination was not issued until four years later. The first type weighed 104 grains, the standard until modified to 103-1/8 grains by the Act of January 18, 1837. As with the dime and half dime, the weight was reduced and arrows placed at the date in 1853. Rays were placed in the field of the reverse during that year only.

# DRAPED BUST (1796–1807)

**AG-3 About Good:** Details clear enough to identify.
**G-4 Good:** Date readable. Bust outlined, but no detail.
**VG-8 Very Good:** All but deepest drapery folds worn smooth. Hairlines nearly gone and curls lacking in detail.
**F-12 Fine:** All drapery lines visible. Hair partly worn.
**VF-20 Very Fine:** Only left side of drapery indistinct.
**EF-40 Extremely Fine:** Hair well outlined and detailed.
**AU-50 About Uncirculated:** Slight trace of wear on shoulder and highest waves of hair.
**MS-60 Uncirculated:** No trace of wear. Light blemishes.
**MS-63 Choice Uncirculated:** Some distracting marks or blemishes in focal areas. Impaired luster possible.

## Small Eagle Reverse (1796)

| | Mintage | AG-3 | G-4 | VG-8 | F-12 | VF-20 | EF-40 | AU-50 | MS-60 | MS-63 |
|---|---|---|---|---|---|---|---|---|---|---|
| 1796 | 6,146 | $2,850 | $5,500 | $7,000 | $14,000 | $18,000 | $25,000 | $30,000 | $42,000 | $65,000 |

## Heraldic Eagle Reverse (1804–1807)

| | Mintage | AG-3 | G-4 | VG-8 | F-12 | VF-20 | EF-40 | AU-50 | MS-60 | MS-63 |
|---|---|---|---|---|---|---|---|---|---|---|
| 1804 | 6,738 | $800 | $1,600 | $2,100 | $3,250 | $5,200 | $10,500 | $20,000 | $28,000 | $65,000 |
| 1805 | 121,394 | 60 | 150 | 200 | 300 | 550 | 1,200 | 2,000 | 3,750 | 6,500 |
| 1806, 6 Over 5 | * | 75 | 200 | 225 | 350 | 600 | 1,400 | 2,200 | 4,000 | 9,000 |
| 1806 | 206,124 | 70 | 160 | 210 | 325 | 575 | 1,200 | 2,100 | 3,750 | 6,000 |
| 1807 | 220,643 | 70 | 160 | 210 | 325 | 575 | 1,200 | 2,100 | 3,750 | 6,000 |

* Included in number below.

# CAPPED BUST (1815–1838)
## Variety 1 – Large Diameter (1815–1828)

**AG-3 About Good:** Details clear enough to identify.
**G-4 Good:** Date, letters, stars legible. Hair under Liberty's headband smooth. Cap lines worn smooth.
**VG-8 Very Good:** Rim well defined. Main details visible. Full LIBERTY on cap. Hair above eye nearly smooth.
**F-12 Fine:** All hair lines visible, but only partial detail visible in drapery. Shoulder clasp distinct.
**VF-20 Very Fine:** All details visible, but some wear evident. Clasp and ear sharp.
**EF-40 Extremely Fine:** All details distinct. Hair well outlined.
**AU-50 About Uncirculated:** Slight trace of wear on tips of curls and above the eye, and on the wing and claw tips.
**MS-60 Uncirculated:** No trace of wear. Light blemishes.
**MS-63 Choice Uncirculated:** Some distracting marks or blemishes in focal areas. Impaired luster possible.

| | Mintage | AG-3 | G-4 | VG-8 | F-12 | VF-20 | EF-40 | AU-50 | MS-60 | MS-63 |
|---|---|---|---|---|---|---|---|---|---|---|
| 1815 ...............89,235 | | $20 | $45 | $55 | $75 | $200 | $600 | $800 | $1,400 | $2,300 |
| 1818, 8 Over 5 ............* | | 18 | 42 | 50 | 70 | 180 | 525 | 775 | 1,500 | 2,500 |
| 1818, Normal Date .....361,174 | | 18 | 42 | 50 | 70 | 180 | 525 | 775 | 1,300 | 2,300 |
| 1819 ...............144,000 | | 18 | 42 | 50 | 70 | 180 | 525 | 775 | 1,300 | 2,300 |
| 1820 ...............127,444 | | 18 | 42 | 50 | 70 | 180 | 525 | 775 | 1,300 | 2,300 |
| 1821 ...............216,851 | | 18 | 42 | 50 | 70 | 180 | 525 | 775 | 1,300 | 2,300 |
| 1822 ................64,080 | | 18 | 42 | 50 | 80 | 200 | 600 | 800 | 1,400 | 2,800 |
| 1822, 25 Over 50c ..........* | | 300 | 700 | 1,400 | 2,400 | 3,250 | 5,500 | 10,000 | 17,500 | |
| 1823, 3 Over 2 .........17,800 | | 7,000 | 15,000 | 18,000 | 22,000 | 25,000 | 35,000 | 65,000 | — | |
| 1824, 4 Over 2 ............** | | 25 | 45 | 65 | 160 | 300 | 800 | 2,000 | 4,750 | |
| 1825 ...............168,000 | | 18 | 42 | 50 | 70 | 180 | 500 | 750 | 1,300 | 2,300 |
| 1827, Original (Curl Base 2 in 25c) ......4,000 | | | | | | | | | | 100,000 |
| 1827, Restrike (Square Base 2 in 25c) .........* | | | | | | | | | | 40,000 |
| 1828 ..............102,000 | | 18 | 42 | 50 | 65 | 175 | 450 | 700 | 1,300 | 2,600 |
| 1828, 25 Over 50c ..........* | | 35 | 65 | 115 | 250 | 500 | 950 | 1,750 | 4,500 | |

\* Included in regular mintage.  \*\* Included in 1825 mintage.

## Variety 2 – Reduced Diameter (1831–1838), Motto Removed

**G-4 Good:** Bust of Liberty well defined. Hair under headband smooth. Date, letters, stars legible. Scant rims.
**VG-8 Very Good:** Details apparent but worn on high spots. Rims strong. Full LIBERTY.
**F-12 Fine:** All hair lines visible. Drapery partly worn. Shoulder clasp distinct.
**VF-20 Very Fine:** Only top spots worn. Clasp sharp. Ear distinct.
**EF-40 Extremely Fine:** Hair details and clasp bold and clear.

**AU-50 About Uncirculated:** Slight trace of wear on hair around forehead, on cheek, and at top and bottom tips of eagle's wings and left claw.
**MS-60 Uncirculated:** No trace of wear. Light blemishes.
**MS-63 Choice Uncirculated:** Some distracting contact marks or blemishes in prime focal areas. Impaired luster possible.

| | Mintage | G-4 | VG-8 | F-12 | VF-20 | EF-40 | AU-50 | MS-60 | MS-63 |
|---|---|---|---|---|---|---|---|---|---|
| 1831 .............398,000 | | $32 | $40 | $45 | $65 | $170 | $290 | $500 | $1,800 |
| 1832 .............320,000 | | 32 | 40 | 45 | 65 | 170 | 290 | 500 | 1,800 |
| 1833 .............156,000 | | 32 | 40 | 50 | 70 | 200 | 320 | 650 | 2,100 |
| 1834 .............286,000 | | 32 | 40 | 45 | 65 | 170 | 290 | 500 | 1,800 |
| 1835 ...........1,952,000 | | 32 | 40 | 45 | 65 | 170 | 290 | 500 | 1,800 |
| 1836 .............472,000 | | 32 | 40 | 45 | 65 | 170 | 290 | 500 | 1,800 |
| 1837 .............252,400 | | 32 | 40 | 45 | 65 | 170 | 290 | 500 | 1,800 |
| 1838 .............366,000 | | 32 | 40 | 45 | 65 | 170 | 290 | 500 | 1,800 |

## LIBERTY SEATED (1838–1891)

**G-4 Good:** Scant rim. LIBERTY on shield worn off. Date and letters legible.
**VG-8 Very Good:** Rim fairly defined, at least three letters in LIBERTY evident.
**F-12 Fine:** LIBERTY complete, but partly weak.
**VF-20 Very Fine:** LIBERTY strong.
**EF-40 Extremely Fine:** Complete LIBERTY and edges of scroll. Clasp clear.
**AU-50 About Uncirculated:** Slight wear on Liberty's knees and breast and on eagle's neck, wing tips, and claws.
**MS-60 Uncirculated:** No trace of wear. Light blemishes.
**MS-63 Choice Uncirculated:** Some distracting marks or blemishes in focal areas. Impaired luster possible.

### Variety 1 – No Motto Above Eagle (1838–1853)

**Small Date**

**Large Date**

*Mintmark location is on reverse, below eagle.*

| | Mintage | G-4 | VG-8 | F-12 | VF-20 | EF-40 | AU-50 | MS-60 | MS-63 |
|---|---|---|---|---|---|---|---|---|---|
| 1838 | 466,000 | $10 | $13 | $20 | $36 | $110 | $220 | $625 | $1,750 |
| 1839 | 491,146 | 10 | 13 | 20 | 35 | 110 | 220 | 625 | 1,750 |
| 1840 | 188,127 | 9 | 12 | 21 | 32 | 70 | 110 | 400 | 1,100 |
| 1840O | 425,200 | 11 | 15 | 27 | 45 | 125 | 225 | 650 | 2,000 |
| 1841 | 120,000 | 18 | 30 | 45 | 65 | 110 | 125 | 425 | 850 |
| 1841O | 452,000 | 10 | 12 | 19 | 32 | 80 | 120 | 350 | 700 |
| 1842, Small Date (Proof only) | | | | | | | | 28,000 | |
| 1842, Large Date | 88,000 | 30 | 40 | 75 | 130 | 175 | 250 | 750 | 1,500 |
| 1842O, Small Date | * | 150 | 250 | 475 | 775 | 1,500 | 3,500 | 7,500 | |
| 1842O, Large Date | 769,000 | 10 | 11 | 17 | 31 | 70 | 125 | 650 | 1,800 |
| 1843 | 645,600 | 9 | 10 | 16 | 22 | 40 | 60 | 225 | 600 |
| 1843O | 968,000 | 10 | 13 | 20 | 45 | 100 | 275 | 900 | 2,200 |
| 1844 | 421,200 | 9 | 10 | 16 | 22 | 40 | 60 | 225 | 600 |
| 1844O | 740,000 | 10 | 11 | 18 | 32 | 80 | 120 | 550 | 1,400 |
| 1845 | 922,000 | 9 | 10 | 16 | 22 | 40 | 60 | 225 | 625 |
| 1846 | 510,000 | 9 | 10 | 16 | 22 | 40 | 60 | 225 | 600 |
| 1847 | 734,000 | 9 | 10 | 16 | 22 | 40 | 60 | 225 | 600 |
| 1847O | 368,000 | 12 | 17 | 27 | 50 | 110 | 275 | 900 | 2,500 |
| 1848 | 146,000 | 11 | 17 | 28 | 50 | 80 | 125 | 450 | 1,100 |
| 1849 | 340,000 | 10 | 12 | 20 | 27 | 70 | 100 | 400 | 700 |
| 1849O | (a) | 175 | 260 | 450 | 950 | 1,600 | 2,500 | 6,000 | — |
| 1850 | 190,800 | 13 | 17 | 25 | 35 | 65 | 100 | 400 | 750 |
| 1850O | 412,000 | 13 | 17 | 25 | 35 | 65 | 180 | 550 | 1,100 |
| 1851 | 160,000 | 15 | 20 | 28 | 50 | 85 | 100 | 400 | 725 |
| 1851O | 88,000 | 65 | 100 | 200 | 300 | 650 | 1,100 | 2,900 | |
| 1852 | 177,060 | 16 | 21 | 30 | 55 | 90 | 110 | 375 | 650 |
| 1852O | 96,000 | 80 | 120 | 175 | 300 | 600 | 1,500 | 3,500 | 12,000 |
| 1853, Recut Date, No Arrows or Rays | 44,200 | 110 | 140 | 175 | 275 | 500 | 750 | 1,300 | 2,000 |

* Included in number below. **a.** Mintage for 1849-O included with 1850-O.

### Variety 2 – Arrows at Date, Rays Around Eagle (1853)

*See next page for chart.*       **1853, 3 Over 4**

| | Mintage | G-4 | VG-8 | F-12 | VF-20 | EF-40 | AU-50 | MS-60 | MS-63 |
|---|---|---|---|---|---|---|---|---|---|
| 1853 | 15,210,020 | $9 | $12 | $15 | $20 | $65 | $125 | $450 | $975 |
| 1853, 3 Over 4 | * | 20 | 35 | 55 | 110 | 160 | 250 | 900 | 2,250 |
| 1853O | 1,332,000 | 9 | 12 | 17 | 30 | 115 | 450 | 1,300 | 4,000 |

* Included in number above.

## Variety 3 – Arrows at Date, No Rays (1854–1855)

| | Mintage | G-4 | VG-8 | F-12 | VF-20 | EF-40 | AU-50 | MS-60 | MS-63 |
|---|---|---|---|---|---|---|---|---|---|
| 1854 | 12,380,000 | $9 | $11 | $14 | $18 | $35 | $100 | $250 | $600 |
| 1854O | 1,484,000 | 9 | 11 | 16 | 20 | 40 | 110 | 325 | 850 |
| 1855 | 2,857,000 | 9 | 11 | 14 | 18 | 35 | 100 | 275 | 650 |
| 1855O | 176,000 | 17 | 25 | 45 | 115 | 160 | 500 | 1,800 | 5,750 |
| 1855S | 396,400 | 17 | 25 | 35 | 60 | 125 | 325 | 900 | 2,500 |

## Variety 1 Resumed, With Weight Standard of Variety 2 (1856–1865)

| | Mintage | G-4 | VG-8 | F-12 | VF-20 | EF-40 | AU-50 | MS-60 | MS-63 | PF-63 |
|---|---|---|---|---|---|---|---|---|---|---|
| 1856 | 7,264,000 | $9 | $11 | $14 | $19 | $27 | $60 | $170 | $300 | $2,600 |
| 1856O | 968,000 | 9 | 11 | 14 | 21 | 40 | 100 | 500 | 825 | |
| 1856S | 286,000 | 15 | 20 | 35 | 80 | 200 | 500 | 1,250 | 4,500 | |
| 1857 | 9,644,000 | 9 | 11 | 14 | 19 | 26 | 60 | 150 | 300 | 1,800 |
| 1857O | 1,180,000 | 9 | 11 | 14 | 19 | 37 | 110 | 500 | 1,200 | |
| 1857S | 82,000 | 25 | 40 | 70 | 150 | 250 | 400 | 1,200 | 3,250 | |
| 1858 | (300+) 7,368,000 | 9 | 11 | 14 | 19 | 26 | 60 | 150 | 300 | 1,000 |
| 1858O | 520,000 | 9 | 11 | 14 | 25 | 50 | 150 | 650 | 1,750 | |
| 1858S | 121,000 | 19 | 32 | 60 | 125 | 600 | 1,250 | 5,000 | — | |
| 1859 | (800) 1,343,200 | 9 | 11 | 14 | 19 | 26 | 60 | 150 | 425 | 650 |
| 1859O | 260,000 | 9 | 14 | 20 | 26 | 50 | 150 | 500 | 1,600 | |
| 1859S | 80,000 | 40 | 60 | 95 | 250 | 1,000 | 5,000 | — | — | |
| 1860 | (1,000) 804,400 | 9 | 11 | 14 | 19 | 26 | 60 | 175 | 300 | 600 |
| 1860O | 388,000 | 9 | 11 | 14 | 20 | 32 | 150 | 450 | 850 | |
| 1860S | 56,000 | 125 | 250 | 450 | 1,500 | 4,500 | 8,250 | — | — | |
| 1861 | (1,000) 4,853,600 | 9 | 11 | 14 | 19 | 26 | 60 | 175 | 350 | 600 |
| 1861S | 96,000 | 27 | 50 | 100 | 225 | 900 | 3,000 | — | — | |
| 1862 | (550) 932,000 | 9 | 11 | 14 | 19 | 26 | 60 | 175 | 350 | 600 |
| 1862S | 67,000 | 20 | 32 | 80 | 110 | 250 | 475 | 1,400 | 3,500 | |
| 1863 | (460) 191,600 | 14 | 18 | 30 | 45 | 70 | 120 | 300 | 450 | 600 |
| 1864 | (470) 93,600 | 30 | 35 | 45 | 70 | 110 | 180 | 300 | 600 | 600 |
| 1864S | 20,000 | 125 | 175 | 300 | 425 | 950 | 1,850 | — | — | |
| 1865 | (500) 58,800 | 25 | 30 | 45 | 70 | 110 | 180 | 300 | 600 | 600 |
| 1865S | 41,000 | 30 | 40 | 60 | 140 | 225 | 450 | 1,250 | 2,000 | |

## Variety 4 – Motto Above Eagle (1866–1873)

| | Mintage | G-4 | VG-8 | F-12 | VF-20 | EF-40 | AU-50 | MS-60 | MS-63 | PF-63 |
|---|---|---|---|---|---|---|---|---|---|---|
| 1866 | (725) 16,800 | $150 | $200 | $225 | $350 | $550 | $700 | $850 | $1,200 | $450 |
| 1866S | 28,000 | 75 | 110 | 200 | 350 | 500 | 900 | 1,600 | 2,500 | |

| | Mintage | G-4 | VG-8 | F-12 | VF-20 | EF-40 | AU-50 | MS-60 | MS-63 | PF-63 |
|---|---|---|---|---|---|---|---|---|---|---|
| 1867 . . . . . . . .(625) . . . .20,000 | | $80 | $100 | $175 | $210 | $260 | $450 | $750 | $1,100 | $450 |
| 1867S . . . . . . . . . . . . . .48,000 | | 85 | 120 | 170 | 300 | 900 | 2,250 | 5,500 | — | |
| 1868 . . . . . . . .(600) . . . .29,400 | | 40 | 60 | 80 | 100 | 125 | 210 | 400 | 700 | 450 |
| 1868S . . . . . . . . . . . . . .96,000 | | 30 | 40 | 50 | 90 | 200 | 350 | 1,100 | 2,800 | |
| 1869 . . . . . . . .(600) . . . .16,000 | | 90 | 110 | 170 | 200 | 275 | 400 | 600 | 1,100 | 450 |
| 1869S . . . . . . . . . . . . . .76,000 | | 30 | 45 | 80 | 125 | 235 | 450 | 1,000 | 2,100 | |
| 1870 . . . . . . . .(1,000) . . . .86,400 | | 20 | 25 | 40 | 60 | 90 | 175 | 400 | 500 | 450 |
| 1870CC . . . . . . . . . . . . . .8,340 | | 3,000 | 4,500 | 6,000 | 8,500 | 13,000 | 22,000 | — | | |
| 1871 . . . . . . . .(960) . . .118,200 | | 11 | 16 | 22 | 40 | 60 | 125 | 225 | 425 | 450 |
| 1871CC . . . . . . . . . . . . . .10,890 | | 750 | 1,500 | 2,400 | 6,500 | 10,000 | 17,500 | — | — | |
| 1871S . . . . . . . . . . . . . .30,900 | | 100 | 150 | 200 | 320 | 500 | 1,200 | 1,800 | 3,000 | |
| 1872 . . . . . . . .(950) . . .182,000 | | 11 | 16 | 22 | 40 | 60 | 100 | 300 | 700 | 450 |
| 1872CC . . . . . . . . . . . . . .22,850 | | 250 | 500 | 750 | 1,300 | 2,750 | 4,500 | 17,000 | | |
| 1872S . . . . . . . . . . . . . .83,000 | | 235 | 450 | 650 | 1,000 | 1,800 | 2,500 | 4,250 | | |
| 1873 . . . . . . . .(650) . . .212,600 | | 11 | 16 | 22 | 35 | 50 | 90 | 200 | 425 | 450 |
| 1873CC . . . . . . . . . . . . . .4,000 | | | | | — | 40,000 | — | — | | |

## Variety 5 – Arrows at Date (1873–1874)

| | Mintage | G-4 | VG-8 | F-12 | VF-20 | EF-40 | AU-50 | MS-60 | MS-63 | PF-63 |
|---|---|---|---|---|---|---|---|---|---|---|
| 1873 . . . . . . . .(540) . . .1,271,160 | | $10 | $11 | $16 | $35 | $90 | $175 | $425 | $700 | $800 |
| 1873CC . . . . . . . . . . . . . .12,462 | | 900 | 1,500 | 4,000 | 6,500 | 9,000 | 12,000 | 25,000 | 40,000 | |
| 1873S . . . . . . . . . . . . . .156,000 | | 11 | 14 | 23 | 45 | 110 | 200 | 600 | 1,000 | |
| 1874 . . . . . . . .(700) . . . .471,200 | | 10 | 11 | 16 | 35 | 90 | 175 | 450 | 750 | 800 |
| 1874S . . . . . . . . . . . . . .392,000 | | 11 | 13 | 20 | 45 | 110 | 175 | 450 | 750 | |

## Variety 4 Resumed, With Weight Standard of Variety 5 (1875–1891)

1877-S, S Over Horizontal S

| | Mintage | G-4 | VG-8 | F-12 | VF-20 | EF-40 | AU-50 | MS-60 | MS-63 | PF-63 |
|---|---|---|---|---|---|---|---|---|---|---|
| 1875 . . . . . . . .(700) . . .4,292,800 | | $9 | $11 | $14 | $18 | $25 | $60 | $125 | $200 | $400 |
| 1875CC . . . . . . . . . . . . . .140,000 | | 25 | 35 | 65 | 125 | 200 | 300 | 800 | 2,000 | |
| 1875S . . . . . . . . . . . . . .680,000 | | 10 | 16 | 23 | 35 | 70 | 125 | 275 | 500 | |
| 1876 . . . . . .(1,150) . .17,816,000 | | 9 | 11 | 14 | 19 | 25 | 60 | 125 | 200 | 400 |
| 1876CC . . . . . . . . . . . . . .4,944,000 | | 16 | 24 | 28 | 30 | 40 | 80 | 200 | 400 | |
| 1876S . . . . . . . . . . . . . .8,596,000 | | 9 | 11 | 14 | 18 | 25 | 60 | 125 | 200 | |
| 1877 . . . . . . . .(510) . .10,911,200 | | 9 | 11 | 14 | 18 | 25 | 60 | 125 | 200 | 400 |
| 1877CC . . . . . . . . . . . . .4,192,000 | | 15 | 22 | 24 | 30 | 40 | 80 | 200 | 350 | |
| 1877S . . . . . . . . . . . . . .8,996,000 | | 9 | 11 | 14 | 19 | 25 | 60 | 125 | 200 | |

*Chart continued on next page.*

| | Mintage | G-4 | VG-8 | F-12 | VF-20 | EF-40 | AU-50 | MS-60 | MS-63 | PF-63 |
|---|---|---|---|---|---|---|---|---|---|---|
| 1877S, S Over Horizontal S .....* | | $12 | $16 | $35 | $50 | $90 | $125 | $300 | $650 | |
| 1878 .......(800) ...2,260,000 | | 9 | 11 | 14 | 19 | 25 | 60 | 125 | 200 | $400 |
| 1878CC ............996,000 | | 11 | 16 | 20 | 30 | 55 | 95 | 250 | 400 | |
| 1878S ............140,000 | | 50 | 100 | 125 | 175 | 300 | 450 | 750 | 1,300 | |
| 1879 .....(1,100) .....13,600 | | 40 | 50 | 75 | 80 | 100 | 135 | 200 | 375 | 400 |
| 1880 .....(1,355) .....13,600 | | 40 | 50 | 75 | 80 | 100 | 135 | 200 | 375 | 400 |
| 1881 .......(975) .....12,000 | | 50 | 65 | 85 | 100 | 120 | 190 | 225 | 400 | 450 |
| 1882 .....(1,100) .....15,200 | | 45 | 50 | 80 | 100 | 110 | 150 | 275 | 375 | 400 |
| 1883 .....(1,039) .....14,400 | | 45 | 50 | 80 | 100 | 110 | 150 | 275 | 375 | 400 |
| 1884 .......(875) .....8,000 | | 90 | 100 | 120 | 125 | 150 | 200 | 350 | 450 | 400 |
| 1885 .......(930) .....13,600 | | 40 | 50 | 75 | 100 | 110 | 200 | 300 | 400 | 400 |
| 1886 .......(886) .....5,000 | | 95 | 110 | 150 | 175 | 275 | 375 | 475 | 500 | 450 |
| 1887 .......(710) .....10,000 | | 80 | 90 | 100 | 125 | 175 | 200 | 300 | 400 | 400 |
| 1888 .......(832) .....10,001 | | 70 | 80 | 90 | 135 | 200 | 225 | 300 | 375 | 400 |
| 1888S ............1,216,000 | | 9 | 11 | 14 | 18 | 25 | 65 | 150 | 275 | |
| 1889 .......(711) .....12,000 | | 50 | 60 | 90 | 110 | 120 | 200 | 300 | 400 | 400 |
| 1890 .......(590) ....80,000 | | 20 | 25 | 35 | 50 | 80 | 125 | 275 | 375 | 400 |
| 1891 ........(600) ...3,920,000 | | 8 | 9 | 11 | 15 | 22 | 65 | 150 | 250 | 400 |
| 18910 ............68,000 | | 50 | 65 | 110 | 325 | 475 | 600 | 1,600 | 2,200 | |
| 1891S ............2,216,000 | | 9 | 11 | 14 | 18 | 25 | 65 | 150 | 250 | |

* Included in 1877S regular mintage (previous page).

# BARBER OR LIBERTY HEAD (1892–1916)

Like other silver coins of this type, the quarter dollars minted from 1892 to 1916 were designed by Charles E. Barber. His initial B is found at the truncation of the neck of Miss Liberty.

**G-4 Good:** Date and legends legible. LIBERTY worn off headband.
**VG-8 Very Good:** Some letters in LIBERTY legible.
**F-12 Fine:** LIBERTY completely legible but not sharp.
**VF-20 Very Fine:** All letters in LIBERTY evenly plain.
**EF-40 Extremely Fine:** LIBERTY bold, its ribbon distinct.
**AU-50 About Uncirculated:** Slight trace of wear above forehead, on cheek, and on eagle's head, wings, and tail.
**MS-60 Uncirculated:** No trace of wear. Light blemishes.
**MS-63 Choice Uncirculated:** Some distracting marks or blemishes in focal areas. Impaired luster possible.

**PF-63 Choice Proof:** Reflective surfaces with only a few blemishes in secondary focal places. No major flaws.

| | Mintage | G-4 | VG-8 | F-12 | VF-20 | EF-40 | AU-50 | MS-60 | MS-63 | PF-63 |
|---|---|---|---|---|---|---|---|---|---|---|
| 1892 .....(1,245) ...8,236,000 | | $6 | $7.00 | $10 | $15 | $30 | $50 | $115 | $175 | $350 |
| 18920 ............2,460,000 | | 7 | 8.00 | 11 | 18 | 35 | 60 | 160 | 210 | |
| 1892S ............964,079 | | 10 | 18.00 | 30 | 50 | 85 | 130 | 210 | 450 | |
| 1893 .......(792) ...5,444,023 | | 6 | 6.25 | 10 | 15 | 30 | 50 | 115 | 165 | 350 |
| 18930 ............3,396,000 | | 6 | 6.25 | 10 | 15 | 35 | 60 | 160 | 220 | |
| 1893S ............1,454,535 | | 7 | 10.00 | 20 | 40 | 70 | 130 | 200 | 500 | |
| 1894 .......(972) ...3,432,000 | | 6 | 6.25 | 10 | 15 | 30 | 60 | 110 | 200 | 350 |
| 18940 ............2,852,000 | | 6 | 6.25 | 10 | 20 | 35 | 90 | 160 | 300 | |
| 1894S ............2,648,821 | | 6 | 6.25 | 11 | 20 | 35 | 90 | 160 | 300 | |
| 1895 .......(880) ...4,440,000 | | 6 | 6.25 | 10 | 15 | 30 | 60 | 110 | 200 | 350 |
| 18950 ............2,816,000 | | 6 | 7.00 | 15 | 27 | 45 | 90 | 185 | 400 | |
| 1895S ............1,764,681 | | 7 | 8.50 | 25 | 50 | 65 | 120 | 225 | 450 | |
| 1896 .......(762) ...3,874,000 | | 6 | 6.25 | 10 | 15 | 32 | 60 | 125 | 200 | 350 |
| 18960 ............1,484,000 | | 10 | 20.00 | 55 | 115 | 170 | 300 | 450 | 850 | |

# QUARTER DOLLARS

| | Mintage | G-4 | VG-8 | F-12 | VF-20 | EF-40 | AU-50 | MS-60 | MS-63 | PF-63 |
|---|---|---|---|---|---|---|---|---|---|---|
| 1896S | 188,039 | $400.00 | $700.00 | $900.00 | $1,500 | $2,000 | $2,900 | $4,000 | $8,250 | |
| 1897 | (731) . .8,140,000 | 6.00 | 6.25 | 10.00 | 15 | 32 | 55 | 100 | 175 | $350 |
| 1897O | 1,414,800 | 7.00 | 12.00 | 40.00 | 100 | 130 | 275 | 425 | 750 | |
| 1897S | 542,229 | 20.00 | 40.00 | 95.00 | 120 | 150 | 275 | 425 | 750 | |
| 1898 | (735) . .11,100,000 | 6.00 | 6.25 | 10.00 | 15 | 35 | 55 | 95 | 150 | 350 |
| 1898O | 1,868,000 | 7.00 | 9.00 | 22.00 | 55 | 110 | 150 | 300 | 650 | |
| 1898S | 1,020,592 | 6.50 | 8.00 | 15.00 | 20 | 35 | 90 | 200 | 600 | |
| 1899 | (846) . .12,624,000 | 6.00 | 6.25 | 10.00 | 15 | 30 | 50 | 90 | 150 | 350 |
| 1899O | 2,644,000 | 6.50 | 7.00 | 10.00 | 16 | 32 | 100 | 200 | 400 | |
| 1899S | 708,000 | 7.00 | 12.00 | 18.00 | 35 | 45 | 125 | 225 | 550 | |
| 1900 | (912) . .10,016,000 | 6.00 | 6.25 | 10.00 | 15 | 30 | 60 | 90 | 150 | 350 |
| 1900O | 3,416,000 | 6.50 | 9.00 | 20.00 | 30 | 50 | 150 | 250 | 400 | |
| 1900S | 1,858,585 | 6.00 | 6.50 | 11.00 | 16 | 30 | 50 | 175 | 450 | |
| 1901 | (813) . .8,892,000 | 6.00 | 6.50 | 9.00 | 15 | 30 | 60 | 100 | 150 | 350 |
| 1901O | 1,612,000 | 18.00 | 25.00 | 60.00 | 110 | 175 | 250 | 400 | 900 | |
| 1901S | 72,664 | 2,800.00 | 6,000.00 | 8,000.00 | 10,000 | 14,000 | 16,000 | 19,000 | 25,000 | |
| 1902 | (777) . .12,196,967 | 6.00 | 6.25 | 8.00 | 15 | 30 | 50 | 95 | 150 | 350 |
| 1902O | 4,748,000 | 6.00 | 6.50 | 15.00 | 30 | 60 | 100 | 200 | 625 | |
| 1902S | 1,524,612 | 6.75 | 8.00 | 20.00 | 35 | 65 | 110 | 220 | 475 | |
| 1903 | (755) . .9,759,309 | 6.00 | 6.25 | 8.00 | 15 | 30 | 50 | 90 | 175 | 350 |
| 1903O | 3,500,000 | 6.00 | 6.50 | 11.00 | 20 | 32 | 100 | 150 | 600 | |
| 1903S | 1,036,000 | 6.50 | 7.50 | 14.00 | 25 | 45 | 100 | 210 | 400 | |
| 1904 | (670) . .9,588,143 | 6.00 | 6.25 | 8.00 | 15 | 30 | 55 | 90 | 150 | 350 |
| 1904O | 2,456,000 | 6.00 | 6.50 | 16.00 | 30 | 90 | 175 | 350 | 600 | |
| 1905 | (727) . .4,967,523 | 6.00 | 6.25 | 8.50 | 15 | 30 | 60 | 100 | 200 | 350 |
| 1905O | 1,230,000 | 6.50 | 10.00 | 35.00 | 65 | 110 | 160 | 200 | 550 | |
| 1905S | 1,884,000 | 6.00 | 7.00 | 16.00 | 22 | 42 | 90 | 175 | 500 | |
| 1906 | (675) . .3,655,760 | 6.00 | 6.25 | 9.00 | 15 | 30 | 50 | 90 | 150 | 350 |
| 1906D | 3,280,000 | 6.00 | 6.25 | 9.00 | 15 | 30 | 60 | 110 | 200 | |
| 1906O | 2,056,000 | 6.00 | 6.25 | 12.00 | 18 | 35 | 90 | 135 | 250 | |
| 1907 | (575) . .7,132,000 | 6.00 | 6.25 | 8.00 | 15 | 30 | 50 | 90 | 175 | 350 |
| 1907D | 2,484,000 | 6.00 | 6.25 | 9.00 | 15 | 30 | 60 | 125 | 350 | |
| 1907O | 4,560,000 | 6.00 | 6.25 | 8.00 | 15 | 30 | 55 | 100 | 250 | |
| 1907S | 1,360,000 | 6.50 | 7.50 | 16.00 | 26 | 55 | 110 | 225 | 420 | |
| 1908 | (545) . .4,232,000 | 6.00 | 6.25 | 8.00 | 15 | 30 | 50 | 110 | 200 | 350 |
| 1908D | 5,788,000 | 6.00 | 6.25 | 8.00 | 15 | 30 | 50 | 110 | 200 | |
| 1908O | 6,244,000 | 6.00 | 6.25 | 8.00 | 15 | 30 | 50 | 110 | 200 | |
| 1908S | 784,000 | 7.00 | 14.00 | 35.00 | 70 | 150 | 200 | 350 | 550 | |
| 1909 | (650) . .9,268,000 | 6.00 | 6.25 | 8.00 | 15 | 30 | 50 | 90 | 175 | 350 |
| 1909D | 5,114,000 | 6.00 | 6.25 | 8.00 | 15 | 30 | 60 | 110 | 160 | |
| 1909O | 712,000 | 8.00 | 17.00 | 35.00 | 95 | 140 | 275 | 400 | 850 | |
| 1909S | 1,348,000 | 6.00 | 6.25 | 13.00 | 19 | 40 | 90 | 150 | 350 | |
| 1910 | (551) . .2,244,000 | 6.00 | 6.25 | 8.00 | 15 | 30 | 60 | 90 | 150 | 350 |
| 1910D | 1,500,000 | 6.00 | 6.25 | 15.00 | 18 | 30 | 110 | 175 | 400 | |
| 1911 | (543) . .3,720,000 | 6.00 | 6.25 | 8.00 | 15 | 30 | 50 | 90 | 150 | 350 |
| 1911D | 933,600 | 6.00 | 6.25 | 30.00 | 90 | 130 | 225 | 325 | 600 | |
| 1911S | 988,000 | 6.00 | 6.25 | 18.00 | 30 | 60 | 120 | 175 | 350 | |
| 1912 | (700) . .4,400,000 | 6.00 | 6.25 | 8.00 | 15 | 30 | 50 | 90 | 150 | 375 |
| 1912S | 708,000 | 6.00 | 7.50 | 15.00 | 18 | 35 | 100 | 175 | 400 | |
| 1913 | (613) . .484,000 | 7.00 | 9.00 | 25.00 | 67 | 185 | 210 | 550 | 600 | 400 |
| 1913D | 1,450,800 | 6.00 | 7.00 | 11.00 | 17 | 35 | 75 | 140 | 185 | |
| 1913S | 40,000 | 750.00 | 1,000.00 | 2,100.00 | 3,000 | 4,400 | 5,000 | 6,000 | 8,500 | |

*Chart continued on next page.*

| | Mintage | G-4 | VG-8 | F-12 | VF-20 | EF-40 | AU-50 | MS-60 | MS-63 | PF-63 |
|---|---|---|---|---|---|---|---|---|---|---|
| 1914 . . . . . . . .(380) . . .6,244,230 | | $6.00 | $6.25 | $8.00 | $15 | $30 | $50 | $90 | $150 | $400 |
| 1914D . . . . . . . . . . . . . .3,046,000 | | 6.00 | 6.25 | 8.00 | 15 | 30 | 50 | 90 | 150 | |
| 1914S . . . . . . . . . . . . . . .264,000 | | 30.00 | 40.00 | 85.00 | 125 | 200 | 300 | 450 | 675 | |
| 1915 . . . . . . . .(450) . . .3,480,000 | | 6.00 | 6.25 | 8.00 | 15 | 30 | 50 | 90 | 150 | 400 |
| 1915D . . . . . . . . . . . . . .3,694,000 | | 6.00 | 6.25 | 8.00 | 15 | 30 | 50 | 90 | 150 | |
| 1915S . . . . . . . . . . . . . . .704,000 | | 6.00 | 6.25 | 9.00 | 16 | 30 | 90 | 125 | 200 | |
| 1916 . . . . . . . . . . . . . . .1,788,000 | | 6.00 | 6.25 | 8.00 | 15 | 30 | 50 | 90 | 150 | |
| 1916D . . . . . . . . . . . . .6,540,800 | | 6.00 | 6.25 | 8.00 | 15 | 30 | 50 | 90 | 150 | |

## STANDING LIBERTY (1916–1930)

This design is by Hermon A. MacNeil, whose initial M is above and to the right of the date. Liberty bears a shield of protection in her left arm, while the right hand holds the olive branch of peace. There was a modification in 1917. The reverse had a new arrangement of stars and the eagle was higher. After 1924 the date was "recessed," thereby giving it greater protection from the effects of circulation.

**G-4 Good:** Date and lettering legible. Top of date worn. Liberty's right leg and toes worn off. Much wear evident on left leg and drapery lines.
**VG-8 Very Good:** Distinct date. Toes faintly visible. Drapery lines visible above Liberty's left leg.
**F-12 Fine:** High curve of right leg flat from thigh to ankle. Only slight wear evident on left leg. Drapery lines over right thigh seen only at sides of leg.
**VF-20 Very Fine:** Garment line across right leg worn, but visible at sides.
**EF-40 Extremely Fine:** Flattened only at high spots. Liberty's toes are sharp. Drapery lines across right leg evident.
**AU-50 About Uncirculated:** Slight trace of wear on head, kneecap, shield's center, and highest point on eagle's body.
**MS-60 Uncirculated:** No trace of wear, but contact marks, surface spots, or faded luster possible.
**MS-63 Choice Uncirculated:** No trace of wear. Light blemishes. Attractive mint luster.

### Variety 1 – No Stars Below Eagle (1916–1917)

*Mintmark location is on obverse, to left of date.*

| | Mintage | G-4 | VG-8 | F-12 | VF-20 | EF-40 | AU-50 | MS-60 | MS-63 |
|---|---|---|---|---|---|---|---|---|---|
| 1916 . . . . . . . . . . . . . . .52,000 | | $1,600 | $2,000 | $3,600 | $4,750 | $5,750 | $6,000 | $7,000 | $9,500 |
| 1917, Variety 1 . . . . .8,740,000 | | 13 | 18 | 26 | 35 | 55 | 100 | 140 | 180 |
| 1917D, Variety 1 . . . .1,509,200 | | 15 | 19 | 28 | 40 | 65 | 110 | 150 | 200 |
| 1917S, Variety 1 . . . .1,952,000 | | 16 | 22 | 30 | 45 | 80 | 125 | 170 | 250 |

### Variety 2 – Stars Below Eagle (1917–1930)
#### *Pedestal Date (1917–1924)*

**1918-S, 8 Over 7**

| | Mintage | G-4 | VG-8 | F-12 | VF-20 | EF-40 | AU-50 | MS-60 | MS-63 |
|---|---|---|---|---|---|---|---|---|---|
| 1917, Variety 2 | 13,880,000 | $11 | $13 | $16 | $18 | $27 | $55 | $100 | $140 |
| 1917D, Variety 2 | 6,224,400 | 18 | 22 | 32 | 40 | 60 | 85 | 125 | 175 |
| 1917S, Variety 2 | 5,552,000 | 18 | 22 | 32 | 40 | 65 | 90 | 125 | 175 |
| 1918 | 14,240,000 | 8 | 9 | 15 | 17 | 25 | 50 | 100 | 145 |
| 1918D | 7,380,000 | 13 | 16 | 26 | 34 | 50 | 85 | 125 | 200 |
| 1918S, Normal Date | 11,072,000 | 9 | 11 | 17 | 20 | 30 | 50 | 120 | 175 |
| 1918S, 8 Over 7 | * | 825 | 1,000 | 1,650 | 2,500 | 3,500 | 7,000 | 10,000 | 21,000 |
| 1919 | 11,324,000 | 18 | 22 | 27 | 35 | 40 | 60 | 100 | 125 |
| 1919D | 1,944,000 | 50 | 70 | 100 | 150 | 225 | 300 | 375 | 800 |
| 1919S | 1,836,000 | 50 | 70 | 100 | 150 | 275 | 325 | 400 | 900 |
| 1920 | 27,860,000 | 8 | 10 | 15 | 20 | 25 | 40 | 100 | 125 |
| 1920D | 3,586,400 | 25 | 30 | 40 | 45 | 65 | 100 | 125 | 450 |
| 1920S | 6,380,000 | 9 | 12 | 16 | 20 | 30 | 50 | 110 | 400 |
| 1921 | 1,916,000 | 85 | 110 | 160 | 200 | 275 | 425 | 625 | 900 |
| 1923 | 9,716,000 | 8 | 10 | 15 | 17 | 20 | 40 | 100 | 150 |
| 1923S | 1,360,000 | 150 | 200 | 240 | 425 | 600 | 800 | 1,000 | 1,700 |
| 1924 | 10,920,000 | 8 | 10 | 12 | 15 | 20 | 50 | 100 | 150 |
| 1924D | 3,112,000 | 25 | 35 | 50 | 65 | 100 | 125 | 150 | 175 |
| 1924S | 2,860,000 | 12 | 15 | 20 | 25 | 60 | 125 | 150 | 500 |

* Included in number above.

### Recessed Date (1925–1930)

| | Mintage | G-4 | VG-8 | F-12 | VF-20 | EF-40 | AU-50 | MS-60 | MS-63 |
|---|---|---|---|---|---|---|---|---|---|
| 1925 | 12,280,000 | $5.50 | $5.75 | $6 | $7 | $16 | $35 | $70 | $140 |
| 1926 | 11,316,000 | 5.50 | 5.75 | 6 | 7 | 16 | 35 | 70 | 140 |
| 1926D | 1,716,000 | 5.50 | 6.00 | 8 | 16 | 27 | 55 | 100 | 170 |
| 1926S | 2,700,000 | 5.50 | 5.75 | 7 | 11 | 50 | 125 | 200 | 400 |
| 1927 | 11,912,000 | 5.50 | 5.75 | 6 | 7 | 16 | 35 | 70 | 140 |
| 1927D | 976,000 | 7.50 | 12.00 | 20 | 35 | 70 | 95 | 160 | 200 |
| 1927S | 396,000 | 16.00 | 21.00 | 50 | 175 | 640 | 1,600 | 2,500 | 4,200 |
| 1928 | 6,336,000 | 5.50 | 5.75 | 6 | 7 | 16 | 35 | 70 | 135 |
| 1928D | 1,627,600 | 5.50 | 5.75 | 6 | 7 | 16 | 35 | 70 | 135 |
| 1928S | 2,644,000 | 5.50 | 5.75 | 6 | 7 | 16 | 35 | 70 | 140 |
| 1929 | 11,140,000 | 5.50 | 5.75 | 6 | 7 | 16 | 35 | 70 | 140 |
| 1929D | 1,358,000 | 5.50 | 5.75 | 6 | 7 | 16 | 35 | 70 | 140 |
| 1929S | 1,764,000 | 5.50 | 5.75 | 6 | 7 | 16 | 35 | 70 | 140 |
| 1930 | 5,632,000 | 5.50 | 5.75 | 6 | 7 | 16 | 35 | 70 | 135 |
| 1930S | 1,556,000 | 5.50 | 5.75 | 6 | 7 | 16 | 35 | 70 | 135 |

## WASHINGTON (1932 TO DATE)

This type was intended to be a commemorative issue marking the 200th anniversary of President Washington's birth. John Flanagan, a New York sculptor, was the designer. The initials JF are found at the base of the neck. The mintmark is on the reverse below the wreath for coins from 1932 to 1964. Starting in 1968, the mintmark was moved to the obverse at the right of the ribbon.

**F-12 Fine:** Hair lines about Washington's ear visible. Tiny feathers on eagle's breast faintly visible.
**VF-20 Very Fine:** Most hair details visible. Wing feathers clear.
**EF-40 Extremely Fine:** Hair lines sharp. Wear spots confined to top of eagle's legs and center of breast.
**MS-60 Uncirculated:** No trace of wear, but many contact marks, surface spotting, or faded luster possible.
**MS-63 Choice Uncirculated:** No trace of wear. Light blemishes. Attractive mint luster.
**MS-64 Uncirculated:** A few scattered contact marks. Good eye appeal and attractive luster.
**MS-65 Gem Uncirculated:** Only light, scattered, non-distracting marks. Strong luster, good eye appeal.
**PF-65 Gem Proof:** Hardly any blemishes, and no flaws.

## Silver Coinage (1932–1964)

| | Mintage | VG-8 | F-12 | VF-20 | EF-40 | MS-60 | MS-63 | MS-65 | PF-65 |
|---|---|---|---|---|---|---|---|---|---|
| 1932 | 5,404,000 | $5.50 | $5.50 | $6.00 | $7.00 | $13 | $23 | $200 | |
| 1932D | 436,800 | 75.00 | 90.00 | 120.00 | 175.00 | 525 | 1,200 | 7,500 | |
| 1932S | 408,000 | 75.00 | 90.00 | 100.00 | 130.00 | 275 | 500 | 2,300 | |
| 1934 | 31,912,052 | 5.00 | 5.00 | 5.00 | 5.50 | 9 | 17 | 45 | |
| 1934D | 3,527,200 | 5.00 | 5.00 | 6.00 | 12.00 | 100 | 175 | 650 | |
| 1935 | 32,484,000 | 5.00 | 5.00 | 5.00 | 5.50 | 9 | 15 | 45 | |
| 1935D | 5,780,000 | 5.00 | 5.00 | 5.50 | 8.00 | 100 | 140 | 450 | |
| 1935S | 5,660,000 | 5.00 | 5.00 | 5.00 | 6.50 | 40 | 60 | 140 | |
| 1936 ....(3,837) | 41,300,000 | 5.00 | 5.00 | 5.00 | 5.50 | 8 | 16 | 40 | $850 |
| 1936D | 5,374,000 | 5.00 | 5.00 | 5.00 | 20.00 | 180 | 350 | 725 | |
| 1936S | 3,828,000 | 5.00 | 5.00 | 5.00 | 6.00 | 40 | 75 | 200 | |
| 1937 ....(5,542) | 19,696,000 | 5.00 | 5.00 | 5.00 | 5.50 | 8 | 15 | 48 | 315 |
| 1937D | 7,189,600 | 5.00 | 5.00 | 5.00 | 6.00 | 25 | 45 | 70 | |
| 1937S | 1,652,000 | 5.00 | 5.00 | 6.00 | 15.00 | 70 | 100 | 150 | |
| 1938 ....(8,045) | 9,472,000 | 5.00 | 5.00 | 5.00 | 6.00 | 30 | 50 | 120 | 200 |
| 1938S | 2,832,000 | 5.00 | 5.00 | 5.00 | 6.50 | 35 | 60 | 125 | |
| 1939 ....(8,795) | 33,540,000 | 5.00 | 5.00 | 5.00 | 5.50 | 6 | 12 | 25 | 150 |
| 1939D | 7,092,000 | 5.00 | 5.00 | 5.00 | 5.50 | 14 | 20 | 50 | |
| 1939S | 2,628,000 | 5.00 | 5.00 | 5.00 | 7.00 | 45 | 65 | 150 | |

| | Mintage | F-12 | VF-20 | EF-40 | MS-60 | MS-63 | MS-65 | PF-65 |
|---|---|---|---|---|---|---|---|---|
| 1940 ........(11,246) | 35,704,000 | $5 | $5 | $5.00 | $7.00 | $12 | $30 | $125 |
| 1940D | 2,797,600 | 5 | 5 | 7.50 | 50.00 | 80 | 140 | |
| 1940S | 8,244,000 | 5 | 5 | 5.00 | 8.00 | 13 | 25 | |
| 1941 ........(15,287) | 79,032,000 | 5 | 5 | 5.00 | 5.50 | 7 | 20 | 100 |
| 1941D | 16,714,800 | 5 | 5 | 6.00 | 12.00 | 22 | 25 | |
| 1941S | 16,080,000 | 5 | 5 | 5.00 | 8.00 | 18 | 25 | |
| 1942 ........(21,123) | 102,096,000 | 5 | 5 | 5.00 | 5.50 | 7 | 10 | 90 |
| 1942D | 17,487,200 | 5 | 5 | 5.00 | 7.00 | 12 | 20 | |
| 1942S | 19,384,000 | 5 | 5 | 6.00 | 27.00 | 45 | 90 | |
| 1943 | 99,700,000 | 5 | 5 | 5.00 | 5.50 | 7 | 20 | |
| 1943D | 16,095,600 | 5 | 5 | 5.00 | 9.00 | 16 | 20 | |
| 1943S | 21,700,000 | 5 | 5 | 5.00 | 9.50 | 19 | 25 | |
| 1944 | 104,956,000 | 5 | 5 | 5.00 | 5.50 | 7 | 18 | |
| 1944D | 14,600,800 | 5 | 5 | 5.00 | 6.00 | 10 | 18 | |
| 1944S | 12,560,000 | 5 | 5 | 5.00 | 7.00 | 12 | 18 | |
| 1945 | 74,372,000 | 5 | 5 | 5.00 | 5.50 | 7 | 18 | |
| 1945D | 12,341,600 | 5 | 5 | 5.00 | 7.00 | 12 | 20 | |
| 1945S | 17,004,001 | 5 | 5 | 5.00 | 6.00 | 7 | 15 | |
| 1946 | 53,436,000 | 5 | 5 | 5.00 | 5.50 | 7 | 16 | |
| 1946D | 9,072,800 | 5 | 5 | 5.00 | 5.50 | 7 | 15 | |
| 1946S | 4,204,000 | 5 | 5 | 5.00 | 5.50 | 7 | 16 | |
| 1947 | 22,556,000 | 5 | 5 | 5.00 | 5.50 | 7 | 15 | |

| | Mintage | F-12 | VF-20 | EF-40 | MS-60 | MS-63 | MS-65 | PF-65 |
|---|---|---|---|---|---|---|---|---|
| 1947D | 15,338,400 | $5 | $5 | $5.00 | $5.50 | $7.00 | $15.00 | |
| 1947S | 5,532,000 | 5 | 5 | 5.00 | 5.50 | 7.00 | 15.00 | |
| 1948 | 35,196,000 | 5 | 5 | 5.00 | 5.50 | 6.00 | 15.00 | |
| 1948D | 16,766,800 | 5 | 5 | 5.00 | 5.50 | 6.50 | 30.00 | |
| 1948S | 15,960,000 | 5 | 5 | 5.00 | 5.50 | 6.50 | 18.00 | |
| 1949 | 9,312,000 | 5 | 5 | 6.00 | 10.00 | 18.00 | 30.00 | |
| 1949D | 10,068,400 | 5 | 5 | 5.00 | 7.50 | 11.00 | 22.00 | |
| 1950 | (51,386) . . .24,920,126 | 5 | 5 | 5.00 | 5.50 | 6.50 | 13.00 | $30.00 |
| 1950D | 21,075,600 | 5 | 5 | 5.00 | 5.50 | 6.50 | 13.00 | |
| 1950D, D Over S | * | | 25 | 75.00 | 125.00 | 175.00 | 500.00 | |
| 1950S | 10,284,004 | 5 | 5 | 6.00 | 6.50 | 7.00 | 25.00 | |
| 1950S, S Over D | * | | 25 | 80.00 | 140.00 | 200.00 | 400.00 | |
| 1951 | (57,500) . . .43,448,102 | 5 | 5 | 5.00 | 5.50 | 6.00 | 14.00 | 27.50 |
| 1951D | 35,354,800 | 5 | 5 | 5.00 | 5.50 | 6.00 | 14.00 | |
| 1951S | 9,048,000 | 5 | 5 | 6.00 | 6.50 | 12.00 | 18.00 | |
| 1952 | (81,980) . . .38,780,093 | 5 | 5 | 5.00 | 5.50 | 6.00 | 11.00 | 25.00 |
| 1952D | 49,795,200 | 5 | 5 | 5.00 | 5.50 | 6.00 | 16.00 | |
| 1952S | 13,707,800 | 5 | 5 | 5.50 | 6.50 | 10.00 | 16.00 | |
| 1953 | (128,800) . . .18,536,120 | 5 | 5 | 5.00 | 5.50 | 6.00 | 16.00 | 22.00 |
| 1953D | 56,112,400 | 5 | 5 | 5.00 | 5.50 | 6.00 | 15.00 | |
| 1953S | 14,016,000 | 5 | 5 | 5.00 | 5.50 | 6.00 | 12.00 | |
| 1954 | (233,300) . . .54,412,203 | 5 | 5 | 5.00 | 5.50 | 6.00 | 13.00 | 12.00 |
| 1954D | 42,305,500 | 5 | 5 | 5.00 | 5.50 | 6.00 | 17.00 | |
| 1954S | 11,834,722 | 5 | 5 | 5.00 | 5.50 | 6.00 | 15.00 | |
| 1955 | (378,200) . . .18,180,181 | 5 | 5 | 5.00 | 5.50 | 6.00 | 12.00 | 12.00 |
| 1955D | 3,182,400 | 5 | 5 | 5.00 | 5.50 | 6.00 | 22.00 | |
| 1956 | (669,384) . . .44,144,000 | 5 | 5 | 5.00 | 5.50 | 6.00 | 8.00 | 7.00 |
| 1956D | 32,334,500 | 5 | 5 | 5.00 | 5.50 | 6.00 | 11.00 | |
| 1957 | (1,247,952) . . .46,532,000 | 5 | 5 | 5.00 | 5.50 | 6.00 | 11.00 | 7.00 |
| 1957D | 77,924,160 | 5 | 5 | 5.00 | 5.50 | 6.00 | 10.00 | |
| 1958 | (875,652) . . . .6,360,000 | 5 | 5 | 5.00 | 5.50 | 6.00 | 9.00 | 7.00 |
| 1958D | 78,124,900 | 5 | 5 | 5.00 | 5.50 | 6.00 | 9.00 | |
| 1959 | (1,149,291) . . .24,384,000 | 5 | 5 | 5.00 | 5.50 | 6.00 | 9.00 | 6.50 |
| 1959D | 62,054,232 | 5 | 5 | 5.00 | 5.50 | 6.00 | 12.00 | |
| 1960 | (1,691,602) . . .29,164,000 | 5 | 5 | 5.00 | 5.00 | 6.00 | 6.50 | 6.00 |
| 1960D | 63,000,324 | 5 | 5 | 5.00 | 5.00 | 5.50 | 6.50 | |
| 1961 | (3,028,244) . . .37,036,000 | 5 | 5 | 5.00 | 5.00 | 5.50 | 6.50 | 6.00 |
| 1961D | 83,656,928 | 5 | 5 | 5.00 | 5.00 | 5.50 | 6.50 | |
| 1962 | (3,218,019) . . .36,156,000 | 5 | 5 | 5.00 | 5.00 | 5.50 | 6.50 | 6.00 |
| 1962D | 127,554,756 | 5 | 5 | 5.00 | 5.00 | 5.50 | 6.50 | |
| 1963 | (3,075,645) . . .74,316,000 | 5 | 5 | 5.00 | 5.00 | 5.50 | 6.50 | 6.00 |
| 1963D | 135,288,184 | 5 | 5 | 5.00 | 5.00 | 5.50 | 6.50 | |
| 1964 | (3,950,762) . .560,390,585 | 5 | 5 | 5.00 | 5.00 | 5.50 | 6.50 | 6.00 |
| 1964D | 704,135,528 | 5 | 5 | 5.00 | 5.00 | 5.50 | 6.50 | |

* Included in number above.

## Clad Coinage and Silver Proofs (1965 to Date)

| | Mintage | MS-63 | MS-65 | PF-65 | | Mintage | MS-63 | MS-65 | PF-65 |
|---|---|---|---|---|---|---|---|---|---|
| 1965 | 1,819,717,540 | $0.30 | $1.50 | | 1968D | 101,534,000 | $0.30 | $1.00 | |
| 1966 | 821,101,500 | 0.30 | 1.00 | | 1968S | (3,041,506) | | | $1.00 |
| 1967 | 1,524,031,848 | 0.30 | 1.00 | | 1969 | 176,212,000 | 0.75 | 1.50 | |
| 1968 | 220,731,500 | 0.50 | 1.50 | | 1969D | 114,372,000 | 0.50 | 2.50 | |

*Chart continued on next page.*

| | Mintage | MS-63 | MS-65 | PF-65 |
|---|---|---|---|---|
| 1969S | (2,934,631) | | | $1.00 |
| 1970 | 136,420,000 | $0.25 | $1.75 | |
| 1970D | 417,341,364 | 0.25 | 1.00 | |
| 1970S | (2,632,810) | | | 1.00 |
| 1971 | 109,284,000 | 0.30 | 1.00 | |
| 1971D | 258,634,428 | 0.30 | 0.50 | |
| 1971S | (3,220,733) | | | 1.00 |
| 1972 | 215,048,000 | 0.30 | 1.00 | |

| | Mintage | MS-63 | MS-65 | PF-65 |
|---|---|---|---|---|
| 1972D | 311,067,732 | $0.30 | $1.50 | |
| 1972S | (3,260,996) | | | $1.00 |
| 1973 | 346,924,000 | 0.30 | 1.50 | |
| 1973D | 232,977,400 | 0.30 | 1.50 | |
| 1973S | (2,760,339) | | | 1.00 |
| 1974 | 801,456,000 | 0.30 | 1.00 | |
| 1974D | 353,160,300 | 0.30 | 1.50 | |
| 1974S | (2,612,568) | | | 1.00 |

## Bicentennial (1776–1976)

| | Mintage | MS-63 | MS-65 | PF-65 |
|---|---|---|---|---|
| 1776–1976, Copper-Nickel Clad | 809,784,016 | $0.30 | $1.00 | |
| 1776–1976D, Copper-Nickel Clad | 860,118,839 | 0.30 | 1.00 | |
| 1776–1976S, Copper-Nickel Clad | (7,059,099) | | | $1.00 |
| 1776–1976S, Silver Clad | 11,000,000 | 1.40 | 2.00 | |
| 1776–1976S, Silver Clad | (4,000,000) | | | 2.00 |

Note: Mintage figures for 1976-S coins are approximate; many were melted in 1982.

## Eagle Reverse Resumed (1977–1998)
### (Dies Slightly Modified to Lower Relief)

| | Mintage | MS-63 | MS-65 | PF-65 |
|---|---|---|---|---|
| 1977 | 468,556,000 | $0.27 | | |
| 1977D | 256,524,978 | 0.27 | $1.00 | |
| 1977S | (3,251,152) | | | $1.00 |
| 1978 | 521,452,000 | 0.27 | 1.50 | |
| 1978D | 287,373,152 | 0.27 | 1.50 | |
| 1978S | (3,127,781) | | | 1.00 |
| 1979 | 515,708,000 | 0.28 | 1.50 | |
| 1979D | 489,789,780 | 0.27 | 1.25 | |
| 1979S | (3,677,175) | | | |
| Filled S | | | | 1.00 |
| Clear S | | | | 2.00 |
| 1980P | 635,832,000 | 0.27 | 1.50 | |
| 1980D | 518,327,487 | 0.27 | 1.25 | |
| 1980S | (3,554,806) | | | 1.00 |
| 1981P | 601,716,000 | 0.27 | 1.50 | |
| 1981D | 575,722,833 | 0.27 | 1.00 | |
| 1981S | (4,063,083) | | | 1.00 |
| 1982P | 500,931,000 | 1.00 | 9.00 | |
| 1982D | 480,042,788 | 0.70 | 7.00 | |
| 1982S | (3,857,479) | | | 1.00 |
| 1983P | 673,535,000 | 4.00 | 21.00 | |
| 1983D | 617,806,446 | 3.00 | 19.00 | |
| 1983S | (3,279,126) | | | 1.00 |

| | Mintage | MS-63 | MS-65 | PF-65 |
|---|---|---|---|---|
| 1984P | 676,545,000 | $0.30 | $2.00 | |
| 1984D | 546,483,064 | 0.30 | 2.00 | |
| 1984S | (3,065,110) | | | $1.00 |
| 1985P | 775,818,962 | 0.50 | 5.00 | |
| 1985D | 519,962,888 | 0.35 | 2.50 | |
| 1985S | (3,362,821) | | | 1.00 |
| 1986P | 551,199,333 | 1.00 | 4.00 | |
| 1986D | 504,298,660 | 3.00 | 9.00 | |
| 1986S | (3,010,497) | | | 1.00 |
| 1987P | 582,499,481 | 0.27 | 2.50 | |
| 1987D | 655,594,696 | 0.27 | 1.00 | |
| 1987S | (4,227,728) | | | 1.00 |
| 1988P | 562,052,000 | 0.50 | 4.00 | |
| 1988D | 596,810,688 | 0.50 | 4.00 | |
| 1988S | (3,262,948) | | | 1.00 |
| 1989P | 512,868,000 | 0.30 | 5.00 | |
| 1989D | 896,535,597 | 0.27 | 1.00 | |
| 1989S | (3,220,194) | | | 1.00 |
| 1990P | 613,792,000 | 0.27 | 4.00 | |
| 1990D | 927,638,181 | 0.28 | 4.00 | |
| 1990S | (3,299,559) | | | 1.75 |
| 1991P | 570,968,000 | 0.30 | 4.00 | |
| 1991D | 630,966,693 | 0.30 | 4.00 | |

| Mintage | MS-63 | MS-65 | PF-65 |
|---|---|---|---|
| 1991S . . . . . . . (2,867,787) | | | $1.25 |
| 1992P . . . . . . 384,764,000 | $0.35 | $5.00 | |
| 1992D . . . . . . 389,777,107 | 0.35 | 5.00 | |
| 1992S . . . . . . . (2,858,981) | | | 1.25 |
| 1992S, Silver . . . (1,317,579) | | | 6.00 |
| 1993P . . . . . . 639,276,000 | 0.30 | 2.00 | |
| 1993D . . . . . . 645,476,128 | 0.30 | 2.00 | |
| 1993S . . . . . . . (2,633,439) | | | 1.25 |
| 1993S, Silver . . . . (761,353) | | | 6.00 |
| 1994P . . . . . . 825,600,000 | 0.30 | 4.00 | |
| 1994D . . . . . . 880,034,110 | 0.30 | 4.00 | |
| 1994S . . . . . . . (2,484,594) | | | 1.00 |
| 1994S, Silver . . . . (785,329) | | | 6.00 |
| 1995P . . . . . 1,004,336,000 | 0.30 | 4.00 | |
| 1995D . . . . . 1,103,216,000 | 0.30 | 3.00 | |

| Mintage | MS-63 | MS-65 | PF-65 |
|---|---|---|---|
| 1995S . . . . . . . (2,117,496) | | | $4.00 |
| 1995S, Silver . . . . (679,985) | | | 6.00 |
| 1996P . . . . . . 925,040,000 | $0.25 | $3.00 | |
| 1996D . . . . . . 906,868,000 | 0.25 | 3.00 | |
| 1996S . . . . . . . (1,750,244) | | | 1.75 |
| 1996S, Silver . . . . (775,021) | | | 6.00 |
| 1997P . . . . . . 595,740,000 | 0.25 | 3.00 | |
| 1997D . . . . . . 599,680,000 | 0.25 | 3.00 | |
| 1997S . . . . . . . (2,055,000) | | | 3.00 |
| 1997S, Silver . . . . (741,678) | | | 6.00 |
| 1998P . . . . . . 896,268,000 | 0.25 | 1.00 | |
| 1998D . . . . . . 821,000,000 | 0.25 | 1.00 | |
| 1998S . . . . . . . (2,086,507) | | | 2.50 |
| 1998S, Silver . . . . (878,792) | | | 6.00 |

## State Quarters (1999–2008)

The United States Mint 50 State Quarters® Program, which began in 1999, produced a series of 50 quarter dollar coins with special designs honoring each state. Five different designs were issued each year during the period 1999 through 2008. States were commemorated in the order of their entrance into statehood.

These are all legal tender coins of standard weight and composition. The obverse side depicting President George Washington was modified to include some of the wording previously used on the reverse. The modification was authorized by special legislation, and carried out by Mint sculptor-engraver William Cousins, whose initials were added to the truncation of Washington's neck adjacent to those of the original designer, John Flanagan.

Each state theme was proposed, and the design approved, by the governor of the state. Final designs were created by Mint personnel.

Circulation coins are made at the Philadelphia and Denver mints. Proof coins are made in San Francisco. Both copper-nickel and silver Proof coins were made each year.

| Mintage | AU-50 | MS-63 | PF-65 |
|---|---|---|---|
| **Delaware** | | | |
| 1999P . . . . . . 373,400,000 | $0.25 | $0.50 | |
| 1999D . . . . . . 401,424,000 | 0.25 | 0.50 | |
| 1999S . . . . . . . (3,713,359) | | | $1.75 |
| 1999S, Silver . . (804,565) | | | 7.00 |
| **Pennsylvania** | | | |
| 1999P . . . . . . 349,000,000 | 0.25 | 0.50 | |
| 1999D . . . . . . 358,332,000 | 0.25 | 0.50 | |
| 1999S . . . . . . . (3,713,359) | | | 1.75 |
| 1999S, Silver . . (804,565) | | | 7.00 |

| Mintage | AU-50 | MS-63 | PF-65 |
|---|---|---|---|
| **New Jersey** | | | |
| 1999P . . . . . . 363,200,000 | $0.25 | $0.30 | |
| 1999D . . . . . . 299,028,000 | 0.25 | 0.35 | |
| 1999S . . . . . . . (3,713,359) | | | $1.75 |
| 1999S, Silver . . (804,565) | | | 7.00 |
| **Georgia** | | | |
| 1999P . . . . . . 451,188,000 | 0.25 | 0.30 | |
| 1999D . . . . . . 488,744,000 | 0.25 | 0.30 | |
| 1999S . . . . . . . (3,713,359) | | | 1.75 |
| 1999S, Silver . . (804,565) | | | 7.00 |

*Chart continued on next page.*

|  | Mintage | AU-50 | MS-63 | PF-65 |
|---|---|---|---|---|
| **Connecticut** | | | | |
| 1999P | 688,744,000 | $0.25 | $0.30 | |
| 1999D | 657,880,000 | 0.25 | 0.30 | |

|  | Mintage | AU-50 | MS-63 | PF-65 |
|---|---|---|---|---|
| **Connecticut** | | | | |
| 1999S | (3,713,359) | | | $1.75 |
| 1999S, Silver | (804,565) | | | 7.00 |

|  | Mintage | AU-50 | MS-63 | PF-65 |
|---|---|---|---|---|
| **Massachusetts** | | | | |
| 2000P | 628,600,000 | $0.25 | $0.30 | |
| 2000D | 535,184,000 | 0.25 | 0.30 | |
| 2000S | (4,020,172) | | | $1.50 |
| 2000S, Silver | (965,421) | | | 6.00 |
| **Maryland** | | | | |
| 2000P | 678,200,000 | 0.25 | 0.30 | |
| 2000D | 556,532,000 | 0.25 | 0.30 | |
| 2000S | (4,020,172) | | | 1.50 |
| 2000S, Silver | (965,421) | | | 6.00 |
| **South Carolina** | | | | |
| 2000P | 742,576,000 | 0.25 | 0.32 | |
| 2000D | 566,208,000 | 0.25 | 0.32 | |

|  | Mintage | AU-50 | MS-63 | PF-65 |
|---|---|---|---|---|
| **South Carolina** | | | | |
| 2000S | (4,020,172) | | | $1.50 |
| 2000S, Silver | (965,421) | | | 6.00 |
| **New Hampshire** | | | | |
| 2000P | 673,040,000 | $0.25 | $0.30 | |
| 2000D | 495,976,000 | 0.25 | 0.30 | |
| 2000S | (4,020,172) | | | 1.50 |
| 2000S, Silver | (965,421) | | | 6.00 |
| **Virginia** | | | | |
| 2000P | 943,000,000 | 0.25 | 0.30 | |
| 2000D | 651,616,000 | 0.25 | 0.30 | |
| 2000S | (4,020,172) | | | 1.50 |
| 2000S, Silver | (965,421) | | | 6.00 |

|  | Mintage | AU-50 | MS-63 | PF-65 |
|---|---|---|---|---|
| **New York** | | | | |
| 2001P | 655,400,000 | $0.25 | $0.30 | |
| 2001D | 619,640,000 | 0.25 | 0.30 | |
| 2001S | (3,094,140) | | | $1.50 |
| 2001S, Silver | (889,697) | | | 6.00 |
| **North Carolina** | | | | |
| 2001P | 627,600,000 | 0.25 | 0.30 | |
| 2001D | 427,876,000 | 0.25 | 0.30 | |
| 2001S | (3,094,140) | | | 1.50 |
| 2001S, Silver | (889,697) | | | 6.00 |
| **Rhode Island** | | | | |
| 2001P | 423,000,000 | 0.25 | 0.30 | |
| 2001D | 447,100,000 | 0.25 | 0.30 | |

|  | Mintage | AU-50 | MS-63 | PF-65 |
|---|---|---|---|---|
| **Rhode Island** | | | | |
| 2001S | (3,094,140) | | | $1.50 |
| 2001S, Silver | (889,697) | | | 6.00 |
| **Vermont** | | | | |
| 2001P | 423,400,000 | $0.25 | $0.30 | |
| 2001D | 459,404,000 | 0.25 | 0.30 | |
| 2001S | (3,094,140) | | | 1.50 |
| 2001S, Silver | (889,697) | | | 6.00 |
| **Kentucky** | | | | |
| 2001P | 353,000,000 | 0.25 | 0.30 | |
| 2001D | 370,564,000 | 0.25 | 0.30 | |
| 2001S | (3,094,140) | | | 1.50 |
| 2001S, Silver | (889,697) | | | 6.00 |

| | Mintage | AU-50 | MS-63 | PF-65 |
|---|---|---|---|---|
| **Tennessee** | | | | |
| 2002P ......361,600,000 | | $0.30 | $0.40 | |
| 2002D ......286,468,000 | | 0.30 | 0.40 | |
| 2002S .......(3,084,245) | | | | $1.50 |
| 2002S, Silver ...(892,229) | | | | 6.00 |
| **Ohio** | | | | |
| 2002P ......217,200,000 | | 0.25 | 0.30 | |
| 2002D ......414,832,000 | | 0.25 | 0.30 | |
| 2002S .......(3,084,245) | | | | 1.50 |
| 2002S, Silver ...(892,229) | | | | 6.00 |
| **Louisiana** | | | | |
| 2002P ......362,000,000 | | 0.25 | 0.30 | |
| 2002D ......402,204,000 | | 0.25 | 0.30 | |

| | Mintage | AU-50 | MS-63 | PF-65 |
|---|---|---|---|---|
| **Louisiana** | | | | |
| 2002S .......(3,084,245) | | | | $1.50 |
| 2002S, Silver ...(892,229) | | | | 6.00 |
| **Indiana** | | | | |
| 2002P ......362,600,000 | | $0.25 | $0.30 | |
| 2002D ......327,200,000 | | 0.25 | 0.30 | |
| 2002S .......(3,084,245) | | | | 1.50 |
| 2002S, Silver ...(892,229) | | | | 6.00 |
| **Mississippi** | | | | |
| 2002P ......290,000,000 | | 0.25 | 0.30 | |
| 2002D ......289,600,000 | | 0.25 | 0.30 | |
| 2002S .......(3,084,245) | | | | 1.50 |
| 2002S, Silver ...(892,229) | | | | 6.00 |

| | Mintage | AU-50 | MS-63 | PF-65 |
|---|---|---|---|---|
| **Illinois** | | | | |
| 2003P ......225,800,000 | | $0.25 | $0.30 | |
| 2003D ......237,400,000 | | 0.25 | 0.30 | |
| 2003S .......(3,408,516) | | | | $1.50 |
| 2003S, Silver ..(1,125,755) | | | | 6.00 |
| **Alabama** | | | | |
| 2003P ......225,000,000 | | 0.25 | 0.30 | |
| 2003D ......232,400,000 | | 0.25 | 0.30 | |
| 2003S .......(3,408,516) | | | | 1.50 |
| 2003S, Silver ..(1,125,755) | | | | 6.00 |
| **Maine** | | | | |
| 2003P ......217,400,000 | | 0.25 | 0.30 | |
| 2003D ......231,400,000 | | 0.25 | 0.30 | |

| | Mintage | AU-50 | MS-63 | PF-65 |
|---|---|---|---|---|
| **Maine** | | | | |
| 2003S .......(3,408,516) | | | | $1.50 |
| 2003S, Silver ..(1,125,755) | | | | 6.00 |
| **Missouri** | | | | |
| 2003P ......225,000,000 | | $0.25 | $0.30 | |
| 2003D ......228,200,000 | | 0.25 | 0.30 | |
| 2003S .......(3,408,516) | | | | 1.50 |
| 2003S, Silver ..(1,125,755) | | | | 6.00 |
| **Arkansas** | | | | |
| 2003P ......228,000,000 | | 0.25 | 0.30 | |
| 2003D ......229,800,000 | | 0.25 | 0.30 | |
| 2003S .......(3,408,516) | | | | 1.50 |
| 2003S, Silver ..(1,125,755) | | | | 6.00 |

| | Mintage | AU-50 | MS-63 | PF-65 |
|---|---|---|---|---|
| **Michigan** | | | | |
| 2004P | 233,800,000 | $0.25 | $0.30 | |
| 2004D | 225,800,000 | 0.25 | 0.30 | |
| 2004S | (2,740,684) | | | $1.50 |
| 2004S, Silver | (1,769,786) | | | 6.00 |
| **Florida** | | | | |
| 2004P | 240,200,000 | 0.25 | 0.30 | |
| 2004D | 241,600,000 | 0.25 | 0.30 | |
| 2004S | (2,740,684) | | | 1.50 |
| 2004S, Silver | (1,769,786) | | | 6.00 |
| **Texas** | | | | |
| 2004P | 278,800,000 | 0.25 | 0.30 | |
| 2004D | 263,000,000 | 0.25 | 0.30 | |

| | Mintage | AU-50 | MS-63 | PF-65 |
|---|---|---|---|---|
| **Texas** | | | | |
| 2004S | (2,740,684) | | | $1.50 |
| 2004S, Silver | (1,769,786) | | | 6.00 |
| **Iowa** | | | | |
| 2004P | 213,800,000 | $0.25 | $0.30 | |
| 2004D | 251,400,000 | 0.25 | 0.30 | |
| 2004S | (2,740,684) | | | 1.50 |
| 2004S, Silver | (1,769,786) | | | 6.00 |
| **Wisconsin** | | | | |
| 2004P | 226,400,000 | 0.25 | 0.30 | |
| 2004D | 226,800,000 | 0.25 | 0.30 | |
| 2004S | (2,740,684) | | | 1.50 |
| 2004S, Silver | (1,769,786) | | | 6.00 |

| | Mintage | AU-50 | MS-63 | PF-65 |
|---|---|---|---|---|
| **California** | | | | |
| 2005P | 257,200,000 | $0.25 | $0.30 | |
| 2005D | 263,200,000 | 0.25 | 0.30 | |
| 2005S | (3,262,960) | | | $1.50 |
| 2005S, Silver | (1,678,649) | | | 6.00 |
| **Minnesota** | | | | |
| 2005P | 239,600,000 | 0.25 | 0.30 | |
| 2005D | 248,400,000 | 0.25 | 0.30 | |
| 2005S | (3,262,960) | | | 1.50 |
| 2005S, Silver | (1,678,649) | | | 6.00 |
| **Oregon** | | | | |
| 2005P | 316,200,000 | 0.25 | 0.30 | |
| 2005D | 404,000,000 | 0.25 | 0.30 | |

| | Mintage | AU-50 | MS-63 | PF-65 |
|---|---|---|---|---|
| **Oregon** | | | | |
| 2005S | (3,262,960) | | | $1.50 |
| 2005S, Silver | (1,678,649) | | | 6.00 |
| **Kansas** | | | | |
| 2005P | 263,400,000 | $0.25 | $0.30 | |
| 2005D | 300,000,000 | 0.25 | 0.30 | |
| 2005S | (3,262,960) | | | 1.50 |
| 2005S, Silver | (1,678,649) | | | 6.00 |
| **West Virginia** | | | | |
| 2005P | 365,400,000 | 0.25 | 0.30 | |
| 2005D | 356,200,000 | 0.25 | 0.30 | |
| 2005S | (3,262,960) | | | 1.50 |
| 2005S, Silver | (1,678,649) | | | 6.00 |

| | Mintage | AU-50 | MS-63 | PF-65 |
|---|---|---|---|---|
| **Nevada** | | | | |
| 2006P | 277,000,000 | $0.25 | $0.30 | |
| 2006D | 312,800,000 | 0.25 | 0.30 | |
| 2006S | (2,882,428) | | | $1.50 |
| 2006S, Silver | (1,585,008) | | | 6.00 |
| **Nebraska** | | | | |
| 2006P | 318,000,000 | 0.25 | 0.30 | |
| 2006D | 273,000,000 | 0.25 | 0.30 | |
| 2006S | (2,882,428) | | | 1.50 |
| 2006S, Silver | (1,585,008) | | | 6.00 |
| **Colorado** | | | | |
| 2006P | 274,800,000 | 0.25 | 0.30 | |
| 2006D | 294,200,000 | 0.25 | 0.30 | |

| | Mintage | AU-50 | MS-63 | PF-65 |
|---|---|---|---|---|
| **Colorado** | | | | |
| 2006S | (2,882,428) | | | $1.50 |
| 2006S, Silver | (1,585,008) | | | 6.00 |
| **North Dakota** | | | | |
| 2006P | 305,800,000 | $0.25 | $0.30 | |
| 2006D | 359,000,000 | 0.25 | 0.30 | |
| 2006S | (2,882,428) | | | 1.50 |
| 2006S, Silver | (1,585,008) | | | 6.00 |
| **South Dakota** | | | | |
| 2006P | 245,000,000 | 0.25 | 0.30 | |
| 2006D | 265,800,000 | 0.25 | 0.30 | |
| 2006S | (2,882,428) | | | 1.50 |
| 2006S, Silver | (1,585,008) | | | 6.00 |

| | Mintage | AU-50 | MS-63 | PF-65 |
|---|---|---|---|---|
| **Montana** | | | | |
| 2007P | 257,000,000 | $0.25 | $0.30 | |
| 2007D | 256,240,000 | 0.25 | 0.30 | |
| 2007S | (2,374,778) | | | $1.50 |
| 2007S, Silver | (1,313,481) | | | 6.00 |
| **Washington** | | | | |
| 2007P | 265,200,000 | 0.25 | 0.30 | |
| 2007D | 280,000,000 | 0.25 | 0.30 | |
| 2007S | (2,374,778) | | | 1.50 |
| 2007S, Silver | (1,313,481) | | | 6.00 |
| **Idaho** | | | | |
| 2007P | 294,600,000 | 0.25 | 0.30 | |
| 2007D | 286,800,000 | 0.25 | 0.30 | |

| | Mintage | AU-50 | MS-63 | PF-65 |
|---|---|---|---|---|
| **Idaho** | | | | |
| 2007S | (2,374,778) | | | $1.50 |
| 2007S, Silver | (1,313,481) | | | 6.00 |
| **Wyoming** | | | | |
| 2007P | 243,600,000 | $0.25 | $0.30 | |
| 2007D | 320,800,000 | 0.25 | 0.30 | |
| 2007S | (2,374,778) | | | 1.50 |
| 2007S, Silver | (1,313,481) | | | 6.00 |
| **Utah** | | | | |
| 2007P | 255,000,000 | 0.25 | 0.30 | |
| 2007D | 253,200,000 | 0.25 | 0.30 | |
| 2007S | (2,374,778) | | | 1.50 |
| 2007S, Silver | (1,313,481) | | | 6.00 |

| | Mintage | AU-50 | MS-63 | PF-65 |
|---|---|---|---|---|
| **Oklahoma** | | | | |
| 2008P | 222,000,000 | $0.25 | $0.30 | |
| 2008D | 194,600,000 | 0.25 | 0.30 | |
| 2008S | (2,078,112) | | | $1.50 |
| 2008S, Silver | (1,192,908) | | | 6.00 |
| **New Mexico** | | | | |
| 2008P | 244,200,000 | 0.25 | 0.30 | |
| 2008D | 244,400,000 | 0.25 | 0.30 | |
| 2008S | (2,078,112) | | | 1.50 |
| 2008S, Silver | (1,192,908) | | | 6.00 |
| **Arizona** | | | | |
| 2008P | 244,600,000 | 0.25 | 0.30 | |
| 2008D | 265,000,000 | 0.25 | 0.30 | |

| | Mintage | AU-50 | MS-63 | PF-65 |
|---|---|---|---|---|
| **Arizona** | | | | |
| 2008S | (2,078,112) | | | $1.50 |
| 2008S, Silver | (1,192,908) | | | 6.00 |
| **Alaska** | | | | |
| 2008P | 251,800,000 | $0.25 | $0.30 | |
| 2008D | 254,000,000 | 0.25 | 0.30 | |
| 2008S | (2,078,112) | | | 1.50 |
| 2008S, Silver | (1,192,908) | | | 6.00 |
| **Hawaii** | | | | |
| 2008P | 254,000,000 | 0.25 | 0.30 | |
| 2008D | 263,600,00 | 0.25 | 0.30 | |
| 2008S | (2,078,112) | | | 1.50 |
| 2008S, Silver | (1,192,908) | | | 6.00 |

Some statehood quarters were accidentally made with "dis-oriented" dies and are valued higher than ordinary pieces. Normal United States coins have dies oriented in "coin alignment," such that the reverse appears upside down when the coin is rotated from right to left. Values for the rotated-die quarters vary according to the amount of shifting. The most valuable are those that are shifted 180 degrees, so that both sides appear upright when the coin is turned over (called *medal alignment*).

Manufacturing varieties showing die doubling or other minor, unintentional characteristics are of interest to collectors and are often worth premium prices.

### District of Columbia and U.S. Territories Quarters (2009)

At the ending of the U.S. Mint 50 State Quarters® Program a new series of quarter-dollar reverse designs was authorized to recognize the District of Columbia and the five U.S. territories: the Commonwealth of Puerto Rico, Guam, American Samoa, the U.S. Virgin Islands, and the Commonwealth of the Northern Mariana Islands. Each of these coins, issued sequentially during 2009, has the portrait of George Washington, as in the past, and is made of the same weight and composition. Each coin commemorates the history, geography, or traditions of the place it represents.

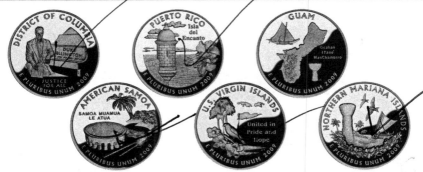

| | Mintage | AU-50 | MS-63 | PF-65 |
|---|---|---|---|---|
| **District of Columbia** | | | | |
| 2009P | 83,600,000 | $0.25 | $0.30 | |
| 2009D | 88,800,000 | 0.25 | 0.30 | |
| 2009S | (2,108,943) | | | $1.50 |
| 2009S, Silver | (993,589) | | | 6.00 |
| **Puerto Rico** | | | | |
| 2009P | 53,200,000 | 0.25 | 0.30 | |
| 2009D | 86,000,000 | 0.25 | 0.30 | |
| 2009S | (2,108,943) | | | 1.50 |
| 2009S, Silver | (993,589) | | | 6.00 |
| **Guam** | | | | |
| 2009P | 45,000,000 | 0.25 | 0.30 | |
| 2009D | 42,600,000 | 0.25 | 0.30 | |
| 2009S | (2,108,943) | | | 1.50 |
| 2009S, Silver | (993,589) | | | 6.00 |

| | Mintage | AU-50 | MS-63 | PF-65 |
|---|---|---|---|---|
| **American Samoa** | | | | |
| 2009P | 42,600,000 | $0.25 | $0.30 | |
| 2009D | 39,600,000 | 0.25 | 0.30 | |
| 2009S | (2,108,943) | | | $1.50 |
| 2009S, Silver | (993,589) | | | 6.00 |
| **U.S. Virgin Islands** | | | | |
| 2009P | 41,000,000 | 0.25 | 0.30 | |
| 2009D | 41,000,000 | 0.25 | 0.30 | |
| 2009S | (2,108,943) | | | 1.50 |
| 2009S, Silver | (993,589) | | | 6.00 |
| **Northern Mariana Islands** | | | | |
| 2009P | 35,200,000 | 0.25 | 0.30 | |
| 2009D | 37,600,000 | 0.25 | 0.30 | |
| 2009S | (2,108,943) | | | 1.50 |
| 2009S, Silver | (993,589) | | | 6.00 |

### *America the Beautiful™ Quarters Program (2010–2021)*

Following up on the popularity of the 50 State Quarters® Program, Congress has authorized the production of new circulating commemorative quarters from 2010 to 2021. The coins honor a site of "natural or historic significance" from each of the 50 states, five U.S. territories, and the District of Columbia. They continue to bear George Washington's portrait on the obverse.

Five designs will be released each year through 2020, with the final coin issued in 2021, in the order the coins' featured locations were designated national parks or national sites. At the discretion of the secretary of the Treasury, this series could be extended an additional 11 years by featuring a second national park or site from each state, district, and territory.

In addition to the circulating quarters, a series of five-ounce silver bullion pieces are being coined each year with designs nearly identical to those of the America the Beautiful™ quarters, with two exceptions: the size, which is three inches in diameter; and the edge, which is marked .999 FINE SILVER 5.0 OUNCE, rather than reeded as on the standard quarters.

| | Mintage | AU-50 | MS-63 | PF-65 |
|---|---|---|---|---|
| **Hot Springs National Park (Arkansas)** | | | | |
| 2010P | 35,600,000 | $0.25 | $0.30 | |
| 2010D | 34,000,000 | 0.25 | 0.30 | |
| 2010S | (1,222,966) | | | $1.50 |
| 2010S, Silver | (693,403) | | | 6.00 |
| **Yellowstone National Park (Wyoming)** | | | | |
| 2010P | 33,600,000 | 0.25 | 0.30 | |
| 2010D | 34,800,000 | 0.25 | 0.30 | |
| 2010S | (1,222,966) | | | 1.50 |
| 2010S, Silver | (693,403) | | | 6.00 |
| **Yosemite National Park (California)** | | | | |
| 2010P | 35,200,000 | 0.25 | 0.30 | |
| 2010D | 34,800,000 | 0.25 | 0.30 | |
| 2010S | (1,222,966) | | | 1.50 |
| 2010S, Silver | (693,403) | | | 6.00 |
| **Grand Canyon National Park (Arizona)** | | | | |
| 2010P | 34,800,000 | 0.25 | 0.30 | |
| 2010D | 35,400,000 | 0.25 | 0.30 | |
| 2010S | (1,222,966) | | | 1.50 |
| 2010S, Silver | (693,403) | | | 6.00 |
| **Mt. Hood National Forest (Oregon)** | | | | |
| 2010P | 34,400,000 | 0.25 | 0.30 | |
| 2010D | 34,400,000 | 0.25 | 0.30 | |
| 2010S | (1,222,966) | | | 1.50 |
| 2010S, Silver | (693,403) | | | 6.00 |

| | Mintage | AU-50 | MS-63 | PF-65 |
|---|---|---|---|---|
| **Gettysburg National Military Park (Pennsylvania)** | | | | |
| 2011P | | $0.25 | $0.30 | |
| 2011S | | 0.25 | 0.30 | |
| 2011S | | | | $1.50 |
| 2011S, Silver | | | | 6.00 |
| **Glacier National Park (Montana)** | | | | |
| 2011P | | 0.25 | 0.30 | |
| 2011D | | 0.25 | 0.30 | |
| 2011S | | | | 1.50 |
| 2011S, Silver | | | | 6.00 |
| **Olympic National Park (Washington)** | | | | |
| 2011P | | 0.25 | 0.30 | |
| 2011D | | 0.25 | 0.30 | |
| 2011S | | | | 1.50 |
| 2011S, Silver | | | | 6.00 |
| **Vicksburg National Military Park (Mississippi)** | | | | |
| 2011P | | 0.25 | 0.30 | |
| 2011D | | 0.25 | 0.30 | |
| 2011S | | | | 1.50 |
| 2011S, Silver | | | | 6.00 |
| **Chickasaw National Recreation Area (Oklahoma)** | | | | |
| 2011P | | 0.25 | 0.30 | |
| 2011D | | 0.25 | 0.30 | |
| 2011S | | | | 1.50 |
| 2011S, Silver | | | | 6.00 |

The half dollar, authorized by the Act of April 2, 1792, was not minted until December, 1794. The weight of the half dollar was 208 grains and its fineness .8924 when first issued. This standard was not changed until 1837 when the Act of January 18, 1837, specified 206-1/4 grains, .900 fine. This fineness continued in use until 1965.

Arrows at the date in 1853 indicate the reduction of weight to 192 grains. During that year only, rays were added to the reverse. Arrows remained in 1854 and 1855. In 1873 the weight was raised by .9 grains and arrows were again placed at the date.

## FLOWING HAIR (1794–1795)

**AG-3 About Good:** Clear enough to identify.
**G-4 Good:** Date and letters sufficient to be legible. Main devices outlined, but lacking in detail.
**VG-8 Very Good:** Major details discernible. Letters well formed but worn.
**F-12 Fine:** Hair ends distinguishable. Top hair lines visible, but otherwise worn smooth.
**VF-20 Very Fine:** Some detail visible in hair in center; other details more bold.
**EF-40 Extremely Fine:** Hair above head and down neck detailed, with slight wear.
**AU-50 About Uncirculated:** All hair visible; slight wear on bust of Liberty and on top edges of eagle's wings, head, and breast.

**2 Leaves Under Wings**     **3 Leaves Under Wings**

| | Mintage | AG-3 | G-4 | VG-8 | F-12 | VF-20 | EF-40 | AU-50 |
|---|---|---|---|---|---|---|---|---|
| 1794 . . . . . . . . . . . . . . . . . . . . . . .23,464 | | $900 | $1,300 | $2,200 | $4,250 | $8,500 | $18,000 | $38,000 |
| 1795 . . . . . . . . . . . . . . . . . . . . .299,680 | | 160 | 335 | 475 | 900 | 2,000 | 5,000 | 8,500 |
| 1795, Recut Date . . . . . . . . . . . . . . . . .* | | 160 | 335 | 475 | 900 | 2,000 | 5,000 | 8,500 |
| 1795, 3 Leaves Under Each Wing . . . . . . .* | | 500 | 800 | 1,000 | 2,000 | 3,000 | 6,500 | 12,000 |

* Included in number above.

## DRAPED BUST (1796–1807)

**AG-3 About Good:** Clear enough to identify.
**G-4 Good:** Date and letters sufficiently clear to be legible. Main devices outlined, but lacking in detail.
**VG-8 Very Good:** Major details discernible. Letters well formed but worn.
**F-12 Fine:** Hair ends distinguishable. Top hair lines visible, but otherwise worn smooth.
**VF-20 Very Fine:** Right side of drapery slightly worn. Left side to curls smooth.
**EF-40 Extremely Fine:** All lines in drapery on bust distinctly visible around to hair curls.
**AU-50 About Uncirculated:** Slight trace of wear on cheek, hair, and shoulder.

### Small Eagle Reverse (1796–1797)

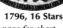

**1796, 16 Stars**                    **1797, 15 Stars**

*See next page for chart.*

| | Mintage | AG-3 | G-4 | VG-8 | F-12 | VF-20 | EF-40 | AU-50 |
|---|---|---|---|---|---|---|---|---|
| 1796, All kinds ................3,918 | | | | | | | | |
| 1796, 15 Stars ................. | | $7,500 | $15,000 | $17,000 | $25,000 | $35,000 | $52,500 | $75,000 |
| 1796, 16 Stars ................. | | 8,000 | 16,000 | 18,000 | 27,000 | 37,000 | 55,000 | 85,000 |
| 1797, 15 Stars ................. | | 7,500 | 15,000 | 17,000 | 25,000 | 35,000 | 52,500 | 75,000 |

## Heraldic Eagle Reverse (1801–1807)

1805, 5 Over 4

1806, 6 Over 5

| | Mintage | G-4 | VG-8 | F-12 | VF-20 | EF-40 | AU-50 | MS-60 |
|---|---|---|---|---|---|---|---|---|
| 1801 ......................30,289 | | $300 | $500 | $1,000 | $1,500 | $4,000 | $6,500 | $17,500 |
| 1802 ......................29,890 | | 300 | 500 | 1,000 | 1,500 | 4,000 | 6,500 | 17,500 |
| 1803 ......................188,234 | | 75 | 100 | 175 | 275 | 650 | 2,000 | 5,000 |
| 1805, All kinds ...............211,722 | | | | | | | | |
| 1805, 5 Over 4 .................. | | 100 | 150 | 275 | 375 | 1,100 | 3,000 | 10,000 |
| 1805, Normal Date .............. | | 90 | 120 | 150 | 250 | 700 | 2,500 | 4,500 |
| 1806, All kinds ...............839,576 | | | | | | | | |
| 1806, Normal Date .............. | | 80 | 100 | 120 | 200 | 485 | 1,300 | 3,000 |
| 1806, 6 Over 5 ................. | | 80 | 100 | 120 | 200 | 500 | 1,500 | 3,500 |
| 1806, 6 Over Inverted 6 ............ | | 90 | 120 | 200 | 500 | 1,200 | 3,000 | 6,000 |
| 1807 ......................301,076 | | 80 | 100 | 120 | 200 | 485 | 1,300 | 3,000 |

## CAPPED BUST, LETTERED EDGE (1807–1836)

John Reich designed this capped-head concept of Liberty. Reich's design of Liberty facing left was used on all U.S. silver denominations for the next 30 years.

**G-4 Good:** Date and letters legible. Bust worn smooth with outline distinct.
**VG-8 Very Good:** LIBERTY faint. Legends distinguishable. Clasp at shoulder visible; curl above it nearly smooth.
**F-12 Fine:** Clasp and adjacent curl clearly outlined with slight details.
**VF-20 Very Fine:** Clasp at shoulder clear. Wear visible on highest point of curl. Hair over brow distinguishable.
**EF-40 Extremely Fine:** Clasp and adjacent curl fairly sharp. Brow and hair above distinct. Curls well defined.
**AU-50 About Uncirculated:** Trace of wear on hair over eye and over ear.
**MS-60 Uncirculated:** No trace of wear. Light blemishes. Possible slide marks from storage handling.
**MS-63 Choice Uncirculated:** Some distracting contact marks or blemishes in prime focal areas. Impaired luster possible.

### First Style (1807–1808)

| | Mintage | G-4 | VG-8 | F-12 | VF-20 | EF-40 | AU-50 | MS-60 | MS-63 |
|---|---|---|---|---|---|---|---|---|---|
| 1807 | 750,500 | $40 | $60 | $100 | $200 | $550 | $1,200 | $2,500 | $4,000 |
| 1808, 8 Over 7 | * | 30 | 40 | 60 | 90 | 200 | 600 | 1,200 | 3,100 |
| 1808 | 1,368,600 | 26 | 33 | 40 | 55 | 125 | 255 | 825 | 1,650 |

* Included in number below.

## Remodeled Portrait and Eagle (1809–1836)

| | Mintage | G-4 | VG-8 | F-12 | VF-20 | EF-40 | AU-50 | MS-60 | MS-63 |
|---|---|---|---|---|---|---|---|---|---|
| 1809 | 1,405,810 | $25 | $29 | $37 | $50 | $100 | $250 | $700 | $1,600 |
| 1810 | 1,276,276 | 25 | 29 | 37 | 50 | 100 | 225 | 675 | 1,500 |
| 1811 | 1,203,644 | 25 | 29 | 35 | 42 | 85 | 185 | 600 | 1,100 |

| 1812, 2 Over 1 | 1813, 50 C. Over UNI | 1814, 4 Over 3 |
|---|---|---|

| | Mintage | G-4 | VG-8 | F-12 | VF-20 | EF-40 | AU-50 | MS-60 | MS-63 |
|---|---|---|---|---|---|---|---|---|---|
| 1812, All kinds | 1,628,059 | | | | | | | | |
| 1812, 2 Over 1 | | $25 | $32 | $40 | $65 | $150 | $250 | $1,000 | $2,200 |
| 1812 | | 25 | 30 | 37 | 55 | 100 | 200 | 500 | 1,000 |
| 1813 | 1,241,903 | 25 | 30 | 37 | 55 | 100 | 185 | 500 | 1,000 |
| 1813, 50 C. Over UNI | * | 25 | 30 | 42 | 70 | 140 | 300 | 700 | 2,100 |
| 1814, All kinds | 1,039,075 | | | | | | | | |
| 1814, 4 Over 3 | | 25 | 30 | 45 | 80 | 150 | 350 | 800 | 2,100 |
| 1814 | | 25 | 30 | 40 | 55 | 100 | 185 | 500 | 1,100 |

* Included in number above.

| 1817, 7 Over 3 | 1817, 7 Over 4 | 1817, "Punctuated" Date |
|---|---|---|

| | Mintage | G-4 | VG-8 | F-12 | VF-20 | EF-40 | AU-50 | MS-60 | MS-63 |
|---|---|---|---|---|---|---|---|---|---|
| 1815, 5 Over 2 | 47,150 | $500 | $750 | $900 | $1,200 | $2,200 | $3,000 | $5,500 | $15,000 |
| 1817, All kinds | 1,215,567 | | | | | | | | |
| 1817, 7 Over 3 | | 30 | 45 | 100 | 200 | 350 | 650 | 1,500 | 4,500 |
| 1817, 7 Over 4 *(8 known)* | | | | 80,000 | 110,000 | 150,000 | | | |
| 1817, Dated 181.7 | * | 25 | 30 | 39 | 50 | 85 | 175 | 475 | 1,000 |
| 1817 | | 25 | 30 | 39 | 45 | 65 | 150 | 450 | 1,000 |

1818, 2nd 8 Over 7

1819, 9 Over 8

1820, 20 Over 19

| | Mintage | G-4 | VG-8 | F-12 | VF-20 | EF-40 | AU-50 | MS-60 | MS-63 |
|---|---|---|---|---|---|---|---|---|---|
| 1818, 2nd 8 Over 7 .........* | | $25 | $30 | $35 | $42 | $65 | $175 | $500 | $1,000 |
| 1818 ...........1,960,322 | | 25 | 30 | 35 | 42 | 65 | 150 | 450 | 925 |
| 1819, 9 Over 8 ...........* | | 25 | 30 | 35 | 42 | 65 | 150 | 450 | 925 |
| 1819 ...........2,208,000 | | 23 | 30 | 35 | 42 | 65 | 150 | 450 | 925 |
| 1820, 20 Over 19 .........* | | 25 | 35 | 40 | 55 | 120 | 300 | 600 | 1,000 |
| 1820 ............751,122 | | 23 | 30 | 35 | 42 | 65 | 150 | 475 | 950 |
| 1821 ...........1,305,797 | | 23 | 30 | 35 | 42 | 65 | 150 | 450 | 950 |
| 1822 ...........1,559,573 | | 23 | 30 | 35 | 42 | 65 | 150 | 475 | 1,000 |
| 1823 ...........1,694,200 | | 23 | 30 | 35 | 42 | 65 | 150 | 400 | 900 |

\* Included in number below.

"Various Dates"
*Probably 4 Over
2 Over 0.*

1824, 4 Over 1

1828, Curl Base,
Knob 2

1828, Square
Base 2

| | Mintage | G-4 | VG-8 | F-12 | VF-20 | EF-40 | AU-50 | MS-60 | MS-63 |
|---|---|---|---|---|---|---|---|---|---|
| 1824, All kinds ...............3,504,954 | | | | | | | | | |
| 1824, 4 Over Various Dates ............. | | $23 | $28 | $34 | $42 | $65 | $150 | $475 | $900 |
| 1824, 4 Over 1 ...................... | | 23 | 28 | 34 | 42 | 65 | 150 | 475 | 900 |
| 1824 .............................. | | 23 | 28 | 34 | 42 | 65 | 150 | 425 | 825 |
| 1825...........................2,943,166 | | 23 | 28 | 34 | 42 | 65 | 150 | 425 | 825 |
| 1826...........................4,004,180 | | 23 | 28 | 34 | 42 | 65 | 150 | 400 | 825 |
| 1827, All kinds ...............5,493,400 | | | | | | | | | |
| 1827, 7 Over 6 ...................... | | 25 | 34 | 40 | 50 | 75 | 150 | 525 | 900 |
| 1827 ............................ | | 23 | 28 | 35 | 45 | 65 | 150 | 425 | 825 |
| 1828, All kinds ...............3,075,200 | | | | | | | | | |
| 1828, Curl Base No Knob 2 ............. | | 23 | 28 | 35 | 45 | 65 | 150 | 425 | 825 |
| 1828, Curl Base Knob 2 ................ | | 25 | 29 | 35 | 45 | 65 | 150 | 425 | 825 |
| 1828, Square Base 2 .................* | | 23 | 28 | 35 | 45 | 65 | 150 | 425 | 825 |
| 1829, 9 Over 7 .....................* | | 23 | 30 | 38 | 50 | 75 | 190 | 500 | 1,250 |
| 1829...........................3,712,156 | | 23 | 28 | 34 | 42 | 65 | 150 | 400 | 850 |
| 1830...........................4,764,800 | | 23 | 28 | 34 | 42 | 65 | 150 | 400 | 850 |
| 1831...........................5,873,660 | | 23 | 28 | 34 | 42 | 65 | 150 | 400 | 850 |
| 1832...........................4,797,000 | | 23 | 28 | 34 | 42 | 65 | 150 | 400 | 850 |
| 1833...........................5,206,000 | | 23 | 28 | 34 | 42 | 65 | 150 | 400 | 850 |
| 1834...........................6,412,004 | | 23 | 28 | 34 | 42 | 65 | 150 | 400 | 850 |
| 1835...........................5,352,006 | | 23 | 28 | 34 | 42 | 65 | 150 | 400 | 850 |
| 1836...........................6,545,000 | | 23 | 28 | 34 | 42 | 65 | 150 | 400 | 850 |
| 1836, 50 Over 00 ...................** | | 30 | 40 | 50 | 70 | 130 | 300 | 800 | 1,700 |

\* Included in number below.  \*\* Included in number above.

## CAPPED BUST, REEDED EDGE (1836–1839)

**G-4 Good:** LIBERTY barely discernible on headband.
**VG-8 Very Good:** Some letters in LIBERTY clear.
**F-12 Fine:** LIBERTY complete but faint.
**VF-20 Very Fine:** LIBERTY sharp. Shoulder clasp clear.
**EF-40 Extremely Fine:** LIBERTY sharp and strong. Hair details visible.
**AU-50 About Uncirculated:** Slight trace of wear on cap, cheek, and hair above forehead, and on eagle's claws, wing tops, and head.
**MS-60 Uncirculated:** No trace of wear. Light blemishes.
**MS-63 Choice Uncirculated:** Some distracting marks or blemishes in focal areas. Impaired luster possible.

### Reverse 50 CENTS (1836–1837)

| | Mintage | G-4 | VG-8 | F-12 | VF-20 | EF-40 | AU-50 | MS-60 | MS-63 |
|---|---|---|---|---|---|---|---|---|---|
| 1836 | 1,200+ | $400 | $500 | $700 | $900 | $1,250 | $2,200 | $4,750 | $8,500 |
| 1837 | 3,629,820 | 24 | 27 | 36 | 55 | 90 | 185 | 500 | 1,100 |

### Reverse HALF DOL. (1838–1839)

On half dollars of 1838 and 1839, the mintmark appears on the obverse; on those thereafter, through 1915, it is on the reverse.

| | Mintage | G-4 | VG-8 | F-12 | VF-20 | EF-40 | AU-50 | MS-60 | MS-63 |
|---|---|---|---|---|---|---|---|---|---|
| 1838 | 3,546,000 | $24 | $27 | $36 | $55 | $100 | $170 | $450 | $1,000 |
| 1838O | 20 | | | | | | 120,000 | 175,000 | |
| 1839 | 1,392,976 | 22 | 27 | 36 | 53 | 90 | 175 | 525 | 1,200 |
| 1839O | 116,000 | 65 | 100 | 135 | 185 | 325 | 600 | 1,500 | 2,750 |

## LIBERTY SEATED (1839–1891)

**G-4 Good:** Scant rim. LIBERTY on shield worn off. Date and letters legible.
**VG-8 Very Good:** Rim fairly defined. Some letters in LIBERTY evident.
**F-12 Fine:** LIBERTY complete, but weak.
**VF-20 Very Fine:** LIBERTY mostly sharp.
**EF-40 Extremely Fine:** LIBERTY entirely sharp. Scroll edges and clasp distinct.
**AU-50 About Uncirculated:** Slight wear on Liberty's breast and knees; eagle's head, claws, and wing tops.
**MS-60 Uncirculated:** No trace of wear. Light blemishes.
**MS-63 Choice Uncirculated:** Some distracting blemishes in prime focal areas. Impaired luster possible.
**PF-63 Choice Proof:** Reflective surfaces with only a few blemishes in secondary focal places. No major flaws.

## Variety 1 – No Motto Above Eagle (1839–1853)

**1842, Small Date**

**1842, Medium Date**

No Drapery From Elbow

Drapery From Elbow (Starting 1839)

| | Mintage | G-4 | VG-8 | F-12 | VF-20 | EF-40 | AU-50 | MS-60 | MS-63 |
|---|---|---|---|---|---|---|---|---|---|
| 1839, No Drapery From Elbow | .......* | $18 | $30 | $50 | $140 | $325 | $500 | $2,600 | $8,500 |
| 1839, Drapery | 1,972,400 | 12 | 15 | 19 | 30 | 50 | 65 | 275 | 950 |
| 1840 | 1,435,008 | 12 | 15 | 21 | 35 | 60 | 70 | 275 | 650 |
| 1840O | 855,100 | 12 | 14 | 18 | 30 | 48 | 60 | 300 | 800 |
| 1841 | 310,000 | 14 | 16 | 22 | 65 | 110 | 140 | 500 | 800 |
| 1841O | 401,000 | 12 | 15 | 19 | 30 | 50 | 65 | 375 | 750 |
| 1842, Small Date | 2,012,764 | 12 | 15 | 20 | 35 | 55 | 70 | 450 | 950 |
| 1842, Medium Date | ** | 12 | 15 | 19 | 30 | 50 | 65 | 300 | 850 |
| 1842O, Small Date | 754,000 | 200 | 375 | 600 | 1,100 | 1,900 | 2,750 | 5,500 | — |
| 1842O, Medium Date | ** | 12 | 14 | 18 | 28 | 45 | 65 | 300 | 1,600 |
| 1843 | 3,844,000 | 12 | 14 | 18 | 28 | 45 | 65 | 300 | 425 |
| 1843O | 2,268,000 | 12 | 14 | 18 | 28 | 45 | 65 | 300 | 450 |
| 1844 | 1,766,000 | 12 | 14 | 18 | 28 | 45 | 65 | 300 | 425 |
| 1844O | 2,005,000 | 12 | 14 | 18 | 28 | 45 | 65 | 300 | 900 |
| 1845 | 589,000 | 13 | 15 | 20 | 32 | 50 | 90 | 380 | 1,200 |
| 1845O | 2,094,000 | 12 | 14 | 17 | 24 | 45 | 65 | 360 | 450 |
| 1846 | 2,210,000 | 12 | 14 | 17 | 24 | 45 | 65 | 300 | 500 |
| 1846, 6 Over Horizontal 6 | ** | 45 | 80 | 125 | 175 | 300 | 500 | 1,100 | 4,000 |
| 1846O | 2,304,000 | 12 | 14 | 17 | 24 | 45 | 75 | 450 | 900 |
| 1847 | 1,156,000 | 12 | 14 | 17 | 24 | 45 | 65 | 300 | 425 |
| 1847O | 2,584,000 | 12 | 14 | 17 | 24 | 45 | 65 | 300 | 1,000 |
| 1848 | 580,000 | 15 | 19 | 28 | 40 | 75 | 180 | 420 | 600 |
| 1848O | 3,180,000 | 12 | 14 | 17 | 24 | 45 | 65 | 360 | 700 |
| 1849 | 1,252,000 | 12 | 14 | 17 | 24 | 45 | 65 | 340 | 700 |
| 1849O | 2,310,000 | 12 | 14 | 17 | 24 | 45 | 65 | 300 | 800 |
| 1850 | 227,000 | 75 | 100 | 175 | 190 | 300 | 350 | 725 | 1,600 |
| 1850O | 2,456,000 | 12 | 14 | 17 | 24 | 45 | 65 | 300 | 575 |
| 1851 | 200,750 | 75 | 125 | 190 | 250 | 275 | 400 | 850 | 1,400 |
| 1851O | 402,000 | 12 | 14 | 18 | 24 | 45 | 65 | 300 | 500 |
| 1852 | 77,130 | 125 | 180 | 280 | 360 | 400 | 550 | 800 | 1,100 |
| 1852O | 144,000 | 20 | 30 | 45 | 70 | 180 | 225 | 1,000 | 3,200 |
| 1853O (3 known) | | | 100,000 | 150,000 | 250,000 | | | | |

* Included in number below. **Included in number above.

## Variety 2 – Arrows at Date, Rays Around Eagle (1853)

| | Mintage | G-4 | VG-8 | F-12 | VF-20 | EF-40 | AU-50 | MS-60 | MS-63 |
|---|---|---|---|---|---|---|---|---|---|
| 1853 . . . . . . . . . . . . | 3,532,708 | $12 | $15 | $20 | $60 | $120 | $300 | $950 | $1,500 |
| 1853O . . . . . . . . . . . | 1,328,000 | 13 | 16 | 22 | 65 | 130 | 340 | 1,400 | 2,000 |

## Variety 3 – Arrows at Date, No Rays (1854–1855)

| | Mintage | G-4 | VG-8 | F-12 | VF-20 | EF-40 | AU-50 | MS-60 | MS-63 |
|---|---|---|---|---|---|---|---|---|---|
| 1854 . . . . . . . . . . . . | 2,982,000 | $12 | $14 | $18 | $30 | $55 | $85 | $360 | $650 |
| 1854O . . . . . . . . . . | 5,240,000 | 12 | 14 | 18 | 30 | 55 | 85 | 360 | 650 |
| 1855, Over 1854 . . . . . . . . . . * | | 15 | 35 | 70 | 120 | 220 | 275 | 800 | 1,400 |
| 1855 . . . . . . . . . . . . . | 759,500 | 12 | 14 | 18 | 30 | 55 | 85 | 360 | 650 |
| 1855O . . . . . . . . . . . | 3,688,000 | 12 | 14 | 18 | 30 | 55 | 85 | 360 | 650 |
| 1855S . . . . . . . . . . . | 129,950 | 150 | 185 | 300 | 600 | 1,400 | 2,750 | 7,000 | — |

* Included in number below.

## Variety 1 Resumed, With Weight Standard of Variety 2 (1856–1866)

| | Mintage | G-4 | VG-8 | F-12 | VF-20 | EF-40 | AU-50 | MS-60 | MS-63 | PF-63 |
|---|---|---|---|---|---|---|---|---|---|---|
| 1856 . . . . . . . . . . . . . . | 938,000 | $12 | $14 | $18 | $23 | $40 | $80 | $220 | $400 | |
| 1856O . . . . . . . . . . . . | 2,658,000 | 12 | 15 | 20 | 24 | 40 | 80 | 220 | 400 | |
| 1856S . . . . . . . . . . . . . | 211,000 | 15 | 20 | 37 | 90 | 200 | 425 | 1,700 | — | |
| 1857 . . . . . . . . . . . . . | 1,988,000 | 12 | 14 | 18 | 23 | 40 | 80 | 220 | 400 | |
| 1857O . . . . . . . . . . . . | 818,000 | 12 | 14 | 20 | 24 | 40 | 80 | 240 | 650 | |
| 1857S . . . . . . . . . . . . . | 158,000 | 18 | 30 | 45 | 85 | 180 | 425 | 1,800 | — | |
| 1858 . . . . . . (300+) . . 4,225,700 | | 12 | 14 | 18 | 28 | 40 | 80 | 220 | 400 | $1,400 |
| 1858O . . . . . . . . . . . . | 7,294,000 | 12 | 14 | 18 | 23 | 40 | 80 | 220 | 400 | |
| 1858S . . . . . . . . . . . . | 476,000 | 14 | 16 | 22 | 30 | 55 | 120 | 525 | 1,500 | |
| 1859 . . . . . . (800) . . . 747,200 | | 12 | 14 | 18 | 23 | 45 | 85 | 225 | 450 | 900 |
| 1859O . . . . . . . . . . . . | 2,834,000 | 12 | 14 | 18 | 23 | 45 | 85 | 225 | 450 | |
| 1859S . . . . . . . . . . . . | 566,000 | 13 | 16 | 22 | 30 | 80 | 85 | 250 | 1,000 | |
| 1860 . . . . . . (1,000) . . . 302,700 | | 13 | 15 | 20 | 28 | 50 | 85 | 225 | 450 | 700 |
| 1860O . . . . . . . . . . . . | 1,290,000 | 12 | 14 | 18 | 23 | 45 | 80 | 225 | 450 | |
| 1860S . . . . . . . . . . . . | 472,000 | 14 | 16 | 22 | 25 | 45 | 80 | 350 | 1,000 | |
| 1861 . . . . . . (1,000) . . 2,887,400 | | 12 | 14 | 18 | 23 | 45 | 80 | 225 | 400 | 700 |
| 1861O . . . . . . . . . . . . | 2,532,633 | 12 | 14 | 18 | 23 | 45 | 80 | 225 | 400 | |
| 1861S . . . . . . . . . . . . | 939,500 | 12 | 14 | 18 | 23 | 45 | 80 | 275 | 425 | |
| 1862 . . . . . . (550) . . . 253,000 | | 14 | 20 | 25 | 50 | 80 | 100 | 450 | 650 | 700 |
| 1862S . . . . . . . . . . . . | 1,352,000 | 12 | 14 | 18 | 23 | 45 | 80 | 275 | 450 | |
| 1863 . . . . . . (460) . . . 503,200 | | 14 | 16 | 22 | 28 | 55 | 85 | 275 | 675 | 700 |
| 1863S . . . . . . . . . . . . | 916,000 | 12 | 14 | 18 | 23 | 45 | 85 | 275 | 450 | |
| 1864 . . . . . . (470) . . . 379,100 | | 15 | 18 | 24 | 32 | 55 | 100 | 275 | 450 | 700 |
| 1864S . . . . . . . . . . . . | 658,000 | 12 | 14 | 18 | 23 | 45 | 85 | 275 | 1,000 | |
| 1865 . . . . . . (500) . . . 511,400 | | 14 | 16 | 22 | 28 | 50 | 90 | 300 | 450 | 700 |
| 1865S . . . . . . . . . . . . | 675,000 | 12 | 14 | 18 | 23 | 45 | 85 | 275 | 400 | |
| 1866S, No Motto . . . . . . . . | 60,000 | 100 | 200 | 300 | 400 | 900 | 1,200 | 2,300 | 5,000 | |

## Variety 4 – Motto Above Eagle (1866–1873)

| | Mintage | G-4 | VG-8 | F-12 | VF-20 | EF-40 | AU-50 | MS-60 | MS-63 | PF-63 |
|---|---|---|---|---|---|---|---|---|---|---|
| 1866 . . . . . . . .(725) . . .744,900 | | $12 | $14 | $17 | $23 | $45 | $80 | $220 | $450 | $550 |
| 1866S . . . . . . . . . . . . . .994,000 | | 12 | 14 | 17 | 23 | 45 | 90 | 320 | 800 | |
| 1867 . . . . . . . .(625) . . .449,300 | | 13 | 16 | 25 | 35 | 65 | 95 | 275 | 500 | 550 |
| 1867S . . . . . . . . . . . . .1,196,000 | | 12 | 14 | 17 | 22 | 45 | 80 | 300 | 650 | |
| 1868 . . . . . . . .(600) . . .417,600 | | 15 | 17 | 23 | 30 | 70 | 120 | 325 | 475 | 550 |
| 1868S . . . . . . . . . . . . .1,160,000 | | 12 | 14 | 17 | 23 | 40 | 90 | 325 | 600 | |
| 1869 . . . . . . . .(600) . . .795,300 | | 12 | 14 | 17 | 23 | 40 | 90 | 275 | 450 | 550 |
| 1869S . . . . . . . . . . . . . .656,000 | | 12 | 14 | 17 | 23 | 42 | 42 | 90 | 350 | 850 | |
| 1870 . . . . . . . .(1,000) . . .633,900 | | 12 | 14 | 17 | 23 | 40 | 80 | 300 | 450 | 550 |
| 1870CC . . . . . . . . . . . . .54,617 | | 325 | 650 | 1,200 | 2,500 | 7,000 | 14,000 | — | — | |
| 1870S . . . . . . . . . . . . .1,004,000 | | 12 | 14 | 17 | 23 | 45 | 95 | 300 | 1,000 | |
| 1871 . . . . . . . .(960) . .1,203,600 | | 12 | 14 | 17 | 23 | 45 | 95 | 275 | 450 | 550 |
| 1871CC . . . . . . . . . . . . .153,950 | | 65 | 100 | 170 | 300 | 900 | 1,500 | 6,500 | 22,000 | |
| 1871S . . . . . . . . . . . . .2,178,000 | | 12 | 14 | 17 | 23 | 42 | 90 | 300 | 500 | |
| 1872 . . . . . . . .(950) . . .880,600 | | 12 | 14 | 17 | 23 | 40 | 90 | 275 | 550 | 550 |
| 1872CC . . . . . . . . . . . . .257,000 | | 30 | 45 | 100 | 200 | 650 | 1,600 | 5,000 | 35,000 | |
| 1872S . . . . . . . . . . . . . .580,000 | | 13 | 16 | 22 | 35 | 75 | 140 | 425 | 1,000 | |
| 1873 . . . . . . . .(600) . . .801,200 | | 12 | 14 | 17 | 23 | 40 | 95 | 250 | 450 | 550 |
| 1873CC . . . . . . . . . . . . .122,500 | | 60 | 100 | 150 | 275 | 650 | 1,900 | 4,500 | 27,000 | |

## Variety 5 – Arrows at Date (1873–1874)

| | Mintage | G-4 | VG-8 | F-12 | VF-20 | EF-40 | AU-50 | MS-60 | MS-63 | PF-63 |
|---|---|---|---|---|---|---|---|---|---|---|
| 1873 . . . . . . . .(550) . .1,815,150 | | $15 | $20 | $25 | $48 | $130 | $160 | $500 | $900 | $1,200 |
| 1873CC . . . . . . . . . . . . .214,560 | | 60 | 95 | 150 | 400 | 800 | 1,100 | 2,750 | 8,500 | |
| 1873S . . . . . . . . . . . . . .228,000 | | 20 | 30 | 45 | 95 | 180 | 300 | 950 | 2,750 | |
| 1874 . . . . . . . .(700) . .2,359,600 | | 15 | 20 | 25 | 48 | 130 | 160 | 500 | 900 | 1,200 |
| 1874CC . . . . . . . . . . . . . .59,000 | | 135 | 225 | 430 | 850 | 1,800 | 3,750 | 6,750 | 11,000 | |
| 1874S . . . . . . . . . . . . . .394,000 | | 18 | 25 | 40 | 90 | 150 | 250 | 875 | 1,600 | |

## Variety 4 Resumed, With Weight Standard of Variety 5 (1875–1891)

| | Mintage | G-4 | VG-8 | F-12 | VF-20 | EF-40 | AU-50 | MS-60 | MS-63 | PF-63 |
|---|---|---|---|---|---|---|---|---|---|---|
| 1875 . . . . . . .(700) | . .6,026,800 | $12 | $14 | $17 | $22 | $35 | $75 | $220 | $300 | $550 |
| 1875CC . . . . . . . . . . . . | .1,008,000 | 12 | 15 | 25 | 35 | 60 | 100 | 275 | 500 | |
| 1875S . . . . . . . . . . . . | .3,200,000 | 12 | 14 | 17 | 22 | 35 | 75 | 220 | 300 | |
| 1876 . . . . . . .(1,150) | .8,418,000 | 12 | 14 | 17 | 22 | 35 | 75 | 220 | 300 | 550 |
| 1876CC . . . . . . . . . . . . | .1,956,000 | 12 | 14 | 17 | 22 | 40 | 80 | 275 | 575 | |
| 1876S . . . . . . . . . . . . | .4,528,000 | 12 | 14 | 17 | 22 | 35 | 75 | 220 | 300 | |
| 1877 . . . . . . .(510) | .8,304,000 | 12 | 14 | 17 | 22 | 35 | 75 | 220 | 300 | 550 |
| 1877CC . . . . . . . . . . . . | .1,420,000 | 12 | 14 | 17 | 22 | 40 | 85 | 260 | 500 | |
| 1877S . . . . . . . . . . . . | .5,356,000 | 12 | 14 | 17 | 22 | 35 | 75 | 220 | 300 | |
| 1878 . . . . . . .(800) | .1,377,600 | 12 | 14 | 17 | 22 | 35 | 75 | 220 | 300 | 550 |
| 1878CC . . . . . . . . . . . . . . | .62,000 | 125 | 200 | 350 | 600 | 1,200 | 2,000 | 3,500 | 10,500 | |
| 1878S . . . . . . . . . . . . | .12,000 | 7,500 | 15,000 | 18,000 | 20,000 | 22,500 | 26,000 | 30,000 | 50,000 | |
| 1879 . . . . . .(1,100) | . . . .4,800 | 90 | 110 | 130 | 170 | 190 | 250 | 350 | 400 | 550 |
| 1880 . . . . . .(1,355) | . . . .8,400 | 90 | 110 | 130 | 170 | 190 | 250 | 350 | 400 | 550 |
| 1881 . . . . . . .(975) | . . . .10,000 | 90 | 110 | 130 | 170 | 190 | 250 | 350 | 400 | 550 |
| 1882 . . . . . .(1,100) | . . . .4,400 | 100 | 120 | 180 | 200 | 210 | 280 | 425 | 400 | 550 |
| 1883 . . . . . .(1,039) | . . . .8,000 | 90 | 110 | 130 | 170 | 190 | 245 | 350 | 400 | 550 |
| 1884 . . . . . . .(875) | . . . .4,400 | 100 | 120 | 180 | 200 | 210 | 280 | 450 | 525 | 550 |
| 1885 . . . . . . .(930) | . . . .5,200 | 100 | 120 | 180 | 200 | 210 | 260 | 475 | 550 | 550 |
| 1886 . . . . . . .(886) | . . . .5,000 | 100 | 120 | 180 | 200 | 210 | 260 | 475 | 550 | 550 |
| 1887 . . . . . . .(710) | . . . .5,000 | 125 | 150 | 180 | 200 | 220 | 270 | 485 | 575 | 550 |
| 1888 . . . . . . .(832) | . . . .12,001 | 90 | 120 | 130 | 170 | 190 | 250 | 425 | 500 | 550 |
| 1889 . . . . . . .(711) | . . . .12,000 | 90 | 110 | 130 | 170 | 190 | 250 | 425 | 500 | 550 |
| 1890 . . . . . . .(590) | . . . .12,000 | 90 | 110 | 130 | 170 | 190 | 250 | 425 | 500 | 550 |
| 1891 . . . . . . .(600) | . . .200,000 | 20 | 25 | 40 | 50 | 65 | 95 | 275 | 370 | 550 |

## BARBER OR LIBERTY HEAD (1892–1915)

Like the dime and quarter dollar, this type was designed by Charles E. Barber, whose initial B is on the truncation of the neck.

**G-4 Good:** Date and legends legible. LIBERTY worn off headband.

**VG-8 Very Good:** Some letters legible in LIBERTY.

**F-12 Fine:** LIBERTY nearly completely legible, but worn.

**VF-20 Very Fine:** All letters in LIBERTY evenly plain.

**EF-40 Extremely Fine:** LIBERTY bold, and its ribbon distinct.

**AU-50 About Uncirculated:** Slight trace of wear above forehead, leaf tips, and cheek, and on eagle's head, tail, and wing tips.

**MS-60 Uncirculated:** No trace of wear. Light blemishes.

**MS-63 Choice Uncirculated:** Some distracting contact marks or blemishes in prime focal areas. Impaired luster possible.

**PF-63 Choice Proof:** Reflective surfaces with only a few blemishes in secondary focal places. No major flaws.

Mintmark location on
reverse, below eagle.

*See next page for chart.*

| | Mintage | G-4 | VG-8 | F-12 | VF-20 | EF-40 | AU-50 | MS-60 | MS-63 | PF-63 |
|---|---|---|---|---|---|---|---|---|---|---|
| 1892 ......(1,245) ...934,000 | | $12 | $15 | $30 | $40 | $125 | $160 | $220 | $400 | $475 |
| 1892O ...........390,000 | | 115 | 150 | 190 | 210 | 250 | 275 | 460 | 850 | |
| 1892S ...........1,029,028 | | 100 | 120 | 175 | 200 | 240 | 300 | 475 | 1,200 | |
| 1893 .......(792) .1,826,000 | | 11 | 12 | 28 | 40 | 100 | 150 | 300 | 700 | 475 |
| 1893O ...........1,389,000 | | 11 | 20 | 32 | 65 | 160 | 200 | 310 | 750 | |
| 1893S ...........740,000 | | 60 | 80 | 100 | 160 | 240 | 325 | 620 | 1,900 | |
| 1894 ......(972) .1,148,000 | | 10 | 20 | 32 | 60 | 130 | 170 | 270 | 500 | 475 |
| 1894O ...........2,138,000 | | 11 | 12 | 30 | 50 | 130 | 160 | 260 | 500 | |
| 1894S ...........4,048,690 | | 11 | 12 | 28 | 45 | 120 | 150 | 255 | 675 | |
| 1895 .......(880) .1,834,338 | | 11 | 12 | 28 | 40 | 110 | 150 | 260 | 500 | 475 |
| 1895O ...........1,766,000 | | 11 | 12 | 28 | 50 | 110 | 165 | 275 | 675 | |
| 1895S ...........1,108,086 | | 12 | 15 | 40 | 70 | 125 | 175 | 275 | 650 | |
| 1896 .......(762) ...950,000 | | 11 | 12 | 28 | 50 | 110 | 150 | 275 | 425 | 500 |
| 1896O ...........924,000 | | 14 | 17 | 60 | 85 | 175 | 300 | 650 | 2,600 | |
| 1896S ...........1,140,948 | | 35 | 45 | 70 | 110 | 185 | 240 | 600 | 1,600 | |
| 1897 .......(731) .2,480,000 | | 11 | 12 | 15 | 35 | 65 | 140 | 220 | 400 | 500 |
| 1897O ...........632,000 | | 50 | 100 | 200 | 325 | 400 | 550 | 800 | 1,600 | |
| 1897S ...........933,900 | | 50 | 75 | 125 | 210 | 350 | 450 | 675 | 1,600 | |
| 1898 .......(735) .2,956,000 | | 11 | 12 | 14 | 30 | 75 | 150 | 200 | 400 | 500 |
| 1898O ...........874,000 | | 10 | 25 | 100 | 125 | 185 | 250 | 475 | 1,600 | |
| 1898S ...........2,358,550 | | 11 | 12 | 22 | 50 | 100 | 150 | 400 | 1,500 | |
| 1899 .......(846) .5,538,000 | | 11 | 12 | 14 | 30 | 65 | 140 | 200 | 400 | 500 |
| 1899O ...........1,724,000 | | 11 | 12 | 22 | 50 | 100 | 160 | 325 | 700 | |
| 1899S ...........1,686,411 | | 11 | 12 | 22 | 45 | 100 | 150 | 300 | 1,000 | |
| 1900 .......(912) .4,762,000 | | 11 | 12 | 14 | 35 | 65 | 140 | 200 | 400 | 475 |
| 1900O ...........2,744,000 | | 11 | 12 | 20 | 40 | 125 | 160 | 325 | 1,450 | |
| 1900S ...........2,560,322 | | 11 | 12 | 18 | 40 | 100 | 140 | 275 | 1,100 | |
| 1901 .......(813) .4,268,000 | | 11 | 12 | 14 | 30 | 60 | 150 | 200 | 400 | 475 |
| 1901O ...........1,124,000 | | 11 | 13 | 25 | 60 | 140 | 200 | 700 | 2,600 | |
| 1901S ...........847,044 | | 14 | 23 | 75 | 160 | 285 | 450 | 900 | 3,100 | |
| 1902 .......(777) .4,922,000 | | 11 | 12 | 14 | 30 | 60 | 150 | 200 | 425 | 475 |
| 1902O ...........2,526,000 | | 11 | 12 | 18 | 35 | 90 | 150 | 350 | 1,750 | |
| 1902S ...........1,460,670 | | 11 | 12 | 20 | 45 | 110 | 165 | 350 | 1,000 | |
| 1903 .......(755) .2,278,000 | | 11 | 12 | 14 | 35 | 70 | 150 | 210 | 750 | 475 |
| 1903O ...........2,100,000 | | 11 | 12 | 16 | 40 | 90 | 160 | 300 | 1,000 | |
| 1903S ...........1,920,772 | | 11 | 12 | 16 | 40 | 95 | 170 | 300 | 950 | |
| 1904 .......(670) .2,992,000 | | 11 | 12 | 14 | 30 | 65 | 140 | 200 | 550 | 475 |
| 1904O ...........1,117,600 | | 11 | 13 | 28 | 90 | 150 | 225 | 550 | 1,500 | |
| 1904S ...........553,038 | | 15 | 27 | 110 | 225 | 450 | 700 | 3,200 | 8,000 | |
| 1905 .......(727) ...662,000 | | 11 | 13 | 30 | 50 | 110 | 140 | 230 | 700 | 475 |
| 1905O ...........505,000 | | 12 | 16 | 40 | 80 | 140 | 175 | 350 | 850 | |
| 1905S ...........2,494,000 | | 11 | 12 | 18 | 40 | 90 | 150 | 300 | 900 | |
| 1906 .......(675) .2,638,000 | | 11 | 12 | 14 | 36 | 75 | 120 | 200 | 400 | 475 |
| 1906D ...........4,028,000 | | 11 | 12 | 15 | 36 | 75 | 120 | 200 | 400 | |
| 1906O ...........2,446,000 | | 11 | 12 | 16 | 38 | 80 | 120 | 275 | 700 | |
| 1906S ...........1,740,154 | | 11 | 12 | 18 | 40 | 90 | 120 | 275 | 525 | |
| 1907 .......(575) .2,598,000 | | 11 | 12 | 14 | 32 | 70 | 120 | 200 | 400 | 475 |
| 1907D ...........3,856,000 | | 11 | 12 | 14 | 32 | 70 | 120 | 200 | 400 | |
| 1907O ...........3,946,600 | | 11 | 12 | 14 | 32 | 70 | 140 | 220 | 400 | |
| 1907S ...........1,250,000 | | 11 | 12 | 23 | 60 | 120 | 275 | 525 | 2,750 | |
| 1908 .......(545) .1,354,000 | | 11 | 12 | 14 | 30 | 70 | 120 | 200 | 400 | 475 |
| 1908D ...........3,280,000 | | 11 | 12 | 14 | 30 | 65 | 120 | 200 | 400 | |
| 1908O ...........5,360,000 | | 11 | 12 | 14 | 30 | 70 | 120 | 210 | 425 | |
| 1908S ...........1,644,828 | | 11 | 12 | 20 | 50 | 110 | 170 | 350 | 1,200 | |
| 1909 .......(650) .2,368,000 | | 11 | 12 | 14 | 30 | 65 | 120 | 200 | 400 | 475 |

| | Mintage | G-4 | VG-8 | F-12 | VF-20 | EF-40 | AU-50 | MS-60 | MS-63 | PF-63 |
|---|---|---|---|---|---|---|---|---|---|---|
| 19090 . . . . . . . . . . . . . .925,400 | | $11 | $12 | $18 | $45 | $120 | $200 | $350 | $850 | |
| 1909S . . . . . . . . . . . . .1,764,000 | | 11 | 12 | 15 | 32 | 90 | 140 | 260 | 550 | |
| 1910 . . . . . . . .(551) . . .418,000 | | 11 | 13 | 28 | 55 | 130 | 150 | 290 | 500 | $475 |
| 1910S . . . . . . . . . . . . .1,948,000 | | 11 | 12 | 15 | 35 | 85 | 130 | 250 | 850 | |
| 1911 . . . . . . . .(543) .1,406,000 | | 11 | 12 | 14 | 28 | 65 | 120 | 180 | 400 | 475 |
| 1911D . . . . . . . . . . . . .695,080 | | 11 | 12 | 15 | 30 | 75 | 125 | 240 | 425 | |
| 1911S . . . . . . . . . . . . .1,272,000 | | 11 | 12 | 15 | 30 | 75 | 130 | 250 | 600 | |
| 1912 . . . . . . . .(700) .1,550,000 | | 11 | 12 | 14 | 28 | 70 | 120 | 200 | 400 | 475 |
| 1912D . . . . . . . . . . . . .2,300,800 | | 11 | 12 | 14 | 28 | 70 | 120 | 200 | 400 | |
| 1912S . . . . . . . . . . . . .1,370,000 | | 11 | 12 | 15 | 30 | 75 | 130 | 240 | 475 | |
| 1913 . . . . . . . .(627) . . .188,000 | | 25 | 30 | 85 | 150 | 220 | 350 | 500 | 800 | 550 |
| 1913D . . . . . . . . . . . . .534,000 | | 11 | 12 | 16 | 35 | 90 | 120 | 225 | 425 | |
| 1913S . . . . . . . . . . . . .604,000 | | 11 | 13 | 20 | 40 | 100 | 140 | 275 | 550 | |
| 1914 . . . . . . . .(380) . . .124,230 | | 60 | 70 | 135 | 220 | 290 | 425 | 600 | 900 | 750 |
| 1914S . . . . . . . . . . . . .992,000 | | 11 | 12 | 15 | 30 | 80 | 140 | 275 | 500 | |
| 1915 . . . . . . . .(450) . . .138,000 | | 40 | 65 | 110 | 150 | 250 | 380 | 600 | 1,100 | 750 |
| 1915D . . . . . . . . . . . . .1,170,400 | | 11 | 12 | 13 | 28 | 60 | 130 | 200 | 400 | |
| 1915S . . . . . . . . . . . . .1,604,000 | | 11 | 12 | 13 | 28 | 60 | 130 | 200 | 400 | |

## LIBERTY WALKING (1916–1947)

This type was designed by Adolph A. Weinman, whose monogram, AW, appears under the tip of the tail feathers. On the 1916 coins and some of the 1917 coins, the mintmark is located on the obverse below the motto.

**G-4 Good:** Rims defined. Motto IN GOD WE TRUST legible.

**VG-8 Very Good:** Motto distinct. About half of skirt lines at left clear.

**F-12 Fine:** All skirt lines evident, but worn in spots. Clear details in sandal below motto.

**VF-20 Very Fine:** Skirt lines sharp, including leg area. Little wear on breast and right arm.

**EF-40 Extremely Fine:** All skirt lines bold.

**AU-50 About Uncirculated:** Slight trace of wear on Liberty's head, knee, and breast tips and on eagle's claws and head.

**MS-60 Uncirculated:** No trace of wear. Light blemishes.

**MS-63 Choice Uncirculated:** Some distracting contact marks or blemishes in prime focal areas. Impaired luster possible.

**PF-63 Choice Proof:** Reflective surfaces with only a few blemishes in secondary focal places. No major flaws.

**PF-65 Gem Proof:** Brilliant surfaces with no noticeable blemishes or flaws. A few scattered, barely noticeable marks or hairlines possible.

1916–1917

1917–1947

**Mintmark Locations**

*Choice Uncirculated well-struck specimens are worth more than values listed.*

| | Mintage | G-4 | VG-8 | F-12 | VF-20 | EF-40 | AU-50 | MS-60 | MS-63 |
|---|---|---|---|---|---|---|---|---|---|
| 1916 . . . . . . . . . . . . . . . . . . . . . . . .608,000 | | $19 | $25 | $40 | $90 | $125 | $150 | $200 | $250 |
| 1916D, Obverse Mintmark . . . . . . . .1,014,400 | | 20 | 26 | 35 | 70 | 115 | 145 | 200 | 300 |
| 1916S, Obverse Mintmark . . . . . . . . .508,000 | | 50 | 65 | 100 | 225 | 325 | 400 | 650 | 1,200 |
| 1917 . . . . . . . . . . . . . . . . . . . . . . .12,292,000 | | 10 | 10 | 11 | 12 | 20 | 35 | 75 | 120 |

*Chart continued on next page.*

| | Mintage | G-4 | VG-8 | F-12 | VF-20 | EF-40 | AU-50 | MS-60 | MS-63 |
|---|---|---|---|---|---|---|---|---|---|
| 1917D, Obverse Mintmark | 765,400 | $10 | $15 | $32 | $70 | $110 | $150 | $275 | $650 |
| 1917D, Reverse Mintmark | 1,940,000 | 11 | 13 | 25 | 60 | 140 | 250 | 450 | 950 |
| 1917S, Obverse Mintmark | 952,000 | 15 | 21 | 60 | 165 | 375 | 700 | 1,300 | 2,500 |
| 1917S, Reverse Mintmark | 5,554,000 | 10 | 11 | 12 | 20 | 38 | 85 | 175 | 900 |
| 1918 | 6,634,000 | 10 | 11 | 12 | 35 | 90 | 150 | 300 | 650 |
| 1918D | 3,853,040 | 10 | 11 | 12 | 45 | 120 | 250 | 650 | 1,400 |
| 1918S | 10,282,000 | 10 | 11 | 12 | 20 | 40 | 100 | 250 | 1,300 |
| 1919 | 962,000 | 10 | 15 | 35 | 150 | 275 | 400 | 650 | 1,800 |
| 1919D | 1,165,000 | 12 | 15 | 40 | 160 | 350 | 850 | 2,500 | 8,500 |
| 1919S | 1,552,000 | 12 | 14 | 35 | 140 | 400 | 900 | 1,600 | 5,200 |
| 1920 | 6,372,000 | 10 | 11 | 12 | 22 | 45 | 85 | 150 | 350 |
| 1920D | 1,551,000 | 10 | 12 | 30 | 120 | 240 | 450 | 750 | 2,200 |
| 1920S | 4,624,000 | 10 | 11 | 13 | 40 | 110 | 220 | 400 | 1,500 |
| 1921 | 246,000 | 95 | 120 | 175 | 450 | 800 | 1,400 | 2,200 | 4,750 |
| 1921D | 208,000 | 175 | 200 | 300 | 500 | 1,000 | 1,800 | 2,500 | 6,500 |
| 1921S | 548,000 | 25 | 35 | 110 | 450 | 2,500 | 4,400 | 7,000 | 15,000 |
| 1923S | 2,178,000 | 10 | 10 | 12 | 55 | 185 | 400 | 1,000 | 1,800 |
| 1927S | 2,392,000 | 10 | 10 | 12 | 25 | 70 | 200 | 600 | 1,200 |
| 1928S | 1,940,000 | 10 | 10 | 14 | 35 | 75 | 220 | 600 | 1,300 |
| 1929D | 1,001,200 | 10 | 10 | 11 | 15 | 45 | 140 | 225 | 400 |
| 1929S | 1,902,000 | 10 | 10 | 11 | 15 | 50 | 140 | 225 | 500 |
| 1933S | 1,786,000 | 10 | 10 | 11 | 13 | 30 | 140 | 320 | 650 |
| 1934 | 6,964,000 | 10 | 10 | 10 | 10 | 10 | 14 | 40 | 50 |
| 1934D | 2,361,000 | 10 | 10 | 10 | 10 | 18 | 45 | 75 | 125 |
| 1934S | 3,652,000 | 10 | 10 | 10 | 10 | 15 | 60 | 175 | 450 |
| 1935 | 9,162,000 | 10 | 10 | 10 | 10 | 10 | 12 | 25 | 40 |
| 1935D | 3,003,800 | 10 | 10 | 10 | 10 | 18 | 30 | 75 | 125 |
| 1935S | 3,854,000 | 10 | 10 | 10 | 10 | 18 | 60 | 125 | 235 |

| | Mintage | G-4 | VG-8 | F-12 | VF-20 | EF-40 | AU-50 | MS-60 | MS-63 | PF-63 | PF-65 |
|---|---|---|---|---|---|---|---|---|---|---|---|
| 1936 . . (3,901) | 12,614,000 | $10 | $10 | $10 | $10 | $10 | $12 | $27 | $40 | $950 | $2,000 |
| 1936D | 4,252,400 | 10 | 10 | 10 | 10 | 12 | 20 | 45 | 60 | | |
| 1936S | 3,884,000 | 10 | 10 | 10 | 10 | 12 | 22 | 75 | 90 | | |
| 1937 . . (5,728) | 9,522,000 | 10 | 10 | 10 | 10 | 10 | 12 | 22 | 35 | 280 | 700 |
| 1937D | 1,676,000 | 10 | 10 | 10 | 10 | 18 | 50 | 120 | 150 | | |
| 1937S | 2,090,000 | 10 | 10 | 10 | 10 | 12 | 32 | 85 | 120 | | |
| 1938 . . (8,152) | 4,110,000 | 10 | 10 | 10 | 10 | 11 | 25 | 35 | 65 | 225 | 450 |
| 1938D | 491,600 | 50 | 60 | 70 | 80 | 95 | 140 | 275 | 350 | | |
| 1939 . . (8,808) | 6,812,000 | 10 | 10 | 10 | 10 | 10 | 12 | 22 | 35 | 200 | 300 |
| 1939D | 4,267,800 | 10 | 10 | 10 | 10 | 10 | 12 | 22 | 40 | | |
| 1939S | 2,552,000 | 10 | 10 | 10 | 10 | 11 | 35 | 70 | 90 | | |

| | Mintage | VG-8 | F-12 | VF-20 | EF-40 | AU-50 | MS-60 | MS-63 | PF-63 | PF-65 |
|---|---|---|---|---|---|---|---|---|---|---|
| 1940 . . . . (11,279) | 9,156,000 | $10 | $10 | $10 | $10 | $10 | $15 | $22 | $200 | $300 |
| 1940S | 4,550,000 | 10 | 10 | 10 | 10 | 11 | 30 | 40 | | |
| 1941 . . . . (15,412) | 24,192,000 | 10 | 10 | 10 | 10 | 10 | 16 | 30 | 200 | 300 |
| 1941D | 11,248,400 | 10 | 10 | 10 | 10 | 11 | 18 | 35 | | |
| 1941S | 8,098,000 | 10 | 10 | 10 | 10 | 15 | 32 | 55 | | |
| 1942 . . . . (21,120) | 47,818,000 | 10 | 10 | 10 | 10 | 10 | 15 | 25 | 200 | 300 |
| 1942D | 10,973,800 | 10 | 10 | 10 | 10 | 11 | 18 | 35 | | |
| 1942S | 12,708,000 | 10 | 10 | 10 | 10 | 11 | 20 | 28 | | |
| 1943 | 53,190,000 | 10 | 10 | 10 | 10 | 10 | 15 | 21 | | |
| 1943D | 11,346,000 | 10 | 10 | 10 | 10 | 11 | 22 | 32 | | |
| 1943S | 13,450,000 | 10 | 10 | 10 | 10 | 11 | 20 | 25 | | |
| 1944 | 28,206,000 | 10 | 10 | 10 | 10 | 10 | 15 | 21 | | |
| 1944D | 9,769,000 | 10 | 10 | 10 | 10 | 11 | 18 | 25 | | |

| | Mintage | VG-8 | F-12 | VF-20 | EF-40 | AU-50 | MS-60 | MS-63 |
|---|---|---|---|---|---|---|---|---|
| 1944S | .8,904,000 | $10 | $10 | $10 | $10 | $11 | $16 | $28 |
| 1945 | .31,502,000 | 10 | 10 | 10 | 10 | 10 | 15 | 21 |
| 1945D | .9,966,800 | 10 | 10 | 10 | 10 | 11 | 15 | 22 |
| 1945S | .10,156,000 | 10 | 10 | 10 | 10 | 11 | 15 | 25 |
| 1946 | .12,118,000 | 10 | 10 | 10 | 10 | 10 | 15 | 21 |
| 1946D | .2,151,000 | 10 | 10 | 10 | 10 | 11 | 16 | 22 |
| 1946S | .3,724,000 | 10 | 10 | 10 | 10 | 11 | 16 | 22 |
| 1947 | .4,094,000 | 10 | 10 | 10 | 10 | 10 | 16 | 22 |
| 1947D | .3,900,600 | 10 | 10 | 10 | 10 | 11 | 16 | 22 |

## FRANKLIN (1948–1963)

The Benjamin Franklin half dollar and the Roosevelt dime were both designed by John R. Sinnock. His initials appear below the shoulder.

**VF-20 Very Fine:** At least half of the lower and upper incused lines on rim of Liberty Bell on reverse visible.
**EF-40 Extremely Fine:** Wear spots at top of end of Franklin's curls and hair at back of ears. Wear evident at top and on lettering of Liberty Bell.
**MS-60 Uncirculated:** No trace of wear. Light blemishes.
**MS-63 Choice Uncirculated:** Some distracting contact marks or blemishes in prime focal areas. Impaired luster possible.
**MS-65 Gem Uncirculated:** Only light, scattered contact marks that are not distracting. Strong luster, good eye appeal.
**PF-63 Choice Proof:** Reflective surfaces with only a few blemishes in secondary focal places. No major flaws.
**PF-65 Gem Proof:** Brilliant surfaces with no noticeable blemishes or flaws. A few scattered, barely noticeable marks or hairlines possible.

**Mintmark Location**

*Choice, well-struck Uncirculated halves with full bell lines command higher prices.*

| | Mintage | VF-20 | EF-40 | MS-60 | MS-63 | MS-65 | PF-63 | PF-65 |
|---|---|---|---|---|---|---|---|---|
| 1948 | .3,006,814 | $10 | $10 | $11 | $14 | $40 | | |
| 1948D | .4,028,600 | 10 | 10 | 11 | 12 | 65 | | |
| 1949 | .5,614,000 | 10 | 10 | 16 | 20 | 70 | | |
| 1949D | .4,120,600 | 10 | 10 | 16 | 23 | 350 | | |
| 1949S | .3,744,000 | 10 | 11 | 25 | 35 | 60 | | |
| 1950 | (51,386) . .7,742,123 | 10 | 10 | 14 | 18 | 50 | $115 | $200 |
| 1950D | .8,031,600 | 10 | 10 | 12 | 17 | 125 | | |
| 1951 | (57,500) . .16,802,102 | 10 | 10 | 11 | 12 | 30 | 65 | 150 |
| 1951D | .9,475,200 | 10 | 10 | 14 | 18 | 75 | | |
| 1951S | .13,696,000 | 10 | 10 | 12 | 16 | 35 | | |
| 1952 | (81,980) . .21,192,093 | 10 | 10 | 11 | 12 | 35 | 35 | 100 |
| 1952D | .25,395,600 | 10 | 10 | 11 | 12 | 60 | | |
| 1952S | .5,526,000 | 10 | 10 | 15 | 20 | 50 | | |
| 1953 | (128,800) . . .2,668,120 | 10 | 10 | 11 | 13 | 35 | 26 | 60 |
| 1953D | .20,900,400 | 10 | 10 | 11 | 12 | 50 | | |
| 1953S | .4,148,000 | 10 | 10 | 12 | 17 | 30 | | |

*Chart continued on next page.*

| | Mintage | VF-20 | EF-40 | MS-60 | MS-63 | MS-65 | PF-63 | PF-65 |
|---|---|---|---|---|---|---|---|---|
| 1954 | (233,300) . .13,188,202 | $10 | $10 | $11 | $12 | $27 | $20 | $45 |
| 1954D | .25,445,580 | 10 | 10 | 11 | 13 | 50 | | |
| 1954S | .4,993,400 | 10 | 10 | 11 | 15 | 22 | | |
| 1955 | (378,200) . . .2,498,181 | 10 | 10 | 12 | 16 | 30 | 20 | 40 |
| 1956 | (669,384) . . .4,032,000 | 10 | 10 | 11 | 14 | 20 | 14 | 20 |
| 1957 | (1,247,952) . . .5,114,000 | 10 | 10 | 11 | 12 | 20 | 12 | 14 |
| 1957D | .19,966,850 | 10 | 10 | 11 | 12 | 22 | | |
| 1958 | (875,652) . . .4,042,000 | 10 | 10 | 11 | 12 | 25 | 12 | 16 |
| 1958D | .23,962,412 | 10 | 10 | 11 | 12 | 20 | | |
| 1959 | (1,149,291) . . .6,200,000 | 10 | 10 | 11 | 12 | 32 | 11 | 12 |
| 1959D | .13,053,750 | 10 | 10 | 11 | 12 | 45 | | |
| 1960 | (1,691,602) . . .6,024,000 | 10 | 10 | 11 | 12 | 50 | 11 | 12 |
| 1960D | .18,215,812 | 10 | 10 | 11 | 12 | 80 | | |
| 1961 | (3,028,244) . . .8,290,000 | 10 | 10 | 11 | 12 | 35 | 11 | 12 |
| 1961D | .20,276,442 | 10 | 10 | 11 | 12 | 60 | | |
| 1962 | (3,218,019) . . .9,714,000 | 10 | 10 | 11 | 12 | 55 | 11 | 12 |
| 1962D | .35,473,281 | 10 | 10 | 11 | 12 | 60 | | |
| 1963 | (3,075,645) . .22,164,000 | 10 | 10 | 11 | 12 | 25 | 11 | 12 |
| 1963D | .67,069,292 | 10 | 10 | 11 | 12 | 25 | | |

## KENNEDY (1964 TO DATE)

Gilroy Roberts, then chief engraver of the Mint, designed the obverse of this coin. His stylized initials are on the truncation of the forceful bust of President John F. Kennedy. The reverse, which uses the eagle from the presidential seal for the motif, is the work of assistant engraver Frank Gasparro.

Mintmark Location (1964)

Mintmark Location (1968 to Date)

### Silver Coinage (1964)

| | Mintage | MS-63 | PF-63 | PF-65 |
|---|---|---|---|---|
| 1964 | (3,950,762) . .273,304,004 | $10 | $11 | $12 |
| 1964D | .156,205,446 | 10 | | |

### Silver Clad Coinage (1965–1970)

| | Mintage | MS-63 | PF-63 | PF-65 |
|---|---|---|---|---|
| 1965 | .65,879,366 | $4 | | |
| 1966 | .108,984,932 | 4 | | |
| 1967 | .295,046,978 | 4 | | |
| 1968D | .246,951,930 | 4 | | |
| 1968S | (3,041,506) | | $4.50 | $5 |
| 1969D | .129,881,800 | $4 | | |
| 1969S | (2,934,631) | | $4.50 | $5 |
| 1970D | .2,150,000 | 10 | | |
| 1970S | (2,632,810) | | 5.00 | 9 |

## Clad Coinage and Silver Proofs (1971 to Date)

| | Mintage | MS-63 | PF-63 | PF-65 | | Mintage | MS-63 | PF-63 | PF-65 |
|---|---|---|---|---|---|---|---|---|---|
| 1971 | 155,164,000 | $0.55 | | | 1973 | 64,964,000 | $0.55 | | |
| 1971D | 302,097,424 | 0.55 | | | 1973D | 83,171,400 | 0.55 | | |
| 1971S | (3,220,733) | | $1.50 | $3.00 | 1973S | (2,760,339) | | $1.50 | $2.50 |
| 1972 | 153,180,000 | 0.60 | | | 1974 | 201,596,000 | 0.55 | | |
| 1972D | 141,890,000 | 0.60 | | | 1974D | 79,066,300 | 0.55 | | |
| 1972S | (3,260,996) | | 1.50 | 3.00 | 1974S | (2,612,568) | | 1.50 | 3.00 |

### Bicentennial (1776–1976)

| | Mintage | MS-63 | PF-63 | PF-65 |
|---|---|---|---|---|
| 1776–1976, Clad | 234,308,000 | $0.55 | | |
| 1776–1976D, Clad | 287,565,248 | 0.55 | | |
| 1776–1976S, Clad | (7,059,099) | | $0.75 | $1.25 |
| 1776–1976S, Silver | 11,000,000 | 4.00 | | |
| 1776–1976S, Silver | (4,000,000) | | 4.50 | 5.00 |

Note: Mintage figures for 1976-S silver coins are approximate; many were melted in 1982.

### Eagle Reverse Resumed (1977 to Date)

| | Mintage | MS-63 | PF-63 | PF-65 | | Mintage | MS-63 | PF-63 | PF-65 |
|---|---|---|---|---|---|---|---|---|---|
| 1977 | 43,598,000 | $0.60 | | | 1982S | (3,857,479) | | $1.00 | $1.50 |
| 1977D | 31,449,106 | 0.60 | | | 1983P | 34,139,000 | $2.50 | | |
| 1977S | (3,251,152) | | $1.00 | $1.25 | 1983D | 32,472,244 | 3.00 | | |
| 1978 | 14,350,000 | 0.60 | | | 1983S | (3,279,126) | | 1.00 | 1.75 |
| 1978D | 13,765,799 | 1.00 | | | 1984P | 26,029,000 | 0.75 | | |
| 1978S | (3,127,781) | | 1.00 | 1.50 | 1984D | 26,262,158 | 0.75 | | |
| 1979 | 68,312,000 | 0.55 | | | 1984S | (3,065,110) | | 1.00 | 2.00 |
| 1979D | 15,815,422 | 0.55 | | | 1985P | 18,706,962 | 2.00 | | |
| 1979S | (3,677,175) | | | | 1985D | 19,814,034 | 1.50 | | |
| Filled S | | | 1.00 | 1.25 | 1985S | (3,362,821) | | 1.00 | 1.75 |
| Clear S | | | 6.00 | 9.00 | 1986P | 13,107,633 | 3.00 | | |
| 1980P | 44,134,000 | 0.55 | | | 1986D | 15,336,145 | 2.50 | | |
| 1980D | 33,456,449 | 0.55 | | | 1986S | (3,010,497) | | 3.00 | 4.50 |
| 1980S | (3,554,806) | | 1.00 | 1.50 | 1987P (a) | 2,890,758 | 2.00 | | |
| 1981P | 29,544,000 | 0.75 | | | 1987D (a) | 2,890,758 | 2.00 | | |
| 1981D | 27,839,533 | 0.55 | | | 1987S | (4,227,728) | | 1.00 | 1.75 |
| 1981S | (4,063,083) | | | | 1988P | 13,626,000 | 1.50 | | |
| Clear S | | | 4.00 | 8.00 | 1988D | 12,000,096 | 1.35 | | |
| Flat S | | | 1.00 | 1.50 | 1988S | (3,262,948) | | 2.00 | 2.50 |
| 1982P | 10,819,000 | 2.00 | | | 1989P | 24,542,000 | 1.00 | | |
| 1982D | 13,140,102 | 2.25 | | | 1989D | 23,000,216 | 1.10 | | |

a. Not issued for circulation.

*Chart continued on next page.*

| | Mintage | MS-63 | PF-63 | PF-65 |
|---|---|---|---|---|
| 1989S | (3,220,194) | | $1.50 | $3.00 |
| 1990P | 22,278,000 | $1.00 | | |
| 1990D | 20,096,242 | 1.10 | | |
| 1990S | (3,299,559) | | 1.50 | 2.00 |
| 1991P | 14,874,000 | 0.70 | | |
| 1991D | 15,054,678 | 1.25 | | |
| 1991S | (2,867,787) | | 4.00 | 4.00 |
| 1992P | 17,628,000 | 0.50 | | |
| 1992D | 17,000,106 | 1.10 | | |
| 1992S | (2,858,981) | | 2.00 | 3.00 |
| 1992S, Silver | (1,317,579) | | 11.00 | 12.00 |
| 1993P | 15,510,000 | 0.50 | | |
| 1993D | 15,000,006 | 0.50 | | |
| 1993S | (2,633,439) | | 3.00 | 5.00 |
| 1993S, Silver | (761,353) | | 12.00 | 17.00 |
| 1994P | 23,718,000 | 0.50 | | |
| 1994D | 23,828,110 | 0.50 | | |
| 1994S | (2,484,594) | | 3.00 | 4.00 |
| 1994S, Silver | (785,329) | | 14.00 | 18.00 |
| 1995P | 26,496,000 | 0.50 | | |
| 1995D | 26,288,000 | 0.50 | | |
| 1995S | (2,117,496) | | 6.00 | 8.00 |
| 1995S, Silver | (679,985) | | 30.00 | 40.00 |
| 1996P | 24,442,000 | 0.50 | | |
| 1996D | 24,744,000 | 0.50 | | |
| 1996S | (1,750,244) | | 3.00 | 5.00 |
| 1996S, Silver | (775,021) | | 15.00 | 20.00 |
| 1997P | 20,882,000 | 0.50 | | |
| 1997D | 19,876,000 | 0.50 | | |
| 1997S | (2,055,000) | | 3.00 | 6.00 |
| 1997S, Silver | (741,678) | | 20.00 | 30.00 |
| 1998P | 15,646,000 | 0.50 | | |
| 1998D | 15,064,000 | 0.50 | | |
| 1998S | (2,086,507) | | 3.00 | 6.00 |
| 1998S, Silver | (878,792) | | 12.00 | 14.00 |
| 1998S, Silver, Matte Finish | (b) | | 100.00 | 125.00 |
| 1999P | 8,900,000 | 0.55 | | |
| 1999D | 10,682,000 | 0.55 | | |
| 1999S | (2,543,401) | | 3.00 | 5.00 |
| 1999S, Silver | (804,565) | | 12.00 | 16.00 |
| 2000P | 22,600,000 | 0.60 | | |
| 2000D | 19,466,000 | 0.60 | | |
| 2000S | (3,082,483) | | 2.00 | 3.00 |
| 2000S, Silver | (965,421) | | 11.00 | 12.00 |

| | Mintage | MS-63 | PF-63 | PF-65 |
|---|---|---|---|---|
| 2001P | 21,200,000 | $0.55 | | |
| 2001D | 19,504,000 | 0.55 | | |
| 2001S | (2,294,909) | | $3.25 | $4.00 |
| 2001S, Silver | (889,697) | | 11.00 | 13.00 |
| 2002P (a) | 3,100,000 | 0.65 | | |
| 2002D (a) | 2,500,000 | 0.65 | | |
| 2002S | (2,319,766) | | 2.00 | 3.00 |
| 2002S, Silver | (892,229) | | 11.00 | 12.00 |
| 2003P (a) | 2,500,000 | 0.65 | | |
| 2003D (a) | 2,500,000 | 0.65 | | |
| 2003S | (2,172,684) | | 2.00 | 3.00 |
| 2003S, Silver | (1,125,755) | | 11.00 | 13.00 |
| 2004P (a) | 2,900,000 | 0.65 | | |
| 2004D (a) | 2,900,000 | 0.65 | | |
| 2004S | (1,789,488) | | 3.00 | 7.00 |
| 2004S, Silver | (1,175,934) | | 11.00 | 13.00 |
| 2005P | 3,800,000 | 0.65 | | |
| 2005D | 3,500,000 | 0.65 | | |
| 2005S | (2,275,000) | | 2.00 | 3.00 |
| 2005S, Silver | (1,069,679) | | 11.00 | 12.00 |
| 2006P (a) | 2,400,000 | 0.65 | | |
| 2006D (a) | 2,000,000 | 0.65 | | |
| 2006S | (2,000,428) | | 2.00 | 3.00 |
| 2006S, Silver | (1,054,008) | | 11.00 | 12.00 |
| 2007P (a) | 2,400,000 | 0.65 | | |
| 2007D (a) | 2,400,000 | 0.65 | | |
| 2007S | (1,702,116) | | 2.00 | 3.00 |
| 2007S, Silver | (875,050) | | 11.00 | 12.00 |
| 2008P (a) | 1,700,000 | 0.65 | | |
| 2008D (a) | 1,700,000 | 0.65 | | |
| 2008S | (1,415,674) | | 2.00 | 3.00 |
| 2008S, Silver | (763,887) | | 11.00 | 12.00 |
| 2009P (a) | 1,900,000 | 0.65 | | |
| 2009D (a) | 1,900,000 | 0.65 | | |
| 2009S | (1,477,967) | | 2.00 | 3.00 |
| 2009S, Silver | (694,406) | | 11.00 | 12.00 |
| 2010P (a) | 1,800,000 | 0.65 | | |
| 2010D (a) | 1,700,000 | 0.65 | | |
| 2010S | 978,016 | | 2.00 | 3.00 |
| 2010S, Silver | 476,999 | | 11.00 | 12.00 |
| 2011P (a) | | 0.65 | | |
| 2011D (a) | | 0.65 | | |
| 2011S | | | 2.00 | 3.00 |
| 2011S, Silver | | | 11.00 | 12.00 |

a. Not issued for circulation. b. Included in commemorative set (see page 219).

The silver dollar was authorized by Congress April 2, 1792. Its weight was specified at 416 grains and its fineness at .8924. The first issues appeared in 1794, and until 1804 all silver dollars had the value stamped on the edge: HUNDRED CENTS, ONE DOLLAR OR UNIT. After a lapse in coinage of the silver dollar during the period 1804 to 1835, coins were made with either plain (1836 only) or reeded edges and the value was placed on the reverse side.

The weight was changed by the law of January 18, 1837, to 412-1/2 grains, fineness .900. The coinage was discontinued by the Act of February 12, 1873, and reauthorized by the Act of February 28, 1878. The silver dollar was again discontinued after 1935, and since then copper-nickel and other base-metal pieces have been coined for circulation. (See also Silver Bullion, page 221.)

## FLOWING HAIR (1794–1795)

**AG-3 About Good:** Clear enough to identify.
**G-4 Good:** Date and letters legible. Main devices outlined, but lacking in detail.
**VG-8 Very Good:** Major details discernible. Letters well formed but worn.
**F-12 Fine:** Hair ends distinguishable. Top hair lines visible, but otherwise worn smooth.
**VF-20 Very Fine:** Some detail visible in hair in center. Other details more bold.
**EF-40 Extremely Fine:** Hair well defined but with some wear.
**AU-50 About Uncirculated:** Slight trace of wear on tips of highest curls; breast feathers usually weak.
**MS-60 Uncirculated:** No trace of wear. Light blemishes.

| | Mintage | AG-3 | G-4 | VG-8 | F-12 | VF-20 | EF-40 | AU-50 | MS-60 |
|---|---|---|---|---|---|---|---|---|---|
| 1794 | 1,758 | $15,000 | $27,000 | $40,000 | $50,000 | $90,000 | $14,000 | $200,000 | — |
| 1795 | 160,295 | 425 | 800 | 1,000 | 2,000 | 3,000 | 8,000 | 12,000 | $28,000 |

## DRAPED BUST (1795–1804)
### Small Eagle Reverse (1795–1798)

**AG-3 About Good:** Clear enough to identify.
**G-4 Good:** Bust outlined, no detail. Date legible, some leaves evident.
**VG-8 Very Good:** Drapery worn except deepest folds. Hair lines smooth.
**F-12 Fine:** All drapery lines distinguishable. Some detail visible in hair lines near cheek and neck.
**VF-20 Very Fine:** Left side of drapery worn smooth.
**EF-40 Extremely Fine:** Drapery distinctly visible. Hair well outlined and detailed.
**AU-50 About Uncirculated:** Slight trace of wear on the bust shoulder and hair to left of forehead, as well as on eagle's breast and top edges of wings.
**MS-60 Uncirculated:** No trace of wear. Light blemishes.

| | Mintage | AG-3 | G-4 | VG-8 | F-12 | VF-20 | EF-40 | AU-50 | MS-60 |
|---|---|---|---|---|---|---|---|---|---|
| 1795, Bust Type | 42,738 | $375 | $650 | $900 | $1,500 | $2,600 | $5,500 | $8,500 | $22,000 |
| 1796 | 79,920 | 375 | 650 | 900 | 1,500 | 2,600 | 5,500 | 8,500 | 22,000 |
| 1797 | 7,776 | 375 | 650 | 900 | 1,500 | 2,600 | 5,500 | 8,500 | 22,000 |
| 1798 | 327,536 | 375 | 650 | 900 | 1,500 | 2,600 | 5,500 | 9,000 | 22,000 |

## Heraldic Eagle Reverse (1798–1804)

**G-4 Good:** Letters and date legible. E PLURIBUS UNUM illegible.
**VG-8 Very Good:** Motto partially legible. Only deepest drapery details visible. All other lines smooth.
**F-12 Fine:** All drapery lines distinguishable. Some detail visible in hair lines near cheek and neck.
**VF-20 Very Fine:** Left side of drapery worn smooth.
**EF-40 Extremely Fine:** Drapery distinct. Hair well detailed.
**AU-50 About Uncirculated:** Slight trace of wear on the bust shoulder and hair to left of forehead, as well as on eagle's breast and top edges of wings.
**MS-60 Uncirculated:** No trace of wear. Light blemishes.

| | Mintage | G-4 | VG-8 | F-12 | VF-20 | EF-40 | AU-50 | MS-60 |
|---|---|---|---|---|---|---|---|---|
| 1798, Heraldic Eagle | * | $450 | $550 | $750 | $1,300 | $2,500 | $5,000 | $11,000 |
| 1799 | 423,515 | 450 | 550 | 750 | 1,300 | 2,500 | 5,000 | 11,000 |
| 1800 | 220,920 | 450 | 550 | 750 | 1,300 | 2,500 | 5,000 | 11,000 |
| 1801 | 54,454 | 450 | 550 | 750 | 1,300 | 2,500 | 5,000 | 11,000 |
| 1802 | 41,650 | 450 | 550 | 750 | 1,300 | 2,500 | 5,000 | 11,000 |
| 1803 | 85,634 | 450 | 550 | 750 | 1,300 | 2,500 | 5,000 | 12,000 |
| 1804, Variety 1, 0 Above Cloud (a) | | | | | *Proof: $3,500,000* | | | |
| 1804, Variety 2, 0 Above Space Between Clouds (a) | | | | | *Proof: $2,500,000* | | | |

* Included in number above. **a.** Numerous counterfeits exist.

## GOBRECHT (1836–1839)

Silver dollars of 1836, 1838, and 1839 were mostly made as patterns and restrikes, but some were made in quantities for general circulation.

| | VF-20 | EF-40 | AU-50 | PF-60 |
|---|---|---|---|---|
| 1836, C. GOBRECHT F. on base. Reverse eagle flying upward amid stars. Plain edge. Although scarce, this is the most common variety and was issued for circulation as regular coinage. | $5,250 | $8,000 | $11,000 | $13,500 |
| 1838, Similar obverse, designer's name omitted, stars added around border. Reverse eagle flying left in plain field. Reeded edge. | 8,750 | 13,500 | 16,000 | 19,000 |
| 1839, Obverse as above. Reverse eagle in plain field. Reeded edge. Issued for circulation as regular coinage. | 8,000 | 11,000 | 14,000 | 16,000 |

## LIBERTY SEATED (1840–1873)

Starting again in 1840, silver dollars were issued for general circulation. The seated figure of Liberty was adopted for the obverse, and a heraldic eagle for the reverse.

**VG-8 Very Good:** Any three letters of LIBERTY at least two-thirds complete.
**F-12 Fine:** All seven letters of LIBERTY visible, though weak.
**VF-20 Very Fine:** LIBERTY strong, but slight wear visible on its ribbon.
**EF-40 Extremely Fine:** Horizontal lines of shield complete. Eagle's eye plain.
**AU-50 About Uncirculated:** Traces of light wear on only the high points of the design. Half of mint luster present.
**MS-60 Uncirculated:** No trace of wear. Light marks or blemishes.
**PF-60 Proof:** Several contact marks, hairlines, or light rubs possible on surface. Luster possibly dull and eye appeal lacking.
**PF-63 Choice Proof:** Reflective surfaces with only a few blemishes in secondary focal places. No major flaws.

### No Motto (1840–1865)

*Location of mintmark, when present, is on reverse, below eagle.*

*See next page for chart.*

| | Mintage | VG-8 | F-12 | VF-20 | EF-40 | AU-50 | MS-60 | PF-60 | PF-63 |
|---|---|---|---|---|---|---|---|---|---|
| 1840 | 61,005 | $160 | $175 | $200 | $350 | $500 | $1,800 | $8,250 | $20,000 |
| 1841 | 173,000 | 125 | 150 | 175 | 285 | 420 | 1,150 | 8,500 | 22,000 |
| 1842 | 184,618 | 125 | 150 | 175 | 285 | 420 | 1,000 | 8,500 | 20,000 |
| 1843 | 165,100 | 125 | 150 | 175 | 285 | 420 | 1,000 | 8,500 | 20,000 |
| 1844 | 20,000 | 130 | 175 | 200 | 325 | 600 | 1,600 | 7,000 | 19,000 |
| 1845 | 24,500 | 140 | 185 | 225 | 350 | 675 | 4,750 | 8,000 | 19,000 |
| 1846 | 110,600 | 125 | 150 | 175 | 285 | 420 | 1,000 | 6,500 | 16,500 |
| 1846O | 59,000 | 150 | 200 | 225 | 325 | 600 | 2,800 | | |
| 1847 | 140,750 | 125 | 150 | 175 | 285 | 420 | 1,000 | 8,250 | 16,500 |
| 1848 | 15,000 | 225 | 285 | 375 | 525 | 900 | 2,100 | 8,250 | 19,000 |
| 1849 | 62,600 | 125 | 150 | 175 | 285 | 375 | 1,100 | 9,500 | 25,000 |
| 1850 | 7,500 | 325 | 350 | 550 | 875 | 1,300 | 3,000 | 8,750 | 17,500 |
| 1850O | 40,000 | 170 | 235 | 400 | 825 | 1,750 | 7,100 | | |
| 1851 | 1,300 | 3,000 | 4,750 | 6,500 | 9,000 | 14,000 | 18,000 | 16,000 | 21,500 |
| 1852 | 1,100 | 2,750 | 4,750 | 6,500 | 8,750 | 14,000 | 17,000 | 17,500 | 23,000 |
| 1853 | 46,110 | 140 | 185 | 235 | 370 | 780 | 1,500 | 13,000 | 23,000 |
| 1854 | 33,140 | 825 | 1,300 | 1,600 | 2,500 | 4,000 | 5,200 | 7,500 | 12,000 |
| 1855 | 26,000 | 600 | 800 | 1,250 | 2,000 | 3,100 | 5,200 | 7,500 | 13,000 |
| 1856 | 63,500 | 225 | 300 | 375 | 800 | 1,400 | 2,800 | 3,750 | 10,000 |
| 1857 | 94,000 | 225 | 300 | 375 | 800 | 1,200 | 1,900 | 3,100 | 5,000 |
| 1858 . . . . . (300+) | | 1,900 | 2,250 | 2,800 | 3,500 | 4,500 | | 5,500 | 8,000 |
| 1859 . . . . . (800) | 255,700 | 160 | 225 | 275 | 350 | 500 | 1,400 | 1,300 | 2,800 |
| 1859O | 360,000 | 125 | 150 | 175 | 285 | 420 | 750 | | |
| 1859S | 20,000 | 200 | 285 | 370 | 1,100 | 2,500 | 8,500 | | |
| 1860 . . . . (1,330) | 217,600 | 130 | 175 | 230 | 325 | 450 | 775 | 1,100 | 2,300 |
| 1860O | 515,000 | 125 | 150 | 175 | 285 | 420 | 700 | | |
| 1861 . . . (1,000) | 77,500 | 325 | 450 | 575 | 700 | 1,350 | 1,850 | 1,100 | 2,300 |
| 1862 . . . . . (550) | 11,540 | 290 | 385 | 490 | 675 | 1,250 | 1,850 | 1,100 | 2,400 |
| 1863 . . . . . (460) | 27,200 | 220 | 255 | 275 | 375 | 800 | 1,700 | 1,100 | 2,400 |
| 1864 . . . . . (470) | 30,700 | 135 | 185 | 300 | 400 | 800 | 2,000 | 1,100 | 2,400 |
| 1865 . . . . . (500) | 46,500 | 135 | 185 | 300 | 400 | 800 | 1,800 | 1,100 | 2,400 |

## With Motto IN GOD WE TRUST (1866–1873)

**Motto IN GOD WE TRUST on Reverse (1866–1873)**

| | Mintage | VG-8 | F-12 | VF-20 | EF-40 | AU-50 | MS-60 | PF-60 | PF-63 |
|---|---|---|---|---|---|---|---|---|---|
| 1866 . . . . . (725) | 48,900 | $140 | $185 | $235 | $350 | $675 | $1,200 | $850 | $2,000 |
| 1867 . . . . . (625) | 46,900 | 140 | 175 | 235 | 325 | 575 | 1,200 | 850 | 2,000 |
| 1868 . . . . . (600) | 162,100 | 125 | 160 | 220 | 260 | 525 | 1,000 | 850 | 2,000 |
| 1869 . . . . . (600) | 423,700 | 125 | 160 | 200 | 260 | 475 | 975 | 850 | 2,000 |

| | Mintage | VG-8 | F-12 | VF-20 | EF-40 | AU-50 | MS-60 | PF-60 | PF-63 |
|---|---|---|---|---|---|---|---|---|---|
| 1870 ....(1,000) ....415,000 | | $130 | $160 | $180 | $250 | $375 | $875 | $850 | $2,000 |
| 1870CC .............11,758 | | 300 | 400 | 600 | 950 | 2,300 | 7,500 | | |
| 1870S ................... | | | 100,000 | 200,000 | 300,000 | 500,000 | 700,000 | | |
| 1871 ......(960) ...1,073,800 | | 130 | 160 | 185 | 250 | 400 | 800 | 850 | 2,000 |
| 1871CC .............1,376 | | 1,400 | 2,200 | 3,000 | 6,000 | 14,000 | 37,000 | | |
| 1872 ......(950) ...1,105,500 | | 130 | 160 | 185 | 250 | 400 | 800 | 850 | 2,000 |
| 1872CC .............3,150 | | 775 | 1,200 | 1,800 | 3,000 | 7,000 | 15,000 | | |
| 1872S .............9,000 | | 200 | 275 | 375 | 900 | 1,700 | 5,500 | | |
| 1873 ......(600) ....293,000 | | 150 | 180 | 200 | 300 | 475 | 975 | 850 | 2,000 |
| 1873CC .............2,300 | | 2,750 | 4,000 | 6,500 | 10,000 | 17,500 | 50,000 | | |

# TRADE DOLLARS (1873–1885)

This trade dollar was issued for circulation in the Orient to compete with dollar-size coins of other countries. It weighed 420 grains compared to 412-1/2 grains, the weight of the regular silver dollar.

**VG-8 Very Good:** About half of mottoes IN GOD WE TRUST (on Liberty's pedestal) and E PLURIBUS UNUM (on obverse ribbon) visible. Rim on both sides well defined.

**F-12 Fine:** Mottoes and LIBERTY legible but worn.

**EF-40 Extremely Fine:** Mottoes and LIBERTY sharp. Only slight wear on rims.

**AU-50 About Uncirculated:** Slight trace of wear on Liberty's left breast and left knee and on hair above ear, as well as on eagle's head, knee, and wing tips.

**MS-60 Uncirculated:** No trace of wear. Light blemishes.

**MS-63 Choice Uncirculated:** Some distracting contact marks or blemishes in prime focal areas. Impaired luster possible.

**PF-63 Choice Proof:** Reflective surfaces with only a few blemishes in secondary focal places. No major flaws.

1875-S, S Over CC

| | Mintage | VG-8 | F-12 | EF-40 | AU-50 | MS-60 | MS-63 | PF-63 |
|---|---|---|---|---|---|---|---|---|
| 1873 .............(865) ....396,635 | | $60 | $70 | $90 | $150 | $425 | $1,850 | $1,900 |
| 1873CC ..................124,500 | | 100 | 175 | 320 | 800 | 3,500 | 10,000 | |
| 1873S ..................703,000 | | 60 | 70 | 90 | 175 | 500 | 1,100 | |
| 1874 .............(700) ....987,100 | | 60 | 70 | 90 | 150 | 275 | 850 | 1,900 |
| 1874CC ..................1,373,200 | | 100 | 150 | 250 | 300 | 700 | 3,800 | |
| 1874S ..................2,549,000 | | 60 | 70 | 90 | 150 | 275 | 850 | |
| 1875 .............(700) ....218,200 | | 80 | 180 | 295 | 500 | 1,000 | 1,700 | 1,900 |
| 1875CC ..................1,573,700 | | 80 | 180 | 285 | 450 | 900 | 1,500 | |
| 1875S ..................4,487,000 | | 60 | 70 | 90 | 150 | 275 | 850 | |
| 1875S, S Over CC .................* | | 125 | 200 | 450 | 700 | 1,500 | 6,000 | |
| 1876 ..........(1,150) ....455,000 | | 60 | 70 | 90 | 150 | 275 | 850 | 1,900 |
| 1876CC ..................509,000 | | 80 | 125 | 225 | 600 | 1,750 | 14,000 | |

* Included in number above.

*Chart continued on next page.*

135

| | Mintage | VG-8 | F-12 | EF-40 | AU-50 | MS-60 | MS-63 | PF-63 |
|---|---|---|---|---|---|---|---|---|
| 1876S | 5,227,000 | $60 | $70 | $90 | $150 | $275 | $850 | |
| 1877 | (510)...3,039,200 | 60 | 70 | 90 | 150 | 275 | 850 | $1,900 |
| 1877CC | 534,000 | 100 | 150 | 300 | 375 | 700 | 3,500 | |
| 1877S | 9,519,000 | 60 | 70 | 90 | 150 | 275 | 850 | |
| 1878 | (900) | | | 600 | | | | 1,900 |
| 1878CC (a) | 97,000 | 250 | 375 | 1,100 | 2,000 | 6,500 | 13,000 | |
| 1878S | 4,162,000 | 60 | 70 | 90 | 150 | 275 | 850 | |
| 1879 | (1,541) | | | 600 | | | | 1,900 |
| 1880 | (1,987) | | | 600 | | | | 1,900 |
| 1881 | (960) | | | 600 | | | | 1,900 |
| 1882 | (1,097) | | | 600 | | | | 1,900 |
| 1883 | (979) | | | 600 | | | | 1,900 |
| 1884 (b) | (10) | | | | | | | 300,000 |
| 1885 (b) | (5) | | | | | | | 950,000 |

**a.** 44,148 trade dollars were melted on July 19, 1878. Many of these may have been 1878-CC. **b.** The trade dollars of 1884 and 1885 were unknown to collectors until 1908. None are listed in the Mint director's report, and numismatists believe that they are not a part of the regular Mint issue.

# MORGAN (1878–1921)

George T. Morgan, formerly a pupil of William Wyon's at the Royal Mint in London, designed the new dollar. His initial M is found at the truncation of the neck, at the last tress. It also appears on the reverse on the left-hand loop of the ribbon.

Sharply struck prooflike coins have a highly reflective surface and usually command substantial premiums.

**VF-20 Very Fine:** Two thirds of hair lines from top of forehead to ear visible. Ear well defined. Feathers on eagle's breast worn.

**EF-40 Extremely Fine:** All hair lines strong and ear bold. Eagle's feathers all plain but with slight wear on breast and wing tips.

**AU-50 About Uncirculated:** Slight trace of wear on the bust shoulder and hair left of forehead, and on eagle's breast and top edges of wings.

**MS-60 Uncirculated:** No trace of wear. Full mint luster present, but may be noticeably marred by scuff marks or bag abrasions.

**MS-63 Choice Uncirculated:** No trace of wear; full mint luster; few noticeable surface marks.

**MS-64 Uncirculated:** A few scattered contact marks. Good eye appeal and attractive luster.

**MS-65 Gem Uncirculated:** Only light, scattered contact marks that are not distracting. Strong luster, good eye appeal.

### 8 Tail Feathers, 1878, Philadelphia Only

*Mintmark location on reverse, below wreath.*

Most Proof Morgan dollars, where indicated in mintage records (quantity shown in parentheses), are valued approximately as follows:
Proof-60 – $600; Proof-63 – $1,300; Proof-65 – $3,000.

*Most Uncirculated silver dollars have scratches or nicks because of handling of mint bags. Choice sharply struck coins with full brilliance and without blemishes are worth more than listed values.*

| | Mintage | VF-20 | EF-40 | AU-50 | MS-60 | MS-63 | MS-65 |
|---|---|---|---|---|---|---|---|
| 1878, 8 Feathers . . . . . . . . . . . .(500) . . . .749,500 | | $22 | $23 | $26 | $70 | $95 | $750 |
| 1878, 7 Feathers . . . . . . . . . . . .(250) . . .9,759,300 | | 22 | 22 | 25 | 35 | 55 | 725 |
| 1878, 7/8 Clear Doubled Feathers . . . . . . . . . . . . .* | | 22 | 24 | 30 | 75 | 140 | 1,400 |
| 1878CC . . . . . . . . . . . . . . . . . . . . . . .2,212,000 | | 52 | 65 | 70 | 120 | 200 | 975 |
| 1878S . . . . . . . . . . . . . . . . . . . . . . . .9,774,000 | | 22 | 22 | 23 | 28 | 42 | 165 |
| 1879 . . . . . . . . . . . . . . .(1,100) . .14,806,000 | | 22 | 22 | 23 | 24 | 32 | 500 |
| 1879CC, CC Over CC . . . . . . . . . . . . . . . . .756,000 | | 75 | 250 | 600 | 2,000 | 3,300 | 13,500 |
| 1879O . . . . . . . . . . . . . . . . . . . . . . . .2,887,000 | | 22 | 23 | 25 | 40 | 125 | 1,650 |
| 1879S . . . . . . . . . . . . . . . . . . . . . . . .9,110,000 | | 22 | 22 | 23 | 24 | 28 | 95 |
| 1880 . . . . . . . . . . . . . . .(1,355) . .12,600,000 | | 22 | 22 | 23 | 24 | 30 | 380 |
| 1880CC . . . . . . . . . . . . . . . . . . . . . . . . .591,000 | | 100 | 130 | 170 | 300 | 350 | 750 |
| 1880O . . . . . . . . . . . . . . . . . . . . . . . .5,305,000 | | 22 | 22 | 23 | 32 | 185 | 9,500 |
| 1880S . . . . . . . . . . . . . . . . . . . . . . . .8,900,000 | | 22 | 22 | 23 | 24 | 28 | 95 |
| 1881 . . . . . . . . . . . . . . .(984) . .9,163,000 | | 22 | 22 | 23 | 24 | 30 | 430 |
| 1881CC . . . . . . . . . . . . . . . . . . . . . . . . .296,000 | | 145 | 185 | 200 | 220 | 280 | 475 |
| 1881O . . . . . . . . . . . . . . . . . . . . . . . .5,708,000 | | 22 | 22 | 23 | 24 | 28 | 730 |
| 1881S . . . . . . . . . . . . . . . . . . . . . . .12,760,000 | | 22 | 22 | 23 | 24 | 28 | 95 |
| 1882 . . . . . . . . . . . . . . .(1,100) . .11,100,000 | | 22 | 22 | 23 | 24 | 30 | 170 |
| 1882CC . . . . . . . . . . . . . . . . . . . . . . .1,133,000 | | 55 | 65 | 70 | 100 | 130 | 250 |
| 1882O . . . . . . . . . . . . . . . . . . . . . . . .6,090,000 | | 22 | 22 | 23 | 24 | 30 | 450 |
| 1882S . . . . . . . . . . . . . . . . . . . . . . . .9,250,000 | | 22 | 22 | 23 | 24 | 28 | 95 |
| 1883 . . . . . . . . . . . . . . .(1,039) . .12,290,000 | | 22 | 22 | 23 | 24 | 28 | 95 |
| 1883CC . . . . . . . . . . . . . . . . . . . . . . .1,204,000 | | 60 | 70 | 80 | 100 | 130 | 235 |
| 1883O . . . . . . . . . . . . . . . . . . . . . . . .8,725,000 | | 22 | 22 | 23 | 24 | 28 | 95 |
| 1883S . . . . . . . . . . . . . . . . . . . . . . . .6,250,000 | | 22 | 25 | 70 | 325 | 1,400 | 15,000 |
| 1884 . . . . . . . . . . . . . . .(875) . .14,070,000 | | 22 | 22 | 23 | 24 | 28 | 135 |
| 1884CC . . . . . . . . . . . . . . . . . . . . . . .1,136,000 | | 70 | 80 | 90 | 115 | 135 | 230 |
| 1884O . . . . . . . . . . . . . . . . . . . . . . . .9,730,000 | | 22 | 22 | 23 | 24 | 28 | 95 |
| 1884S . . . . . . . . . . . . . . . . . . . . . . . .3,200,000 | | 22 | 25 | 240 | 2,500 | 15,000 | 99,500 |
| 1885 . . . . . . . . . . . . . . .(930) . .17,787,000 | | 22 | 22 | 23 | 24 | 28 | 95 |
| 1885CC . . . . . . . . . . . . . . . . . . . . . . . . .228,000 | | 250 | 275 | 290 | 310 | 350 | 775 |
| 1885O . . . . . . . . . . . . . . . . . . . . . . . .9,185,000 | | 22 | 22 | 23 | 24 | 28 | 95 |
| 1885S . . . . . . . . . . . . . . . . . . . . . . . .1,497,000 | | 22 | 25 | 50 | 90 | 135 | 800 |
| 1886 . . . . . . . . . . . . . . .(886) . .19,963,000 | | 22 | 22 | 23 | 24 | 28 | 95 |
| 1886O . . . . . . . . . . . . . . . . . . . . . . .10,710,000 | | 22 | 25 | 50 | 325 | 1,900 | 95,000 |
| 1886S . . . . . . . . . . . . . . . . . . . . . . . . .750,000 | | 30 | 40 | 60 | 140 | 235 | 1,500 |
| 1887 . . . . . . . . . . . . . . .(710) . .20,290,000 | | 22 | 22 | 23 | 24 | 28 | 95 |
| 1887O . . . . . . . . . . . . . . . . . . . . . . .11,550,000 | | 22 | 22 | 23 | 24 | 65 | 1,200 |
| 1887S . . . . . . . . . . . . . . . . . . . . . . . .1,771,000 | | 22 | 22 | 23 | 60 | 125 | 1,500 |
| 1888 . . . . . . . . . . . . . . .(833) . .19,183,000 | | 22 | 22 | 23 | 24 | 28 | 100 |
| 1888O . . . . . . . . . . . . . . . . . . . . . . .12,150,000 | | 22 | 22 | 23 | 24 | 30 | 210 |
| 1888S . . . . . . . . . . . . . . . . . . . . . . . . .657,000 | | 80 | 95 | 110 | 150 | 210 | 1,600 |
| 1889 . . . . . . . . . . . . . . .(811) . .21,726,000 | | 22 | 22 | 23 | 24 | 28 | 95 |
| 1889CC . . . . . . . . . . . . . . . . . . . . . . . .350,000 | | 775 | 1,850 | 3,750 | 11,000 | 17,000 | 155,000 |
| 1889O . . . . . . . . . . . . . . . . . . . . . . .11,875,000 | | 22 | 22 | 25 | 75 | 200 | 2,200 |

* Included in number above.

*Chart continued on next page.*

| | Mintage | VF-20 | EF-40 | AU-50 | MS-60 | MS-63 | MS-65 |
|---|---|---|---|---|---|---|---|
| 1889S . . . . . . . . . . | 700,000 | $28 | $37 | $55 | $125 | $225 | $900 |
| 1890 . . . .(590) . . | 16,802,000 | 22 | 22 | 23 | 24 | 30 | 950 |
| 1890CC . . . . . . . . | 2,309,041 | 60 | 80 | 95 | 180 | 450 | 3,000 |
| 1890O . . . . . . . . . | 10,701,000 | 22 | 22 | 23 | 30 | 55 | 750 |
| 1890S . . . . . . . . . | 8,230,373 | 22 | 22 | 23 | 30 | 55 | 450 |
| 1891 . . . .(650) . . | 8,693,556 | 22 | 22 | 23 | 30 | 90 | 3,000 |
| 1891CC . . . . . . . . | 1,618,000 | 60 | 75 | 100 | 200 | 450 | 2,300 |
| 1891O . . . . . . . . . | 7,954,529 | 22 | 23 | 25 | 75 | 180 | 3,350 |
| 1891S . . . . . . . . . | 5,296,000 | 22 | 22 | 23 | 25 | 70 | 600 |
| 1892 . . .(1,245) . . | 1,036,000 | 22 | 23 | 40 | 85 | 210 | 1,850 |
| 1892CC . . . . . . . . | 1,352,000 | 125 | 220 | 300 | 750 | 1,200 | 4,600 |
| 1892O . . . . . . . . . | 2,744,000 | 22 | 23 | 35 | 85 | 165 | 2,300 |
| 1892S . . . . . . . . . | 1,200,000 | 50 | 140 | 1,000 | 16,500 | 33,000 | 100,000 |
| 1893 . . . .(792) . . | 378,000 | 100 | 130 | 175 | 325 | 700 | 3,400 |
| 1893CC . . . . . . . . | 677,000 | 225 | 800 | 975 | 1,800 | 3,600 | 27,000 |
| 1893O . . . . . . . . . | 300,000 | 150 | 275 | 460 | 1,100 | 3,750 | 110,000 |
| 1893S . . . . . . . . . | 100,000 | 3,500 | 4,800 | 12,000 | 42,000 | 80,000 | 275,000 |
| 1894 . . . .(972) . . | 110,000 | 800 | 1,000 | 1,300 | 2,500 | 3,500 | 17,000 |
| 1894O . . . . . . . . . | 1,723,000 | 27 | 50 | 130 | 325 | 2,100 | 23,000 |
| 1894S . . . . . . . . . | 1,260,000 | 40 | 67 | 185 | 310 | 600 | 3,000 |
| 1895 . . . .(880) . . | | | 15,000 (a) | 18,000 (a) | 23,000 (a) | 30,000 (a) | 42,000 (a) |
| 1895O . . . . . . . . . | 450,000 | 220 | 350 | 800 | 8,500 | 24,000 | 105,000 |
| 1895S . . . . . . . . . | 400,000 | 175 | 325 | 775 | 1,900 | 3,000 | 11,000 |
| 1896 . . . .(762) . . | 9,976,000 | 22 | 22 | 23 | 24 | 28 | 95 |
| 1896O . . . . . . . . . | 4,900,000 | 22 | 23 | 90 | 550 | 4,000 | 90,000 |
| 1896S . . . . . . . . . | 5,000,000 | 30 | 95 | 375 | 675 | 1,500 | 8,600 |
| 1897 . . . .(731) . . | 2,822,000 | 22 | 22 | 23 | 24 | 28 | 125 |
| 1897O . . . . . . . . . | 4,004,000 | 22 | 23 | 60 | 360 | 2,750 | 28,000 |
| 1897S . . . . . . . . . | 5,825,000 | 22 | 22 | 23 | 30 | 55 | 300 |
| 1898 . . . .(735) . . | 5,884,000 | 22 | 22 | 23 | 24 | 29 | 126 |
| 1898O . . . . . . . . . | 4,440,000 | 22 | 22 | 23 | 24 | 28 | 95 |
| 1898S . . . . . . . . . | 4,102,000 | 24 | 28 | 45 | 135 | 225 | 1,000 |
| 1899 . . . .(846) . . | 330,000 | 90 | 120 | 150 | 200 | 225 | 500 |
| 1899O . . . . . . . . . | 12,290,000 | 22 | 22 | 23 | 24 | 28 | 95 |
| 1899S . . . . . . . . . | 2,562,000 | 24 | 28 | 60 | 170 | 260 | 900 |
| 1900 . . . .(912) . . | 8,830,000 | 22 | 22 | 23 | 24 | 28 | 95 |
| 1900O . . . . . . . . . | 12,590,000 | 22 | 22 | 23 | 24 | 28 | 100 |
| 1900S . . . . . . . . . | 3,540,000 | 24 | 26 | 45 | 150 | 225 | 750 |
| 1901 . . . .(813) . . | 6,962,000 | 28 | 55 | 250 | 1,100 | 8,500 | 115,000 |
| 1901O . . . . . . . . . | 13,320,000 | 22 | 22 | 23 | 24 | 28 | 100 |
| 1901S . . . . . . . . . | 2,284,000 | 24 | 26 | 75 | 250 | 370 | 1,900 |
| 1902 . . . .(777) . . | 7,994,000 | 22 | 22 | 23 | 27 | 55 | 225 |
| 1902O . . . . . . . . . | 8,636,000 | 22 | 22 | 23 | 25 | 28 | 95 |
| 1902S . . . . . . . . . | 1,530,000 | 70 | 100 | 135 | 200 | 325 | 1,400 |
| 1903 . . . .(755) . . | 4,652,000 | 26 | 32 | 36 | 45 | 50 | 130 |
| 1903O . . . . . . . . . | 4,450,000 | 200 | 210 | 225 | 240 | 260 | 425 |
| 1903S . . . . . . . . . | 1,241,000 | 90 | 185 | 900 | 2,000 | 3,250 | 5,250 |
| 1904 . . . .(650) . . | 2,788,000 | 22 | 22 | 24 | 45 | 150 | 1,900 |

a. Values are for Proofs.

| | Mintage | VF-20 | EF-40 | AU-50 | MS-60 | MS-63 | MS-65 |
|---|---|---|---|---|---|---|---|
| 1904O | 3,720,000 | $22 | $22 | $23 | $24 | $28 | $95 |
| 1904S | 2,304,000 | 35 | 120 | 320 | 675 | 1,600 | 4,000 |
| 1921 | 44,690,000 | 22 | 22 | 23 | 24 | 25 | 90 |
| 1921D | 20,345,000 | 22 | 22 | 23 | 24 | 32 | 175 |
| 1921S | 21,695,000 | 22 | 22 | 23 | 24 | 32 | 610 |

# PEACE (1921–1935)

Anthony de Francisci, a medalist, designed this dollar. His monogram is located in the field of the coin under the neck of Liberty.

**VF-20 Very Fine:** Hair over eye well worn. Some strands over ear well defined. Some eagle feathers on top and outside edge of right wing visible.

**EF-40 Extremely Fine:** Hair lines over brow and ear are strong, though slightly worn. Outside wing feathers at right and those at top visible but faint.

**AU-50 About Uncirculated:** Slight trace of wear. Most luster present, although marred by contact marks.

**MS-60 Uncirculated:** No trace of wear. Full mint luster, but possibly noticeably marred by stains, surface marks, or bag abrasions.

**MS-63 Choice Uncirculated:** Some distracting contact marks or blemishes in prime focal areas. Impaired luster possible.

**MS-64 Uncirculated:** A few scattered contact marks. Good eye appeal and attractive luster.

**MS-65 Gem Uncirculated:** Only light, scattered, non-distracting contact marks. Strong luster, good eye appeal.

**PF-65 Choice Proof:** Satin surfaces, no noticeable blemishes or flaws.

*Mintmark location on reverse, below ONE.*

*Most Uncirculated silver dollars have scratches or nicks because of handling of mint bags. Choice sharply struck coins with full brilliance and without blemishes are worth more than listed values.*

| | Mintage | VF-20 | EF-40 | AU-50 | MS-60 | MS-63 | MS-65 | PF-65 |
|---|---|---|---|---|---|---|---|---|
| 1921 | 1,006,473 | $50 | $60 | $75 | $125 | $240 | $1,300 | $22,000 |
| 1922 | 51,737,000 | 22 | 22 | 23 | 24 | 25 | 80 | 30,000 |
| 1922D | 15,063,000 | 22 | 22 | 23 | 24 | 26 | 200 | |
| 1922S | 17,475,000 | 22 | 22 | 23 | 24 | 33 | 1,250 | |
| 1923 | 30,800,000 | 22 | 22 | 23 | 24 | 25 | 85 | |
| 1923D | 6,811,000 | 22 | 22 | 23 | 25 | 65 | 575 | |
| 1923S | 19,020,000 | 22 | 22 | 23 | 25 | 40 | 3,250 | |
| 1924 | 11,811,000 | 22 | 22 | 23 | 24 | 25 | 85 | |
| 1924S | 1,728,000 | 22 | 22 | 30 | 100 | 235 | 4,800 | |
| 1925 | 10,198,000 | 22 | 22 | 23 | 24 | 25 | 85 | |
| 1925S | 1,610,000 | 22 | 22 | 24 | 33 | 90 | 12,000 | |
| 1926 | 1,939,000 | 22 | 22 | 23 | 25 | 40 | 175 | |

*Chart continued on next page.*                               **139**

| | Mintage | VF-20 | EF-40 | AU-50 | MS-60 | MS-63 | MS-65 |
|---|---|---|---|---|---|---|---|
| 1926D | 2,348,700 | $22 | $22 | $23 | $31 | $85 | $275 |
| 1926S | 6,980,000 | 22 | 22 | 23 | 24 | 50 | 425 |
| 1927 | 848,000 | 22 | 22 | 23 | 37 | 85 | 1,400 |
| 1927D | 1,268,900 | 22 | 22 | 45 | 80 | 200 | 2,800 |
| 1927S | 866,000 | 22 | 22 | 40 | 75 | 200 | 5,750 |
| 1928 | 360,649 | 215 | 245 | 275 | 325 | 390 | 2,300 |
| 1928S | 1,632,000 | 22 | 22 | 25 | 85 | 325 | 12,000 |
| 1934 | 954,057 | 22 | 22 | 23 | 60 | 100 | 450 |
| 1934D | 1,569,500 | 22 | 22 | 24 | 70 | 185 | 925 |
| 1934S | 1,011,000 | 35 | 85 | 250 | 900 | 2,000 | 4,800 |
| 1935 | 1,576,000 | 22 | 22 | 23 | 45 | 65 | 335 |
| 1935S | 1,964,000 | 22 | 22 | 50 | 125 | 235 | 700 |

## EISENHOWER (1971–1978)
### Eagle Reverse (1971–1974)

Honoring both President Dwight D. Eisenhower and the first landing of man on the moon, this design is the work of Chief Engraver Frank Gasparro, whose initials are on the truncation and below the eagle. The reverse is an adaptation of the official *Apollo 11* insignia.

*Mintmark location is above date.*

| | Mintage | EF-40 | MS-63 | PF-63 | PF-65 |
|---|---|---|---|---|---|
| 1971, Copper-Nickel Clad | 47,799,000 | $1.05 | $1.75 | | |
| 1971D, Copper-Nickel Clad | 68,587,424 | 1.05 | 1.30 | | |
| 1971S, Silver Clad | (4,265,234) . . .6,868,530 | | 9.00 | $10.00 | $13.00 |
| 1972, Copper-Nickel Clad | 75,890,000 | 1.05 | 1.30 | | |
| 1972D, Copper-Nickel Clad | 92,548,511 | 1.05 | 1.30 | | |
| 1972S, Silver Clad | (1,811,631) . . .2,193,056 | | 9.00 | 10.00 | 12.00 |
| 1973, Copper-Nickel Clad **(a)** | 2,000,056 | 1.50 | 5.50 | | |
| 1973D, Copper-Nickel Clad **(a)** | 2,000,000 | 1.50 | 5.50 | | |
| 1973S, Copper-Nickel Clad | (2,760,339) . . . . . . . . . | | | 3.00 | 7.00 |
| 1973S, Silver Clad | (1,013,646) . . .1,883,140 | | 9.00 | 11.00 | 18.50 |
| 1974, Copper-Nickel Clad | 27,366,000 | 1.05 | 2.00 | | |
| 1974D, Copper-Nickel Clad | 45,517,000 | 1.05 | 2.00 | | |
| 1974S, Copper-Nickel Clad | (2,612,568) . . . . . . . . . | | | 2.50 | 3.50 |
| 1974S, Silver Clad | (1,306,579) . . .1,900,156 | | 9.00 | 10.00 | 12.00 |

**a.** 1,769,258 of each sold only in sets and not released for circulation. Unissued coins destroyed at mint.

## Bicentennial (1776–1976)

Obverse

Reverse Variety 2    Reverse Variety 1

*Variety 1: Design in low relief, bold lettering on reverse.*
*Variety 2: Sharp design, delicate lettering on reverse.*

| | Mintage | EF-40 | MS-63 | PF-63 | PF-65 |
|---|---|---|---|---|---|
| 1776–1976, Copper-Nickel Clad, Variety 1 | 4,019,000 | $1.10 | $3.00 | | |
| 1776–1976, Copper-Nickel Clad, Variety 2 | 113,318,000 | 1.10 | 1.50 | | |
| 1776–1976D, Copper-Nickel Clad, Variety 1 | 21,048,710 | 1.10 | 1.50 | | |
| 1776–1976D, Copper-Nickel Clad, Variety 2 | 82,179,564 | 1.10 | 1.50 | | |
| 1776–1976S, Copper-Nickel Clad, Variety 1 | (2,845,450) | | | $2.50 | $5.50 |
| 1776–1976S, Copper-Nickel Clad, Variety 2 | (4,149,730) | | | 2.50 | 3.50 |
| 1776–1976S, Silver Clad, Variety 1 | 11,000,000 | | 9.00 | | |
| 1776–1976S, Silver Clad, Variety 1 | (4,000,000) | | | 10.00 | 13.00 |

## Eagle Reverse Resumed (1977–1978)

| | Mintage | EF-40 | MS-63 | PF-63 | PF-65 |
|---|---|---|---|---|---|
| 1977, Copper-Nickel Clad | 12,596,000 | $1.05 | $2.00 | | |
| 1977D, Copper-Nickel Clad | 32,983,006 | 1.05 | 1.50 | | |
| 1977S, Copper-Nickel Clad | (3,251,152) | | | $2.50 | $4.00 |
| 1978, Copper-Nickel Clad | 25,702,000 | 1.05 | 1.25 | | |
| 1978D, Copper-Nickel Clad | 33,012,890 | 1.05 | 1.50 | | |
| 1978S, Copper-Nickel Clad | (3,127,781) | | | 2.50 | 4.75 |

## SUSAN B. ANTHONY (1979–1999)

Filled S    Clear S

| | Mintage | MS-63 |
|---|---|---|
| 1979P, Narrow Rim | 360,222,000 | $1 |
| 1979P, Wide Rim | * | 10 |
| 1979D | 288,015,744 | 1 |

* Included in number above.

*Chart continued on next page.*

| | Mintage | MS-63 | PF-63 | PF-65 |
|---|---|---|---|---|
| 1979S | 109,576,000 | $1.00 | | |
| 1979S, Proof, Filled S | (3,677,175) | | $2.50 | $4.00 |
| 1979S, Proof, Clear S | * | | 20.00 | 40.00 |
| 1980P | 27,610,000 | 1.05 | | |
| 1980D | 41,628,708 | 1.05 | | |
| 1980S | 20,422,000 | 1.05 | | |
| 1980S, Proof | (3,554,806) | | 2.50 | 5.00 |
| 1981P | 3,000,000 | 2.00 | | |
| 1981D | 3,250,000 | 2.00 | | |
| 1981S | 3,492,000 | 2.00 | | |
| 1981S, Proof, First S | (4,063,083) | | 2.50 | 4.00 |
| 1981S, Proof, Clear S | * | | 90.00 | 125.00 |
| 1999P | 29,592,000 | 1.25 | | |
| 1999P, Proof | (75,000) | | 10.00 | 15.00 |
| 1999D | 11,776,000 | 1.25 | | |

* Included in number above.

## SACAGAWEA (2000–2008)

The design of this coin was selected in national competition from among 120 submissions that were considered by a panel appointed by Treasury Secretary Robert Rubin. The adopted motif depicts Sacagawea, a young Native American Shoshone, as rendered by artist Glenna Goodacre. On her back she carries Jean Baptiste, her infant son. The reverse shows an eagle in flight, designed by Mint engraver Thomas D. Rogers Sr.

The composition exemplifies the spirit of Liberty, Peace, and Freedom shown by Sacagawea in her conduct as interpreter and guide to explorers Meriwether Lewis and William Clark during their famed journey westward from the great northern plains to the Pacific.

These coins have a distinctive golden color and a plain edge to distinguish them from other denominations or coins of a similar size. The change in composition and appearance was mandated under the United States Dollar Coin Act of 1997.

Several distinctive finishes can be identified on the Sacagawea dollars as a result of the Mint attempting to adjust the dies, blanks, strikes, or finishing to produce coins with minimal spotting and a better surface color. One group of 5,000 pieces dated 2000 with a special finish were presented to sculptor Glenna Goodacre in payment for the obverse design. Unexplained error coins made from mismatched dies (a state quarter obverse combined with a Sacagawea dollar reverse) are extremely rare.

| | Mintage | MS-63 | PF-63 | PF-65 |
|---|---|---|---|---|
| 2000P | 767,140,000 | $1 | | |
| 2000D | 518,916,000 | 1 | | |
| 2000S | (4,047,904) | | $3 | $6 |

# SILVER AND RELATED DOLLARS

| | Mintage | MS-63 | PF-63 | PF-65 |
|---|---|---|---|---|
| 2001P | . . . . . . .62,468,000 | $1.00 | | |
| 2001D | . . . . . . .70,939,500 | 1.00 | | |
| 2001S | . . . . . . .(3,183,740) | | $18 | $30 |
| 2002P (a) | . . . . . .3,865,610 | 1.10 | | |
| 2002D (a) | . . . . . .3,732,000 | 1.10 | | |
| 2002S | . . . . . . .(3,211,995) | | 8 | 15 |
| 2003P | . . . . . . . .3,080,000 | 1.20 | | |
| 2003D | . . . . . . . .3,080,000 | 1.20 | | |
| 2003S | . . . . . . .(3,298,439) | | 4 | 8 |
| 2004P | . . . . . . . .2,660,000 | 1.10 | | |
| 2004D | . . . . . . . .2,660,000 | 1.10 | | |
| 2004S | . . . . . . .(2,965,422) | | 4 | 8 |

| | Mintage | MS-63 | PF-63 | PF-65 |
|---|---|---|---|---|
| 2005P | . . . . . . . .2,520,000 | $1.10 | | |
| 2005D | . . . . . . . .2,520,000 | 1.10 | | |
| 2005S | . . . . . . .(3,344,679) | | $3 | $5 |
| 2006P | . . . . . . . .4,900,000 | 1.10 | | |
| 2006D | . . . . . . . .2,800,000 | 1.10 | | |
| 2006S | . . . . . . .(3,054,436) | | 3 | 5 |
| 2007P (a) | . . . . . .3,640,000 | 1.10 | | |
| 2007D (a) | . . . . . .3,920,000 | 1.10 | | |
| 2007S | . . . . . . .(2,577,166) | | 3 | 5 |
| 2008P (a) | . . . . . .9,800,000 | 1.10 | | |
| 2008D (a) | . . . .14,840,000 | 1.10 | | |
| 2008S | . . . . . . .(2,169,561) | | 3 | 5 |

a. Not issued for circulation.

## NATIVE AMERICAN (2009 TO DATE)

**Agriculture (2009)**  **Great Law of Peace (2010)**  **Wampanoag Treaty (2011)**

| | Mintage | MS-65 | PF-65 |
|---|---|---|---|
| 2009P, Agriculture | . . . . . .37,380,000 | $1.10 | |
| 2009D, Agriculture | . . . . .33,880,000 | 1.10 | |
| 2009S, Agriculture | . . . . .(1,994,998) | | $3 |
| 2010P, Great Law | . . . . . .32,060,000 | 1.10 | |
| 2010D, Great Law | . . . . . .42,980,000 | 1.10 | |

| | Mintage | MS-65 | PF-65 |
|---|---|---|---|
| 2010S, Great Law | . . . . . .(1,455,015) | | $3 |
| 2011P, Wampanoag Treaty | . . . . . . . . | $1.10 | |
| 2011D, Wampanoag Treaty | . . . . . . . . | 1.10 | |
| 2011S, Wampanoag Treaty | . . . . . . . . | | 3 |

## PRESIDENTIAL (2007–2016)

Four different coins, each bearing the image of a former U.S. president, are issued each year in the order that the presidents served. The size and composition of these coins is the same as that of the Sacagawea dollars that are also made each year. A companion series of $10 gold bullion coins (listed in the Bullion section) honors the spouse of each president.

**Presidential Dollars Reverse**

**Date, Mintmark, and Motto Incused on Edge (Motto Moved to Obverse in 2009)**

| | Mintage | MS-65 | PF-65 |
|---|---|---|---|
| 2007P, Washington | 176,680,000 | $1 | |
| 2007D, Washington | 163,680,000 | 1 | |
| 2007S, Washington | (3,965,989) | | $3 |
| 2007P, J. Adams | 112,420,000 | 1 | |
| 2007D, J. Adams | 112,140,000 | 1 | |
| 2007S, J. Adams | (3,965,989) | | 3 |

| | Mintage | MS-65 | PF-65 |
|---|---|---|---|
| 2007P, Jefferson | 100,800,000 | $1 | |
| 2007D, Jefferson | 102,810,000 | 1 | |
| 2007S, Jefferson | (3,965,989) | | $3 |
| 2007P, Madison | 84,560,000 | 1 | |
| 2007D, Madison | 87,780,000 | 1 | |
| 2007S, Madison | (3,965,989) | | 3 |

| | Mintage | MS-65 | PF-65 |
|---|---|---|---|
| 2008P, Monroe | 64,260,000 | $1 | |
| 2008D, Monroe | 60,230,000 | 1 | |
| 2008S, Monroe | (3,083,940) | | $3 |
| 2008P, J.Q. Adams | 57,540,000 | 1 | |
| 2008D, J.Q. Adams | 57,720,000 | 1 | |
| 2008S, J.Q. Adams | (3,083,940) | | 3 |

| | Mintage | MS-65 | PF-65 |
|---|---|---|---|
| 2008P, Jackson | 61,180,000 | $1 | |
| 2008D, Jackson | 61,070,000 | 1 | |
| 2008S, Jackson | (3,083,940) | | $3 |
| 2008P, Van Buren | 51,520,000 | 1 | |
| 2008D, Van Buren | 50,960,000 | 1 | |
| 2008S, Van Buren | (3,083,940) | | 3 |

Note: Errors have been reported in the Presidential dollar series, including coins minted without edge lettering. Depending on their rarity, dealers may pay a premium for such errors.

| | Mintage | MS-65 | PF-65 |
|---|---|---|---|
| 2009P, Harrison | 43,260,000 | $1 | |
| 2009D, Harrison | 55,160,000 | 1 | |
| 2009S, Harrison | (2,800,298) | | $3 |
| 2009P, Tyler | 43,540,000 | 1 | |
| 2009D, Tyler | 43,540,000 | 1 | |
| 2009S, Tyler | (2,800,298) | | 3 |

| | Mintage | MS-65 | PF-65 |
|---|---|---|---|
| 2009P, Polk | 46,620,000 | $1 | |
| 2009D, Polk | 41,720,000 | 1 | |
| 2009S, Polk | (2,800,298) | | $3 |
| 2009P, Taylor | 41,580,000 | 1 | |
| 2009D, Taylor | 36,680,000 | 1 | |
| 2009S, Taylor | (2,800,298) | | 3 |

| | Mintage | MS-65 | PF-65 |
|---|---|---|---|
| 2010P, Fillmore | 37,520,000 | $1 | |
| 2010D, Fillmore | 36,960,000 | 1 | |
| 2010S, Fillmore | (1,932,092) | | $3 |
| 2010P, Pierce | 38,220,000 | 1 | |
| 2010D, Pierce | 38,360,000 | 1 | |
| 2010S, Pierce | (1,932,092) | | 3 |

| | Mintage | MS-65 | PF-65 |
|---|---|---|---|
| 2010P, Buchanan | 36,820,000 | $1 | |
| 2010D, Buchanan | 36,540,000 | 1 | |
| 2010S, Buchanan | (1,932,092) | | $3 |
| 2010P, Lincoln | 49,000,000 | 1 | |
| 2010D, Lincoln | 48,020,000 | 1 | |
| 2010S, Lincoln | (1,932,092) | | 3 |

| | Mintage | MS-65 | PF-65 |
|---|---|---|---|
| 2011P, Johnson | | $1 | |
| 2011D, Johnson | | 1 | |
| 2011S, Johnson | | | $3 |
| 2011P, Grant | | 1 | |
| 2011D, Grant | | 1 | |
| 2011S, Grant | | | 3 |

| | Mintage | MS-65 | PF-65 |
|---|---|---|---|
| 2011P, Hayes | | $1 | |
| 2011D, Hayes | | 1 | |
| 2011S, Hayes | | | $3 |
| 2011P, Garfield | | 1 | |
| 2011D, Garfield | | 1 | |
| 2011S, Garfield | | | 3 |

Presidential dollar designs scheduled for 2012 are as follows: Chester Arthur, Grover Cleveland (two coins for his two terms in office), and Benjamin Harrison.

Coinage of the gold dollar was authorized by the Act of March 3, 1849. The weight was 25.8 grains, fineness .900. The first type, struck until 1854, is known as the Liberty Head type.

In 1854, the piece was made larger in diameter and thinner. The design was changed to a feather headdress on a female, generally referred to as the Indian Princess Head type. In 1856 the type was changed slightly by enlarging the size of the head.

## LIBERTY HEAD (1849–1854)

**VF-20 Very Fine:** LIBERTY on headband complete and legible. Knobs on coronet defined.
**EF-40 Extremely Fine:** Slight wear on Liberty's hair. Knobs on coronet sharp.
**AU-50 About Uncirculated:** Trace of wear on headband. Nearly full luster.
**AU-55 Choice About Uncirculated:** Evidence of friction on design high points.
**MS-60 Uncirculated:** No trace of wear. Light marks and blemishes.
**MS-63 Choice Uncirculated:** Some distracting contact marks or blemishes in prime focal areas. Impaired luster possible.

| | Mintage | VF-20 | EF-40 | AU-50 | AU-55 | MS-60 | MS-63 |
|---|---|---|---|---|---|---|---|
| 1849, Open Wreath, No L on Truncation | 688,567 | $165 | $195 | $215 | $225 | $475 | $1,150 |
| 1849, Close Wreath | * | 165 | 195 | 215 | 225 | 475 | 950 |
| 1849C | 11,634 | 750 | 1,100 | 1,700 | 2,000 | 5,500 | 12,500 |
| 1849D | 21,588 | 900 | 1,350 | 1,850 | 2,250 | 3,750 | 8,750 |
| 1849O | 215,000 | 165 | 185 | 250 | 375 | 550 | 2,500 |
| 1850 | 481,953 | 160 | 185 | 200 | 215 | 300 | 900 |
| 1850C | 6,966 | 800 | 1,000 | 1,850 | 3,000 | 5,500 | 20,000 |
| 1850D | 8,382 | 950 | 1,300 | 2,150 | 3,500 | 8,000 | 17,500 |
| 1850O | 14,000 | 215 | 300 | 550 | 1,000 | 2,200 | 4,500 |
| 1851 | 3,317,671 | 160 | 185 | 200 | 210 | 275 | 900 |
| 1851C | 41,267 | 800 | 1,100 | 1,350 | 1,750 | 2,500 | 4,750 |
| 1851D | 9,882 | 900 | 1,250 | 1,650 | 2,000 | 3,850 | 11,500 |
| 1851O | 290,000 | 170 | 195 | 215 | 225 | 575 | 1,800 |
| 1852 | 2,045,351 | 160 | 185 | 200 | 210 | 275 | 900 |
| 1852C | 9,434 | 750 | 1,000 | 1,350 | 1,600 | 3,250 | 7,500 |
| 1852D | 6,360 | 800 | 1,250 | 1,750 | 1,850 | 6,500 | 18,500 |
| 1852O | 140,000 | 165 | 190 | 250 | 450 | 850 | 2,550 |
| 1853 | 4,076,051 | 160 | 185 | 200 | 210 | 275 | 900 |
| 1853C | 11,515 | 750 | 1,000 | 1,550 | 1,850 | 3,750 | 9,000 |
| 1853D | 6,583 | 900 | 1,200 | 1,850 | 3,000 | 6,500 | 18,500 |
| 1853O | 290,000 | 165 | 190 | 200 | 225 | 450 | 1,600 |
| 1854 | 855,502 | 160 | 185 | 200 | 210 | 275 | 900 |
| 1854D | 2,935 | 950 | 2,250 | 3,850 | 4,750 | 8,000 | 22,500 |
| 1854S | 14,632 | 275 | 500 | 600 | 850 | 1,850 | 3,750 |

* Included in number above.

## INDIAN PRINCESS HEAD,
## SMALL HEAD (1854–1856)

**VF-20 Very Fine:** Feather-curl tips on headdress outlined but details worn.

**EF-40 Extremely Fine:** Slight wear on tips of feather curls on headdress.

**AU-50 About Uncirculated:** Trace of wear on feathers, nearly full luster.

**AU-55 Choice About Uncirculated:** Evidence of friction on design high points. Most of original mint luster present.

**MS-60 Uncirculated:** No trace of wear. Light marks and blemishes.

**MS-63 Choice Uncirculated:** Some distracting contact marks or blemishes in prime focal areas. Impaired luster possible.

**PF-63 Choice Proof:** Reflective surfaces with only a few blemishes in secondary focal areas. No major flaws.

| | Mintage | VF-20 | EF-40 | AU-50 | AU-55 | MS-60 | MS-63 | PF-63 |
|---|---|---|---|---|---|---|---|---|
| 1854 | .783,943 | $230 | $325 | $425 | $700 | $1,350 | $6,750 | $100,000 |
| 1855 | .758,269 | 230 | 325 | 425 | 700 | 1,350 | 6,750 | 110,000 |
| 1855C | .9,803 | 1,000 | 2,500 | 6,500 | 8,500 | 15,000 | | |
| 1855D | .1,811 | 3,500 | 7,500 | 17,000 | 23,000 | 37,500 | 65,000 | |
| 1855O | .55,000 | 350 | 475 | 1,100 | 1,750 | 5,000 | 18,500 | |
| 1856S | .24,600 | 575 | 900 | 1,850 | 2,100 | 4,750 | 22,500 | |

## INDIAN PRINCESS HEAD,
## LARGE HEAD (1856–1889)

**VF-20 Very Fine:** Slight detail in curled feathers in headdress. Details worn smooth at eyebrow, hair below headdress, and behind ear and bottom curl.

**EF-40 Extremely Fine:** Slight wear above and to right of eye and on top of curled feathers.

**AU-50 About Uncirculated:** Trace of wear on feathers, nearly full luster.

**AU-55 Choice About Uncirculated:** Evidence of friction on design high points. Most of original mint luster present.

**MS-60 Uncirculated:** No trace of wear. Light marks and blemishes.

**MS-63 Choice Uncirculated:** Some distracting contact marks or blemishes in prime focal areas. Impaired luster possible.

**PF-63 Choice Proof:** Reflective surfaces with only a few blemishes in secondary focal places. No major flaws.

| | Mintage | VF-20 | EF-40 | AU-50 | AU-55 | MS-60 | MS-63 | PF-63 |
|---|---|---|---|---|---|---|---|---|
| 1856 | .1,762,936 | $160 | $180 | $200 | $225 | $250 | $700 | $17,500 |
| 1856D | .1,460 | 2,750 | 4,250 | 5,000 | 6,500 | 19,000 | 45,000 | |
| 1857 | .774,789 | 160 | 180 | 200 | 225 | 250 | 700 | 8,500 |
| 1857C | .13,280 | 775 | 1,100 | 2,100 | 2,750 | 7,500 | 22,000 | |
| 1857D | .3,533 | 900 | 1,350 | 2,750 | 3,500 | 7,000 | 25,000 | |
| 1857S | .10,000 | 375 | 450 | 850 | 1,100 | 4,250 | 14,000 | |
| 1858 | .117,995 | 160 | 180 | 200 | 225 | 250 | 700 | 5,000 |
| 1858D | .3,477 | 900 | 1,150 | 2,250 | 2,750 | 6,500 | 17,000 | |

*Chart continued on next page.* **147**

| | Mintage | VF-20 | EF-40 | AU-50 | AU-55 | MS-60 | MS-63 | PF-63 |
|---|---|---|---|---|---|---|---|---|
| 1858S | .10,000 | $275 | $375 | $1,000 | $1,300 | $4,250 | $12,500 | |
| 1859 | (80)...168,244 | 165 | 200 | 215 | 235 | 275 | 825 | $4,500 |
| 1859C | .5,235 | 800 | 1,150 | 2,250 | 2,750 | 7,250 | 23,500 | |
| 1859D | .4,952 | 900 | 1,250 | 2,100 | 2,500 | 6,750 | 16,500 | |
| 1859S | .15,000 | 225 | 275 | 875 | 1,150 | 4,250 | 10,000 | |
| 1860 | (154)...36,514 | 165 | 200 | 215 | 235 | 275 | 750 | 4,000 |
| 1860D | .1,566 | 1,800 | 2,750 | 5,500 | 6,750 | 12,500 | 40,000 | |
| 1860S | .13,000 | 275 | 375 | 575 | 775 | 2,000 | 4,500 | |
| 1861 | (349)...527,150 | 160 | 195 | 205 | 225 | 275 | 750 | 4,000 |
| 1861D | .1,250 | 6,500 | 12,500 | 24,500 | 28,500 | 40,000 | 67,500 | |
| 1862 | (35)...1,361,355 | 160 | 195 | 205 | 225 | 275 | 750 | 4,250 |
| 1863 | (50).....6,200 | 450 | 1,000 | 2,250 | 2,750 | 4,500 | 7,500 | 5,000 |
| 1864 | (50).....5,900 | 300 | 375 | 650 | 850 | 950 | 2,250 | 6,000 |
| 1865 | (25).....3,725 | 300 | 450 | 600 | 700 | 1,150 | 2,250 | 5,000 |
| 1866 | (30).....7,100 | 300 | 375 | 550 | 750 | 800 | 1,650 | 4,750 |
| 1867 | (50).....5,200 | 300 | 375 | 500 | 650 | 850 | 1,650 | 5,000 |
| 1868 | (25).....10,500 | 225 | 325 | 375 | 550 | 750 | 1,650 | 5,000 |
| 1869 | (25).....5,900 | 275 | 375 | 500 | 600 | 775 | 1,500 | 5,000 |
| 1870 | (35).....6,300 | 225 | 325 | 375 | 475 | 650 | 1,250 | 5,000 |
| 1870S | .3,000 | 375 | 550 | 950 | 1,100 | 1,850 | 4,500 | |
| 1871 | (30).....3,900 | 225 | 325 | 375 | 475 | 600 | 1,100 | 4,500 |
| 1872 | (30).....3,500 | 225 | 300 | 375 | 475 | 675 | 1,500 | 5,000 |
| 1873, Close 3 | (25).....1,800 | 300 | 600 | 675 | 775 | 1,150 | 2,500 | 8,500 |
| 1873, Open 3 | .123,300 | 160 | 180 | 200 | 215 | 275 | 750 | |
| 1874 | (20)...198,800 | 160 | 180 | 205 | 215 | 275 | 750 | 6,000 |
| 1875 | (20).......400 | 1,600 | 2,850 | 3,750 | 4,500 | 6,750 | 9,000 | 12,000 |
| 1876 | (45).....3,200 | 225 | 275 | 375 | 425 | 500 | 850 | 4,000 |
| 1877 | (20).....3,900 | 185 | 275 | 375 | 425 | 500 | 850 | 5,000 |
| 1878 | (20).....3,000 | 185 | 275 | 375 | 425 | 500 | 850 | 4,500 |
| 1879 | (30).....3,000 | 185 | 225 | 250 | 275 | 350 | 800 | 4,500 |
| 1880 | (36).....1,600 | 185 | 200 | 215 | 235 | 350 | 750 | 4,000 |
| 1881 | (87).....7,620 | 185 | 200 | 215 | 225 | 350 | 800 | 4,000 |
| 1882 | (125).....5,000 | 185 | 225 | 250 | 275 | 350 | 800 | 4,500 |
| 1883 | (207).....10,800 | 185 | 225 | 250 | 265 | 350 | 800 | 4,000 |
| 1884 | (1,006).....5,230 | 185 | 215 | 225 | 235 | 350 | 775 | 4,000 |
| 1885 | (1,105).....11,156 | 185 | 225 | 250 | 265 | 350 | 800 | 3,750 |
| 1886 | (1,016).....5,000 | 180 | 200 | 215 | 225 | 350 | 800 | 3,750 |
| 1887 | (1,043).....7,500 | 180 | 200 | 215 | 225 | 350 | 800 | 3,750 |
| 1888 | (1,079).....15,501 | 170 | 185 | 200 | 215 | 325 | 750 | 3,750 |
| 1889 | (1,779).....28,950 | 165 | 185 | 200 | 215 | 325 | 750 | 3,750 |

Although authorized by the Act of April 2, 1792, coinage of quarter eagles ($2.50 gold coins) was not begun until 1796.

## CAPPED BUST TO RIGHT (1796–1807)

**F-12 Fine:** Hair worn smooth on high spots. E PLURIBUS UNUM on ribbon weak but legible.
**VF-20 Very Fine:** Some wear on high spots.
**EF-40 Extremely Fine:** Only slight wear on Liberty's hair and cheek.
**AU-50 About Uncirculated:** Trace of wear on cap, hair, cheek, and drapery.
**AU-55 Choice About Uncirculated:** Evidence of friction on design high points. Some original mint luster.
**MS-60 Uncirculated:** No trace of wear. Light blemishes.

No Stars on Obverse (1796)          Stars on Obverse (1796–1807)

| | Mintage | F-12 | VF-20 | EF-40 | AU-50 | AU-55 | MS-60 |
|---|---|---|---|---|---|---|---|
| 1796, No Stars on Obverse | .963 | $35,000 | $50,000 | $65,000 | $85,000 | $100,000 | $165,000 |
| 1796, Stars on Obverse | .432 | 25,000 | 35,000 | 50,000 | 75,000 | 95,000 | 135,000 |
| 1797 | .427 | 10,000 | 15,000 | 25,000 | 35,000 | 45,000 | 100,000 |
| 1798 | .1,094 | 3,000 | 5,000 | 9,000 | 16,500 | 21,000 | 50,000 |
| 1802, 2 Over 1 | .3,035 | 3,000 | 5,000 | 9,000 | 14,500 | 16,500 | 22,500 |
| 1804, 13-Star Reverse | .* | 20,000 | 35,000 | 75,000 | 125,000 | 150,000 | 250,000 |
| 1804, 14-Star Reverse | .3,327 | 3,000 | 5,000 | 8,500 | 12,500 | 15,000 | 20,000 |
| 1805 | .1,781 | 3,000 | 5,000 | 8,500 | 12,500 | 15,000 | 20,000 |
| 1806, 6/4, 8 Stars Left, 5 Right | .1,136 | 3,500 | 5,500 | 8,500 | 12,500 | 15,000 | 20,000 |
| 1806, 6/5, 7 Stars Left, 6 Right | .480 | 4,500 | 6,500 | 10,000 | 15,000 | 25,000 | 50,000 |
| 1807 | .6,812 | 3,000 | 5,000 | 8,500 | 12,500 | 15,000 | 20,000 |

\* Included in number below.

## CAPPED BUST TO LEFT, LARGE SIZE (1808)

**F-12 Fine:** E PLURIBUS UNUM on reverse, and LIBERTY on headband, legible but weak.
**VF-20 Very Fine:** Motto and LIBERTY clear.
**EF-40 Extremely Fine:** All details of hair plain.
**AU-50 About Uncirculated:** Trace of wear above eye, on top of cap, and on cheek and hair.
**AU-55 Choice About Uncirculated:** Evidence of friction on design high points. Some original mint luster present.
**MS-60 Uncirculated:** No trace of wear. Light blemishes.

| | Mintage | F-12 | VF-20 | EF-40 | AU-50 | AU-55 | MS-60 |
|---|---|---|---|---|---|---|---|
| 1808 | .2,710 | $17,550 | $25,000 | $35,000 | $65,000 | $75,000 | $115,000 |

## CAPPED HEAD TO LEFT (1821–1834)

Those dated 1829 to 1834 are smaller in diameter than the 1821 to 1827 pieces.

Large Diameter                    Reduced Diameter

*See next page for chart.*

| | Mintage | F-12 | VF-20 | EF-40 | AU-50 | AU-55 | MS-60 |
|---|---|---|---|---|---|---|---|
| 1821 | 6,448 | $4,000 | $5,500 | $7,500 | $10,000 | $14,000 | $21,000 |
| 1824, 4 Over 1 | 2,600 | 4,000 | 5,500 | 7,500 | 9,500 | 13,000 | 21,000 |
| 1825 | 4,434 | 4,500 | 6,000 | 7,500 | 9,500 | 13,000 | 20,000 |
| 1826, 6 Over 6 | 760 | 4,500 | 6,000 | 8,000 | 10,000 | 14,000 | 27,500 |
| 1827 | 2,800 | 4,000 | 6,000 | 8,500 | 10,000 | 15,000 | 22,000 |
| 1829 | 3,403 | 3,500 | 4,500 | 5,500 | 8,000 | 10,000 | 13,500 |
| 1830 | 4,540 | 3,500 | 4,500 | 5,500 | 8,000 | 10,000 | 13,500 |
| 1831 | 4,520 | 3,500 | 4,500 | 5,500 | 8,000 | 10,000 | 13,500 |
| 1832 | 4,400 | 3,500 | 4,500 | 5,500 | 8,000 | 10,000 | 13,500 |
| 1833 | 4,160 | 3,500 | 4,500 | 5,500 | 8,000 | 10,000 | 13,500 |
| 1834, With Motto | 4,000 | 5,500 | 7,500 | 10,000 | 15,000 | 20,000 | 32,500 |

## CLASSIC HEAD, NO MOTTO ON REVERSE (1834–1839)

In 1834, the quarter eagle was redesigned. A ribbon binding the hair, bearing the word LIBERTY, replaced the Liberty cap. The motto was omitted from the reverse.

**F-12 Fine:** LIBERTY on headband legible and complete. Curl under ear outlined but no detail.

**VF-20 Very Fine:** LIBERTY plain; detail in hair curl.

**EF-40 Extremely Fine:** Small amount of wear on top of hair and below L in LIBERTY. Wear evident on wing.

**AU-50 About Uncirculated:** Trace of wear on coronet and hair above ear.

**AU-55 Choice About Uncirculated:** Evidence of friction on design high points. Some of original mint luster present.

**MS-60 Uncirculated:** No trace of wear. Light blemishes.

**MS-63 Choice Uncirculated:** Some distracting contact marks or blemishes in prime focal areas. Impaired luster possible.

*Mintmark location.*

| | Mintage | F-12 | VF-20 | EF-40 | AU-50 | AU-55 | MS-60 | MS-63 |
|---|---|---|---|---|---|---|---|---|
| 1834, No Motto | 112,234 | $225 | $375 | $600 | $900 | $1,100 | $2,750 | $7,500 |
| 1835 | 131,402 | 250 | 375 | 600 | 900 | 1,100 | 2,750 | 7,500 |
| 1836 | 547,986 | 225 | 375 | 600 | 900 | 1,100 | 2,750 | 7,500 |
| 1837 | 45,080 | 275 | 500 | 750 | 950 | 1,150 | 3,000 | 10,000 |
| 1838 | 47,030 | 250 | 450 | 650 | 850 | 1,100 | 2,750 | 7,500 |
| 1838C | 7,880 | 900 | 1,350 | 2,500 | 5,750 | 8,000 | 16,000 | 30,000 |
| 1839 | 27,021 | 375 | 575 | 800 | 1,150 | 1,400 | 3,500 | 13,500 |
| 1839C | 18,140 | 950 | 1,500 | 3,500 | 4,250 | 6,500 | 17,500 | 30,000 |
| 1839D | 13,674 | 1,100 | 1,600 | 3,750 | 5,500 | 8,000 | 22,000 | 40,000 |
| 1839O | 17,781 | 375 | 675 | 1,100 | 1,850 | 2,200 | 5,000 | 15,000 |

## LIBERTY HEAD (1840–1907)

*Mintmark location.*

**4** Plain 4

**4** Crosslet 4

| | Mintage | VF-20 | EF-40 | AU-50 | AU-55 | MS-60 | MS-63 |
|---|---|---|---|---|---|---|---|
| 1840 | 18,859 | $275 | $500 | $1,600 | $2,000 | $4,000 | $8,000 |
| 1840C | 12,822 | 1,000 | 1,500 | 2,250 | 2,750 | 7,500 | 20,000 |
| 1840D | 3,532 | 1,850 | 4,500 | 6,500 | 8,250 | 20,000 | |
| 1840O | 33,580 | 275 | 500 | 1,250 | 1,500 | 6,500 | 15,000 |

| | Mintage | VF-20 | EF-40 | AU-50 | AU-55 | MS-60 | MS-63 |
|---|---|---|---|---|---|---|---|
| 1841 .............................(unknown) | | $40,000 | $75,000 | $95,000 | $120,000 | | |
| 1841C ...........................10,281 | | 1,000 | 1,350 | 2,250 | 2,750 | $10,000 | $30,000 |
| 1841D ...........................4,164 | | 1,550 | 3,000 | 6,000 | 7,500 | 15,000 | 35,000 |
| 1842 .............................2,823 | | 850 | 2,000 | 4,000 | 5,500 | 12,500 | 30,000 |
| 1842C ...........................6,729 | | 1,550 | 2,250 | 4,500 | 6,250 | 15,000 | 30,000 |
| 1842D ...........................4,643 | | 1,500 | 3,000 | 6,500 | 8,250 | 25,000 | 55,000 |
| 1842O ...........................19,800 | | 275 | 650 | 1,500 | 2,200 | 6,500 | 20,000 |
| 1843 .............................100,546 | | 275 | 300 | 500 | 750 | 1,500 | 4,500 |
| 1843C ...........................26,064 | | 1,000 | 1,250 | 2,000 | 3,000 | 5,000 | 13,000 |
| 1843D ...........................36,209 | | 1,000 | 1,500 | 1,800 | 2,500 | 4,500 | 20,000 |
| 1843O ...........................364,002 | | 275 | 300 | 325 | 375 | 1,000 | 4,500 |
| 1844 .............................6,784 | | 275 | 500 | 1,350 | 1,800 | 5,000 | 13,500 |
| 1844C ...........................11,622 | | 1,000 | 1,500 | 3,500 | 4,500 | 12,000 | 32,500 |
| 1844D ...........................17,332 | | 1,200 | 1,350 | 2,000 | 2,500 | 4,500 | 18,000 |
| 1845 .............................91,051 | | 275 | 300 | 315 | 450 | 750 | 3,500 |
| 1845D ...........................19,460 | | 1,100 | 1,350 | 2,000 | 3,000 | 6,500 | 25,000 |
| 1845O ...........................4,000 | | 650 | 1,500 | 5,500 | 7,500 | 13,500 | 32,500 |
| 1846 .............................21,598 | | 275 | 300 | 500 | 750 | 3,500 | 15,000 |
| 1846C ...........................4,808 | | 1,200 | 2,000 | 3,500 | 5,000 | 12,500 | 23,500 |
| 1846D ...........................19,303 | | 1,250 | 1,850 | 2,500 | 3,500 | 6,500 | 20,000 |
| 1846O ...........................62,000 | | 275 | 325 | 750 | 950 | 3,000 | 12,500 |
| 1847 .............................29,814 | | 275 | 300 | 500 | 650 | 2,200 | 5,000 |
| 1847C ...........................23,226 | | 1,000 | 1,350 | 2,000 | 3,000 | 4,500 | 10,000 |
| 1847D ...........................15,784 | | 1,100 | 1,500 | 2,000 | 3,000 | 5,500 | 15,000 |
| 1847O ...........................124,000 | | 275 | 300 | 750 | 1,250 | 3,000 | 13,500 |
| 1848 .............................6,500 | | 375 | 550 | 1,250 | 1,450 | 3,500 | 9,500 |

## CAL. Gold Quarter Eagle (1848)

In 1848, about 230 ounces of gold were sent to Secretary of War William L. Marcy by Colonel R.B. Mason, military governor of California. The gold was turned over to the Mint and made into quarter eagles. The distinguishing mark CAL. was punched above the eagle on the reverse side, while the coins were in the die.

**CAL. Above Eagle on Reverse (1848)**

| | Mintage | VF-20 | EF-40 | AU-50 | AU-55 | MS-60 | MS-63 |
|---|---|---|---|---|---|---|---|
| 1848, CAL. Above Eagle ................1,389 | | $21,500 | $27,500 | $35,000 | $45,000 | $60,000 | $85,000 |
| 1848C ...........................16,788 | | 900 | 1,450 | 2,250 | 3,000 | 8,500 | 25,000 |
| 1848D ...........................13,771 | | 1,000 | 1,500 | 2,350 | 2,750 | 6,500 | 22,000 |
| 1849 .............................23,294 | | 275 | 300 | 550 | 650 | 1,500 | 4,750 |
| 1849C ...........................10,220 | | 950 | 1,450 | 3,250 | 4,250 | 12,500 | 3,500 |
| 1849D ...........................10,945 | | 1,000 | 1,500 | 2,250 | 2,850 | 9,500 | 25,000 |
| 1850 .............................252,923 | | 275 | 300 | 325 | 375 | 675 | 2,500 |
| 1850C ...........................9,148 | | 950 | 1,350 | 2,250 | 2,750 | 7,000 | 25,000 |
| 1850D ...........................12,148 | | 1,000 | 1,500 | 2,350 | 2,850 | 10,000 | 30,000 |

*Chart continued on next page.*

| | Mintage | VF-20 | EF-40 | AU-50 | AU-55 | MS-60 | MS-63 | PF-63 |
|---|---|---|---|---|---|---|---|---|
| 1850O | 84,000 | $275 | $300 | $700 | $850 | $2,750 | $10,000 | |
| 1851 | 1,372,748 | 275 | 300 | 315 | 325 | 400 | 850 | |
| 1851C | 14,923 | 1,000 | 1,450 | 2,200 | 2,500 | 6,000 | 21,000 | |
| 1851D | 11,264 | 1,100 | 1,600 | 2,400 | 2,750 | 6,500 | 25,000 | |
| 1851O | 148,000 | 275 | 325 | 500 | 650 | 2,500 | 9,500 | |
| 1852 | 1,159,681 | 275 | 300 | 315 | 325 | 400 | 900 | |
| 1852C | 9,772 | 950 | 1,500 | 2,750 | 3,250 | 9,500 | 23,500 | |
| 1852D | 4,078 | 1,000 | 2,000 | 4,500 | 5,500 | 10,000 | 32,000 | |
| 1852O | 140,000 | 275 | 300 | 550 | 750 | 3,000 | 7,500 | |
| 1853 | 1,404,668 | 275 | 300 | 315 | 325 | 400 | 900 | |
| 1853D | 3,178 | 1,350 | 2,250 | 3,500 | 4,000 | 8,500 | 35,000 | |
| 1854 | 596,258 | 275 | 300 | 315 | 325 | 400 | 950 | |
| 1854C | 7,295 | 950 | 1,500 | 3,000 | 4,500 | 7,500 | 25,000 | |
| 1854D | 1,760 | 2,250 | 4,750 | 7,500 | 9,500 | 16,500 | 50,000 | |
| 1854O | 153,000 | 300 | 325 | 350 | 400 | 1,000 | 6,000 | |
| 1854S | 246 | 100,000 | 150,000 | 250,000 | | | | |
| 1855 | 235,480 | 275 | 300 | 315 | 325 | 400 | 1,000 | |
| 1855C | 3,677 | 1,100 | 2,000 | 3,000 | 3,500 | 14,500 | 30,000 | |
| 1855D | 1,123 | 2,250 | 5,000 | 8,500 | 11,000 | 35,000 | 60,000 | |
| 1856 | 384,240 | 275 | 300 | 315 | 325 | 400 | 900 | $40,000 |
| 1856C | 7,913 | 950 | 1,850 | 2,500 | 3,000 | 8,500 | 22,000 | |
| 1856D | 874 | 4,500 | 8,500 | 22,500 | 27,500 | 50,000 | 95,000 | |
| 1856O | 21,100 | 275 | 475 | 850 | 1,150 | 4,500 | 20,000 | |
| 1856S | 72,120 | 300 | 325 | 650 | 750 | 2,750 | 7,500 | |
| 1857 | 214,130 | 275 | 300 | 315 | 325 | 400 | 1,000 | 35,000 |
| 1857D | 2,364 | 1,000 | 1,800 | 2,500 | 3,000 | 8,000 | 22,000 | |
| 1857O | 34,000 | 275 | 325 | 650 | 850 | 3,000 | 9,500 | |
| 1857S | 69,200 | 300 | 325 | 650 | 850 | 3,000 | 9,500 | |
| 1858 | 47,377 | 275 | 300 | 315 | 325 | 700 | 1,150 | 25,000 |
| 1858C | 9,056 | 950 | 1,500 | 2,500 | 3,000 | 7,000 | 25,000 | |
| 1859 (80) | 39,364 | 275 | 300 | 315 | 350 | 850 | 2,250 | 15,000 |
| 1859D | 2,244 | 1,250 | 2,000 | 2,500 | 4,000 | 12,500 | 45,000 | |
| 1859S | 15,200 | 300 | 675 | 1,550 | 1,850 | 3,000 | 12,500 | |
| 1860 (112) | 22,563 | 275 | 300 | 315 | 325 | 750 | 2,000 | 15,000 |
| 1860C | 7,469 | 1,000 | 1,500 | 2,500 | 5,000 | 13,500 | 25,000 | |
| 1860S | 35,600 | 275 | 450 | 750 | 900 | 2,500 | 10,000 | |
| 1861 (90) | 1,283,788 | 275 | 300 | 315 | 325 | 550 | 1,250 | 15,000 |
| 1861S | 24,000 | 3,250 | 600 | 2,000 | 3,000 | 5,000 | 11,500 | |
| 1862, 2 Over 1 | * | 650 | 1,350 | 2,750 | 3,500 | 6,500 | 10,000 | |
| 1862 (35) | 98,508 | 275 | 400 | 1,250 | 1,550 | 5,000 | 11,000 | 13,500 |
| 1862S | 8,000 | 500 | 1,350 | 3,000 | 4,000 | 12,500 | 25,000 | |
| 1863, Proof only (30) | | | | | | | | 35,000 |
| 1863S | 10,800 | 375 | 1,000 | 2,250 | 3,500 | 9,000 | 20,000 | |
| 1864 (50) | 2,824 | 4,000 | 9,500 | 15,000 | 20,000 | 35,000 | | 12,000 |
| 1865 (25) | 1,520 | 3,000 | 5,000 | 12,000 | 15,000 | 27,500 | | 12,000 |
| 1865S | 23,376 | 275 | 475 | 950 | 1,350 | 3,000 | 7,000 | |
| 1866 (30) | 3,080 | 750 | 2,500 | 4,000 | 5,500 | 8,000 | 18,000 | 9,000 |
| 1866S | 38,960 | 275 | 450 | 925 | 1,550 | 4,500 | 14,000 | |
| 1867 (50) | 3,200 | 300 | 500 | 750 | 1,250 | 3,500 | 6,000 | 9,000 |
| 1867S | 28,000 | 275 | 425 | 1,000 | 1,350 | 3,000 | 8,000 | |
| 1868 (25) | 3,600 | 275 | 300 | 450 | 675 | 1,250 | 5,000 | 9,000 |

* Included in number below.

| | Mintage | VF-20 | EF-40 | AU-50 | AU-55 | MS-60 | MS-63 | PF-63 |
|---|---|---|---|---|---|---|---|---|
| 1868S | 34,000 | $275 | $300 | $750 | $950 | $2,500 | $8,000 | |
| 1869 | (25) 4,320 | 275 | 325 | 450 | 850 | 2,000 | 7,500 | $7,000 |
| 1869S | 29,500 | 275 | 350 | 550 | 1,000 | 2,750 | 6,000 | |
| 1870 | (35) 4,520 | 275 | 325 | 500 | 900 | 2,750 | 6,500 | 7,500 |
| 1870S | 16,000 | 275 | 300 | 550 | 1,150 | 3,000 | 10,000 | |
| 1871 | (30) 5,320 | 275 | 300 | 425 | 600 | 1,500 | 3,000 | 7,500 |
| 1871S | 22,000 | 275 | 300 | 400 | 550 | 1,500 | 3,000 | |
| 1872 | (30) 3,000 | 300 | 550 | 750 | 1,650 | 3,000 | 10,000 | 6,500 |
| 1872S | 18,000 | 275 | 300 | 600 | 1,100 | 3,250 | 8,000 | |
| 1873 | (25) 178,000 | 275 | 300 | 315 | 325 | 400 | 900 | 6,000 |
| 1873S | 27,000 | 275 | 300 | 500 | 750 | 1,800 | 5,500 | |
| 1874 | (20) 3,920 | 275 | 300 | 450 | 700 | 1,500 | 4,500 | 8,500 |
| 1875 | (20) 400 | 2,750 | 4,500 | 7,500 | 9,000 | 18,000 | 30,000 | 20,000 |
| 1875S | 11,600 | 275 | 300 | 500 | 850 | 2,500 | 6,000 | |
| 1876 | (45) 4,176 | 275 | 450 | 600 | 1,100 | 2,250 | 4,500 | 6,500 |
| 1876S | 5,000 | 275 | 400 | 600 | 1,300 | 2,000 | 6,750 | |
| 1877 | (20) 1,632 | 275 | 550 | 750 | 1,150 | 2,000 | 6,500 | 6,500 |
| 1877S | 35,400 | 275 | 300 | 315 | 325 | 450 | 1,750 | |
| 1878 | (20) 286,240 | 275 | 300 | 315 | 325 | 400 | 875 | 9,000 |
| 1878S | 178,000 | 275 | 300 | 315 | 325 | 400 | 1,250 | |
| 1879 | (30) 88,960 | 275 | 300 | 315 | 325 | 400 | 900 | 6,500 |
| 1879S | 43,500 | 275 | 300 | 315 | 325 | 400 | 3,250 | |
| 1880 | (36) 2,960 | 325 | 350 | 500 | 650 | 1,000 | 2,500 | 6,500 |
| 1881 | (51) 640 | 1,250 | 2,000 | 4,500 | 5,000 | 7,500 | 15,000 | 6,500 |
| 1882 | (67) 4,000 | 275 | 300 | 325 | 375 | 500 | 2,000 | 5,000 |
| 1883 | (82) 1,920 | 275 | 350 | 600 | 900 | 1,800 | 5,000 | 5,000 |
| 1884 | (73) 1,950 | 275 | 300 | 425 | 575 | 1,000 | 2,500 | 5,000 |
| 1885 | (87) 800 | 575 | 1,250 | 1,850 | 2,000 | 3,000 | 5,000 | 5,000 |
| 1886 | (88) 4,000 | 275 | 300 | 325 | 375 | 750 | 2,000 | 5,000 |
| 1887 | (122) 6,160 | 275 | 300 | 315 | 325 | 550 | 2,000 | 4,750 |
| 1888 | (97) 16,001 | 275 | 300 | 315 | 325 | 400 | 900 | 4,750 |
| 1889 | (48) 17,600 | 275 | 300 | 315 | 325 | 400 | 900 | 4,750 |
| 1890 | (93) 8,720 | 275 | 300 | 315 | 325 | 400 | 1,000 | 4,750 |
| 1891 | (80) 10,960 | 275 | 300 | 315 | 325 | 400 | 900 | 4,750 |
| 1892 | (105) 2,440 | 275 | 300 | 315 | 325 | 450 | 1,500 | 4,750 |
| 1893 | (106) 30,000 | 275 | 300 | 315 | 325 | 400 | 900 | 4,750 |
| 1894 | (122) 4,000 | 275 | 300 | 325 | 350 | 450 | 1,250 | 4,750 |
| 1895 | (119) 6,000 | 275 | 300 | 315 | 325 | 400 | 900 | 4,750 |
| 1896 | (132) 19,070 | 275 | 300 | 315 | 325 | 400 | 850 | 4,750 |
| 1897 | (136) 29,768 | 275 | 300 | 315 | 325 | 400 | 850 | 4,750 |
| 1898 | (165) 24,000 | 275 | 300 | 315 | 325 | 400 | 850 | 4,750 |
| 1899 | (150) 27,200 | 275 | 300 | 315 | 325 | 400 | 850 | 4,750 |
| 1900 | (205) 67,000 | 275 | 300 | 315 | 325 | 400 | 850 | 4,750 |
| 1901 | (223) 91,100 | 275 | 300 | 315 | 325 | 400 | 850 | 4,750 |
| 1902 | (193) 133,540 | 275 | 300 | 315 | 325 | 400 | 850 | 4,750 |
| 1903 | (197) 201,060 | 275 | 300 | 315 | 325 | 400 | 850 | 4,750 |
| 1904 | (170) 160,790 | 275 | 300 | 315 | 325 | 400 | 850 | 4,750 |
| 1905 | (144) 217,800 | 275 | 300 | 315 | 325 | 400 | 850 | 4,750 |
| 1906 | (160) 176,330 | 275 | 300 | 315 | 325 | 400 | 850 | 4,750 |
| 1907 | (154) 336,294 | 275 | 300 | 315 | 325 | 400 | 850 | 4,750 |

## INDIAN HEAD (1908–1929)

Bela Lyon Pratt designed this coin and the similar $5 gold piece. Its design features no raised rim, and the main devices and legends are in sunken relief below the surface of the coin.

**VF-20 Very Fine:** Hair-cord knot distinct. Feathers at top of head clear. Cheekbone worn.

**EF-40 Extremely Fine:** Cheekbone, war bonnet, and headband feathers slightly worn.

**AU-50 About Uncirculated:** Trace of wear on cheekbone and headdress.

**MS-60 Uncirculated:** No trace of wear. Light blemishes.

**MS-63 Choice Uncirculated:** Some distracting contact marks or blemishes in prime focal areas. Impaired luster possible.

**MS-64 Uncirculated:** A few scattered contact marks visible. Good eye appeal and attractive luster.

**Matte PF-63 Choice Proof:** Few blemishes in secondary focal areas. No major flaws. Matte surfaces.

*Mintmark location is on reverse, to left of arrows.*

| | Mintage | VF-20 | EF-40 | AU-50 | MS-60 | MS-63 | MS-64 | MATTE PF-63 |
|---|---|---|---|---|---|---|---|---|
| 1908 ............(236) ....564,821 | | $250 | $275 | $300 | $325 | $800 | $1,350 | $6,000 |
| 1909 ............(139) ....441,760 | | 250 | 275 | 300 | 325 | 1,200 | 2,250 | 6,000 |
| 1910 ............(682) ....492,000 | | 250 | 275 | 300 | 325 | 1,100 | 2,250 | 6,000 |
| 1911 ............(191) ....704,000 | | 250 | 275 | 300 | 325 | 900 | 1,250 | 6,000 |
| 1911D ...................55,680 | | 2,500 | 3,250 | 3,750 | 6,500 | 15,000 | 22,500 | |
| 1912 ............(197) ....616,000 | | 250 | 275 | 300 | 325 | 1,200 | 2,500 | 6,000 |
| 1913 ............(165) ....722,000 | | 250 | 275 | 300 | 325 | 900 | 1,500 | 6,000 |
| 1914 ............(117) ....240,000 | | 250 | 275 | 300 | 450 | 3,750 | 8,500 | 6,000 |
| 1914D ...................448,000 | | 250 | 275 | 300 | 350 | 1,200 | 3,000 | |
| 1915 ............(100) ....606,000 | | 250 | 275 | 300 | 325 | 850 | 1,350 | 7,500 |
| 1925D ...................578,000 | | 250 | 275 | 300 | 325 | 725 | 1,150 | |
| 1926 ....................446,000 | | 250 | 275 | 300 | 325 | 725 | 1,150 | |
| 1927 ....................388,000 | | 250 | 275 | 300 | 325 | 725 | 1,150 | |
| 1928 ....................416,000 | | 250 | 275 | 300 | 325 | 725 | 1,150 | |
| 1929 ....................532,000 | | 250 | 275 | 300 | 325 | 725 | 1,150 | |

The three-dollar gold piece was authorized by the Act of February 21, 1853. Coinage was struck beginning in 1854. It was never popular and saw very little circulation.

**VF-20 Very Fine:** Eyebrow, hair about forehead and ear, and bottom curl all worn smooth. Faint details visible on curled feather-ends of headdress.

**EF-40 Extremely Fine:** Light wear above and to right of eye, and on top of curled feathers.

**AU-50 About Uncirculated:** Trace of wear on top of curled feathers and in hair above and to right of eye.

**AU-55 Choice About Uncirculated:** Evidence of friction on design high points. Much of original mint luster present.

**MS-60 Uncirculated:** No trace of wear. Light blemishes.

**MS-63 Choice Uncirculated:** Some distracting contact marks or blemishes in prime focal areas. Impaired luster possible.

*Mintmark location is on reverse, below wreath.*

**PF-63 Choice Proof:** Reflective surfaces with only a few blemishes in secondary focal places. No major flaws.

| | Mintage | VF-20 | EF-40 | AU-50 | AU-55 | MS-60 | MS-63 | PF-63 |
|---|---|---|---|---|---|---|---|---|
| 1854 | 138,618 | $700 | $900 | $1,150 | $1,250 | $2,000 | $5,000 | $50,000 |
| 1854D | 1,120 | 7,500 | 15,000 | 25,000 | 35,000 | 65,000 | | |
| 1854O | 24,000 | 875 | 1,750 | 3,000 | 3,500 | 15,000 | 25,000 | |
| 1855 | 50,555 | 650 | 900 | 1,200 | 1,500 | 2,000 | 6,000 | 30,000 |
| 1855S | 6,600 | 950 | 1,850 | 5,000 | 7,500 | 17,500 | 65,000 | |
| 1856 | 26,010 | 700 | 1,000 | 1,250 | 1,800 | 2,100 | 6,000 | 20,000 |
| 1856S | 34,500 | 750 | 1,150 | 2,250 | 4,500 | 8,500 | 17,500 | |
| 1857 | 20,891 | 700 | 975 | 1,250 | 2,000 | 2,100 | 7,000 | 18,500 |
| 1857S | 14,000 | 775 | 1,750 | 4,500 | 6,000 | 15,000 | | |
| 1858 | 2,133 | 825 | 1,300 | 2,000 | 3,500 | 6,000 | 13,500 | 18,500 |
| 1859 | (80) 15,558 | 700 | 900 | 1,250 | 1,500 | 2,000 | 6,000 | 18,000 |
| 1860 | (119) 7,036 | 725 | 950 | 1,250 | 1,650 | 2,100 | 6,000 | 9,000 |
| 1860S | 7,000 | 775 | 1,500 | 5,000 | 7,500 | 14,000 | 35,000 | |
| 1861 | (113) 5,959 | 700 | 900 | 1,500 | 1,750 | 3,000 | 7,000 | 12,000 |
| 1862 | (35) 5,750 | 700 | 900 | 1,500 | 1,750 | 3,000 | 7,000 | 10,000 |
| 1863 | (39) 5,000 | 750 | 950 | 1,500 | 1,750 | 3,000 | 7,000 | 10,000 |
| 1864 | (50) 2,630 | 750 | 1,000 | 1,500 | 1,750 | 3,000 | 7,000 | 10,000 |
| 1865 | (25) 1,140 | 1,000 | 2,000 | 4,000 | 5,000 | 7,000 | 13,000 | 15,000 |
| 1866 | (30) 4,000 | 750 | 950 | 1,350 | 1,750 | 3,000 | 7,500 | 10,000 |
| 1867 | (50) 2,600 | 750 | 950 | 1,350 | 1,750 | 3,000 | 7,500 | 10,000 |
| 1868 | (25) 4,850 | 700 | 900 | 1,350 | 1,750 | 2,750 | 7,500 | 10,000 |
| 1869 | (25) 2,500 | 700 | 900 | 1,350 | 1,750 | 3,000 | 8,000 | 10,000 |
| 1870 | (35) 3,500 | 700 | 900 | 1,500 | 1,850 | 3,000 | 8,000 | 10,000 |
| 1870S *(unique)* | | — | | | | | | |
| 1871 | (30) 1,300 | 725 | 1,000 | 1,350 | 1,750 | 3,200 | 7,000 | 10,000 |
| 1872 | (30) 2,000 | 725 | 1,000 | 1,350 | 1,750 | 3,200 | 7,000 | 10,000 |
| 1873, Open 3 (Original) | (25) | 3,500 | 5,500 | 15,000 | 20,000 | | | |
| 1873, Close 3 | | 2,750 | 4,500 | 7,500 | 12,500 | 24,000 | 35,000 | 20,000 |
| 1874 | (20) 41,800 | 650 | 850 | 1,200 | 1,250 | 2,000 | 5,000 | 22,000 |
| 1875, Proof only | (20) | | | 37,500 | 55,000 | | | 85,000 |
| 1876, Proof only | (45) | | | 12,500 | 17,500 | | | 27,500 |
| 1877 | (20) 1,468 | 1,250 | 3,000 | 6,000 | 8,000 | 15,000 | 30,000 | 15,000 |
| 1878 | (20) 82,304 | 700 | 900 | 1,100 | 1,250 | 2,000 | 4,750 | 15,000 |
| 1879 | (30) 3,000 | 750 | 925 | 1,250 | 1,850 | 2,100 | 5,250 | 12,000 |
| 1880 | (36) 1,000 | 750 | 1,350 | 1,750 | 1,900 | 2,500 | 5,250 | 12,000 |
| 1881 | (54) 500 | 1,250 | 2,250 | 3,750 | 4,750 | 5,750 | 11,000 | 12,000 |
| 1882 | (76) 1,500 | 750 | 950 | 1,350 | 1,750 | 2,500 | 5,250 | 9,000 |
| 1883 | (89) 900 | 750 | 1,250 | 1,750 | 2,250 | 2,750 | 5,500 | 9,000 |
| 1884 | (106) 1,000 | 750 | 1,350 | 1,750 | 2,250 | 2,750 | 5,500 | 9,000 |
| 1885 | (109) 801 | 775 | 1,350 | 1,850 | 2,250 | 3,500 | 9,000 | 10,000 |
| 1886 | (142) 1,000 | 750 | 1,250 | 1,850 | 2,250 | 3,250 | 6,000 | 9,000 |
| 1887 | (160) 6,000 | 725 | 950 | 1,350 | 1,750 | 2,500 | 5,000 | 9,000 |
| 1888 | (291) 5,000 | 700 | 900 | 1,150 | 1,300 | 2,200 | 5,000 | 9,000 |
| 1889 | (129) 2,300 | 700 | 900 | 1,150 | 1,300 | 2,000 | 5,000 | 9,000 |

## STELLA (1879–1880)

These pattern coins were first suggested by the Hon. John A. Kasson, then U.S. envoy extraordinary and minister plenipotentiary to Austria-Hungary. It was through the efforts of Dr. W.W. Hubbell, who patented the alloy goloid (used in making another pattern piece, the goloid metric dollar) that we have these beautiful and interesting coins.

The $4 Stella—so called because of the five-pointed star on the reverse—was envisioned by Kasson as America's answer to various foreign gold coins popular in the international market. The British sovereign, Italy's 20 lire, and the 20 pesetas of Spain were three such coins: each smaller than a U.S. $5 gold piece, they were used widely in international trade.

The Stella was one of many proposals made to Congress for an international trade coin, and one of only several that made it to pattern coin form (others include the 1868 $5 and 1874 Bickford $10).

Odds were stacked against the Stella from the start. The denomination of four U.S. dollars didn't match any of the coin's European counterparts, and at any rate the U.S. double eagle ($20 coin)—already used in international commerce—was a more convenient medium of exchange. The Stella was never minted in quantities for circulation.

There are two distinct types in both years of issue. Charles E. Barber designed the Flowing Hair type, and George T. Morgan the Coiled Hair. They were struck as patterns in gold, aluminum, copper, and white metal. Only those struck in gold are listed.

**Flowing Hair**                                        **Coiled Hair**

| | Mintage | EF-40 | AU-50 | PF-60 | PF-63 | PF-65 |
|---|---|---|---|---|---|---|
| 1879, Flowing Hair | (425+) | $67,500 | $80,000 | $90,000 | $115,000 | $155,000 |
| 1879, Coiled Hair (12 known) | | 100,000 | 125,000 | 150,000 | 225,000 | 450,000 |
| 1880, Flowing Hair (17 known) | | 75,000 | 85,000 | 115,000 | 135,000 | 275,000 |
| 1880, Coiled Hair (18 known) | | 175,000 | 200,000 | 250,000 | 400,000 | 700,000 |

The half eagle ($5 gold coin) was the first gold coin struck for the United States. It was authorized to be coined by the Act of April 2, 1792. The first type weighed 135 grains, of .91667 fineness. The weight was changed by the Act of June 28, 1834, to 129 grains, of .899225 fineness. Fineness became .900 by the Act of January 18, 1837.

## CAPPED BUST TO RIGHT (1795–1807)

**F-12 Fine:** Liberty's hair worn smooth but with distinct outline. For heraldic type, E PLURIBUS UNUM faint but legible.
**VF-20 Very Fine:** Slight to noticeable wear on high spots such as hair, turban, and eagle's head and wings.
**EF-40 Extremely Fine:** Slight wear on hair and highest part of cheek.
**AU-50 About Uncirculated:** Trace of wear on cap, hair, cheek, and drapery.
**MS-60 Uncirculated:** No trace of wear. Light blemishes.
**MS-63 Choice Uncirculated:** Some distracting marks or blemishes in focal areas. Impaired luster possible.

### Small Eagle Reverse (1795–1798)

1795
Obverse

1795
Reverse

1796, 6 Over 5

1797, 15 Stars

1797, 16 Stars

| | Mintage | F-12 | VF-20 | EF-40 | AU-50 | AU-55 | MS-60 | MS-63 |
|---|---|---|---|---|---|---|---|---|
| 1795, Small Eagle | 8,707 | $13,000 | $18,000 | $23,000 | $32,000 | $40,000 | $55,000 | $125,000 |
| 1796, 6 Over 5 | 6,196 | 15,000 | 19,000 | 30,000 | 50,000 | 65,000 | 90,000 | 175,000 |
| 1797, 15 Stars | 3,609 | 16,500 | 21,000 | 37,500 | 75,000 | 100,000 | 150,000 | |
| 1797, 16 Stars | * | 16,000 | 20,000 | 34,000 | 70,000 | 90,000 | 145,000 | |
| 1798, Small Eagle *(7 known)* | | 75,000 | 150,000 | 200,000 | 250,000 | 450,000 | — | |

* Included in number above.

### Heraldic Eagle Reverse (1795–1807)

| | Mintage | F-12 | VF-20 | EF-40 | AU-50 | AU-55 | MS-60 | MS-63 |
|---|---|---|---|---|---|---|---|---|
| 1795, Heraldic Eagle | * | $10,000 | $15,000 | $20,000 | $35,000 | $40,000 | $65,000 | $115,000 |
| 1797, 7 Over 5 | * | 8,000 | 12,000 | 22,000 | 45,000 | 50,000 | 100,000 | |
| 1798, Large 8, 13-Star Reverse | 24,867 | 3,000 | 4,000 | 6,000 | 8,500 | 11,000 | 20,000 | |
| 1798, Large 8, 14-Star Reverse | ** | 3,000 | 4,250 | 8,000 | 15,000 | 20,000 | 50,000 | |
| 1799 | 7,451 | 2,500 | 3,500 | 5,500 | 9,000 | 12,000 | 18,000 | 45,000 |
| 1800 | 37,628 | 2,500 | 3,500 | 5,500 | 7,500 | 8,500 | 11,000 | 23,000 |

* Included in number below. ** Included in number above.

*Chart continued on next page.*

| | Mintage | F-12 | VF-20 | EF-40 | AU-50 | AU-55 | MS-60 | MS-63 |
|---|---|---|---|---|---|---|---|---|
| 1802, 2 Over 1 | 53,176 | $2,500 | $3,500 | $5,500 | $7,500 | $8,500 | $11,000 | $20,000 |
| 1803, 3 Over 2 | 33,506 | 2,500 | 3,500 | 5,500 | 7,500 | 8,500 | 11,000 | 22,000 |
| 1804 | 30,475 | 2,500 | 3,500 | 5,500 | 7,500 | 8,500 | 11,000 | 22,000 |
| 1805 | 33,183 | 2,500 | 3,500 | 5,500 | 7,500 | 8,500 | 11,000 | 22,000 |
| 1806 | 64,093 | 2,500 | 3,500 | 5,500 | 7,500 | 8,500 | 11,000 | 22,000 |
| 1807 | 32,488 | 2,500 | 3,500 | 5,500 | 7,500 | 8,500 | 11,000 | 22,000 |

## CAPPED BUST TO LEFT (1807–1812)

**F-12 Fine:** LIBERTY on cap legible but partly weak.
**VF-20 Very Fine:** Headband edges slightly worn. LIBERTY bold.
**EF-40 Extremely Fine:** Slight wear on highest portions of hair; 80% of major curls plain.
**AU-50 About Uncirculated:** Trace of wear above eye and on top of cap, cheek, and hair.
**AU-55 Choice About Uncirculated:** Evidence of friction on design high points. Some mint luster present.
**MS-60 Uncirculated:** No trace of wear. Light blemishes.
**MS-63 Choice Uncirculated:** Some distracting contact marks or blemishes in prime focal areas. Impaired luster possible.

| | Mintage | F-12 | VF-20 | EF-40 | AU-50 | AU-55 | MS-60 | MS-63 |
|---|---|---|---|---|---|---|---|---|
| 1807 | 51,605 | $2,000 | $3,000 | $4,000 | $6,000 | $7,000 | $9,000 | $20,000 |
| 1808, All kinds | 55,578 | | | | | | | |
| 1808, 8 Over 7 | | 2,250 | 3,500 | 4,500 | 7,000 | 9,000 | 12,000 | 25,000 |
| 1808 | | 2,000 | 3,000 | 4,000 | 6,000 | 7,000 | 9,000 | 18,000 |
| 1809, 9 Over 8 | 33,875 | 2,000 | 3,000 | 4,000 | 6,000 | 7,000 | 9,000 | 18,000 |
| 1810 | 100,287 | 2,000 | 3,000 | 4,000 | 6,000 | 7,000 | 9,000 | 18,000 |
| 1811 | 99,581 | 2,000 | 3,000 | 4,000 | 6,000 | 7,000 | 9,000 | 18,000 |
| 1812 | 58,087 | 2,000 | 3,000 | 4,000 | 6,000 | 7,000 | 9,000 | 18,000 |

## CAPPED HEAD TO LEFT (1813–1834)

Large Diameter

Reduced Diameter

### Large Diameter (1813–1829)

| | Mintage | F-12 | VF-20 | EF-40 | AU-50 | AU-55 | MS-60 | MS-63 |
|---|---|---|---|---|---|---|---|---|
| 1813 | 95,428 | $2,500 | $3,000 | $4,500 | $6,500 | $7,500 | $8,500 | $15,000 |
| 1814, 4 Over 3 | 15,454 | 3,500 | 5,000 | 6,000 | 8,500 | 10,000 | 14,000 | 24,000 |
| 1815 | 635 | 25,000 | 40,000 | 100,000 | 150,000 | 175,000 | 225,000 | 275,000 |
| 1818 | 48,588 | 3,500 | 5,000 | 8,500 | 11,000 | 13,000 | 16,000 | 30,000 |
| 1819 | 51,723 | 6,500 | 12,000 | 25,000 | 35,000 | 40,000 | 50,000 | 65,000 |
| 1820 | 263,806 | 4,000 | 5,500 | 9,500 | 11,500 | 14,000 | 16,000 | 28,000 |
| 1821 | 34,641 | 10,000 | 15,000 | 30,000 | 50,000 | 65,000 | 90,000 | 125,000 |
| 1822 (3 known) | 17,796 | | | 3,000,000 | | | | |
| 1823 | 14,485 | 3,500 | 5,000 | 10,000 | 12,000 | 15,000 | 17,500 | 30,000 |

| | Mintage | F-12 | VF-20 | EF-40 | AU-50 | AU-55 | MS-60 | MS-63 |
|---|---|---|---|---|---|---|---|---|
| 1824 ....................17,340 | | $4,000 | $6,000 | $24,000 | $30,000 | $35,000 | $45,000 | $65,000 |
| 1825, 5 Over Partial 4 .........29,060 | | 4,000 | 6,000 | 20,000 | 25,000 | 30,000 | 40,000 | 60,000 |
| 1825, 5 Over 4 *(2 known)* ...........* | | | | 250,000 | | | | |
| 1826 ....................18,069 | | 4,000 | 6,000 | 15,000 | 20,000 | 22,500 | 30,000 | 50,000 |
| 1827 ....................24,913 | | 4,500 | 7,500 | 18,000 | 20,000 | 25,000 | 40,000 | 60,000 |
| 1828, 8 Over 7 *(5 known)* ...........** | | 15,000 | 25,000 | 50,000 | 65,000 | 75,000 | 100,000 | 300,000 |
| 1828 ....................28,029 | | 4,500 | 7,500 | 18,000 | 20,000 | 25,000 | 40,000 | 60,000 |
| 1829, Large Date .............57,442 | | 12,500 | 25,000 | 50,000 | 65,000 | 75,000 | 85,000 | 125,000 |

\* Included in number above. \*\* Included in number below.

## Reduced Diameter (1829–1834)

| | Mintage | F-12 | VF-20 | EF-40 | AU-50 | AU-55 | MS-60 | MS-63 |
|---|---|---|---|---|---|---|---|---|
| 1829, Small Date ..................* | | $25,000 | $45,000 | $60,000 | $85,000 | $100,000 | $150,000 | $200,000 |
| 1830 ....................126,351 | | 10,000 | 20,000 | 30,000 | 35,000 | 40,000 | 50,000 | 70,000 |
| 1831 ....................140,594 | | 10,000 | 20,000 | 30,000 | 35,000 | 40,000 | 50,000 | 70,000 |
| 1832, Curved-Base 2, | | | | | | | | |
|    12 Stars *(5 known)* ........157,487 | | 30,000 | 45,000 | 65,000 | 85,000 | | | |
| 1832, Square-Base 2, 13 Stars ........** | | 10,000 | 20,000 | 30,000 | 35,000 | 40,000 | 50,000 | 70,000 |
| 1833 ....................193,630 | | 10,000 | 20,000 | 30,000 | 35,000 | 40,000 | 50,000 | 70,000 |
| 1834 ....................50,141 | | 10,000 | 20,000 | 30,000 | 35,000 | 40,000 | 50,000 | 70,000 |

\* Included in mintage for 1829, Large Date (previous page). \*\* Included in number above.

## CLASSIC HEAD (1834–1838)

| | Mintage | F-12 | VF-20 | EF-40 | AU-50 | AU-55 | MS-60 | MS-63 |
|---|---|---|---|---|---|---|---|---|
| 1834 ....................657,460 | | $375 | $425 | $600 | $850 | $1,100 | $3,000 | $7,500 |
| 1835 ....................371,534 | | 375 | 425 | 600 | 1,000 | 1,200 | 3,200 | 7,500 |
| 1836 ....................553,147 | | 375 | 425 | 600 | 1,000 | 1,200 | 3,200 | 9,500 |
| 1837 ....................207,121 | | 375 | 450 | 600 | 1,300 | 1,500 | 3,500 | 12,000 |
| 1838 ....................286,588 | | 375 | 425 | 600 | 1,250 | 1,500 | 3,500 | 9,000 |
| 1838C ....................17,179 | | 1,000 | 1,800 | 3,500 | 7,500 | 9,500 | 25,000 | 50,000 |
| 1838D ....................20,583 | | 1,100 | 1,750 | 3,250 | 6,500 | 9,000 | 20,000 | 40,000 |

## LIBERTY HEAD (1839–1908)
### Variety 1 – No Motto Above Eagle (1839–1866)

**VF-20 Very Fine:** LIBERTY on coronet bold. Major lines show in curls on neck.
**EF-40 Extremely Fine:** Details clear in curls on neck. Slight wear on top and lower part of coronet and on hair.
**AU-50 About Uncirculated:** Trace of wear on coronet and hair above eye.
**AU-55 Choice About Uncirculated:** Evidence of friction on design high points. Some original mint luster.
**MS-60 Uncirculated:** No trace of wear. Light blemishes.
**MS-63 Choice Uncirculated:** Some distracting contact marks or blemishes in prime focal areas. Impaired luster possible.

*Mintmark: 1839, above date;*
*1840–1908, below eagle.*

**PF-63 Choice Proof:** Attractive reflective surfaces with only a few blemishes in secondary focal places. No major flaws.

| 1842, Large Date | Small Letters | Large Letters |
|---|---|---|

| | Mintage | VF-20 | EF-40 | AU-50 | AU-55 | MS-60 | MS-63 | PF-63 |
|---|---|---|---|---|---|---|---|---|
| 1839 | 118,143 | $425 | $450 | $675 | $875 | $2,500 | $15,000 | |
| 1839C | 17,205 | 1,250 | 2,000 | 3,500 | 5,000 | 12,500 | 35,000 | |
| 1839D | 18,939 | 1,500 | 3,250 | 4,750 | 6,750 | 15,000 | | |
| 1840 | 137,382 | 400 | 415 | 750 | 950 | 2,200 | 6,750 | |
| 1840C | 18,992 | 1,200 | 2,000 | 3,500 | 5,000 | 12,500 | 35,000 | |
| 1840D | 22,896 | 1,200 | 2,000 | 4,000 | 5,500 | 10,000 | 25,000 | |
| 1840O | 40,120 | 400 | 415 | 1,100 | 1,500 | 6,000 | 20,000 | |
| 1841 | 15,833 | 400 | 415 | 900 | 1,100 | 3,000 | 7,000 | $50,000 |
| 1841C | 21,467 | 1,200 | 1,700 | 2,200 | 2,600 | 8,500 | 25,000 | |
| 1841D | 29,392 | 1,200 | 1,750 | 2,200 | 2,600 | 8,000 | 18,000 | |
| 1842, Small Letters | 27,578 | 400 | 415 | 1,350 | 1,550 | 7,500 | 12,000 | 60,000 |
| 1842, Large Letters | * | 525 | 1,100 | 1,850 | 2,250 | 8,250 | 13,500 | |
| 1842C, Small Date | 27,432 | 5,000 | 12,500 | 20,000 | 25,000 | 50,000 | | |
| 1842C, Large Date | * | 1,200 | 1,500 | 2,200 | 2,600 | 8,500 | 23,000 | |
| 1842D, Small Date | 59,608 | 1,200 | 1,600 | 2,200 | 2,600 | 8,500 | 23,000 | |
| 1842D, Large Date | * | 1,750 | 4,000 | 8,500 | 12,500 | 30,000 | | |
| 1842O | 16,400 | 700 | 1,500 | 5,000 | 8,000 | 13,000 | 30,000 | |
| 1843 | 611,205 | 400 | 415 | 425 | 475 | 1,350 | 7,500 | |
| 1843C | 44,277 | 1,100 | 1,600 | 2,500 | 3,500 | 7,000 | 22,500 | |
| 1843D | 98,452 | 1,300 | 1,650 | 2,000 | 2,500 | 7,000 | 15,000 | |
| 1843O, Small Letters | 19,075 | 450 | 1,000 | 1,500 | 2,000 | 11,500 | 32,500 | |
| 1843O, Large Letters | 82,000 | 425 | 875 | 1,250 | 1,850 | 7,500 | 18,000 | |
| 1844 | 340,330 | 400 | 415 | 425 | 450 | 1,500 | 6,000 | |
| 1844C | 23,631 | 1,300 | 2,000 | 3,500 | 4,500 | 13,500 | 25,000 | |
| 1844D | 88,982 | 1,100 | 1,650 | 2,000 | 2,500 | 6,000 | 17,500 | |
| 1844O | 364,600 | 400 | 415 | 425 | 575 | 3,250 | 10,000 | |
| 1845 | 417,099 | 400 | 415 | 425 | 450 | 1,500 | 7,000 | |
| 1845D | 90,629 | 1,250 | 1,700 | 2,250 | 2,750 | 6,750 | 16,000 | |
| 1845O | 41,000 | 450 | 550 | 1,850 | 2,500 | 6,000 | 15,000 | |
| 1846, Large Date | 395,942 | 400 | 415 | 425 | 500 | 1,650 | 8,500 | |
| 1846, Small Date | * | 400 | 415 | 425 | 450 | 1,350 | 7,500 | |
| 1846C | 12,995 | 1,200 | 2,000 | 3,500 | 4,750 | 13,500 | 37,500 | |
| 1846D | 80,294 | 1,250 | 1,650 | 2,500 | 3,500 | 7,500 | 15,000 | |
| 1846O | 58,000 | 450 | 650 | 2,000 | 2,500 | 7,000 | 18,500 | |
| 1847 | 915,981 | 400 | 415 | 425 | 450 | 1,350 | 4,750 | |
| 1847C | 84,151 | 1,200 | 1,600 | 2,250 | 2,750 | 7,500 | 20,000 | |
| 1847D | 64,405 | 1,250 | 1,600 | 2,250 | 2,750 | 6,000 | 12,500 | |
| 1847O | 12,000 | 1,250 | 3,000 | 5,500 | 7,000 | 16,000 | 25,000 | |
| 1848 | 260,775 | 400 | 415 | 425 | 450 | 1,450 | 8,000 | |
| 1848C | 64,472 | 1,200 | 1,650 | 2,100 | 2,750 | 12,500 | 30,000 | |
| 1848D | 47,465 | 1,250 | 1,750 | 2,100 | 2,750 | 8,500 | 18,500 | |
| 1849 | 133,070 | 400 | 415 | 475 | 575 | 1,850 | 9,000 | |
| 1849C | 64,823 | 1,250 | 1,600 | 2,200 | 2,650 | 6,500 | 15,000 | |
| 1849D | 39,036 | 1,250 | 1,650 | 2,250 | 2,650 | 7,500 | 20,000 | |
| 1850 | 64,491 | 400 | 475 | 675 | 825 | 2,500 | 14,000 | |

* Included in number above.

| | Mintage | VF-20 | EF-40 | AU-50 | AU-55 | MS-60 | MS-63 | PF-63 |
|---|---|---|---|---|---|---|---|---|
| 1850C | 63,591 | $1,250 | $1,500 | $2,250 | $2,650 | $7,000 | $13,000 | |
| 1850D | 43,984 | 1,350 | 1,750 | 2,750 | 3,250 | 16,500 | | |
| 1851 | 377,505 | 400 | 415 | 425 | 450 | 1,750 | 7,000 | |
| 1851C | 49,176 | 1,250 | 1,650 | 2,350 | 2,800 | 8,000 | 30,000 | |
| 1851D | 62,710 | 1,200 | 1,750 | 2,250 | 2,750 | 8,250 | 16,000 | |
| 1851O | 41,000 | 500 | 1,000 | 2,600 | 3,250 | 8,000 | 15,000 | |
| 1852 | 573,901 | 400 | 415 | 425 | 450 | 1,200 | 5,500 | |
| 1852C | 72,574 | 1,200 | 1,500 | 2,200 | 2,750 | 4,500 | 16,500 | |
| 1852D | 91,584 | 1,250 | 1,650 | 2,100 | 2,650 | 6,500 | 18,000 | |
| 1853 | 305,770 | 400 | 415 | 425 | 450 | 1,250 | 6,000 | |
| 1853C | 65,571 | 1,250 | 1,650 | 2,200 | 2,750 | 5,000 | 18,000 | |
| 1853D | 89,678 | 1,300 | 1,750 | 2,100 | 2,600 | 5,250 | 15,000 | |
| 1854 | 160,675 | 400 | 415 | 425 | 450 | 1,500 | 6,000 | |
| 1854C | 39,283 | 1,200 | 1,650 | 2,650 | 3,250 | 9,000 | 25,000 | |
| 1854D | 56,413 | 1,200 | 1,500 | 2,100 | 2,500 | 6,000 | 20,000 | |
| 1854O | 46,000 | 425 | 475 | 1,050 | 1,500 | 5,000 | 16,500 | |
| 1854S *(3 known)* | 268 | | | — | 750,000 | — | | |
| 1855 | 117,098 | 400 | 415 | 425 | 450 | 1,500 | 5,500 | |
| 1855C | 39,788 | 1,200 | 1,650 | 2,250 | 2,650 | 9,000 | 30,000 | |
| 1855D | 22,432 | 1,250 | 1,750 | 2,250 | 2,650 | 9,500 | 27,500 | |
| 1855O | 11,100 | 550 | 1,550 | 3,000 | 3,500 | 13,500 | | |
| 1855S | 61,000 | 425 | 675 | 1,550 | 2,000 | 8,750 | | |
| 1856 | 197,990 | 400 | 415 | 425 | 450 | 1,650 | 6,500 | |
| 1856C | 28,457 | 1,200 | 1,600 | 2,250 | 2,650 | 13,000 | 25,000 | — |
| 1856D | 19,786 | 1,250 | 1,750 | 2,500 | 3,000 | 7,500 | 25,000 | |
| 1856O | 10,000 | 550 | 875 | 3,000 | 3,500 | 9,500 | | |
| 1856S | 105,100 | 425 | 475 | 700 | 975 | 4,500 | 18,500 | |
| 1857 | 98,188 | 400 | 415 | 425 | 450 | 1,500 | 5,500 | — |
| 1857C | 31,360 | 1,200 | 1,650 | 2,250 | 2,650 | 5,250 | 18,500 | |
| 1857D | 17,046 | 1,250 | 1,700 | 2,400 | 2,750 | 8,000 | 24,000 | |
| 1857O | 13,000 | 550 | 1,000 | 2,750 | 3,500 | 10,000 | 32,500 | |
| 1857S | 87,000 | 425 | 450 | 675 | 900 | 6,000 | 12,500 | |
| 1858 | 15,136 | 400 | 415 | 475 | 575 | 2,400 | 6,000 | — |
| 1858C | 38,856 | 1,200 | 1,650 | 2,250 | 2,650 | 6,000 | 22,500 | |
| 1858D | 15,362 | 1,250 | 1,750 | 2,450 | 2,850 | 8,000 | 23,000 | |
| 1858S | 18,600 | 550 | 1,750 | 3,500 | 4,500 | 20,000 | | |
| 1859 | (80) 16,734 | 400 | 475 | 575 | 650 | 4,500 | 12,500 | $30,000 |
| 1859C | 31,847 | 1,200 | 1,650 | 2,500 | 3,250 | 8,500 | 27,000 | |
| 1859D | 10,366 | 1,250 | 1,750 | 2,250 | 3,000 | 7,000 | 30,000 | |
| 1859S | 13,220 | 800 | 2,000 | 3,250 | 4,500 | 16,000 | | |
| 1860 | (62) 19,763 | 400 | 450 | 750 | 900 | 2,500 | 10,000 | 25,000 |
| 1860C | 14,813 | 1,300 | 1,750 | 2,600 | 3,250 | 8,000 | 15,000 | |
| 1860D | 14,635 | 1,350 | 1,800 | 2,600 | 3,250 | 8,500 | 32,000 | |
| 1860S | 21,200 | 650 | 1,400 | 3,000 | 3,850 | 16,000 | | |
| 1861 | (66) 688,084 | 400 | 415 | 425 | 450 | 1,300 | 5,000 | 25,000 |
| 1861C | 6,879 | 1,500 | 2,500 | 4,500 | 6,000 | 16,000 | 55,000 | |
| 1861D | 1,597 | 6,000 | 12,000 | 20,000 | 25,000 | 50,000 | 100,000 | |
| 1861S | 18,000 | 650 | 2,500 | 3,500 | 5,000 | 24,000 | | |
| 1862 | (35) 4,430 | 500 | 1,400 | 2,400 | 2,850 | 12,000 | 28,000 | 25,000 |
| 1862S | 9,500 | 2,000 | 3,500 | 5,500 | 6,750 | 27,500 | | |
| 1863 | (30) 2,442 | 800 | 2,500 | 3,500 | 4,500 | 16,000 | | 25,000 |
| 1863S | 17,000 | 950 | 2,500 | 5,000 | 7,000 | 22,000 | | |
| 1864 | (50) 4,170 | 500 | 1,250 | 2,750 | 3,500 | 8,000 | | 25,000 |
| 1864S | 3,888 | 2,750 | 10,000 | 16,000 | 20,000 | 32,500 | | |
| 1865 | (25) 1,270 | 875 | 3,250 | 6,750 | 7,750 | 13,500 | | 25,000 |
| 1865S | 27,612 | 750 | 1,500 | 3,000 | 3,850 | 10,000 | 20,000 | |
| 1866S | 9,000 | 1,200 | 2,500 | 7,500 | 9,000 | 25,000 | | |

## Variety 2 – Motto Above Eagle (1866–1908)

**VF-20 Very Fine:** Half of hair lines above coronet missing. Hair curls under ear evident, but worn. Motto and its ribbon sharp.
**EF-40 Extremely Fine:** Small amount of wear on top of hair and below L in LIBERTY. Wear evident on wing tips and neck of eagle.
**AU-50 About Uncirculated:** Trace of wear on tip of coronet and hair above eye.
**AU-55 Choice About Uncirculated:** Evidence of friction on design high points. Some original mint luster present.
**MS-60 Uncirculated:** No trace of wear. Light blemishes.
**MS-63 Choice Uncirculated:** Some distracting contact marks or blemishes in prime focal areas. Impaired luster possible.
**PF-63 Choice Proof:** Reflective surfaces with only a few blemishes in secondary focal places. No major flaws.

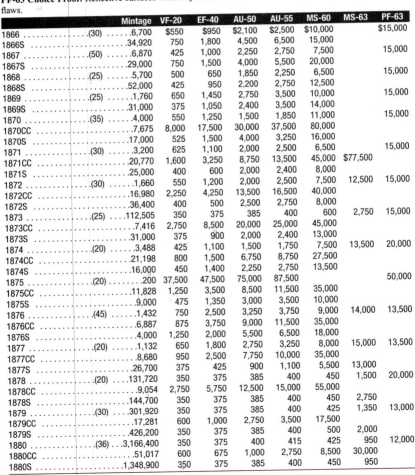

| | Mintage | VF-20 | EF-40 | AU-50 | AU-55 | MS-60 | MS-63 | PF-63 |
|---|---|---|---|---|---|---|---|---|
| 1866 . . . . . . . . . . . .(30) . . . . .6,700 | | $550 | $950 | $2,100 | $2,500 | $10,000 | | $15,000 |
| 1866S . . . . . . . . . . . . . . . .34,920 | | 750 | 1,800 | 4,500 | 6,500 | 15,000 | | |
| 1867 . . . . . . . . . . . .(50) . . . . .6,870 | | 425 | 1,000 | 2,250 | 2,750 | 7,500 | | 15,000 |
| 1867S . . . . . . . . . . . . . . . . .29,000 | | 750 | 1,500 | 4,000 | 5,500 | 20,000 | | |
| 1868 . . . . . . . . . . . .(25) . . . . .5,700 | | 500 | 650 | 1,850 | 2,250 | 6,500 | | 15,000 |
| 1868S . . . . . . . . . . . . . . . . .52,000 | | 425 | 950 | 2,200 | 2,750 | 12,500 | | |
| 1869 . . . . . . . . . . . .(25) . . . . .1,760 | | 650 | 1,450 | 2,750 | 3,500 | 10,000 | | 15,000 |
| 1869S . . . . . . . . . . . . . . . . .31,000 | | 375 | 1,050 | 2,400 | 3,500 | 14,000 | | |
| 1870 . . . . . . . . . . . .(35) . . . . .4,000 | | 550 | 1,250 | 1,500 | 1,850 | 11,000 | | 15,000 |
| 1870CC . . . . . . . . . . . . . . . . .7,675 | | 8,000 | 17,500 | 30,000 | 37,500 | 80,000 | | |
| 1870S . . . . . . . . . . . . . . . . .17,000 | | 525 | 1,500 | 4,000 | 3,250 | 16,000 | | |
| 1871 . . . . . . . . . . . .(30) . . . . .3,200 | | 625 | 1,100 | 2,000 | 2,500 | 6,500 | | 15,000 |
| 1871CC . . . . . . . . . . . . . . . .20,770 | | 1,600 | 3,250 | 8,750 | 13,500 | 45,000 | $77,500 | |
| 1871S . . . . . . . . . . . . . . . . .25,000 | | 400 | 600 | 2,000 | 2,400 | 8,000 | | |
| 1872 . . . . . . . . . . . .(30) . . . . .1,660 | | 550 | 1,200 | 2,000 | 2,500 | 7,500 | 12,500 | 15,000 |
| 1872CC . . . . . . . . . . . . . . . .16,980 | | 2,250 | 4,250 | 13,500 | 16,500 | 40,000 | | |
| 1872S . . . . . . . . . . . . . . . . .36,400 | | 400 | 500 | 2,500 | 2,750 | 8,000 | | |
| 1873 . . . . . . . . . . . .(25) . . . .112,505 | | 350 | 375 | 385 | 400 | 600 | 2,750 | 15,000 |
| 1873CC . . . . . . . . . . . . . . . . .7,416 | | 2,750 | 8,500 | 20,000 | 25,000 | 45,000 | | |
| 1873S . . . . . . . . . . . . . . . . .31,000 | | 375 | 900 | 2,000 | 2,400 | 13,000 | | |
| 1874 . . . . . . . . . . . .(20) . . . . .3,488 | | 425 | 1,100 | 1,500 | 1,750 | 7,500 | 13,500 | 20,000 |
| 1874CC . . . . . . . . . . . . . . . .21,198 | | 800 | 1,500 | 6,750 | 8,750 | 27,500 | | |
| 1874S . . . . . . . . . . . . . . . . .16,000 | | 450 | 1,400 | 2,250 | 2,750 | 13,500 | | |
| 1875 . . . . . . . . . . . .(20) . . . . . . .200 | | 37,500 | 47,500 | 75,000 | 87,500 | | | 50,000 |
| 1875CC . . . . . . . . . . . . . . . .11,828 | | 1,250 | 3,500 | 8,500 | 11,500 | 35,000 | | |
| 1875S . . . . . . . . . . . . . . . . . .9,000 | | 475 | 1,350 | 3,000 | 3,500 | 10,000 | | |
| 1876 . . . . . . . . . . . .(45) . . . . .1,432 | | 750 | 2,500 | 3,250 | 3,750 | 9,000 | 14,000 | 13,500 |
| 1876CC . . . . . . . . . . . . . . . . .6,887 | | 875 | 3,750 | 9,000 | 11,500 | 35,000 | | |
| 1876S . . . . . . . . . . . . . . . . . .4,000 | | 1,250 | 2,000 | 5,500 | 6,500 | 18,000 | | |
| 1877 . . . . . . . . . . . .(20) . . . . .1,132 | | 650 | 1,800 | 2,750 | 3,250 | 8,000 | 15,000 | 13,500 |
| 1877CC . . . . . . . . . . . . . . . . .8,680 | | 950 | 2,500 | 7,750 | 10,000 | 35,000 | | |
| 1877S . . . . . . . . . . . . . . . . .26,700 | | 375 | 425 | 900 | 1,100 | 5,500 | 13,000 | |
| 1878 . . . . . . . . . . . .(20) . . . .131,720 | | 350 | 375 | 385 | 400 | 450 | 1,500 | 20,000 |
| 1878CC . . . . . . . . . . . . . . . . .9,054 | | 2,750 | 5,750 | 12,500 | 15,000 | 55,000 | | |
| 1878S . . . . . . . . . . . . . . . .144,700 | | 350 | 375 | 385 | 400 | 450 | 2,750 | |
| 1879 . . . . . . . . . . . .(30) . . . .301,920 | | 350 | 375 | 385 | 400 | 425 | 1,350 | 13,000 |
| 1879CC . . . . . . . . . . . . . . . .17,281 | | 600 | 1,000 | 2,750 | 3,500 | 17,500 | | |
| 1879S . . . . . . . . . . . . . . . .426,200 | | 350 | 375 | 385 | 400 | 500 | 2,000 | |
| 1880 . . . . . . . . . . . .(36) . . .3,166,400 | | 350 | 375 | 400 | 415 | 425 | 950 | 12,000 |
| 1880CC . . . . . . . . . . . . . . . .51,017 | | 600 | 675 | 1,000 | 2,750 | 8,500 | 30,000 | |
| 1880S . . . . . . . . . . . . . . .1,348,900 | | 350 | 375 | 385 | 400 | 450 | 950 | |

| | Mintage | VF-20 | EF-40 | AU-50 | AU-55 | MS-60 | MS-63 | PF-63 |
|---|---|---|---|---|---|---|---|---|
| 1881 . . . . . . . . . . . . . .(42) . . .5,708,802 | | $350 | $375 | $400 | $415 | $425 | $950 | $12,000 |
| 1881CC . . . . . . . . . . . . . . . . . .13,886 | | 650 | 1,250 | 5,000 | 7,500 | 16,500 | 50,000 | |
| 1881S . . . . . . . . . . . . . . . . . . .969,000 | | 350 | 375 | 385 | 400 | 450 | 950 | |
| 1882 . . . . . . . . . . . . . .(48) . . .2,514,520 | | 350 | 375 | 385 | 400 | 450 | 950 | 11,000 |
| 1882CC . . . . . . . . . . . . . . . . . .82,817 | | 500 | 600 | 750 | 1,000 | 7,000 | 30,000 | |
| 1882S . . . . . . . . . . . . . . . . . . .969,000 | | 350 | 375 | 385 | 400 | 425 | 925 | |
| 1883 . . . . . . . . . . . . . .(61) . . . .233,400 | | 350 | 375 | 385 | 400 | 450 | 1,000 | 11,000 |
| 1883CC . . . . . . . . . . . . . . . . . .12,598 | | 550 | 875 | 2,750 | 3,750 | 15,000 | | |
| 1883S . . . . . . . . . . . . . . . . . . .83,200 | | 350 | 375 | 385 | 400 | 600 | 1,800 | |
| 1884 . . . . . . . . . . . . . .(48) . . . .191,030 | | 350 | 375 | 385 | 400 | 450 | 1,200 | 11,000 |
| 1884CC . . . . . . . . . . . . . . . . . .16,402 | | 600 | 850 | 2,500 | 3,750 | 16,500 | | |
| 1884S . . . . . . . . . . . . . . . . . . .177,000 | | 350 | 375 | 385 | 400 | 450 | 1,100 | |
| 1885 . . . . . . . . . . . . . .(66) . . . .601,440 | | 350 | 375 | 385 | 400 | 450 | 950 | 10,000 |
| 1885S . . . . . . . . . . . . . . . . . .1,211,500 | | 350 | 375 | 385 | 400 | 450 | 950 | |
| 1886 . . . . . . . . . . . . . .(72) . . .388,360 | | 350 | 375 | 385 | 400 | 450 | 900 | 10,000 |
| 1886S . . . . . . . . . . . . . . . . . .3,268,000 | | 350 | 375 | 385 | 400 | 450 | 900 | |
| 1887, Proof Only . . . . . .(87) . . . . . . . . . . . | | | | | | | | 42,500 |
| 1887S . . . . . . . . . . . . . . . . . .1,912,000 | | 350 | 375 | 385 | 400 | 450 | 900 | |
| 1888 . . . . . . . . . . . . . .(95) . . . . .18,201 | | 350 | 375 | 385 | 400 | 500 | 1,100 | 10,000 |
| 1888S . . . . . . . . . . . . . . . . . .293,900 | | 350 | 375 | 385 | 400 | 700 | 2,000 | |
| 1889 . . . . . . . . . . . . . .(45) . . . . .7,520 | | 350 | 375 | 385 | 400 | 675 | 1,800 | 10,000 |
| 1890 . . . . . . . . . . . . . .(88) . . . . .4,240 | | 350 | 375 | 385 | 425 | 1,250 | 3,500 | 10,000 |
| 1890CC . . . . . . . . . . . . . . . . . .53,800 | | 550 | 650 | 750 | 875 | 1,300 | 6,000 | |
| 1891 . . . . . . . . . . . . . .(53) . . . .61,360 | | 385 | 400 | 415 | 425 | 450 | 1,200 | 9,500 |
| 1891CC . . . . . . . . . . . . . . . . . .208,000 | | 500 | 600 | 750 | 850 | 1,200 | 2,500 | |
| 1892 . . . . . . . . . . . . . .(92) . . . .753,480 | | 350 | 375 | 385 | 400 | 425 | 950 | 9,500 |
| 1892CC . . . . . . . . . . . . . . . . . .82,968 | | 500 | 600 | 750 | 850 | 1,250 | 5,000 | |
| 1892O . . . . . . . . . . . . . . . . . . .10,000 | | 450 | 650 | 875 | 1,150 | 2,350 | | |
| 1892S . . . . . . . . . . . . . . . . . . .298,400 | | 350 | 375 | 385 | 400 | 450 | 1,500 | |
| 1893 . . . . . . . . . . . . . .(77) . . .1,528,120 | | 350 | 375 | 385 | 400 | 425 | 900 | 9,500 |
| 1893CC . . . . . . . . . . . . . . . . . .60,000 | | 500 | 550 | 650 | 850 | 1,150 | 5,000 | |
| 1893O . . . . . . . . . . . . . . . . . . .110,000 | | 400 | 425 | 450 | 475 | 700 | 4,000 | |
| 1893S . . . . . . . . . . . . . . . . . . .224,000 | | 350 | 375 | 400 | 415 | 450 | 925 | |
| 1894 . . . . . . . . . . . . . .(75) . . . .957,880 | | 350 | 375 | 385 | 400 | 425 | 900 | 9,500 |
| 1894O . . . . . . . . . . . . . . . . . . .16,600 | | 400 | 425 | 450 | 475 | 850 | 4,500 | |
| 1894S . . . . . . . . . . . . . . . . . . .55,900 | | 350 | 385 | 400 | 450 | 1,800 | 6,000 | |
| 1895 . . . . . . . . . . . . . .(81) . . .1,345,855 | | 350 | 375 | 400 | 415 | 425 | 900 | 9,500 |
| 1895S . . . . . . . . . . . . . . . . . . .112,000 | | 375 | 385 | 400 | 450 | 1,850 | 3,500 | |
| 1896 . . . . . . . . . . . . . .(103) . . . .58,960 | | 350 | 375 | 385 | 400 | 425 | 900 | 8,500 |
| 1896S . . . . . . . . . . . . . . . . . . .155,400 | | 375 | 385 | 400 | 450 | 750 | 3,500 | |
| 1897 . . . . . . . . . . . . . .(83) . . . .867,800 | | 350 | 375 | 385 | 400 | 425 | 900 | 8,500 |
| 1897S . . . . . . . . . . . . . . . . . . .354,000 | | 350 | 375 | 385 | 400 | 550 | 3,250 | |
| 1898 . . . . . . . . . . . . . .(75) . . . .633,420 | | 350 | 375 | 385 | 400 | 425 | 900 | 8,500 |
| 1898S . . . . . . . . . . . . . . . . . .1,397,400 | | 350 | 375 | 400 | 415 | 450 | 925 | |
| 1899 . . . . . . . . . . . . . .(99) . . .1,710,630 | | 350 | 375 | 400 | 415 | 425 | 900 | 8,500 |
| 1899S . . . . . . . . . . . . . . . . . .1,545,000 | | 350 | 375 | 400 | 425 | 450 | 925 | |
| 1900 . . . . . . . . . . . . . .(230) . . .1,405,500 | | 350 | 375 | 400 | 415 | 425 | 900 | 8,500 |
| 1900S . . . . . . . . . . . . . . . . . . .329,000 | | 350 | 375 | 400 | 415 | 450 | 1,000 | |
| 1901 . . . . . . . . . . . . . .(140) . . . .615,900 | | 350 | 375 | 400 | 415 | 425 | 900 | 8,500 |
| 1901S, 1 Over 0 . . . . . . . . .3,648,000 | | 350 | 375 | 400 | 415 | 450 | 1,100 | |
| 1901S . . . . . . . . . . . . . . . . . . . . . . .* | | 350 | 375 | 385 | 400 | 425 | 900 | |
| 1902 . . . . . . . . . . . . . .(162) . . . .172,400 | | 350 | 375 | 400 | 415 | 425 | 900 | 8,500 |
| 1902S . . . . . . . . . . . . . . . . . . .939,000 | | 350 | 375 | 400 | 415 | 425 | 900 | |
| 1903 . . . . . . . . . . . . . .(154) . . . .226,870 | | 350 | 375 | 400 | 415 | 425 | 900 | 8,500 |
| 1903S . . . . . . . . . . . . . . . . . .1,855,000 | | 350 | 375 | 400 | 415 | 425 | 900 | |

* Included in number above.

*Chart continued on next page.*

| | Mintage | VF-20 | EF-40 | AU-50 | AU-55 | MS-60 | MS-63 | PF-63 |
|---|---|---|---|---|---|---|---|---|
| 1904 . . . . . . . . . . . . . . (136) . . . . | 392,000 | $350 | $375 | $400 | $415 | $425 | $900 | $8,500 |
| 1904S . . . . . . . . . . . . . . . . . . . . . | 97,000 | 350 | 375 | 400 | 415 | 550 | 2,200 | |
| 1905 . . . . . . . . . . . . . . (108) . . . . | 302,200 | 350 | 375 | 400 | 415 | 425 | 900 | 8,500 |
| 1905S . . . . . . . . . . . . . . . . . . . . . | 880,700 | 350 | 375 | 400 | 415 | 450 | 1,300 | |
| 1906 . . . . . . . . . . . . . . (85) . . . . | 348,735 | 350 | 375 | 400 | 415 | 425 | 900 | 8,500 |
| 1906D . . . . . . . . . . . . . . . . . . . . . | 320,000 | 350 | 375 | 400 | 415 | 425 | 925 | |
| 1906S . . . . . . . . . . . . . . . . . . . . . | 598,000 | 350 | 375 | 400 | 415 | 425 | 925 | |
| 1907 . . . . . . . . . . . . . . (92) . . . . | 626,100 | 350 | 375 | 385 | 400 | 425 | 900 | 8,500 |
| 1907D . . . . . . . . . . . . . . . . . . . . . | 888,000 | 350 | 375 | 400 | 415 | 425 | 925 | |
| 1908 . . . . . . . . . . . . . . . . . . . . . | 421,874 | 350 | 375 | 400 | 415 | 425 | 900 | 8,500 |

## INDIAN HEAD (1908–1929)

This type conforms in design to the quarter eagle of the same date. The sunken-relief designs and lettering make the Indian Head a unique series, along with the quarter eagle, in United States coinage.

**VF-20 Very Fine:** Noticeable wear on large middle feathers and tip of eagle's wing.
**EF-40 Extremely Fine:** Cheekbone, war bonnet, and head-band feathers slightly worn. Feathers on eagle's upper wing show considerable wear.
**AU-50 About Uncirculated:** Trace of wear on cheekbone and headdress.
**AU-55 Choice About Uncirculated:** Evidence of friction on design high points. Much of original mint luster present.
**MS-60 Uncirculated:** No trace of wear. Light blemishes.
**MS-63 Choice Uncirculated:** Some distracting contact marks or blemishes in prime focal areas. Impaired luster possible.
**Matte PF-63 Choice Proof:** Matte surfaces with few blemishes in secondary focal places. No major flaws.

Mintmark Location

*Scarcer coins with well-struck mintmarks command higher prices.*

| | Mintage | VF-20 | EF-40 | AU-50 | AU-55 | MS-60 | MS-63 | MATTE PF-63 |
|---|---|---|---|---|---|---|---|---|
| 1908 . . . . . . . . . . . (167) . . . | 577,845 | $375 | $385 | $400 | $415 | $475 | $1,550 | $9,000 |
| 1908D . . . . . . . . . . . . . . . . . | 148,000 | 375 | 385 | 400 | 415 | 475 | 1,550 | |
| 1908S . . . . . . . . . . . . . . . . . | 82,000 | 400 | 450 | 475 | 500 | 950 | 5,000 | |
| 1909 . . . . . . . . . . . (78) . . . | 627,060 | 375 | 385 | 400 | 415 | 475 | 1,550 | 9,000 |
| 1909D . . . . . . . . . . . . . . . . . | 3,423,560 | 375 | 385 | 400 | 415 | 475 | 1,550 | |
| 1909O . . . . . . . . . . . . . . . . . | 34,200 | 2,500 | 3,750 | 6,000 | 8,500 | 20,000 | 60,000 | |
| 1909S . . . . . . . . . . . . . . . . . | 297,200 | 400 | 415 | 425 | 435 | 1,000 | 8,000 | |
| 1910 . . . . . . . . . . . (250) . . . | 604,000 | 375 | 385 | 400 | 415 | 475 | 1,550 | 9,000 |
| 1910D . . . . . . . . . . . . . . . . . | 193,600 | 375 | 385 | 400 | 415 | 475 | 2,500 | |
| 1910S . . . . . . . . . . . . . . . . . | 770,200 | 375 | 385 | 400 | 425 | 650 | 5,000 | |
| 1911 . . . . . . . . . . . (139) . . . | 915,000 | 375 | 385 | 400 | 415 | 475 | 1,550 | 9,000 |
| 1911D . . . . . . . . . . . . . . . . . | 72,500 | 425 | 650 | 950 | 1,250 | 5,000 | 35,000 | |
| 1911S . . . . . . . . . . . . . . . . . | 1,416,000 | 375 | 400 | 415 | 425 | 650 | 3,500 | |
| 1912 . . . . . . . . . . . (144) . . . | 790,000 | 375 | 385 | 400 | 415 | 475 | 1,550 | 9,000 |
| 1912S . . . . . . . . . . . . . . . . . | 392,000 | 375 | 385 | 400 | 425 | 1,100 | 10,000 | |
| 1913 . . . . . . . . . . . (99) . . . | 915,901 | 375 | 385 | 400 | 415 | 475 | 1,550 | 9,000 |
| 1913S . . . . . . . . . . . . . . . . . | 408,000 | 375 | 385 | 400 | 415 | 1,200 | 10,000 | |
| 1914 . . . . . . . . . . . (125) . . . | 247,000 | 375 | 385 | 400 | 415 | 475 | 1,550 | 9,000 |
| 1914D . . . . . . . . . . . . . . . . . | 247,000 | 375 | 385 | 400 | 415 | 475 | 1,750 | |
| 1914S . . . . . . . . . . . . . . . . . | 263,000 | 375 | 385 | 400 | 415 | 1,000 | 10,000 | |
| 1915 . . . . . . . . . . . (75) . . . | 588,000 | 375 | 385 | 400 | 415 | 475 | 1,550 | 9,000 |
| 1915S . . . . . . . . . . . . . . . . . | 164,000 | 375 | 385 | 400 | 450 | 1,500 | 12,500 | |
| 1916S . . . . . . . . . . . . . . . . . | 240,000 | 375 | 385 | 400 | 415 | 550 | 5,000 | |
| 1929 . . . . . . . . . . . . . . . . . | 662,000 | 6,500 | 9,500 | 10,500 | 12,500 | 13,500 | 26,500 | |

Coinage authorization, specified weights, and fineness of the eagle coins conform to those of the half eagle. The small eagle reverse was used until 1797, when the large, heraldic eagle replaced it.

## CAPPED BUST TO RIGHT (1795–1804)

**F-12 Fine:** Details on turban and head obliterated.
**VF-20 Very Fine:** Hair lines in curls on neck and details under turban and over forehead worn but distinguishable.
**EF-40 Extremely Fine:** Definite wear on hair to left of eye and strand of hair across and around turban, as well as on eagle's wing tips.
**AU-50 About Uncirculated:** Trace of wear on cap, hair, cheek, and drapery.
**AU-55 Choice About Uncirculated:** Evidence of friction on design high points. Most of original mint luster present.
**MS-60 Uncirculated:** No trace of wear. Light blemishes.
**MS-63 Choice Uncirculated:** Some distracting contact marks or blemishes in prime focal areas. Impaired luster possible.

### Small Eagle Reverse (1795–1797)

| | Mintage | F-12 | VF-20 | EF-40 | AU-50 | AU-55 | MS-60 | MS-63 |
|---|---|---|---|---|---|---|---|---|
| 1795 | 5,583 | $20,000 | $25,000 | $35,000 | $45,000 | $52,500 | $80,000 | $175,000 |
| 1796 | 4,146 | 23,000 | 27,000 | 40,000 | 50,000 | 57,500 | 87,500 | 200,000 |
| 1797, Small Eagle | 3,615 | 25,000 | 32,500 | 50,000 | 75,000 | 90,000 | 115,000 | |

### Heraldic Eagle Reverse (1797–1804)

| | Mintage | F-12 | VF-20 | EF-40 | AU-50 | AU-55 | MS-60 | MS-63 |
|---|---|---|---|---|---|---|---|---|
| 1797, Large Eagle | 10,940 | $7,000 | $9,500 | $15,000 | $16,500 | $18,500 | $32,500 | $80,000 |
| 1798, 8 Over 7, 9 Stars Left, 4 Rt | 900 | 10,000 | 13,000 | 25,000 | 35,000 | 40,000 | 75,000 | 175,000 |
| 1798, 8 Over 7, 7 Stars Left, 6 Rt | 842 | 23,000 | 27,500 | 45,000 | 85,000 | 120,000 | 200,000 | |
| 1799 | 37,449 | 6,500 | 7,750 | 12,000 | 16,000 | 17,500 | 20,000 | 50,000 |
| 1800 | 5,999 | 6,500 | 7,750 | 12,000 | 16,000 | 17,500 | 20,000 | 50,000 |
| 1801 | 44,344 | 6,500 | 7,750 | 12,000 | 16,000 | 17,500 | 20,000 | 50,000 |
| 1803 | 15,017 | 6,500 | 7,750 | 12,000 | 16,000 | 17,500 | 20,000 | 50,000 |
| 1804 | 3,757 | 12,000 | 15,000 | 23,000 | 35,000 | 42,500 | 55,000 | 150,000 |

# LIBERTY HEAD, NO MOTTO ABOVE EAGLE (1838–1866)

In 1838 the weight and diameter of the eagle were reduced and the obverse and reverse were redesigned. Liberty now faced left and the word LIBERTY was placed on the coronet.

**VF-20 Very Fine:** Hair lines above coronet partly worn. Curls under ear worn but defined.

**EF-40 Extremely Fine:** Small amount of wear on top of hair and below L in LIBERTY. Wear evident on wing tips and neck of eagle.

**AU-50 About Uncirculated:** Trace of wear on tip of coronet and hair above eye.

**AU-55 Choice About Uncirculated:** Evidence of friction on design high points. Some of original mint luster present.

Mintmark is on reverse, below eagle.

**MS-60 Uncirculated:** No trace of wear. Light blemishes.

**MS-63 Choice Uncirculated:** Some distracting contact marks or blemishes in prime focal areas. Impaired luster possible.

**PF-63 Choice Proof:** Attractive reflective surfaces with only a few blemishes in secondary focal places. No major flaws.

|  | Mintage | VF-20 | EF-40 | AU-50 | AU-55 | MS-60 | MS-63 | PF-63 |
|---|---|---|---|---|---|---|---|---|
| 1838 | 7,200 | $2,000 | $4,750 | $10,000 | $12,500 | $30,000 | $75,000 | |
| 1839, Large Letters | 25,801 | 850 | 1,500 | 4,000 | 5,000 | 20,000 | 40,000 | |
| 1839, Small Letters | 12,447 | 1,100 | 2,300 | 4,500 | 6,000 | 22,000 | 70,000 | |
| 1840 | 47,338 | 750 | 850 | 950 | 1,200 | 7,000 | | |
| 1841 | 63,131 | 750 | 775 | 825 | 1,000 | 5,500 | 22,000 | |
| 1841O | 2,500 | 2,250 | 4,750 | 13,500 | 17,500 | 32,500 | | |
| 1842 | 81,507 | 750 | 800 | 900 | 1,075 | 10,000 | 22,000 | |
| 1842O | 27,400 | 750 | 850 | 2,000 | 2,500 | 13,500 | | |
| 1843 | 75,462 | 750 | 775 | 1,000 | 1,250 | 12,000 | | |
| 1843O | 175,162 | 775 | 800 | 900 | 1,100 | 8,500 | 32,000 | |
| 1844 | 6,361 | 900 | 2,000 | 3,500 | 4,000 | 10,000 | | |
| 1844O | 118,700 | 750 | 800 | 1,250 | 1,550 | 8,750 | | |
| 1845 | 26,153 | 750 | 800 | 1,250 | 1,550 | 10,000 | | |
| 1845O | 47,500 | 775 | 800 | 1,800 | 2,250 | 10,000 | 30,000 | |
| 1846 | 20,095 | 750 | 900 | 3,500 | 4,000 | 14,000 | | |
| 1846O | 81,780 | 775 | 850 | 2,500 | 3,250 | 10,000 | 25,000 | |
| 1847 | 862,258 | 750 | 775 | 800 | 825 | 2,500 | 15,000 | |
| 1847O | 571,500 | 775 | 800 | 825 | 875 | 4,000 | 13,000 | |
| 1848 | 145,484 | 750 | 775 | 800 | 825 | 3,500 | 15,000 | — |
| 1848O | 35,850 | 775 | 800 | 2,350 | 2,750 | 11,000 | 20,000 | |
| 1849 | 653,618 | 750 | 775 | 800 | 850 | 2,500 | 10,000 | |
| 1849O | 23,900 | 800 | 1,600 | 4,000 | 5,250 | 18,000 | | |
| 1850 | 291,451 | 750 | 775 | 800 | 825 | 2,750 | 13,000 | |
| 1850O | 57,500 | 800 | 875 | 1,250 | 1,500 | 12,000 | | |
| 1851 | 176,328 | 750 | 775 | 800 | 825 | 3,000 | 15,000 | |
| 1851O | 263,000 | 750 | 800 | 875 | 1,000 | 4,500 | 17,000 | |
| 1852 | 263,106 | 750 | 775 | 800 | 825 | 3,500 | 16,000 | |
| 1852O | 18,000 | 800 | 950 | 2,500 | 3,250 | 18,000 | | |
| 1853, 3 Over 2 | 201,253 | 850 | 900 | 1,500 | 1,750 | 10,000 | | |
| 1853 | * | 750 | 775 | 800 | 825 | 2,500 | 13,000 | |
| 1853O | 51,000 | 800 | 825 | 900 | 1,000 | 8,500 | | |
| 1854 | 54,250 | 750 | 775 | 800 | 825 | 3,500 | | |
| 1854O | 52,500 | 800 | 825 | 850 | 1,450 | 6,500 | 23,000 | |
| 1854S | 123,826 | 800 | 850 | 950 | 1,150 | 6,500 | 25,000 | |
| 1855 | 121,701 | 750 | 775 | 800 | 825 | 3,000 | 12,000 | — |
| 1855O | 18,000 | 875 | 1,250 | 4,500 | 6,500 | 18,000 | | |

* Included in number above.

| | Mintage | VF-20 | EF-40 | AU-50 | AU-55 | MS-60 | MS-63 | PF-63 |
|---|---|---|---|---|---|---|---|---|
| 1855S | 9,000 | $1,500 | $2,300 | $4,250 | $6,000 | $19,000 | | |
| 1856 | 60,490 | 750 | 775 | 800 | 825 | 2,500 | $12,000 | — |
| 18560 | 14,500 | 800 | 1,100 | 22,750 | 3,500 | 12,000 | | |
| 1856S | 68,000 | 750 | 800 | 900 | 1,100 | 6,000 | | |
| 1857 | 16,606 | 750 | 800 | 1,250 | 1,450 | 7,000 | | |
| 18570 | 5,500 | 900 | 1,250 | 3,000 | 3,750 | 20,000 | | — |
| 1857S | 26,000 | 775 | 900 | 1,500 | 1,850 | 7,000 | 13,000 | |
| 1858 | 2,521 | 3,500 | 6,000 | 8,500 | 10,500 | 25,000 | | — |
| 18580 | 20,000 | 800 | 900 | 1,250 | 1,500 | 6,000 | 23,000 | |
| 1858S | 11,800 | 1,100 | 2,000 | 3,000 | 3,750 | 22,000 | | |
| 1859 (80) | 16,013 | 775 | 800 | 850 | 900 | 6,000 | 12,000 | $45,000 |
| 18590 | 2,300 | 3,250 | 7,500 | 15,000 | 20,000 | 40,000 | | |
| 1859S | 7,000 | 1,550 | 3,000 | 8,500 | 11,000 | 30,000 | | |
| 1860 (50) | 15,055 | 750 | 775 | 900 | 1,000 | 5,000 | 12,000 | 31,000 |
| 18600 | 11,100 | 850 | 1,150 | 2,250 | 2,750 | 8,000 | | |
| 1860S | 5,000 | 1,850 | 3,250 | 8,000 | 10,000 | 27,500 | | |
| 1861 (69) | 113,164 | 750 | 775 | 800 | 825 | 4,000 | 12,000 | 30,000 |
| 1861S | 15,500 | 1,000 | 1,850 | 4,000 | 5,000 | 22,000 | | |
| 1862 (35) | 10,960 | 750 | 850 | 1,500 | 1,750 | 8,000 | 18,000 | 30,000 |
| 1862S | 12,500 | 1,250 | 2,250 | 3,250 | 4,000 | 24,000 | | |
| 1863 (30) | 1,218 | 2,750 | 5,500 | 8,500 | 9,500 | 30,000 | 50,000 | 30,000 |
| 1863S | 10,000 | 1,250 | 2,400 | 6,000 | 8,000 | 15,000 | | |
| 1864 (50) | 3,530 | 1,250 | 2,500 | 5,000 | 7,500 | 10,000 | | 30,000 |
| 1864S | 2,500 | 3,000 | 7,000 | 14,000 | 16,000 | 36,000 | | |
| 1865 (25) | 3,980 | 1,300 | 2,500 | 4,000 | 6,000 | 23,000 | 37,500 | 30,000 |
| 1865S | 16,700 | 2,350 | 4,000 | 10,000 | 12,500 | 30,000 | 50,000 | |
| 1866S | 8,500 | 1,600 | 2,200 | 7,000 | 8,500 | 30,000 | | |

## LIBERTY HEAD, MOTTO ABOVE EAGLE (1866–1907)

**VF-20 Very Fine:** Half of hair lines over coronet visible. Curls under ear worn but defined. IN GOD WE TRUST and its ribbon sharp.
**EF-40 Extremely Fine:** Small amount of wear on top of hair and below L in LIBERTY. Wear evident on wing tips and neck of eagle.
**AU-50 About Uncirculated:** Trace of wear on hair above eye and on coronet.
**AU-55 Choice About Uncirculated:** Evidence of friction on design high points. Some of original mint luster present.

*Mintmark is on reverse, below eagle.*

**MS-60 Uncirculated:** No trace of wear. Light blemishes.
**MS-63 Choice Uncirculated:** Some distracting marks or blemishes in focal areas. Impaired luster possible.
**PF-63 Choice Proof:** Reflective surfaces with only a few blemishes in secondary focal areas. No major flaws.

| | Mintage | VF-20 | EF-40 | AU-50 | AU-55 | MS-60 | MS-63 | PF-63 |
|---|---|---|---|---|---|---|---|---|
| 1866 (30) | 3,750 | $750 | $1,350 | $3,000 | $3,500 | $15,000 | | $25,000 |
| 1866S | 11,500 | 1,100 | 2,500 | 4,500 | 5,500 | 16,000 | | |
| 1867 (50) | 3,090 | 1,100 | 1,650 | 2,500 | 3,500 | 15,000 | | 25,000 |
| 1867S | 9,000 | 1,500 | 3,500 | 5,000 | 6,500 | 25,000 | | |
| 1868 (25) | 10,630 | 750 | 775 | 1,000 | 1,100 | 10,000 | | 25,000 |
| 1868S | 13,500 | 1,000 | 1,300 | 2,250 | 2,500 | 13,000 | | |
| 1869 (25) | 1,830 | 1,050 | 1,500 | 2,500 | 3,000 | 18,000 | | 25,000 |
| 1869S | 6,430 | 1,050 | 1,500 | 2,750 | 3,250 | 13,000 | | |
| 1870 (35) | 3,990 | 750 | 950 | 1,450 | 1,650 | 12,500 | | 22,500 |
| 1870CC | 5,908 | 15,000 | 27,500 | 55,000 | 80,000 | | | |
| 1870S | 8,000 | 800 | 1,350 | 3,250 | 4,500 | 20,000 | | |
| 1871 (30) | 1,790 | 1,000 | 1,600 | 2,500 | 3,000 | 11,000 | | 22,500 |
| 1871CC | 8,085 | 2,250 | 4,250 | 12,500 | 15,000 | 40,000 | | |

*Chart continued on next page.*

| | Mintage | VF-20 | EF-40 | AU-50 | AU-55 | MS-60 | MS-63 | PF-63 |
|---|---|---|---|---|---|---|---|---|
| 1871S | 16,500 | $875 | $1,350 | $3,000 | $4,500 | $15,000 | | |
| 1872 .........(30) ......1,620 | | 1,400 | 2,000 | 5,000 | 6,000 | 10,000 | $23,000 | $23,500 |
| 1872CC | 4,600 | 2,500 | 6,000 | 15,000 | 20,000 | 45,000 | | |
| 1872S | 17,300 | 750 | 800 | 1,100 | 1,500 | 11,000 | | |
| 1873 .........(25) ......800 | | 3,250 | 7,500 | 12,500 | 15,000 | 30,000 | | 25,000 |
| 1873CC | 4,543 | 2,750 | 7,500 | 25,000 | 32,500 | 50,000 | | |
| 1873S | 12,000 | 900 | 1,300 | 2,500 | 3,000 | 15,000 | | |
| 1874 .........(20) ......53,140 | | 725 | 735 | 750 | 775 | 1,200 | 4,500 | 25,000 |
| 1874CC | 16,767 | 1,100 | 2,000 | 6,000 | 7,500 | 32,500 | | |
| 1874S | 10,000 | 900 | 1,550 | 3,250 | 3,500 | 25,000 | | |
| 1875 .........(20) ......100 | | 47,500 | 67,500 | 87,500 | | | | 95,000 |
| 1875CC | 7,715 | 3,250 | 6,000 | 13,000 | 25,000 | 65,000 | | |
| 1876 .........(45) ......687 | | 1,800 | 3,500 | 10,000 | 11,500 | 30,000 | | 20,000 |
| 1876CC | 4,696 | 2,850 | 5,000 | 12,500 | 14,500 | 40,000 | | |
| 1876S | 5,000 | 875 | 1,300 | 2,750 | 3,500 | 22,000 | | |
| 1877 .........(20) ......797 | | 2,150 | 3,500 | 7,250 | 8,500 | 22,500 | | 20,000 |
| 1877CC | 3,332 | 2,250 | 5,250 | 10,000 | 12,500 | 35,000 | | |
| 1877S | 17,000 | 725 | 735 | 1,100 | 1,250 | 18,000 | | |
| 1878 .........(20) ......73,780 | | 725 | 735 | 750 | 765 | 800 | 5,000 | 20,000 |
| 1878CC | 3,244 | 2,750 | 6,750 | 13,500 | 15,000 | 45,000 | | |
| 1878S | 26,100 | 725 | 735 | 850 | 1,000 | 7,500 | 20,000 | |
| 1879 .........(30) ......384,740 | | 725 | 735 | 750 | 765 | 775 | 2,500 | 17,500 |
| 1879CC | 1,762 | 4,250 | 8,750 | 17,500 | 20,000 | 45,000 | | |
| 1879O | 1,500 | 1,600 | 3,500 | 8,500 | 10,000 | 25,000 | | |
| 1879S | 224,000 | 725 | 735 | 750 | 765 | 775 | 4,500 | |
| 1880 .........(36) ..1,644,840 | | 725 | 735 | 750 | 765 | 775 | 2,500 | 17,500 |
| 1880CC | 11,190 | 875 | 950 | 1,250 | 1,550 | 10,000 | | |
| 1880O | 9,200 | 750 | 825 | 1,100 | 1,350 | 5,500 | | |
| 1880S | 506,250 | 725 | 735 | 750 | 765 | 775 | 2,500 | |
| 1881 .........(40) ..3,877,220 | | 725 | 735 | 750 | 765 | 775 | 1,250 | 17,500 |
| 1881CC | 24,015 | 775 | 850 | 1,050 | 1,250 | 4,000 | 15,000 | |
| 1881O | 8,350 | 750 | 850 | 975 | 1,150 | 5,000 | | |
| 1881S | 970,000 | 725 | 735 | 750 | 765 | 775 | 2,500 | |
| 1882 .........(40) ..2,324,440 | | 725 | 735 | 750 | 765 | 775 | 1,250 | 15,000 |
| 1882CC | 6,764 | 850 | 1,050 | 2,500 | 2,750 | 15,000 | 30,000 | |
| 1882O | 10,820 | 800 | 850 | 1,000 | 1,150 | 4,250 | 12,500 | |
| 1882S | 132,000 | 725 | 735 | 750 | 765 | 775 | 3,500 | |
| 1883 .........(40) ....208,700 | | 725 | 735 | 750 | 765 | 775 | 2,500 | 15,000 |
| 1883CC | 12,000 | 800 | 850 | 2,150 | 2,500 | 10,000 | | |
| 1883O | 800 | 3,500 | 9,500 | 15,000 | 17,500 | 37,500 | | |
| 1883S | 38,000 | 725 | 735 | 750 | 765 | 775 | 6,000 | |
| 1884 .........(45) ....76,860 | | 725 | 735 | 750 | 765 | 775 | 3,000 | 15,000 |
| 1884CC | 9,925 | 850 | 1,050 | 2,150 | 2,500 | 7,500 | | |
| 1884S | 124,250 | 725 | 735 | 750 | 765 | 775 | 3,500 | |
| 1885 .........(65) ....253,462 | | 725 | 735 | 750 | 765 | 775 | 2,250 | 12,500 |
| 1885S | 228,000 | 725 | 735 | 750 | 765 | 775 | 1,850 | |
| 1886 .........(60) ....236,100 | | 725 | 735 | 750 | 765 | 775 | 3,000 | 12,500 |
| 1886S | 826,000 | 700 | 715 | 725 | 735 | 750 | 1,250 | |
| 1887 .........(80) ....53,600 | | 725 | 735 | 750 | 765 | 775 | 4,000 | 12,000 |
| 1887S | 817,000 | 725 | 735 | 750 | 765 | 775 | 2,000 | |
| 1888 .........(75) ....132,921 | | 725 | 735 | 750 | 765 | 775 | 4,000 | 12,000 |
| 1888O | 21,335 | 750 | 800 | 850 | 875 | 950 | 4,000 | |
| 1888S | 648,700 | 725 | 735 | 750 | 765 | 775 | 1,350 | |
| 1889 .........(45) ....4,440 | | 725 | 735 | 750 | 765 | 1,500 | 4,500 | 12,000 |
| 1889S | 425,400 | 725 | 735 | 750 | 765 | 775 | 1,250 | |
| 1890 .........(63) ....57,980 | | 725 | 735 | 750 | 765 | 800 | 3,500 | 10,000 |
| 1890CC | 17,500 | 800 | 850 | 900 | 950 | 1,750 | 8,500 | |
| 1891 .........(48) ....91,820 | | 700 | 715 | 725 | 735 | 750 | 2,500 | 10,000 |

| | Mintage | VF-20 | EF-40 | AU-50 | AU-55 | MS-60 | MS-63 | PF-63 |
|---|---|---|---|---|---|---|---|---|
| 1891CC | 103,732 | $800 | $850 | $875 | $925 | $1,350 | $5,250 | |
| 1892 | (72) ....797,480 | 700 | 715 | 725 | 735 | 750 | 1,250 | $10,000 |
| 1892CC | 40,000 | 800 | 850 | 900 | 925 | 2,500 | 7,250 | |
| 1892O | 28,688 | 700 | 715 | 725 | 735 | 750 | 5,000 | |
| 1892S | 115,500 | 700 | 715 | 725 | 735 | 750 | 2,500 | |
| 1893 | (55) ..1,840,840 | 700 | 715 | 725 | 735 | 750 | 1,250 | 10,000 |
| 1893CC | 14,000 | 800 | 850 | 900 | 1,250 | 5,000 | 15,000 | |
| 1893O | 17,000 | 750 | 775 | 800 | 825 | 900 | 4,500 | |
| 1893S | 141,350 | 725 | 735 | 750 | 765 | 775 | 2,500 | |
| 1894 | (43) ..2,470,735 | 700 | 715 | 725 | 735 | 750 | 1,250 | 10,000 |
| 1894O | 107,500 | 725 | 750 | 775 | 800 | 850 | 4,000 | |
| 1894S | 25,000 | 725 | 750 | 775 | 800 | 2,000 | 8,250 | |
| 1895 | (56) ....567,770 | 700 | 715 | 725 | 735 | 750 | 1,250 | 10,000 |
| 1895O | 98,000 | 700 | 715 | 725 | 735 | 750 | 4,250 | |
| 1895S | 49,000 | 725 | 735 | 750 | 765 | 1,500 | 5,000 | |
| 1896 | (78) .....76,270 | 700 | 715 | 725 | 735 | 750 | 1,800 | 10,000 |
| 1896S | 123,750 | 725 | 735 | 750 | 765 | 1,500 | 7,000 | |
| 1897 | (69) ..1,000,090 | 700 | 715 | 725 | 735 | 750 | 1,250 | 10,000 |
| 1897O | 42,500 | 750 | 765 | 775 | 785 | 800 | 3,500 | |
| 1897S | 234,750 | 700 | 715 | 725 | 735 | 750 | 3,500 | |
| 1898 | (67) ....812,130 | 700 | 715 | 725 | 735 | 750 | 1,250 | 10,000 |
| 1898S | 473,600 | 700 | 715 | 725 | 735 | 750 | 3,000 | |
| 1899 | (86) ..1,262,219 | 700 | 715 | 725 | 735 | 750 | 1,250 | 10,000 |
| 1899O | 37,047 | 725 | 735 | 750 | 765 | 775 | 3,500 | |
| 1899S | 841,000 | 725 | 735 | 750 | 765 | 800 | 2,250 | |
| 1900 | (120) ...293,840 | 700 | 715 | 725 | 735 | 750 | 1,250 | 10,000 |
| 1900S | 81,000 | 725 | 735 | 750 | 765 | 800 | 4,000 | |
| 1901 | (85) ..1,718,740 | 700 | 715 | 725 | 735 | 750 | 1,250 | 10,000 |
| 1901O | 72,041 | 700 | 715 | 725 | 735 | 775 | 2,500 | |
| 1901S | 2,812,750 | 700 | 715 | 725 | 735 | 750 | 1,250 | |
| 1902 | (113) ...82,400 | 700 | 715 | 725 | 735 | 750 | 2,000 | 10,000 |
| 1902S | 469,500 | 700 | 715 | 725 | 735 | 750 | 1,250 | |
| 1903 | (96) ....125,830 | 700 | 715 | 725 | 735 | 750 | 1,250 | 10,000 |
| 1903O | 112,771 | 700 | 715 | 725 | 735 | 750 | 2,250 | |
| 1903S | 538,000 | 700 | 715 | 725 | 735 | 750 | 1,250 | |
| 1904 | (108) ...161,930 | 700 | 715 | 725 | 735 | 750 | 1,500 | 10,000 |
| 1904O | 108,950 | 700 | 715 | 725 | 735 | 750 | 2,500 | |
| 1905 | (86) ...200,992 | 700 | 715 | 725 | 735 | 750 | 1,250 | 10,000 |
| 1905S | 369,250 | 700 | 715 | 725 | 735 | 750 | 4,000 | |
| 1906 | (77) ...165,420 | 700 | 715 | 725 | 735 | 750 | 1,250 | 10,000 |
| 1906D | 981,000 | 700 | 715 | 725 | 735 | 750 | 1,250 | |
| 1906O | 86,895 | 700 | 715 | 725 | 735 | 750 | 3,000 | |
| 1906S | 457,000 | 700 | 715 | 725 | 735 | 750 | 2,750 | |
| 1907 | (74) ..1,203,899 | 700 | 715 | 725 | 735 | 750 | 1,250 | 10,000 |
| 1907D | 1,030,000 | 700 | 715 | 725 | 735 | 750 | 1,325 | |
| 1907S | 210,500 | 725 | 735 | 750 | 765 | 775 | 3,750 | |

## INDIAN HEAD (1907–1933)

**VF-20 Very Fine:** Bonnet feathers worn near band. Wear visible on high points of hair.

**EF-40 Extremely Fine:** Slight wear on cheekbone and headdress feathers. Slight wear visible on eagle's eye and left wing.

**AU-50 About Uncirculated:** Trace of wear on hair above eye and on forehead.

**AU-55 Choice About Uncirculated:** Evidence of friction on design high points. Much of original mint luster present.

**MS-60 Uncirculated:** No trace of wear. Light blemishes.

**MS-63 Choice Uncirculated:** Some distracting contact marks or blemishes in prime focal areas. Impaired luster possible.

**Matte PF-63 Choice Proof:** Matte surfaces with few blemishes in secondary focal places. No major flaws.

**No Motto**
*Mintmark is above
left tip of branch on
1908-D No Motto.*

**With Motto
IN GOD WE TRUST**
*Mintmark is at left
of arrow points.*

*Gem Uncirculated (MS-65) coins are rare and worth substantial premiums.*

| | Mintage | VF-20 | EF-40 | AU-50 | AU-55 | MS-60 | MS-63 |
|---|---|---|---|---|---|---|---|
| 1907, Wire Rim, Periods | .500 | $10,000 | $13,500 | $17,500 | $19,000 | $23,000 | $32,500 |
| 1907, Rounded Rim, Periods Before and After *E*PLURIBUS*UNUM* | .50 | 25,000 | 35,000 | 45,000 | 50,000 | 65,000 | 85,000 |
| 1907, No Periods | .239,406 | 725 | 735 | 745 | 765 | 800 | 2,500 |
| 1908, No Motto | .33,500 | 725 | 735 | 745 | 765 | 850 | 3,000 |
| 1908D, No Motto | .210,000 | 725 | 735 | 745 | 765 | 850 | 4,250 |

## Variety 2 – Motto on Reverse (1908–1933)

| | Mintage | VF-20 | EF-40 | AU-50 | AU-55 | MS-60 | MS-63 | MATTE PF-63 |
|---|---|---|---|---|---|---|---|---|
| 1908 ...(116) | .341,370 | $700 | $715 | $725 | $735 | $750 | $1,800 | $12,000 |
| 1908D | .836,500 | 700 | 715 | 725 | 735 | 750 | 4,500 | |
| 1908S | .59,850 | 725 | 750 | 775 | 825 | 2,250 | 7,750 | |
| 1909 ...(74) | .184,789 | 700 | 715 | 725 | 735 | 775 | 2,500 | 12,000 |
| 1909D | .121,540 | 700 | 715 | 725 | 750 | 800 | 4,000 | |
| 1909S | .292,350 | 700 | 715 | 725 | 750 | 825 | 4,000 | |
| 1910 ...(204) | .318,500 | 700 | 715 | 725 | 735 | 775 | 1,250 | 12,000 |
| 1910D | .2,356,640 | 700 | 715 | 725 | 735 | 775 | 1,250 | |
| 1910S | .811,000 | 700 | 715 | 725 | 735 | 850 | 5,500 | |
| 1911 ...(95) | .505,500 | 700 | 715 | 725 | 735 | 775 | 1,250 | 12,000 |
| 1911D | .30,100 | 750 | 950 | 1,150 | 2,250 | 5,500 | 22,500 | |
| 1911S | .51,000 | 725 | 750 | 775 | 800 | 850 | 6,500 | |
| 1912 ...(83) | .405,000 | 700 | 715 | 725 | 735 | 775 | 1,250 | 12,000 |
| 1912S | .300,000 | 725 | 750 | 775 | 800 | 850 | 5,000 | |
| 1913 ...(71) | .442,000 | 700 | 715 | 725 | 735 | 775 | 1,250 | 12,000 |
| 1913S | .66,000 | 725 | 750 | 800 | 1,000 | 3,000 | 20,000 | |
| 1914 ...(50) | .151,000 | 700 | 715 | 725 | 735 | 775 | 1,500 | 12,000 |
| 1914D | .343,500 | 700 | 715 | 725 | 735 | 775 | 1,500 | |
| 1914S | .208,000 | 700 | 715 | 725 | 735 | 850 | 5,000 | |
| 1915 ...(75) | .351,000 | 700 | 715 | 725 | 735 | 775 | 1,500 | 13,500 |
| 1915S | .59,000 | 700 | 725 | 750 | 800 | 2,250 | 11,000 | |
| 1916S | .138,500 | 700 | 725 | 750 | 800 | 850 | 4,000 | |
| 1920S | .126,500 | 8,500 | 12,500 | 15,000 | 17,500 | 27,500 | 67,500 | |
| 1926 | .1,014,000 | 700 | 715 | 725 | 735 | 775 | 1,050 | |
| 1930S | .96,000 | 5,000 | 6,500 | 8,500 | 9,500 | 15,000 | 27,500 | |
| 1932 | .4,463,000 | 700 | 715 | 725 | 735 | 775 | 1,050 | |
| 1933 | .312,500 | 75,000 | 85,000 | 100,000 | 115,000 | 165,000 | 185,000 | |

This largest denomination of all regular United States issues was authorized to be coined by the Act of March 3, 1849. The coin's weight was set at 516 grains, and its fineness at .900. A single $20 gold pattern of 1849 resides in the Smithsonian.

## LIBERTY HEAD (1849–1907)

**VF-20 Very Fine:** LIBERTY on crown bold; prongs on crown defined; lower half worn flat. Hair worn about ear.

**EF-40 Extremely Fine:** Trace of wear on rounded prongs of crown and down hair curls. Minor bagmarks.

**AU-50 About Uncirculated:** Trace of wear on hair over eye and on coronet.

**AU-55 Choice About Uncirculated:** Evidence of friction on design high points. Some of original mint luster present.

**MS-60 Uncirculated:** No trace of wear. Light blemishes.

**MS-63 Choice Uncirculated:** Some distracting marks or blemishes in focal areas. Impaired luster possible.

**PF-63 Choice Proof:** Reflective surfaces with only a few blemishes in secondary focal areas. No major flaws.

### Without Motto on Reverse (1849–1866)

*Mintmark is below eagle.*

| | Mintage | VF-20 | EF-40 | AU-50 | AU-55 | MS-60 | MS-63 | PF-63 |
|---|---|---|---|---|---|---|---|---|
| 1850 | 1,170,261 | $1,500 | $1,700 | $2,500 | $3,250 | $7,250 | $32,500 | |
| 1850O | 141,000 | 1,550 | 3,000 | 5,500 | 8,500 | 32,500 | | |
| 1851 | 2,087,155 | 1,400 | 1,450 | 1,550 | 1,600 | 2,500 | 15,000 | |
| 1851O | 315,000 | 1,550 | 2,450 | 3,750 | 5,000 | 14,000 | 47,500 | |
| 1852 | 2,053,026 | 1,400 | 1,450 | 1,550 | 1,600 | 2,500 | 12,500 | |
| 1852O | 190,000 | 1,550 | 2,500 | 3,500 | 5,000 | 15,500 | 35,000 | |
| 1853 | 1,261,326 | 1,400 | 1,450 | 1,550 | 1,600 | 3,000 | 16,000 | |
| 1853O | 71,000 | 1,600 | 1,800 | 3,250 | 5,500 | 22,500 | | |
| 1854 | 757,899 | 1,400 | 1,450 | 1,550 | 1,650 | 6,500 | 17,500 | |
| 1854O | 3,250 | 75,000 | 125,000 | 220,000 | 280,000 | 475,000 | | |
| 1854S | 141,468 | 1,500 | 1,550 | 2,600 | 3,250 | 4,250 | 11,000 | |
| 1855 | 364,666 | 1,400 | 1,450 | 1,550 | 1,650 | 6,500 | 30,000 | |
| 1855O | 8,000 | 2,750 | 11,000 | 25,000 | 30,000 | 65,000 | | |
| 1855S | 879,675 | 1,400 | 1,450 | 1,600 | 1,800 | 5,500 | 11,000 | |
| 1856 | 329,878 | 1,400 | 1,450 | 1,550 | 1,650 | 5,750 | 18,500 | |
| 1856O | 2,250 | 75,000 | 125,000 | 225,000 | 300,000 | 425,000 | | |
| 1856S | 1,189,750 | 1,400 | 1,450 | 1,550 | 1,700 | 4,250 | 11,000 | |
| 1857 | 439,375 | 1,400 | 1,450 | 1,550 | 1,650 | 2,650 | 15,000 | |
| 1857O | 30,000 | 1,850 | 2,250 | 4,750 | 6,500 | 25,000 | 67,500 | |
| 1857S | 970,500 | 1,450 | 1,500 | 1,600 | 1,650 | 2,750 | 6,000 | |
| 1858 | 211,714 | 1,450 | 1,500 | 1,650 | 2,200 | 3,250 | 22,500 | |
| 1858O | 35,250 | 1,850 | 2,750 | 4,750 | 6,750 | 27,500 | | |
| 1858S | 846,710 | 1,450 | 1,550 | 1,650 | 1,700 | 6,500 | | |
| 1859 | (80) 43,597 | 1,650 | 2,000 | 3,250 | 5,500 | 22,500 | | $75,000 |
| 1859O | 9,100 | 3,750 | 13,500 | 22,500 | 27,500 | 77,500 | | |
| 1859S | 636,445 | 1,400 | 1,450 | 1,500 | 1,550 | 3,750 | 25,000 | |
| 1860 | (59) 577,670 | 1,400 | 1,450 | 1,500 | 1,550 | 2,750 | 10,000 | 52,500 |
| 1860O | 6,600 | 3,750 | 11,000 | 21,000 | 26,500 | 75,000 | | |
| 1860S | 544,950 | 1,450 | 1,500 | 1,600 | 1,650 | 5,500 | 10,000 | |

*Chart continued on next page.*

| | Mintage | VF-20 | EF-40 | AU-50 | AU-55 | MS-60 | MS-63 | PF-63 |
|---|---|---|---|---|---|---|---|---|
| 1861 . . . . . . . . . . . .(66) . . .2,976,453 | | $1,400 | $1,450 | $1,475 | $1,500 | $2,750 | $7,500 | $50,000 |
| 1861O . . . . . . . . . . . . . . . . . . . .17,741 | | 3,250 | 10,000 | 27,500 | 37,500 | 62,500 | | |
| 1861S . . . . . . . . . . . . . . . . . . . .768,000 | | 1,400 | 1,450 | 1,600 | 1,650 | 6,500 | 22,000 | |
| 1862 . . . . . . . . . . . .(35) . . . .92,133 | | 1,450 | 1,950 | 3,750 | 5,000 | 11,000 | 26,500 | 42,500 |
| 1862S . . . . . . . . . . . . . . . . . . . .854,173 | | 1,400 | 1,450 | 1,600 | 1,800 | 6,500 | 22,000 | |
| 1863 . . . . . . . . . . . .(30) . . .142,790 | | 1,400 | 1,550 | 2,650 | 3,250 | 13,250 | 24,500 | 42,500 |
| 1863S . . . . . . . . . . . . . . . . . . . .966,570 | | 1,400 | 1,450 | 1,600 | 1,800 | 5,000 | 22,500 | |
| 1864 . . . . . . . . . . . .(50) . . .204,235 | | 1,400 | 1,450 | 1,600 | 1,800 | 7,500 | | 42,500 |
| 1864S . . . . . . . . . . . . . . . . . . . .793,660 | | 1,400 | 1,450 | 1,500 | 1,600 | 5,500 | 22,500 | |
| 1865 . . . . . . . . . . . .(25) . . .351,175 | | 1,400 | 1,450 | 1,500 | 1,550 | 4,250 | 13,250 | 42,500 |
| 1865S . . . . . . . . . . . . . . . . . . .1,042,500 | | 1,400 | 1,450 | 1,500 | 1,550 | 3,000 | 6,750 | |
| 1866S . . . . . . . . . . . . . . . . . . . .120,000 | | 2,250 | 5,500 | 22,500 | 32,500 | 85,000 | | |

## Motto Above Eagle (1866–1907)
### *Value TWENTY D. (1866–1876)*

| | Mintage | VF-20 | EF-40 | AU-50 | AU-55 | MS-60 | MS-63 | PF-63 |
|---|---|---|---|---|---|---|---|---|
| 1866 . . . . . . . . . . . .(30) . . .698,745 | | $1,350 | $1,375 | $1,450 | $1,550 | $5,500 | $16,500 | $42,500 |
| 1866S . . . . . . . . . . . . . . . . . . . .842,250 | | 1,350 | 1,375 | 1,450 | 3,250 | 11,250 | | |
| 1867 . . . . . . . . . . . .(50) . . .251,015 | | 1,350 | 1,375 | 1,450 | 1,550 | 2,150 | 12,500 | 42,500 |
| 1867S . . . . . . . . . . . . . . . . . . . .920,750 | | 1,350 | 1,375 | 1,600 | 1,750 | 7,500 | | |
| 1868 . . . . . . . . . . . .(25) . . . .98,575 | | 1,350 | 1,375 | 1,600 | 1,750 | 7,500 | 37,500 | 42,500 |
| 1868S . . . . . . . . . . . . . . . . . . . .837,500 | | 1,350 | 1,375 | 1,450 | 1,500 | 8,500 | 30,000 | |
| 1869 . . . . . . . . . . . .(25) . . .175,130 | | 1,350 | 1,375 | 1,450 | 1,500 | 5,500 | 16,250 | 42,500 |
| 1869S . . . . . . . . . . . . . . . . . . . .686,750 | | 1,350 | 1,375 | 1,450 | 1,500 | 5,500 | 32,500 | |
| 1870 . . . . . . . . . . . .(35) . . .155,150 | | 1,350 | 1,375 | 1,450 | 1,500 | 6,250 | 32,500 | 42,500 |
| 1870CC . . . . . . . . . . . . . . . . . . . . .3,789 | | 135,000 | 200,000 | 300,000 | 400,000 | | | |
| 1870S . . . . . . . . . . . . . . . . . . . .982,000 | | 1,350 | 1,375 | 1,400 | 1,500 | 3,500 | 22,500 | |
| 1871 . . . . . . . . . . . .(30) . . . .80,120 | | 1,350 | 1,375 | 1,400 | 1,450 | 2,850 | 16,000 | 40,000 |
| 1871CC . . . . . . . . . . . . . . . . . . . .17,387 | | 6,250 | 12,500 | 32,500 | 35,000 | 65,000 | | |
| 1871S . . . . . . . . . . . . . . . . . . . .928,000 | | 1,350 | 1,375 | 1,400 | 1,500 | 3,250 | 16,000 | |
| 1872 . . . . . . . . . . . .(30) . . .251,850 | | 1,350 | 1,375 | 1,400 | 1,450 | 2,500 | 16,500 | 40,000 |
| 1872CC . . . . . . . . . . . . . . . . . . . .26,900 | | 2,000 | 3,700 | 7,500 | 8,750 | 26,500 | | |
| 1872S . . . . . . . . . . . . . . . . . . . .780,000 | | 1,350 | 1,375 | 1,400 | 1,450 | 2,250 | 15,500 | |
| 1873 . . . . . . . . . . . .(25) . .1,709,800 | | 1,350 | 1,375 | 1,400 | 1,450 | 2,100 | 8,500 | 42,500 |
| 1873CC . . . . . . . . . . . . . . . . . . . .22,410 | | 2,650 | 3,750 | 7,750 | 9,750 | 25,000 | | |
| 1873S . . . . . . . . . . . . . . . . . . .1,040,600 | | 1,350 | 1,375 | 1,400 | 1,450 | 1,750 | 13,250 | |
| 1874 . . . . . . . . . . . .(20) . . .366,780 | | 1,350 | 1,375 | 1,400 | 1,450 | 1,650 | 12,000 | 42,500 |
| 1874CC . . . . . . . . . . . . . . . . . . .115,085 | | 1,550 | 1,950 | 2,650 | 3,000 | 8,750 | 40,000 | |
| 1874S . . . . . . . . . . . . . . . . . . .1,214,000 | | 1,350 | 1,375 | 1,400 | 1,450 | 1,600 | 16,000 | |
| 1875 . . . . . . . . . . . .(20) . . .295,720 | | 1,350 | 1,375 | 1,400 | 1,450 | 1,600 | 8,500 | 67,500 |
| 1875CC . . . . . . . . . . . . . . . . . . .111,151 | | 1,550 | 1,650 | 1,800 | 2,200 | 3,500 | 16,250 | |
| 1875S . . . . . . . . . . . . . . . . . . .1,230,000 | | 1,350 | 1,375 | 1,400 | 1,450 | 1,650 | 9,500 | |
| 1876 . . . . . . . . . . . .(45) . . .583,860 | | 1,350 | 1,375 | 1,400 | 1,450 | 1,600 | 8,500 | 42,500 |
| 1876CC . . . . . . . . . . . . . . . . . . .138,441 | | 1,550 | 1,650 | 1,800 | 2,350 | 6,500 | 26,500 | |
| 1876S . . . . . . . . . . . . . . . . . . .1,597,000 | | 1,350 | 1,375 | 1,400 | 1,450 | 1,650 | 8,500 | |

## Value TWENTY DOLLARS (1877–1907)

| | Mintage | VF-20 | EF-40 | AU-50 | AU-55 | MS-60 | MS-63 | PF-63 |
|---|---|---|---|---|---|---|---|---|
| 1877 ............(20) ....397,650 | | $1,350 | $1,375 | $1,400 | $1,450 | $1,550 | $8,250 | $26,500 |
| 1877CC ...............42,565 | | 1,600 | 1,850 | 3,250 | 4,500 | 14,250 | | |
| 1877S ...............1,735,000 | | 1,350 | 1,375 | 1,400 | 1,425 | 1,500 | 11,000 | |
| 1878 ............(20) ....543,625 | | 1,350 | 1,375 | 1,400 | 1,425 | 1,500 | 8,750 | 26,500 |
| 1878CC ...............13,180 | | 2,250 | 3,250 | 5,750 | 7,750 | 22,000 | | |
| 1878S ...............1,739,000 | | 1,350 | 1,375 | 1,400 | 1,425 | 1,500 | 12,500 | |
| 1879 ............(30) ....207,600 | | 1,350 | 1,375 | 1,400 | 1,425 | 1,500 | 10,500 | 25,000 |
| 1879CC ...............10,708 | | 2,650 | 3,750 | 7,500 | 10,500 | 26,500 | | |
| 1879O ...............2,325 | | 7,750 | 13,250 | 26,500 | 36,500 | 65,000 | 95,000 | |
| 1879S ...............1,223,800 | | 1,350 | 1,375 | 1,400 | 1,425 | 1,500 | 25,000 | |
| 1880 ............(36) ....51,420 | | 1,350 | 1,375 | 1,400 | 1,425 | 3,250 | 16,500 | 25,000 |
| 1880S ...............836,000 | | 1,350 | 1,375 | 1,400 | 1,425 | 1,500 | 11,000 | |
| 1881 ............(61) ....2,199 | | 7,500 | 12,500 | 22,500 | 25,000 | 50,000 | | 25,000 |
| 1881S ...............727,000 | | 1,350 | 1,375 | 1,400 | 1,425 | 1,500 | 13,000 | |
| 1882 ............(59) ....571 | | 10,000 | 32,500 | 55,000 | 67,500 | 100,000 | 150,000 | 25,000 |
| 1882CC ...............39,140 | | 1,500 | 1,650 | 1,850 | 2,750 | 7,500 | 37,500 | |
| 1882S ...............1,125,000 | | 1,350 | 1,375 | 1,400 | 1,425 | 1,500 | 11,000 | |
| 1883, Proof only ......(92) | | | | | | | | 55,000 |
| 1883CC ...............59,962 | | 1,500 | 1,650 | 1,850 | 2,000 | 6,500 | 18,500 | |
| 1883S ...............1,189,000 | | 1,350 | 1,375 | 1,400 | 1,425 | 1,500 | 5,500 | |
| 1884, Proof only ......(71) | | | | | | | | 55,000 |
| 1884CC ...............81,139 | | 1,500 | 1,650 | 1,850 | 2,250 | 4,500 | 13,500 | |
| 1884S ...............916,000 | | 1,350 | 1,375 | 1,400 | 1,425 | 1,500 | 4,500 | |
| 1885 ............(77) ....751 | | 6,500 | 9,500 | 14,250 | 16,500 | 42,500 | 67,500 | 25,000 |
| 1885CC ...............9,450 | | 2,250 | 3,250 | 5,500 | 6,750 | 12,750 | 32,500 | |
| 1885S ...............683,500 | | 1,350 | 1,375 | 1,400 | 1,425 | 1,500 | 3,750 | |
| 1886 ............(106) ....1,000 | | 7,750 | 12,500 | 26,500 | 32,500 | 55,000 | 75,000 | 25,000 |
| 1887, Proof only .....(121) | | | | | | | | 55,000 |
| 1887S ...............283,000 | | 1,350 | 1,375 | 1,400 | 1,425 | 1,500 | 11,000 | |
| 1888 ............(105) ....226,161 | | 1,350 | 1,375 | 1,400 | 1,425 | 1,500 | 6,500 | 25,000 |
| 1888S ...............859,600 | | 1,350 | 1,375 | 1,400 | 1,425 | 1,500 | 3,250 | |
| 1889 ............(41) ....44,070 | | 1,350 | 1,375 | 1,400 | 1,425 | 1,500 | 9,000 | 26,500 |
| 1889CC ...............30,945 | | 1,650 | 1,850 | 2,350 | 2,750 | 5,500 | 13,500 | |
| 1889S ...............774,700 | | 1,350 | 1,375 | 1,400 | 1,425 | 1,500 | 4,500 | |
| 1890 ............(55) ....75,940 | | 1,350 | 1,375 | 1,400 | 1,425 | 1,500 | 7,000 | 25,000 |
| 1890CC ...............91,209 | | 1,600 | 1,850 | 2,100 | 2,350 | 4,250 | 22,500 | |
| 1890S ...............802,750 | | 1,350 | 1,375 | 1,400 | 1,425 | 1,500 | 4,500 | |
| 1891 ............(52) ....1,390 | | 5,000 | 10,000 | 14,000 | 16,500 | 42,500 | 75,000 | 25,000 |
| 1891CC ...............5,000 | | 4,250 | 7,750 | 9,500 | 12,500 | 18,250 | 36,500 | |
| 1891S ...............1,288,125 | | 1,350 | 1,375 | 1,400 | 1,425 | 1,500 | 2,500 | |
| 1892 ............(93) ....4,430 | | 1,500 | 2,350 | 3,750 | 5,000 | 8,000 | 26,500 | 25,000 |

*Chart continued on next page.*

| | Mintage | VF-20 | EF-40 | AU-50 | AU-55 | MS-60 | MS-63 | PF-63 |
|---|---|---|---|---|---|---|---|---|
| 1892CC | 27,265 | $1,650 | $1,850 | $2,250 | $2,650 | $5,500 | $25,000 | |
| 1892S | 930,150 | 1,350 | 1,375 | 1,400 | 1,425 | 1,500 | 2,650 | |
| 1893 | (59) 344,280 | 1,350 | 1,375 | 1,400 | 1,425 | 1,500 | 2,000 | $25,000 |
| 1893CC | 18,402 | 1,750 | 1,900 | 2,350 | 2,650 | 5,500 | 25,000 | |
| 1893S | 996,175 | 1,350 | 1,375 | 1,400 | 1,425 | 1,500 | 2,200 | |
| 1894 | (50) 1,368,940 | 1,350 | 1,375 | 1,400 | 1,425 | 1,500 | 2,350 | 25,000 |
| 1894S | 1,048,550 | 1,350 | 1,375 | 1,400 | 1,425 | 1,500 | 2,350 | |
| 1895 | (51) 1,114,605 | 1,350 | 1,375 | 1,400 | 1,425 | 1,500 | 1,850 | 25,000 |
| 1895S | 1,143,500 | 1,350 | 1,375 | 1,400 | 1,425 | 1,500 | 1,850 | |
| 1896 | (128) 792,535 | 1,350 | 1,375 | 1,400 | 1,425 | 1,500 | 1,850 | 25,000 |
| 1896S | 1,403,925 | 1,350 | 1,375 | 1,400 | 1,425 | 1,500 | 1,850 | |
| 1897 | (86) 1,383,175 | 1,350 | 1,375 | 1,400 | 1,425 | 1,500 | 1,850 | 25,000 |
| 1897S | 1,470,250 | 1,350 | 1,375 | 1,400 | 1,425 | 1,500 | 1,850 | |
| 1898 | (75) 170,395 | 1,350 | 1,375 | 1,400 | 1,425 | 1,500 | 3,000 | 25,000 |
| 1898S | 2,575,175 | 1,350 | 1,375 | 1,400 | 1,425 | 1,500 | 1,850 | |
| 1899 | (84) 1,669,300 | 1,350 | 1,375 | 1,400 | 1,425 | 1,500 | 1,850 | 25,000 |
| 1899S | 2,010,300 | 1,350 | 1,375 | 1,400 | 1,425 | 1,500 | 1,850 | |
| 1900 | (124) 1,874,460 | 1,350 | 1,375 | 1,400 | 1,425 | 1,500 | 1,850 | 25,000 |
| 1900S | 2,459,500 | 1,350 | 1,375 | 1,400 | 1,425 | 1,500 | 1,850 | |
| 1901 | (96) 111,430 | 1,350 | 1,375 | 1,400 | 1,425 | 1,500 | 1,850 | 25,000 |
| 1901S | 1,596,000 | 1,350 | 1,375 | 1,400 | 1,425 | 1,500 | 1,850 | |
| 1902 | (114) 31,140 | 1,350 | 1,375 | 1,400 | 1,425 | 1,500 | 8,500 | 25,000 |
| 1902S | 1,753,625 | 1,350 | 1,375 | 1,400 | 1,425 | 1,500 | 2,500 | |
| 1903 | (158) 287,270 | 1,350 | 1,375 | 1,400 | 1,425 | 1,500 | 1,850 | 25,000 |
| 1903S | 954,000 | 1,350 | 1,375 | 1,400 | 1,425 | 1,500 | 2,000 | |
| 1904 | (98) 6,256,699 | 1,350 | 1,375 | 1,400 | 1,425 | 1,500 | 1,850 | 25,000 |
| 1904S | 5,134,175 | 1,350 | 1,375 | 1,400 | 1,425 | 1,500 | 2,000 | |
| 1905 | (92) 58,919 | 1,350 | 1,375 | 1,400 | 1,425 | 1,500 | 10,000 | 25,000 |
| 1905S | 1,813,000 | 1,350 | 1,375 | 1,400 | 1,425 | 1,500 | 1,900 | |
| 1906 | (94) 69,596 | 1,350 | 1,375 | 1,400 | 1,425 | 1,500 | 5,500 | 25,000 |
| 1906D | 620,250 | 1,350 | 1,375 | 1,400 | 1,425 | 1,500 | 2,100 | |
| 1906S | 2,065,750 | 1,350 | 1,375 | 1,400 | 1,425 | 1,500 | 2,000 | |
| 1907 | (78) 1,451,786 | 1,350 | 1,375 | 1,400 | 1,425 | 1,500 | 1,850 | 25,000 |
| 1907D | 842,250 | 1,350 | 1,375 | 1,400 | 1,425 | 1,500 | 1,950 | |
| 1907S | 2,165,800 | 1,350 | 1,375 | 1,400 | 1,425 | 1,500 | 2,000 | |

## SAINT-GAUDENS (1907–1933)

The $20 gold piece designed by Augustus Saint-Gaudens is considered by many to be the most beautiful United States coin. The first coins issued were slightly more than 12,000 high-relief pieces struck for general circulation. The relief is much higher than that of later issues and the date 1907 is in Roman numerals. A few of the Proof coins were made using the lettered-edge collar from the Ultra High Relief version. These can be distinguished by a pronounced bottom left serif on the N in UNUM, and other minor differences. Flat-relief double eagles were issued later in 1907 with Arabic numerals, and continued through 1933.

The field of the rare, Ultra High Relief experimental pieces is extremely concave and connects directly with the edge without any border, giving it a sharp knifelike appearance. Liberty's skirt shows two folds on the side of her right leg; the Capitol building in the background at left is very small; the sun, on the reverse side, has 14 rays, as opposed to the regular high-relief coins, which have only 13 rays extending from the sun. High-relief Proofs are trial or experimental pieces.

**VF-20 Very Fine:** Minor wear on Liberty's legs and toes. Eagle's left wing and breast feathers worn.
**EF-40 Extremely Fine:** Drapery lines on chest visible. Wear on left breast, knee, and below. Eagle's feathers on breast and right wing bold.
**AU-50 About Uncirculated:** Trace of wear on nose, breast, and knee. Wear visible on eagle's wings.
**AU-55 Choice About Uncirculated:** Evidence of friction on design high points. Most of mint luster remains.
**MS-60 Uncirculated:** No trace of wear. Light marks or blemishes.
**MS-63 Select Uncirculated:** Some distracting contact marks or blemishes in prime focal areas. Impaired luster possible.
**Matte PF-63 Choice Proof:** Matte surfaces with only a few blemishes in secondary focal places. No major flaws.

## Ultra High Relief Pattern, MCMVII (1907)

| | PF-67 |
| --- | --- |
| 1907, Ultra High Relief, Plain Edge *(unique)* .................................................. | — |
| 1907, Ultra High Relief, Lettered Edge ......................................................... | — |

## Without Motto IN GOD WE TRUST (1907–1908)
### *High Relief, MCMVII (1907)*

| | Mintage | VF-20 | EF-40 | AU-50 | AU-55 | MS-60 | MS-63 | PF |
| --- | --- | --- | --- | --- | --- | --- | --- | --- |
| 1907, High Relief, Roman Numerals (MCMVII), Wire Rim .........12,367 | | $6,000 | $7,000 | $8,500 | $9,000 | $11,000 | $20,000 | — |

### *Arabic Numerals, No Motto (1907–1908)*

| Mintmark is on obverse, above date. | No Motto | Motto IN GOD WE TRUST (1908–1933) |
| --- | --- | --- |

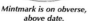

| | Mintage | VF-20 | EF-40 | AU-50 | AU-55 | MS-60 | MS-63 | MATTE PF-63 |
| --- | --- | --- | --- | --- | --- | --- | --- | --- |
| 1907 .....................361,667 | | $1,350 | $1,375 | $1,400 | $1,415 | $1,475 | $1,650 | |
| 1908 ...................4,271,551 | | 1,350 | 1,375 | 1,400 | 1,415 | 1,475 | 1,575 | |
| 1908D ....................663,750 | | 1,350 | 1,375 | 1,400 | 1,415 | 1,475 | 1,575 | |
| 1908, With Motto .....(101) ....156,258 | | 1,350 | 1,375 | 1,400 | 1,415 | 1,475 | 1,600 | $17,500 |
| 1908D, With Motto ............349,500 | | 1,350 | 1,375 | 1,400 | 1,415 | 1,475 | 1,575 | |
| 1908S, With Motto ............22,000 | | 1,650 | 2,500 | 5,500 | 5,750 | 8,750 | 16,500 | |

1909, 9 Over 8

| | Mintage | VF-20 | EF-40 | AU-50 | AU-55 | MS-60 | MS-63 | MATTE PF-63 |
|---|---|---|---|---|---|---|---|---|
| 1909, 9 Over 8 .................* | | $1,350 | $1,375 | $1,400 | $1,415 | $1,500 | $3,500 | |
| 1909 ..........(67) ...161,282 | | 1,350 | 1,375 | 1,400 | 1,415 | 1,500 | 2,450 | $17,500 |
| 1909D ................52,500 | | 1,350 | 1,375 | 1,400 | 1,415 | 1,500 | 5,500 | |
| 1909S ...............2,774,925 | | 1,350 | 1,375 | 1,400 | 1,415 | 1,475 | 1,575 | |
| 1910 ..........(167) ...482,000 | | 1,350 | 1,375 | 1,400 | 1,415 | 1,475 | 1,575 | 17,500 |
| 1910D ................429,000 | | 1,350 | 1,375 | 1,400 | 1,415 | 1,475 | 1,575 | |
| 1910S ...............2,128,250 | | 1,350 | 1,375 | 1,400 | 1,415 | 1,475 | 1,575 | |
| 1911 ..........(100) ...197,250 | | 1,350 | 1,375 | 1,400 | 1,415 | 1,475 | 1,850 | 17,500 |
| 1911D ................846,500 | | 1,350 | 1,375 | 1,400 | 1,415 | 1,475 | 1,575 | |
| 1911S ................775,750 | | 1,350 | 1,375 | 1,400 | 1,415 | 1,475 | 1,575 | |
| 1912 ..........(74) ...149,750 | | 1,350 | 1,375 | 1,400 | 1,415 | 1,475 | 2,450 | 17,500 |
| 1913 ..........(58) ...168,780 | | 1,350 | 1,375 | 1,400 | 1,415 | 1,475 | 2,500 | 17,500 |
| 1913D ................393,500 | | 1,350 | 1,375 | 1,400 | 1,415 | 1,475 | 1,575 | |
| 1913S ................34,000 | | 1,350 | 1,375 | 1,500 | 1,550 | 1,700 | 3,500 | |
| 1914 ..........(70) ...95,250 | | 1,350 | 1,375 | 1,400 | 1,415 | 1,475 | 2,750 | 17,500 |
| 1914D ................453,000 | | 1,350 | 1,375 | 1,400 | 1,415 | 1,475 | 1,575 | |
| 1914S ...............1,498,000 | | 1,350 | 1,375 | 1,400 | 1,415 | 1,475 | 1,575 | |
| 1915 ..........(50) ...152,000 | | 1,350 | 1,375 | 1,400 | 1,415 | 1,475 | 1,900 | 20,000 |
| 1915S ................567,500 | | 1,350 | 1,375 | 1,400 | 1,415 | 1,475 | 1,575 | |
| 1916S ................796,000 | | 1,350 | 1,375 | 1,400 | 1,415 | 1,475 | 1,575 | |
| 1920 ................228,250 | | 1,350 | 1,375 | 1,400 | 1,415 | 1,475 | 1,575 | |
| 1920S ................558,000 | | 10,000 | 15,000 | 22,000 | 26,000 | 42,000 | 75,000 | |
| 1921 ................528,500 | | 22,000 | 35,000 | 45,000 | 50,000 | 80,000 | 175,000 | |
| 1922 ...............1,375,500 | | 1,350 | 1,375 | 1,400 | 1,415 | 1,475 | 1,575 | |
| 1922S ...............2,658,000 | | 1,350 | 1,375 | 1,500 | 1,600 | 2,200 | 4,500 | |
| 1923 ................566,000 | | 1,350 | 1,375 | 1,400 | 1,415 | 1,475 | 1,575 | |
| 1923D ...............1,702,250 | | 1,350 | 1,375 | 1,400 | 1,415 | 1,475 | 1,575 | |
| 1924 ...............4,323,500 | | 1,350 | 1,375 | 1,400 | 1,415 | 1,475 | 1,575 | |
| 1924D ...............3,049,500 | | 1,450 | 1,500 | 1,650 | 1,750 | 3,250 | 7,850 | |
| 1924S ...............2,927,500 | | 1,450 | 1,500 | 1,650 | 1,800 | 3,250 | 8,500 | |
| 1925 ...............2,831,750 | | 1,350 | 1,375 | 1,400 | 1,415 | 1,475 | 1,575 | |
| 1925D ...............2,938,500 | | 1,650 | 1,850 | 2,250 | 2,750 | 3,750 | 8,750 | |
| 1925S ...............3,776,500 | | 1,750 | 2,000 | 2,750 | 3,250 | 7,850 | 14,500 | |
| 1926 ................816,750 | | 1,350 | 1,375 | 1,400 | 1,415 | 1,475 | 1,575 | |
| 1926D ................481,000 | | 6,000 | 11,000 | 14,000 | 17,500 | 21,000 | 26,000 | |
| 1926S ...............2,041,500 | | 1,650 | 1,850 | 2,200 | 2,500 | 2,750 | 4,650 | |
| 1927 ...............2,946,750 | | 1,350 | 1,375 | 1,400 | 1,415 | 1,475 | 1,575 | |
| 1927D ................180,000 | | | 250,000 | 300,000 | 350,000 | 500,000 | 850,000 | |
| 1927S ...............3,107,000 | | 4,000 | 7,000 | 9,000 | 11,000 | 16,000 | 35,000 | |
| 1928 ...............8,816,000 | | 1,350 | 1,375 | 1,400 | 1,415 | 1,475 | 1,575 | |
| 1929 ...............1,779,750 | | 7,500 | 10,000 | 12,000 | 13,000 | 15,000 | 26,000 | |
| 1930S ................74,000 | | 20,000 | 30,000 | 35,000 | 40,000 | 50,000 | 75,000 | |
| 1931 ...............2,938,250 | | 7,500 | 10,000 | 15,000 | 20,000 | 30,000 | 50,000 | |
| 1931D ................106,500 | | 7,500 | 10,000 | 14,000 | 18,000 | 27,500 | 60,000 | |
| 1932 ...............1,101,750 | | 7,500 | 10,000 | 14,000 | 18,000 | 22,000 | 50,000 | |
| 1933 ................445,500 | | | | | None placed in circulation. | | | |

* Included in number below.

Collecting United States commemorative coins is like gathering snapshots for an album of important events, places, and people in the nation's history. Because they represent so many different aspects of America—from wars and Olympic games to presidents, state parks, and historical landmarks, every collector can assemble a set with its own special significance.

All U.S. commemorative coins are issued as legal tender, though in most cases the precious metal of the coins surpasses their face values. The weight and fineness for commemoratives follow those of standard-issue gold, silver, and clad coins.

# CLASSIC COMMEMORATIVE SILVER AND GOLD

(1892–1893) World's Columbian Exposition Half Dollar

| | Distribution | AU-50 | MS-60 | MS-63 | MS-65 |
|---|---|---|---|---|---|
| 1892, World's Columbian Exposition half dollar . . . . . . . . . . . . . . .950,000 | | $11 | $16 | $40 | $285 |
| 1893, Same type. . . . . . . . . . . . . . . . . . . . . . . . . . . . . . . . . . . . . .1,550,405 | | 11 | 16 | 38 | 250 |

(1893) World's Columbian Exposition, Isabella Quarter Dollar

| | Distribution | AU-50 | MS-60 | MS-63 | MS-65 |
|---|---|---|---|---|---|
| 1893, World's Columbian Exposition, Chicago, quarter dollar . . . . . .24,214 | | $300 | $350 | $400 | $1,500 |

(1900) Lafayette Dollar

| | Distribution | AU-50 | MS-60 | MS-63 | MS-65 |
|---|---|---|---|---|---|
| 1900, Lafayette silver dollar . . . . . . . . . . . . . . . . . . . . . . . . . . . . . .36,026 | | $300 | $450 | $1,000 | $5,750 |

### (1903) Louisiana Purchase Exposition

| | Distribution | AU-50 | MS-60 | MS-63 | MS-65 |
|---|---|---|---|---|---|
| 1903, Louisiana Purchase / Thomas Jefferson gold dollar | 17,500 | $300 | $400 | $500 | $1,100 |
| 1903, Louisiana Purchase / William McKinley gold dollar | 17,500 | 300 | 400 | 500 | 1,100 |

### (1904–1905) Lewis and Clark Exposition

| | Distribution | AU-50 | MS-60 | MS-63 | MS-65 |
|---|---|---|---|---|---|
| 1904, Lewis and Clark Exposition gold dollar | 10,025 | $500 | $700 | $1,000 | $5,000 |
| 1905, Lewis and Clark Exposition gold dollar | 10,041 | 600 | 800 | 1,300 | 9,500 |

### (1915) Panama-Pacific Exposition

| | Distribution | AU-50 | MS-60 | MS-63 | MS-65 |
|---|---|---|---|---|---|
| 1915S, Panama-Pacific Exposition half dollar | 27,134 | $250 | $300 | $400 | $1,300 |
| 1915S, Panama-Pacific Exposition gold dollar | 15,000 | 325 | 375 | 450 | 850 |
| 1915S, Panama-Pacific Exposition gold $2.50 | 6,749 | 900 | 1,200 | 2,100 | 3,750 |
| 1915S, Panama-Pacific Exposition gold $50 Round | 483 | 30,000 | 36,000 | 45,000 | 100,000 |

(1915) Panama-Pacific Exposition

| | Distribution | AU-50 | MS-60 | MS-63 | MS-65 |
|---|---|---|---|---|---|
| 1915S, Panama-Pacific Exposition gold $50 Octagonal ............. | 645 | $30,000 | $36,500 | $46,000 | $105,000 |

(1916–1917) McKinley Memorial

| | Distribution | AU-50 | MS-60 | MS-63 | MS-65 |
|---|---|---|---|---|---|
| 1916, McKinley Memorial gold dollar ...................... | 15,000 | $300 | $350 | $400 | $950 |
| 1917, McKinley Memorial gold dollar ...................... | 5,000 | 350 | 400 | 500 | 1,500 |

(1918) Illinois Centennial

| | Distribution | AU-50 | MS-60 | MS-63 | MS-65 |
|---|---|---|---|---|---|
| 1918, Illinois Centennial half dollar ....................... | 100,058 | $70 | $80 | $90 | $260 |

(1920) Maine Centennial

| | Distribution | AU-50 | MS-60 | MS-63 | MS-65 |
|---|---|---|---|---|---|
| 1920, Maine Centennial half dollar ....................... | 50,028 | $70 | $90 | $110 | $250 |

(1920–1921) Pilgrim Tercentenary

With 1921 in Field
on Obverse

| | Distribution | AU-50 | MS-60 | MS-63 | MS-65 |
|---|---|---|---|---|---|
| 1920, Pilgrim Tercentenary half dollar . . . . . . . . . . . . . . . . . . . .152,112 | | $45 | $60 | $70 | $200 |
| 1921, Same, With Date Added in Field . . . . . . . . . . . . . . . . . . . . . .20,053 | | 90 | 110 | 120 | 250 |

(1921) Missouri Centennial

With 2★4 in Field

| | Distribution | AU-50 | MS-60 | MS-63 | MS-65 |
|---|---|---|---|---|---|
| 1921, Missouri Centennial half dollar, "2★4" in Field . . . . . . . . . . .9,400 | | $350 | $450 | $600 | $2,000 |
| 1921, Missouri Centennial half dollar, Plain . . . . . . . . . . . . . . . . .11,400 | | 210 | 360 | 475 | 1,900 |

(1921) Alabama Centennial

Without 2X2 in Field

| | Distribution | AU-50 | MS-60 | MS-63 | MS-65 |
|---|---|---|---|---|---|
| 1921, Alabama Centennial half dollar, Plain . . . . . . . . . . . . . . . . . . . . . .35,000 | | $100 | $125 | $150 | $800 |
| 1921, Alabama Centennial half dollar, With "2X2" in Field of Obverse . . .30,000 | | 160 | 185 | 275 | 850 |

(1922) Grant Memorial

| | Distribution | AU-50 | MS-60 | MS-63 | MS-65 |
|---|---|---|---|---|---|
| 1922, Grant Memorial, With Star* half dollar .................4,256 | | $525 | $725 | $1,000 | $4,000 |
| 1922, Same type, No Star in Obv Field ......................67,405 | | 65 | 75 | 90 | 450 |
| 1922, Grant Memorial, With Star* gold dollar .................5,016 | | 900 | 1,000 | 1,200 | 1,600 |
| 1922, Grant Memorial, No Star in Obv Field ...................5,016 | | 900 | 1,000 | 1,200 | 1,700 |

* Fake stars usually have a flattened spot on the reverse.

(1923) Monroe Doctrine Centennial

| | Distribution | AU-50 | MS-60 | MS-63 | MS-65 |
|---|---|---|---|---|---|
| 1923S, Monroe Doctrine Centennial half dollar ..............274,077 | | $30 | $40 | $82 | $1,000 |

(1924) Huguenot-Walloon Tercentenary

| | Distribution | AU-50 | MS-60 | MS-63 | MS-65 |
|---|---|---|---|---|---|
| 1924, Huguenot-Walloon Tercentenary half dollar ............142,080 | | $75 | $80 | $95 | $225 |

(1925) Lexington-Concord Sesquicentennial

| | Distribution | AU-50 | MS-60 | MS-63 | MS-65 |
|---|---|---|---|---|---|
| 1925, Lexington-Concord Sesquicentennial half dollar . . . . . . . . . | 162,013 | $50 | $67 | $85 | $375 |

(1925) Stone Mountain Memorial

| | Distribution | AU-50 | MS-60 | MS-63 | MS-65 |
|---|---|---|---|---|---|
| 1925, Stone Mountain Memorial half dollar . . . . . . . . . . . . . . . . | 1,314,709 | $30 | $42 | $48 | $135 |

(1925) California Diamond Jubilee

| | Distribution | AU-50 | MS-60 | MS-63 | MS-65 |
|---|---|---|---|---|---|
| 1925S, California Diamond Jubilee half dollar . . . . . . . . . . . . . . . . | 86,594 | $100 | $110 | $180 | $520 |

(1925) Fort Vancouver Centennial

| | Distribution | AU-50 | MS-60 | MS-63 | MS-65 |
|---|---|---|---|---|---|
| 1925, Fort Vancouver Centennial half dollar . . . . . . . . . . . . . . . . | 14,994 | $180 | $225 | $250 | $735 |

**(1926) Sesquicentennial of American Independence**

| | Distribution | AU-50 | MS-60 | MS-63 | MS-65 |
|---|---|---|---|---|---|
| 1926, Sesquicentennial of American Independence half dollar ....141,120 | | $50 | $65 | $80 | $1,950 |
| 1926, Sesquicentennial of American Independence gold $2.50 ....46,019 | | 235 | 280 | 400 | 1,800 |

**(1926–1939) Oregon Trail Memorial**

| | Distribution | AU-50 | MS-60 | MS-63 | MS-65 |
|---|---|---|---|---|---|
| 1926, Oregon Trail Memorial half dollar ......................47,955 | | $75 | $95 | $100 | $180 |
| 1926S, Same type, S Mint .............................83,055 | | 75 | 95 | 100 | 180 |
| 1928, Oregon Trail Memorial half dollar (same as 1926) ..........6,028 | | 95 | 110 | 120 | 200 |
| 1933D, Oregon Trail Memorial half dollar .....................5,008 | | 195 | 210 | 250 | 330 |
| 1934D, Oregon Trail Memorial half dollar .....................7,006 | | 95 | 110 | 120 | 210 |
| 1936, Oregon Trail Memorial half dollar .....................10,006 | | 85 | 100 | 130 | 180 |
| 1936S, Same type, S Mint .............................5,006 | | 85 | 100 | 130 | 200 |
| 1937D, Oregon Trail Memorial half dollar ....................12,008 | | 85 | 100 | 130 | 180 |
| 1938, Oregon Trail Memorial half dollar (same as 1926) ..........6,006 | | | | | |
| 1938D, Same type, D Mint .............................6,005 | | Set: | 250 | 300 | 500 |
| 1938S, Same type, S Mint .............................6,006 | | | | | |
| 1939, Oregon Trail Memorial half dollar (same as 1926) ..........3,004 | | | | | |
| 1939D, Same type, D Mint .............................3,004 | | Set: | 850 | 925 | 1,100 |
| 1939S, Same type, S Mint .............................3,005 | | | | | |
| Oregon Trail Memorial half dollar, single type coin .................... | | 75 | 95 | 100 | 180 |

**(1927) Vermont Sesquicentennial**

| | Distribution | AU-50 | MS-60 | MS-63 | MS-65 |
|---|---|---|---|---|---|
| 1927, Vermont Sesquicentennial (Battle of Bennington) half dollar .....28,142 | | $130 | $160 | $175 | $530 |

(1928) Hawaiian Sesquicentennial

| | Distribution | AU-50 | MS-60 | MS-63 | MS-65 |
|---|---|---|---|---|---|
| 1928, Hawaiian Sesquicentennial half dollar .....................10,008 | | $1,200 | $1,450 | $1,800 | $3,750 |
| 1928, Hawaiian Sesquicentennial, Sandblast Proof Presentation Piece ..... (50) | | | | 6,500 | 14,500 |

(1934) Maryland Tercentenary

| | Distribution | AU-50 | MS-60 | MS-63 | MS-65 |
|---|---|---|---|---|---|
| 1934, Maryland Tercentenary half dollar .....................25,015 | | $85 | $95 | $100 | $200 |

(1934–1938) Texas Independence Centennial

| | Distribution | AU-50 | MS-60 | MS-63 | MS-65 |
|---|---|---|---|---|---|
| 1934, Texas Independence Centennial half dollar ..............61,463 | | $75 | $80 | $90 | $135 |
| 1935, Texas Independence Centennial half dollar (same as 1934) ...9,996 | | | | | |
| 1935D, Same type, D Mint .....................10,007 | | *Set:* | 200 | 225 | 425 |
| 1935S, Same type, S Mint .....................10,008 | | | | | |
| 1936, Texas Independence Centennial half dollar (same as 1934) ...8,911 | | | | | |
| 1936D, Same type, D Mint .....................9,039 | | *Set:* | 200 | 225 | 425 |
| 1936S, Same type, S Mint .....................9,055 | | | | | |
| 1937, Texas Independence Centennial half dollar (same as 1934) ...6,571 | | | | | |
| 1937D, Same type, D Mint .....................6,605 | | *Set:* | 200 | 225 | 425 |
| 1937S, Same type, S Mint .....................6,637 | | | | | |

# COMMEMORATIVES

| | Distribution | AU-50 | MS-60 | MS-63 | MS-65 |
|---|---|---|---|---|---|
| 1938, Texas Independence Centennial half dollar (same as 1934) . . .3,780 | | | | | |
| 1938D, Same type, D Mint . . . . . . . . . . . . . . . . . . . . . . . . . . . . . . . . . .3,775 | | Set: | $375 | $400 | $750 |
| 1938S, Same type, S Mint . . . . . . . . . . . . . . . . . . . . . . . . . . . . . . . . .3,814 | | | | | |
| Texas Independence Centennial half dollar, single type coin . . . . . . . . . . . . | | $75 | 80 | 90 | 135 |

**(1934–1938) Daniel Boone Bicentennial**   **1934 Added on Reverse**

| | Distribution | AU-50 | MS-60 | MS-63 | MS-65 |
|---|---|---|---|---|---|
| 1934, Daniel Boone Bicentennial half dollar . . . . . . . . . . . . . . . . . .10,007 | | $75 | $85 | $90 | $140 |
| 1935, Daniel Boone Bicentennial half dollar . . . . . . . . . . . . . . . . . . .10,010 | | | | | |
| 1935D, Same type, D Mint . . . . . . . . . . . . . . . . . . . . . . . . . . . . . . . . .5,005 | | Set: | 200 | 250 | 400 |
| 1935S, Same type, S Mint . . . . . . . . . . . . . . . . . . . . . . . . . . . . . . . . .5,005 | | | | | |
| 1935, Same as 1934 but Small 1934 on reverse . . . . . . . . . . . . . .10,008 | | | | | |
| 1935D, Same type, D Mint . . . . . . . . . . . . . . . . . . . . . . . . . . . . . . . . .2,003 | | Set: | 400 | 475 | 1,100 |
| 1935S, Same type, S Mint . . . . . . . . . . . . . . . . . . . . . . . . . . . . . . . . .2,004 | | | | | |
| 1936, Daniel Boone Bicentennial half dollar (same as preceding) . . .12,012 | | | | | |
| 1936D, Same type, D Mint . . . . . . . . . . . . . . . . . . . . . . . . . . . . . . . . .5,005 | | Set: | 200 | 250 | 400 |
| 1936S, Same type, S Mint . . . . . . . . . . . . . . . . . . . . . . . . . . . . . . . . .5,006 | | | | | |
| 1937, Daniel Boone Bicentennial half dollar (same as preceding) . . . .9,810 | | | | | |
| 1937D, Same type, D Mint . . . . . . . . . . . . . . . . . . . . . . . . . . . . . . . . .2,506 | | Set: | 380 | 450 | 750 |
| 1937S, Same type, S Mint . . . . . . . . . . . . . . . . . . . . . . . . . . . . . . . . .2,506 | | | | | |
| 1938, Daniel Boone Bicentennial half dollar (same as preceding) . . . .2,100 | | | | | |
| 1938D, Same type, D Mint . . . . . . . . . . . . . . . . . . . . . . . . . . . . . . . . .2,100 | | Set: | 550 | 675 | 900 |
| 1938S, Same type, S Mint . . . . . . . . . . . . . . . . . . . . . . . . . . . . . . . . .2,100 | | | | | |
| Daniel Boone Bicentennial half dollar, single type coin . . . . . . . . . . . . . . . | | 75 | 85 | 90 | 140 |

**(1935) Connecticut Tercentenary**

| | Distribution | AU-50 | MS-60 | MS-63 | MS-65 |
|---|---|---|---|---|---|
| 1935, Connecticut Tercentenary half dollar . . . . . . . . . . . . . . . . . . .25,018 | | $135 | $165 | $180 | $275 |

**(1935–1939)
Arkansas Centennial**

| | Distribution | AU-50 | MS-60 | MS-63 | MS-65 |
|---|---|---|---|---|---|
| 1935, Arkansas Centennial half dollar ........................13,012 | | | | | |
| 1935D, Same type, D Mint .................................5,505 | Set: | $165 | $220 | $400 | |
| 1935S, Same type, S Mint.................................5,506 | | | | | |
| 1936, Arkansas Centennial half dollar (same as 1935 but 1936 on rev) . .9,660 | | | | | |
| 1936D, Same type, D Mint .................................9,660 | Set: | 165 | 220 | 425 | |
| 1936S, Same type, S Mint.................................9,662 | | | | | |
| 1937, Arkansas Centennial half dollar (same as 1935) ..............5,505 | | | | | |
| 1937D, Same type, D mint .................................5,505 | Set: | 180 | 225 | 500 | |
| 1937S, Same type, S mint.................................5,506 | | | | | |
| 1938, Arkansas Centennial half dollar (same as 1935) ..............3,156 | | | | | |
| 1938D, Same type, D Mint .................................3,155 | Set: | 250 | 265 | 900 | |
| 1938S, Same type, S Mint.................................3,156 | | | | | |
| 1939, Arkansas Centennial half dollar (same as 1935) ..............2,104 | | | | | |
| 1939D, Same type, D Mint .................................2,104 | Set: | 525 | 625 | 1,650 | |
| 1939S, Same type, S Mint.................................2,105 | | | | | |
| Arkansas Centennial half dollar, single type coin ........................ | | $45 | 60 | 70 | 100 |

**(1936) Arkansas
Centennial – Robinson**

| | Distribution | AU-50 | MS-60 | MS-63 | MS-65 |
|---|---|---|---|---|---|
| 1936, Arkansas Centennial (Robinson) half dollar ..............25,265 | $75 | $85 | $100 | $215 |

**(1935) Hudson, New
York, Sesquicentennial**

| | Distribution | AU-50 | MS-60 | MS-63 | MS-65 |
|---|---|---|---|---|---|
| 1935, Hudson, New York, Sesquicentennial half dollar ..........10,008 | $375 | $485 | $665 | $1,200 |

**(1935–1936) California-Pacific International Exposition**

| | Distribution | AU-50 | MS-60 | MS-63 | MS-65 |
|---|---|---|---|---|---|
| 1935S, California-Pacific International Exposition half dollar ......70,132 | | $50 | $65 | $80 | $95 |
| 1936D, California-Pacific International Exposition half dollar ......30,092 | | 50 | 75 | 85 | 100 |

**(1935) Old Spanish Trail**

| | Distribution | AU-50 | MS-60 | MS-63 | MS-65 |
|---|---|---|---|---|---|
| 1935, Old Spanish Trail half dollar .........................10,008 | | $575 | $725 | $800 | $1,200 |

**(1936) Providence, Rhode Island, Tercentenary**

| | Distribution | AU-50 | MS-60 | MS-63 | MS-65 |
|---|---|---|---|---|---|
| 1936, Providence, Rhode Island, Tercentenary half dollar ........20,013 | | | | | |
| 1936D, Same type, D Mint ..............................15,010 | | *Set:* | $170 | $190 | $410 |
| 1936S, Same type, S Mint ..............................15,011 | | | | | |
| Providence, Rhode Island, Tercentenary half dollar, single type coin ...... | | $55 | 60 | 70 | 140 |

**(1936) Cleveland Centennial / Great Lakes Exposition**

| | Distribution | AU-50 | MS-60 | MS-63 | MS-65 |
|---|---|---|---|---|---|
| 1936, Cleveland Centennial / Great Lakes Exposition half dollar . . . .50,030 | | $65 | $70 | $75 | $100 |

**(1936) Wisconsin Territorial Centennial**

| | Distribution | AU-50 | MS-60 | MS-63 | MS-65 |
|---|---|---|---|---|---|
| 1936, Wisconsin Territorial Centennial half dollar . . . . . . . . . . . . . .25,015 | | $120 | $140 | $150 | $200 |

**(1936) Cincinnati Music Center**

| | Distribution | AU-50 | MS-60 | MS-63 | MS-65 |
|---|---|---|---|---|---|
| 1936, Cincinnati Music Center half dollar . . . . . . . . . . . . . . . . . . . . .5,005 | | | | | |
| 1936D, Same type, D Mint . . . . . . . . . . . . . . . . . . . . . . . . . . . . . . .5,005 | | Set: | $450 | $500 | $1,200 |
| 1936S, Same type, S Mint . . . . . . . . . . . . . . . . . . . . . . . . . . . . . . .5,006 | | | | | |
| Cincinnati Music Center half dollar, single type coin . . . . . . . . . . . . . . . . . | | $140 | 150 | 160 | 390 |

(1936) Long Island Tercentenary

| | Distribution | AU-50 | MS-60 | MS-63 | MS-65 |
|---|---|---|---|---|---|
| 1936, Long Island Tercentenary half dollar . . . . . . . . . . . . . . . . . . . .81,826 | $50 | $60 | $65 | $215 |

(1936) York County, Maine, Tercentenary

| | Distribution | AU-50 | MS-60 | MS-63 | MS-65 |
|---|---|---|---|---|---|
| 1936, York County, Maine, Tercentenary half dollar . . . . . . . . . . . . .25,015 | $120 | $130 | $140 | $175 |

(1936) Bridgeport, Connecticut, Centennial

| | Distribution | AU-50 | MS-60 | MS-63 | MS-65 |
|---|---|---|---|---|---|
| 1936, Bridgeport, Connecticut, Centennial half dollar . . . . . . . . . . .25,015 | $75 | $85 | $110 | $160 |

(1936) Lynchburg, Virginia, Sesquicentennial

| | Distribution | AU-50 | MS-60 | MS-63 | MS-65 |
|---|---|---|---|---|---|
| 1936, Lynchburg, Virginia, Sesquicentennial half dollar . . . . . . . . . .20,013 | $125 | $140 | $160 | $210 |

(1936) Elgin, Illinois, Centennial

| | Distribution | AU-50 | MS-60 | MS-63 | MS-65 |
|---|---|---|---|---|---|
| 1936, Elgin, Illinois, Centennial half dollar . . . . . . . . . . . . . . . . . . . .20,015 | | $125 | $140 | $160 | $190 |

(1936) Albany, New York, Charter

| | Distribution | AU-50 | MS-60 | MS-63 | MS-65 |
|---|---|---|---|---|---|
| 1936, Albany, New York, Charter half dollar . . . . . . . . . . . . . . . . . . .17,671 | | $170 | $180 | $190 | $225 |

(1936) San Francisco – Oakland Bay Bridge Opening

| | Distribution | AU-50 | MS-60 | MS-63 | MS-65 |
|---|---|---|---|---|---|
| 1936S, San Francisco–Oakland Bay Bridge Opening half dollar . . . .71,424 | | $90 | $100 | $110 | $200 |

(1936) Delaware Tercentenary

| | Distribution | AU-50 | MS-60 | MS-63 | MS-65 |
|---|---|---|---|---|---|
| 1936, Delaware Tercentenary half dollar . . . . . . . . . . . . . . . . . . . .20,993 | | $150 | $170 | $180 | $250 |

(1936) Columbia, South Carolina, Sesquicentennial

| | Distribution | AU-50 | MS-60 | MS-63 | MS-65 |
|---|---|---|---|---|---|
| 1936, Columbia, South Carolina, Sesquicentennial half dollar ......9,007 | | | | | |
| 1936D, Same type, D Mint ...............................8,009 | *Set:* | $425 | $475 | $600 |
| 1936S, Same type, S Mint ...............................8,007 | | | | | |
| Columbia, South Carolina, Sesquicentennial half dollar, single type coin ... | | $145 | 150 | 160 | 190 |

(1936) Battle of Gettysburg Anniversary

| | Distribution | AU-50 | MS-60 | MS-63 | MS-65 |
|---|---|---|---|---|---|
| 1936, Battle of Gettysburg Anniversary half dollar .............26,928 | | $235 | $275 | $300 | $450 |

(1936) Norfolk, Virginia, Bicentennial

| | Distribution | AU-50 | MS-60 | MS-63 | MS-65 |
|---|---|---|---|---|---|
| 1936, Norfolk, Virginia, Bicentennial half dollar ................16,936 | | $230 | $250 | $275 | $300 |

(1937) Roanoke Island, North Carolina, 350th Anniversary

| | Distribution | AU-50 | MS-60 | MS-63 | MS-65 |
|---|---|---|---|---|---|
| 1937, Roanoke Island, North Carolina, 350th Anniversary half dollar .... | 29,030 | $120 | $130 | $150 | $175 |

(1937) Battle of Antietam Anniversary

| | Distribution | AU-50 | MS-60 | MS-63 | MS-65 |
|---|---|---|---|---|---|
| 1937, Battle of Antietam Anniversary half dollar | 18,028 | $355 | $375 | $400 | $510 |

(1938) New Rochelle, New York, 250th Anniversary

| | Distribution | AU-50 | MS-60 | MS-63 | MS-65 |
|---|---|---|---|---|---|
| 1938, New Rochelle, New York, 250th Anniversary half dollar | 15,266 | $200 | $225 | $250 | $325 |

(1946) Iowa Centennial

| | Distribution | AU-50 | MS-60 | MS-63 | MS-65 |
|---|---|---|---|---|---|
| 1946, Iowa Centennial half dollar | 100,057 | $65 | $70 | $80 | $90 |

(1946–1951) Booker T. Washington Memorial

| | Distribution | AU-50 | MS-60 | MS-63 | MS-65 |
|---|---|---|---|---|---|
| 1946, Booker T. Washington Memorial half dollar **(a)** | 700,546 | | | | |
| 1946D, Same type, D Mint | 50,000 | Set: | $32 | $42 | $90 |
| 1946S, Same type, S Mint | 500,279 | | | | |
| 1947, Booker T. Washington Memorial half dollar (same as 1946) | 6,000 | | | | |
| 1947D, Same type, D Mint | 6,000 | Set: | 50 | 75 | 150 |
| 1947S, Same type, S Mint | 6,000 | | | | |
| 1948, Booker T. Washington Memorial half dollar (same as 1946) | 8,005 | | | | |
| 1948D, Same type, D Mint | 8,005 | Set: | 95 | 110 | 160 |
| 1948S, Same type, S Mint | 8,005 | | | | |
| 1949, Booker T. Washington Memorial half dollar (same as 1946) | 6,004 | | | | |
| 1949D, Same type, D Mint | 6,004 | Set: | 135 | 145 | 190 |
| 1949S, Same type, S Mint | 6,004 | | | | |
| 1950, Booker T. Washington Memorial half dollar (same as 1946) | 6,004 | | | | |
| 1950D, Same type, D Mint | 6,004 | Set: | 80 | 90 | 130 |
| 1950S, Same type, S Mint | 62,091 | | | | |
| 1951, Booker T. Washington Memorial half dollar (same as 1946) | 210,082 | | | | |
| 1951D, Same type, D Mint | 7,004 | Set: | 80 | 90 | 120 |
| 1951S, Same type, S Mint | 7,004 | | | | |
| Booker T. Washington Memorial, single type coin | | $10 | 12 | 15 | 25 |

**a.** Minted; quantity melted unknown.

(1951–1954) Carver/Washington Commemorative

| | Distribution | AU-50 | MS-60 | MS-63 | MS-65 |
|---|---|---|---|---|---|
| 1951, Carver/Washington half dollar | 20,018 | | | | |
| 1951D, Same type, D Mint | 10,004 | Set: | $65 | $80 | $310 |
| 1951S, Same type, S Mint | 10,004 | | | | |
| 1952, Carver/Washington half dollar (same as 1951) | 1,106,292 | | | | |
| 1952D, Same type, D Mint | 8,006 | Set: | 65 | 80 | 225 |
| 1952S, Same type, S Mint | 8,006 | | | | |

*Chart continued on next page.*

| | Distribution | AU-50 | MS-60 | MS-63 | MS-65 |
|---|---|---|---|---|---|
| 1953, Carver/Washington half dollar (same as 1951) | 8,003 | | | | |
| 1953D, Same type, D Mint | 8,003 | Set: | $65 | $80 | $300 |
| 1953S, Same type, S Mint | 88,020 | | | | |
| 1954, Carver/Washington half dollar (same as 1951) | 12,006 | | | | |
| 1954D, Same type, D Mint | 12,006 | Set: | 65 | 80 | 225 |
| 1954S, Same type, S Mint | 42,024 | | | | |
| Carver/Washington half dollar, single type coin | | $10 | 12 | 15 | 25 |

# MODERN COMMEMORATIVES

**(1982) George Washington 250th Anniversary of Birth**

| | Distribution | MS-67 | PF-67 |
|---|---|---|---|
| 1982D, George Washington 250th Anniversary half dollar | 2,210,458 | $10 | |
| 1982S, Same type, S mint, Proof | (4,894,044) | | $11 |

**(1983–1984) Los Angeles Olympiad**

| | Distribution | MS-67 | PF-67 |
|---|---|---|---|
| 1983P, Discus Thrower silver dollar | 294,543 | $22 | |
| 1983D, Same type, D Mint | 174,014 | 22 | |
| 1983S, Same type, S Mint | (1,577,025) ....174,014 | 22 | $23 |

(1983–1984) Los Angeles Olympiad

| | Distribution | MS-67 | PF-67 |
|---|---|---|---|
| 1984P, Olympic Coliseum silver dollar | 217,954 | $22 | |
| 1984D, Same type, D Mint | 116,675 | 23 | |
| 1984S, Same type, S Mint | (1,801,210) ....116,675 | 23 | $23 |
| 1984P, Olympic Torch Bearers gold $10 | (33,309) | | 700 |
| 1984D, Same type, D Mint | (34,533) | | 710 |
| 1984S, Same type, S Mint | (48,551) | | 700 |
| 1984W, Same type, W Mint | (381,085) .....75,886 | 700 | 700 |

(1986) Statue of Liberty Centennial

| | Distribution | MS-67 | PF-67 |
|---|---|---|---|
| 1986D, Statue of Liberty Centennial half dollar | 928,008 | $4.50 | |
| 1986S, Same type, S Mint, Proof | (6,925,627) | | $4.50 |
| 1986P, Statue of Liberty Centennial silver dollar | 723,635 | 23.00 | |
| 1986S, Same type, S Mint, Proof | (6,414,638) | | 23.00 |
| 1986W, Statue of Liberty Centennial gold $5 | (404,013) .....95,248 | 350.00 | 350.00 |

(1987) U.S. Constitution Bicentennial

|  | Distribution | MS-67 | PF-67 |
|---|---|---|---|
| 1987P, U.S. Constitution Bicentennial silver dollar | .451,629 | $23 | |
| 1987S, Same type, S Mint, Proof | .(2,747,116) | | $23 |
| 1987W, U.S. Constitution Bicentennial gold $5 | .(651,659) ....214,225 | 350 | 350 |

(1988) Seoul Olympiad

|  | Distribution | MS-67 | PF-67 |
|---|---|---|---|
| 1988D, Seoul Olympiad silver dollar | .191,368 | $23 | |
| 1988S, Same type, S Mint, Proof | .(1,359,366) | | $23 |
| 1988W, Seoul Olympiad gold $5 | .(281,465) .....62,913 | 350 | 350 |

(1989) Congress Bicentennial

|  | Distribution | MS-67 | PF-67 |
|---|---|---|---|
| 1989D, Congress Bicentennial half dollar .................................163,753 | | $6 | |
| 1989S, Same type, S Mint, Proof ...........................(767,897) ........... | | | $6 |
| 1989D, Congress Bicentennial silver dollar ................................135,203 | | 22 | |
| 1989S, Same type, S Mint, Proof ...........................(762,198) ........... | | | 23 |
| 1989W, Congress Bicentennial gold $5 .........................(164,690) .....46,899 | | 350 | 350 |

(1990) Eisenhower Centennial

|  | Distribution | MS-67 | PF-67 |
|---|---|---|---|
| 1990W, Eisenhower Centennial silver dollar ..............................241,669 | | $23 | |
| 1990P, Same type, P Mint, Proof ...........................(1,144,461) ........... | | | $24 |

(1991) **Mount Rushmore Golden Anniversary**

| | Distribution | MS-67 | PF-67 |
|---|---|---|---|
| 1991D, Mount Rushmore Golden Anniversary half dollar ........................172,754 | | $25 | |
| 1991S, Same type, S Mint, Proof ...........................(753,257) .......... | | | $25 |
| 1991P, Mount Rushmore Golden Anniversary silver dollar ......................133,139 | | 30 | |
| 1991S, Same type, S Mint, Proof ...........................(738,419) .......... | | | 28 |
| 1991W, Mount Rushmore Golden Anniversary gold $5 .............(111,991) .....31,959 | | 375 | 360 |

(1991) **Korean War Memorial**

| | Distribution | MS-67 | PF-67 |
|---|---|---|---|
| 1991D, Korean War Memorial silver dollar ..................................213,049 | | $22 | |
| 1991P, Same type, P Mint, Proof ...............................(618,488) .......... | | | $24 |

**(1991) United Service Organizations**

| | Distribution | MS-67 | PF-67 |
|---|---|---|---|
| 1991D, USO silver dollar | 124,958 | $22 | |
| 1991S, Same type, S Mint, Proof | (321,275) | | $24 |

**(1992) XXV Olympiad**

| | Distribution | MS-67 | PF-67 |
|---|---|---|---|
| 1992P, XXV Olympiad clad half dollar | 161,607 | $7 | |
| 1992S, Same type, S Mint, Proof | (519,645) | | $750 |
| 1992D, XXV Olympiad silver dollar | 187,552 | 23 | |
| 1992S, Same type, S Mint, Proof | (504,505) | | 25.00 |
| 1992W, XXV Olympiad gold $5 | (77,313) .....27,732 | 375 | 350.00 |

(1992) White House 200th Anniversary

| | Distribution | MS-67 | PF-67 |
|---|---|---|---|
| 1992D, White House 200th Anniversary silver dollar | 123,803 | $24 | |
| 1992W, Same type, W Mint, Proof | (375,851) | | $24 |

(1992) Christopher Columbus Quincentenary

| | Distribution | MS-67 | PF-67 |
|---|---|---|---|
| 1992D, Christopher Columbus Quincentenary half dollar | 135,702 | $9 | |
| 1992S, Same type, S Mint, Proof | (390,154) | | $8 |
| 1992D, Christopher Columbus Quincentenary silver dollar | 106,949 | 27 | |
| 1992P, Same type, P Mint, Proof | (385,241) | | 28 |
| 1992W, Christopher Columbus Quincentenary gold $5 | (79,730) 24,329 | 375 | 350 |

(1993) Bill of Rights

| | Distribution | MS-67 | PF-67 |
|---|---|---|---|
| 1993W, Bill of Rights silver half dollar . . . . . . . . . . . . . . . . . . . . . . . . . . . . . . . . . . . .193,346 | | $15 | |
| 1993S, Same type, S Mint, Proof . . . . . . . . . . . . . . . . . . . . . . . . . . . .(586,315) . . . . . . . . . . | | | $13 |
| 1993D, Bill of Rights silver dollar . . . . . . . . . . . . . . . . . . . . . . . . . . . . . . . . . . . . . . .98,383 | | 22 | |
| 1993S, Same type, S Mint, Proof . . . . . . . . . . . . . . . . . . . . . . . . . . . .(534,001) . . . . . . . . . . | | | 23 |
| 1993W, Bill of Rights gold $5 . . . . . . . . . . . . . . . . . . . . . . . . . . . . . . . . .(78,651) . . . . .23,266 | | 375 | 350 |

(1991–1995) 50th Anniversary of World War II

| | Distribution | MS-67 | PF-67 |
|---|---|---|---|
| (1993P) 1991–1995 World War II clad half dollar . . . . . . . . . . . . . . . . .(317,396) . . . .197,072 | | $20 | $18 |

*Entry continued on next page.*

(1991–1995) 50th Anniversary of World War II

|  | Distribution | MS-67 | PF-67 |
|---|---|---|---|
| (1993D) 1991–1995 World War II silver dollar | 107,240 | $25 | |
| (1993W) Same type, W Mint, Proof | (342,041) | | $30 |
| (1993W) 1991–1995 World War II gold $5 | (67,026) .....23,672 | 375 | 350 |

(1994) World Cup Tournament

|  | Distribution | MS-67 | PF-67 |
|---|---|---|---|
| 1994D, World Cup Tournament clad half dollar | 168,208 | $7 | |
| 1994P, Same type, P Mint, Proof | (609,354) | | $6 |
| 1994D, World Cup Tournament silver dollar | 81,524 | 23 | |
| 1994S, Same type, S Mint, Proof | (577,090) | | 26 |
| 1994W, World Cup Tournament gold $5 | (89,614) .....22,447 | 350 | 370 |

(1993 [1994]) Thomas Jefferson

| | Distribution | MS-67 | PF-67 |
|---|---|---|---|
| 1993 (1994) Thomas Jefferson silver dollar, P Mint | 266,927 | $22 | |
| 1993 (1994) Same type, S Mint, Proof | (332,891) | | $23 |

(1994) Vietnam Veterans Memorial

| | Distribution | MS-67 | PF-67 |
|---|---|---|---|
| 1994W, Vietnam Veterans Memorial silver dollar | 57,290 | $65 | |
| 1994P, Same type, P Mint, Proof | (227,671) | | $52 |

(1994) U.S. Prisoner of War Museum

| | Distribution | MS-67 | PF-67 |
|---|---|---|---|
| 1994W, U.S. Prisoner of War Museum silver dollar | 54,893 | $70 | |
| 1994P, Same type, P Mint, Proof | (224,449) | | $32 |

(1994) Women in Military Service Memorial

| | Distribution | MS-67 | PF-67 |
|---|---|---|---|
| 1994W, Women in Military Service Memorial silver dollar | 69,860 | $30 | |
| 1994P, Same type, P Mint, Proof | (241,278) | | $30 |

(1994) U.S. Capitol Bicentennial

| | Distribution | MS-67 | PF-67 |
|---|---|---|---|
| 1994D, U.S. Capitol Bicentennial silver dollar | 68,332 | $22 | |
| 1994S, Same type, S Mint, Proof | (279,579) | | $27 |

(1995) Civil War Battlefield Preservation

| | Distribution | MS-67 | PF-67 |
|---|---|---|---|
| 1995S, Civil War Battlefield Preservation clad half dollar | 119,520 | $30 | |
| 1995S, Same type, S Mint, Proof | (330,002) | | $28 |

#### (1995) Civil War Battlefield Preservation

| | Distribution | MS-67 | PF-67 |
|---|---|---|---|
| 1995P, Civil War Battlefield Preservation silver dollar | 45,866 | $55 | |
| 1995S, Same type, S Mint, Proof | (437,114) | | $55 |
| 1995W, Civil War Battlefield Preservation gold $5 | 12,735 | 700 | |
| 1995W, Same type, W Mint, Proof | (55,246) | | 370 |

#### (1995) XXVI Olympiad

| | Distribution | MS-67 | PF-67 |
|---|---|---|---|
| 1995S, XXVI Olympiad, Basketball clad half dollar | 171,001 | $15 | |
| 1995S, Same type, S Mint, Proof | (169,655) | | $13 |
| 1995S, XXVI Olympiad, Baseball clad half dollar | 164,605 | 15 | |
| 1995S, Same type, S Mint, Proof | (118,087) | | 13 |
| 1996S, XXVI Olympiad, Swimming clad half dollar | 49,533 | 110 | |
| 1996S, Same type, S Mint, Proof | (114,315) | | 25 |

*Chart continued on next page.*

**205**

| | Distribution | MS-67 | PF-67 |
|---|---|---|---|
| 1996S, XXVI Olympiad, Soccer clad half dollar | 52,836 | $105 | |
| 1996S, Same type, S Mint, Proof | (112,412) | | $65 |
| 1995D, XXVI Olympiad, Gymnastics silver dollar | 42,497 | 45 | |
| 1995P, Same type, P Mint, Proof | (182,676) | | 30 |
| 1995D, XXVI Olympiad, Paralympics silver dollar | 28,649 | 60 | |
| 1995P, Same type, P Mint, Proof | (138,337) | | 45 |
| 1995D, XXVI Olympiad, Track and Field silver dollar | 24,976 | 60 | |
| 1995P, Same type, P mint, Proof | (136,935) | | 35 |
| 1995D, XXVI Olympiad, Cycling silver dollar | 19,662 | 110 | |
| 1995P, Same type, P Mint, Proof | (118,795) | | 35 |
| 1996D, XXVI Olympiad, Tennis silver dollar | 15,983 | 225 | |
| 1996P, Same type, P Mint, Proof | (92,016) | | 65 |
| 1996D, XXVI Olympiad, Paralympics silver dollar | 14,497 | 250 | |
| 1996P, Same type, P Mint, Proof | (84,280) | | 60 |
| 1996D, XXVI Olympiad, Rowing silver dollar | 16,258 | 260 | |
| 1996P, Same type, P Mint, Proof | (151,890) | | 50 |
| 1996D, XXVI Olympiad, High Jump silver dollar | 15,697 | 290 | |
| 1996P, Same type, P Mint, Proof | (124,502) | | 45 |
| 1995W, XXVI Olympiad, Torch Runner gold $5 | 14,675 | 680 | |
| 1995W, Same type, W Mint, Proof | (57,442) | | 350 |
| 1995W, XXVI Olympiad, Stadium gold $5 | 10,579 | 1,600 | |
| 1995W, Same type, W Mint, Proof | (43,124) | | 450 |
| 1996W, XXVI Olympiad, Flag Bearer gold $5 | 9,174 | 1,600 | |
| 1996W, Same type, W Mint, Proof | (32,886) | | 450 |
| 1996W, XXVI Olympiad, Cauldron gold $5 | 9,210 | 1,600 | |
| 1996W, Same type, W Mint, Proof | (38,555) | | 450 |

(1995) Special Olympics World Games

| | Distribution | MS-67 | PF-67 |
|---|---|---|---|
| 1995W, Special Olympics World Games silver dollar | 89,301 | $23 | |
| 1995P, Same type, P Mint, Proof | (351,764) | | $22 |

### (1996) National Community Service

| | Distribution | MS-67 | PF-67 |
|---|---|---|---|
| 1996S, National Community Service silver dollar ...............................23,500 | | $160 | |
| 1996S, Same type, S Mint, Proof ..............................(101,543)........... | | | $55 |

### (1996) Smithsonian Institution 150th Anniversary

| | Distribution | MS-67 | PF-67 |
|---|---|---|---|
| 1996D, Smithsonian Institution 150th Anniversary silver dollar ....................31,320 | | $100 | |
| 1996P, Same type, P Mint, Proof ..............................(129,152)........... | | | $40 |
| 1996W, Smithsonian Institution 150th Anniversary gold $5 .........................9,068 | | 800 | |
| 1996W, Same type, W Mint, Proof ..............................(21,772)........... | | | 385 |

### (1997) U.S. Botanic Garden

| | Distribution | MS-67 | PF-67 |
|---|---|---|---|
| 1997P, U.S. Botanic Garden silver dollar ...................................58,505 | | $30 | |
| 1997P, Same type, P Mint, Proof ..............................(189,671)........... | | | $28 |

**(1997) Jackie Robinson**

| | Distribution | MS-67 | PF-67 |
|---|---|---|---|
| 1997S, Jackie Robinson silver dollar | 30,180 | $75 | |
| 1997S, Same type, S Mint, Proof | (110,002) | | $75 |
| 1997W, Jackie Robinson gold $5 | 5,174 | 3,250 | |
| 1997W, Same type, W Mint, Proof | (24,072) | | 450 |

**(1997) Franklin D. Roosevelt**

| | Distribution | MS-67 | PF-67 |
|---|---|---|---|
| 1997W, Franklin D. Roosevelt gold $5 | 11,894 | $825 | |
| 1997W, Same type, W Mint, Proof | (29,474) | | $350 |

**(1997) National Law Enforcement Officers Memorial**

| | Distribution | MS-67 | PF-67 |
|---|---|---|---|
| 1997P, National Law Enforcement Officers Memorial silver dollar | 28,575 | $125 | |
| 1997P, Same type, P Mint, Proof | (110,428) | | $80 |

(1998) Robert F. Kennedy

| | Distribution | MS-67 | PF-67 |
|---|---|---|---|
| 1998S, Robert F. Kennedy silver dollar .................................106,422 | | $26 | |
| 1998S, Same type, S Mint, Proof .............................(99,020) ........... | | | $35 |

(1998) Black Revolutionary War Patriots

| | Distribution | MS-67 | PF-67 |
|---|---|---|---|
| 1998S, Black Revolutionary War Patriots silver dollar ..........................37,210 | | $120 | |
| 1998S, Same type, S Mint, Proof .............................(75,070) ........... | | | $75 |

(1999) Dolley Madison

| | Distribution | MS-67 | PF-67 |
|---|---|---|---|
| 1999P, Dolley Madison silver dollar .......................................89,104 | | $30 | |
| 1999P, Same type, P Mint, Proof .............................(224,403) ........... | | | $23 |

**(1999) George Washington Death Bicentennial**

| | Distribution | MS-67 | PF-67 |
|---|---|---|---|
| 1999W, George Washington Death Bicentennial gold $5 ...........................22,511 | | $350 | |
| 1999W, Same type, W Mint, Proof ...............................(41,693) ........... | | | $350 |

**(1999) Yellowstone National Park**

| | Distribution | MS-67 | PF-67 |
|---|---|---|---|
| 1999P, Yellowstone National Park silver dollar ................................23,614 | | $40 | |
| 1999S, Same type, S Mint, Proof ...........................(128,646) ........... | | | $35 |

**(2000) Library of Congress Bicentennial**

| | Distribution | MS-67 | PF-67 |
|---|---|---|---|
| 2000P, Library of Congress Bicentennial silver dollar ..........................53,264 | | $37 | |
| 2000P, Same type, P Mint, Proof ...............................(198,503) ........... | | | $37 |
| 2000W, Library of Congress Bicentennial bimetallic (gold/platinum) $10 ...............7,261 | | 4,000 | |
| 2000W, Same type, W Mint, Proof ...............................(27,445) ........... | | | 850 |

**(2000) Leif Ericson Millennium**

| | Distribution | MS-67 | PF-67 |
|---|---|---|---|
| 2000P, Leif Ericson Millennium silver dollar | 28,150 | $75 | |
| 2000P, Same type, P Mint, Proof | (144,748) | | $55 |

**(2001) American Buffalo Commemorative**

| | Distribution | MS-67 | PF-67 |
|---|---|---|---|
| 2001D, American Buffalo silver dollar | 227,131 | $150 | |
| 2001P, Same type, P Mint, Proof | (272,869) | | $150 |

**(2001) Capitol Visitor Center**

| | Distribution | MS-67 | PF-67 |
|---|---|---|---|
| 2001P, U.S. Capitol Visitor Center clad half dollar | 99,157 | $10 | |
| 2001P, Same type, P Mint, Proof | (77,962) | | $12 |

*Entry continued on next page.*

**(2001) Capitol Visitor Center**

| | Distribution | MS-67 | PF-67 |
|---|---|---|---|
| 2001P, U.S. Capitol Visitor Center silver dollar | .35,380 | $24 | |
| 2001P, Same type, P Mint, Proof | .(143,793) | | $30 |
| 2001W, U.S. Capitol Visitor Center gold $5 | .6,761 | 1,500 | |
| 2001W, Same type, W Mint, Proof | .(27,652) | | 350 |
| 2002P, Salt Lake Olympic Games silver dollar | .40,257 | 25 | |
| 2002P, Same type, P Mint, Proof | .(166,864) | | 30 |
| 2002W, Salt Lake Olympic Games gold $5 | .10,585 | 375 | |
| 2002W, Same type, W Mint, Proof | .(32,877) | | 350 |
| 2002W, West Point Bicentennial silver dollar | .103,201 | 22 | |
| 2002W, Same type, W Mint, Proof | .(288,293) | | 22 |
| 2003P, First Flight Centennial clad half dollar | .57,122 | 11 | |
| 2003P, Same type, P Mint, Proof | .(109,710) | | 12 |
| 2003P, First Flight Centennial silver dollar | .53,533 | 26 | |
| 2003P, Same type, P Mint, Proof | .(190,240) | | 24 |
| 2003W, First Flight Centennial gold $10 | .10,009 | 750 | |
| 2003W, Same type, W Mint, Proof | .(21,676) | | 700 |
| 2004P, Thomas Alva Edison silver dollar | .92,510 | 24 | |
| 2004P, Same type, P Mint, Proof | .(211,055) | | 27 |
| 2004P, Lewis and Clark Bicentennial silver dollar | .142,015 | 22 | |
| 2004P, Same type, P Mint, Proof | .(351,989) | | 22 |
| 2005P, Chief Justice John Marshall silver dollar | .67,096 | 23 | |
| 2005P, Same type, P Mint, Proof | .(196,753) | | 25 |
| 2005P, Marine Corps 230th Anniversary silver dollar | .49,671 | 30 | |
| 2005P, Same type, P Mint, Proof | .(548,810) | | 32 |
| 2006P, Benjamin Franklin "Scientist" silver dollar | .58,000 | 25 | |
| 2006P, Same type, P Mint, Proof | .(142,000) | | 35 |
| 2006P, Benjamin Franklin "Founding Father" silver dollar | .58,000 | 25 | |
| 2006P, Same type, P Mint, Proof | .(142,000) | | 35 |
| 2006S, San Francisco Old Mint Centennial silver dollar | .67,100 | 30 | |
| 2006S, Same type, S Mint, Proof | .(160,870) | | 30 |

# COMMEMORATIVES

| | Distribution | MS-67 | PF-67 |
|---|---|---|---|
| 2006S, San Francisco Old Mint Centennial gold $5 | 17,500 | $350 | |
| 2006S, Same type, S Mint, Proof | (44,174) | | $350 |
| 2007P, Jamestown 400th Anniversary silver dollar | | 25 | |
| 2007P, Same type, P Mint, Proof | | | 28 |
| 2007W, Jamestown 400th Anniversary gold $5 | | 350 | |
| 2007W, Same type, W Mint, Proof | | | 350 |
| 2007P, Little Rock Central High School Desegregation silver dollar | 124,678 | 25 | |
| 2007S, Same type, S Mint, Proof | (66,093) | | 28 |
| 2008S, Bald Eagle clad half dollar | 120,180 | 7 | |
| 2008S, Same type, S Mint, Proof | (220,577) | | 8 |
| 2008P, Bald Eagle silver dollar | 119,204 | 28 | |
| 2008P, Same type, P Mint, Proof | (294,601) | | 32 |
| 2008W, Bald Eagle gold $5 | 19,009 | 350 | |
| 2008W, Same type, W Mint, Proof | (59,269) | | 350 |
| 2009P, Louis Braille Bicentennial silver dollar | 82,639 | 24 | |
| 2009P, Same type, P Mint, Proof | (135,235) | | 25 |
| 2009P, Abraham Lincoln Bicentennial silver dollar | 125,000 | 30 | |
| 2009P, Same type, P Mint, Proof | (325,000) | | 32 |
| 2010W, American Veterans Disabled for Life silver dollar | 77,859 | 24 | |
| 2010W, Same type, W mint, Proof | (189,881) | | 25 |
| 2010P, Boy Scouts of America Centennial silver dollar | 105,000 | 24 | |
| 2010P, Same type, S Mint, Proof | (245,000) | | 25 |
| 2011P, Medal of Honor silver dollar | | 24 | |
| 2011S, Same type, S Mint, Proof | | | 25 |
| 2011P, Medal of Honor gold $5 | | 350 | |
| 2011S, Same type, S Mint, Proof | | | 350 |
| 2011P, U.S. Army half dollar | | 9 | |
| 2011S, Same type, S Mint, Proof | | | 10 |
| 2011P, U.S. Army silver dollar | | 27 | |
| 2011S, Same type, S Mint, Proof | | | 29 |
| 2011P, U.S. Army gold $5 | | 375 | |
| 2011S, Same type, S Mint, Proof | | | 380 |

## GOVERNMENT COMMEMORATIVE SETS

*Values are for commemorative coins and sets in all of their original packaging.*

| | Value |
|---|---|
| **(1983–1984) Los Angeles Olympiad** | |
| 1983 and 1984 Proof dollars | $45 |
| 1983 and 1984 6-coin set. One each of 1983 and 1984 dollars, both Proof and Uncirculated gold $10 **(a)** | 1,450 |
| 1983 3-piece collector set. 1983 P, D, and S Uncirculated dollars | 66 |
| 1984 3-piece collector set. 1984 P, D, and S Uncirculated dollars | 70 |
| 1983 and 1984 gold and silver Uncirculated set. One each of 1983 and 1984 Uncirculated dollar and one 1984 Uncirculated gold $10 | 744 |
| 1983 and 1984 gold and silver Proof set. One each of 1983 and 1984 Proof dollars and one 1984 Proof gold $10 | 744 |

a. Packaged in cherrywood box.

| | Value |
|---|---|

### (1986) Statue of Liberty

| | |
|---|---|
| 2-coin set. Proof silver dollar and clad half dollar | $28 |
| 3-coin set. Proof silver dollar, clad half dollar, and gold $5 | 380 |
| 2-coin set. Uncirculated silver dollar and clad half dollar | 28 |
| 2-coin set. Uncirculated and Proof gold $5 | 580 |
| 3-coin set. Uncirculated silver dollar, clad half dollar, and gold $5 | 380 |
| 6-coin set. One each of Proof and Uncirculated half dollar, silver dollar, and gold $5 **(a)** | 760 |

### (1987) Constitution

| | |
|---|---|
| 2-coin set. Uncirculated silver dollar and gold $5 | 375 |
| 2-coin set. Proof silver dollar and gold $5 | 375 |
| 4-coin set. One each of Proof and Uncirculated silver dollar and gold $5 **(a)** | 750 |

### (1988) Seoul Olympiad

| | |
|---|---|
| 2-coin set. Uncirculated silver dollar and gold $5 | 375 |
| 2-coin set. Proof silver dollar and gold $5 | 375 |
| 4-coin set. One each of Proof and Uncirculated silver dollar and gold $5 **(a)** | 750 |

### (1989) Congress

| | |
|---|---|
| 2-coin set. Proof clad half dollar and silver dollar | 30 |
| 3-coin set. Proof clad half dollar, silver dollar, and gold $5 | 380 |
| 2-coin set. Uncirculated clad half dollar and silver dollar | 28 |
| 3-coin set. Uncirculated clad half dollar, silver dollar, and gold $5 | 380 |
| 6-coin set. One each of Proof and Uncirculated clad half dollar, silver dollar, gold $5 **(a)** | 760 |

### (1991) Mount Rushmore

| | |
|---|---|
| 2-coin set. Uncirculated clad half dollar and silver dollar | 55 |
| 2-coin set. Proof clad half dollar and silver dollar | 53 |
| 3-coin set. Uncirculated clad half dollar, silver dollar, and gold $5 | 430 |
| 3-coin set. Proof half dollar, silver dollar, and gold $5 | 415 |
| 6-coin set. One each of Proof and Uncirculated clad half dollar, silver dollar, and gold $5 **(a)** | 845 |

### (1992) XXV Olympiad

| | |
|---|---|
| 2-coin set. Uncirculated clad half dollar and silver dollar | 30 |
| 2-coin set. Proof clad half dollar and silver dollar | 33 |
| 3-coin set. Uncirculated clad half dollar, silver dollar, and gold $5 | 405 |
| 3-coin set. Proof half dollar, silver dollar, and gold $5 | 385 |
| 6-coin set. One each of Proof and Uncirculated clad half dollar, silver dollar, and gold $5 **(a)** | 790 |

### (1992) Christopher Columbus

| | |
|---|---|
| 2-coin set. Uncirculated clad half dollar and silver dollar | 36 |
| 2-coin set. Proof clad half dollar and silver dollar | 36 |
| 3-coin set. Uncirculated clad half dollar, silver dollar, and gold $5 | 410 |
| 3-coin set. Proof half dollar, silver dollar, and gold $5 | 385 |
| 6-coin set. One each of Proof and Uncirculated clad half dollar, silver dollar, and gold $5 **(a)** | 795 |

### (1993) Bill of Rights

| | |
|---|---|
| 2-coin set. Uncirculated silver half dollar and silver dollar | 37 |
| 2-coin set. Proof silver half dollar and silver dollar | 36 |
| 3-coin set. Uncirculated silver half dollar, silver dollar, and gold $5 | 410 |
| 3-coin set. Proof half dollar, silver dollar, and gold $5 | 385 |
| 6-coin set. One each of Proof and Uncirculated silver half dollar, silver dollar, and gold $5 **(a)** | 795 |
| "Young Collector" set. Silver half dollar | 15 |
| Educational set. Silver half dollar and James Madison medal | 16 |
| Proof silver half dollar and 25-cent stamp | 15 |

a. Packaged in cherrywood box.

| | Value |
|---|---|

### (1993) World War II

| | |
|---|---|
| 2-coin set. Uncirculated clad half dollar and silver dollar | $45 |
| 2-coin set. Proof clad half dollar and silver dollar | 50 |
| 3-coin set. Uncirculated clad half dollar, silver dollar, and gold $5 | 420 |
| 3-coin set. Proof clad half dollar, silver dollar, and gold $5 | 400 |
| 6-coin set. One each of Proof and Uncirculated clad half dollar, silver dollar, and gold $5 **(a)** | 820 |
| "Young Collector" set. Clad half dollar | 23 |
| Victory Medal set. Uncirculated clad half dollar and reproduction medal | 25 |

### (1993) Thomas Jefferson

| | |
|---|---|
| 3-piece set (issued in 1994). Silver dollar, Jefferson nickel, and $2 note | 40 |

### (1994) World Cup Soccer

| | |
|---|---|
| 2-coin set. Uncirculated clad half dollar and silver dollar | 30 |
| 2-coin set. Proof clad half dollar and silver dollar | 32 |
| 3-coin set. Uncirculated clad half dollar, silver dollar, and gold $5 | 380 |
| 3-coin set. Proof clad half dollar, silver dollar, and gold $5 | 400 |
| 6-coin set. One each of Proof and Uncirculated clad half dollar, silver dollar, and gold $5 **(a)** | 780 |
| "Young Collector" set. Uncirculated clad half dollar | 9 |
| "Special Edition" set. Proof clad half dollar and silver dollar | 26 |

### (1994) U.S. Veterans

| | |
|---|---|
| 3-coin set. Uncirculated POW, Vietnam, and Women in Military Service silver dollars | 165 |
| 3-coin set. Proof POW, Vietnam, and Women in Military Service silver dollars | 115 |

### (1995) Special Olympics

| | |
|---|---|
| 2-coin set. Proof Special Olympics silver dollar, 1995S Kennedy half dollar | 60 |

### (1995) Civil War Battlefield Preservation

| | |
|---|---|
| 2-coin set. Uncirculated clad half dollar and silver dollar | 85 |
| 2-coin set. Proof clad half dollar and silver dollar | 85 |
| 3-coin set. Uncirculated clad half dollar, silver dollar, and gold $5 | 785 |
| 3-coin set. Proof clad half dollar, silver dollar, and gold $5 | 455 |
| 6-coin set. One each of Proof and Uncirculated clad half dollar, silver dollar, and gold $5 **(a)** | 1,235 |
| "Young Collector" set. Uncirculated clad half dollar | 35 |
| 2-coin "Union" set. Clad half dollar and silver dollar | 85 |
| 3-coin "Union" set. Clad half dollar, silver dollar, and gold $5 | 525 |

### (1995–1996) Centennial Olympic Games

| | |
|---|---|
| 4-coin set #1. Uncirculated half dollar (Basketball), dollars (Gymnastics, Paralympics), gold $5 (Torch Bearer) | 800 |
| 4-coin set #2. Proof half dollar (Basketball), dollars (Gymnastics, Paralympics), gold $5 (Torch Bearer) | 430 |
| 2-coin set #1: Proof silver dollars (Gymnastics, Paralympics) | 65 |
| "Young Collector" set. Uncirculated Basketball, Baseball, Swimming, or Soccer half dollar | — |
| 1995–1996 16-coin Uncirculated set. One each of all Uncirculated coins **(a)** | 7,025 |
| 1995–1996 16-coin Proof set. One each of all Proof coins **(a)** | 2,180 |
| 1995–1996 8-coin Proof silver dollars set | 370 |
| 1995–1996 32-coin set. One each of all Uncirculated and Proof coins **(a)** | 9,200 |

### (1996) National Community Service

| | |
|---|---|
| Proof silver dollar and Saint-Gaudens stamp | 70 |

### (1996) Smithsonian Institution 150th Anniversary

| | |
|---|---|
| 2-coin set. Proof silver dollar and gold $5 | 425 |
| 4-coin set. One each of Proof and Uncirculated silver dollar and gold $5 **(a)** | 1,325 |
| "Young Collector" set. Proof silver dollar | 55 |

**a.** Packaged in cherrywood box.

| | Value |
|---|---|

**(1997) U.S. Botanic Garden**
"Coinage and Currency" set. Uncirculated silver dollar, Jefferson nickel, and $1 note .............. $150

**(1997) Jackie Robinson**
2-coin set. Proof silver dollar and gold $5 .......................................... 525
4-coin set. One each of Proof and Uncirculated silver dollar and gold $5 **(a)** ...................... 3,850
3-piece "Legacy" set. Baseball card, pin, and gold $5 **(a)** .................................. 700

**(1997) Franklin D. Roosevelt**
2-coin set. One each of Proof and Uncirculated gold $5 .................................... 1,175

**(1997) National Law Enforcement Officers Memorial**
Insignia set. Silver dollar, lapel pin, and patch ........................................ 150

**(1998) Robert F. Kennedy**
2-coin set. RFK silver dollar and JFK silver half dollar ................................... 175
2-coin set. Proof and Uncirculated RFK silver dollars ................................... 60

**(1998) Black Revolutionary War Patriots**
2-coin set. Proof and Uncirculated silver dollars ...................................... 200
"Young Collector" set. Uncirculated silver dollar ...................................... 125
Black Revolutionary War Patriots set. Silver dollar and four stamps .................... 100

**(1999) Dolley Madison Commemorative**
2-coin set. Proof and Uncirculated silver dollars ...................................... 50

**(1999) George Washington Death**
2-coin set. One each of Proof and Uncirculated gold $5 .................................... 700

**(1999) Yellowstone National Park**
2-coin set. One each of Proof and Uncirculated silver dollars ............................. 75

**(2000) Leif Ericson Millennium**
2-coin set. Proof silver dollar and Icelandic 1,000 kronur ................................ 90

**(2000) Millennium Coin and Currency Set**
3-piece set. Uncirculated 2000 Sacagawea dollar; Uncirculated 2000 Silver Eagle;
George Washington $1 note, series 1999 ........................................... 55

**(2001) American Buffalo**
2-coin set. One each of Proof and Uncirculated silver dollar ............................. 300
"Coinage and Currency" set. Uncirculated American Buffalo silver dollar, face reprint of 1899
$5 Indian Chief Silver Certificate, 1987 Chief Red Cloud 10¢ stamp, 2001 Bison 21¢ stamp ........ 190

**(2001) U.S. Capitol Visitor Center**
3-coin set. Proof clad half dollar, silver dollar, and gold $5 ............................. 395

**(2002) Salt Lake Olympic Games**
2-coin set. Proof silver dollar and gold $5 ........................................... 380
4-coin set. One each of Proof and Uncirculated silver dollar and gold $5 ...................... 780

**(2003) First Flight Centennial**
3-coin set. Proof clad half dollar, silver dollar, and gold $5 ............................. 735

**(2003) Legacies of Freedom™**
Uncirculated 2003 $1 American Eagle silver bullion coin and an Uncirculated 2002 £2 Silver Britannia coin    60

**(2004) Thomas A. Edison**
Edison set. Uncirculated silver dollar and light bulb ................................... 40

**(2004) Lewis and Clark**
Coin and Pouch set. Proof silver dollar and beaded pouch .............................. 130
"Coinage and Currency" set. Uncirculated silver dollar, Sacagawea golden dollar, two 2005 nickels,
replica 1901 $10 Bison note, silver-plated Peace Medal replica, three stamps, two booklets ........ 60

a. Packaged in cherrywood box.

| | Value |
|---|---|

**(2004) Westward Journey Nickel Series™**
Westward Journey Nickel Series™ Coin and Medal set. Proof Sacagawea golden dollar,
two 2004 Proof nickels, silver-plated Peace Medal replica . . . . . . . . . . . . . . . . . . . . . . . . . . . . . . . $35

**(2005) Westward Journey Nickel Series™**
Westward Journey Nickel Series™ Coin and Medal set. Proof Sacagawea golden dollar,
two 2005 Proof nickels, silver-plated Peace Medal replica . . . . . . . . . . . . . . . . . . . . . . . . . . . . . . . 32

**(2005) Chief Justice John Marshall**
"Coin and Chronicles" set. Uncirculated silver dollar, booklet, BEP intaglio portrait . . . . . . . . . . . . . . . . . 35

**(2005) American Legacy**
American Legacy Collection. Proof Marine Corps dollar, Proof John Marshall dollar, 11-piece Proof set . . 110

**(2005) Marine Corps 230th Anniversary**
Marine Corps Uncirculated silver dollar and stamp set . . . . . . . . . . . . . . . . . . . . . . . . . . . . . . . . . . . . 42

**(2006) Benjamin Franklin**
"Coin and Chronicles" set. Uncirculated "Scientist" silver dollar, four stamps,
four stamps, *Poor Richard's Almanack* replica, intaglio print . . . . . . . . . . . . . . . . . . . . . . . . . . . . . . . 40

**(2006) American Legacy**
American Legacy Collection. Proof 2006P Benjamin Franklin, Founding Father silver dollar;
Proof 2006S San Francisco Old Mint silver dollar; Proof cent, nickel, dime, quarter,
half dollar, and dollar . . . . . . . . . . . . . . . . . . . . . . . . . . . . . . . . . . . . . . . . . . . . . . . . . . . . . . . . . . . . . 85

**(2007) American Legacy**
American Legacy Collection. 16 Proof coins for 2007: five state quarters; four Presidential dollars;
Jamestown and Little Rock Central High School Desegregation silver dollars; Proof cent, nickel,
dime, half dollar, and dollar . . . . . . . . . . . . . . . . . . . . . . . . . . . . . . . . . . . . . . . . . . . . . . . . . . . . . . . . 95

**(2007) Little Rock Central High School Desegregation**
Little Rock Coin and Medal set. Proof 2007P silver dollar, bronze medal . . . . . . . . . . . . . . . . . . . . . . . 120

**(2008) Bald Eagle**
3-piece set. Proof clad half dollar, silver dollar, and gold $5 . . . . . . . . . . . . . . . . . . . . . . . . . . . . . . . . 385
Bald Eagle Coin and Medal Set. Uncirculated silver dollar, bronze medal . . . . . . . . . . . . . . . . . . . . . . . 32
"Young Collector" set. Uncirculated clad half dollar . . . . . . . . . . . . . . . . . . . . . . . . . . . . . . . . . . . . . . 10

**(2008) American Legacy**
American Legacy Collection. 15 Proof coins for 2008: cent, nickel, dime, half dollar, and dollar;
five state quarters; four Presidential dollars; Bald Eagle dollar . . . . . . . . . . . . . . . . . . . . . . . . . . . . . 100

**(2009) Louis Braille**
Uncirculated silver dollar in tri-folded package . . . . . . . . . . . . . . . . . . . . . . . . . . . . . . . . . . . . . . . . . . . 30

**(2009) Abraham Lincoln Coin and Chronicles**
Four Proof 2009S cents and Abraham Lincoln Proof silver dollar . . . . . . . . . . . . . . . . . . . . . . . . . . . . 110

**(2011) Medal of Honor**
2-coin set. Proof silver dollar and gold $5 . . . . . . . . . . . . . . . . . . . . . . . . . . . . . . . . . . . . . . . . . . . . . 465
4-coin set. One each Proof and Uncirculated silver dollar and gold $5 . . . . . . . . . . . . . . . . . . . . . . . . . 900

## PROOF COINS AND SETS

Proof coins can usually be distinguished by their sharpness of detail, high wire edge, and extremely brilliant, mirrorlike surface. Proofs are sold by the Mint at a premium.

Proof coins were not struck during 1943–1949 or 1965–1967. Sets from 1936 through 1972 include the cent, nickel, dime, quarter, and half dollar; from 1973 through 1981 the dollar was also included. *Values shown are for original unblemished sets.*

Figures in parentheses represent the total number of full sets minted.

| Year | Mintage | Issue Price | Current Value | Year | Mintage | Issue Price | Current Value |
|---|---|---|---|---|---|---|---|
| 1936 | (3,837) | $1.89 | $5,000.00 | 1978S | (3,127,781) | $9.00 | $4.75 |
| 1937 | (5,542) | 1.89 | 2,500.00 | 1979S, Filled S | (3,677,175) | 9.00 | 4.00 |
| 1938 | (8,045) | 1.89 | 1,200.00 | 1979S, Clear S | * | 9.00 | 50.00 |
| 1939 | (8,795) | 1.89 | 1,000.00 | 1980S | (3,554,806) | 10.00 | 3.50 |
| 1940 | (11,246) | 1.89 | 900.00 | 1981S | (4,063,083) | 11.00 | 3.75 |
| 1941 | (15,287) | 1.89 | 900.00 | 1982S | (3,857,479) | 11.00 | 2.00 |
| 1942, Both nickels | (21,120) | 1.89 | 835.00 | 1983S | (3,138,765) | 11.00 | 3.00 |
| 1942, One nickel | * | 1.89 | 800.00 | 1983S, Prestige set | | | |
| 1950 | (51,386) | 2.10 | 500.00 | (Olympic dollar) | (140,361) | 59.00 | 43.00 |
| 1951 | (57,500) | 2.10 | 400.00 | 1984S | (2,748,430) | 11.00 | 3.50 |
| 1952 | (81,980) | 2.10 | 165.00 | 1984S, Prestige set | | | |
| 1953 | (128,800) | 2.10 | 140.00 | (Olympic dollar) | (316,680) | 59.00 | 24.00 |
| 1954 | (233,300) | 2.10 | 70.00 | 1985S | (3,362,821) | 11.00 | 2.90 |
| 1955, Box pack | (378,200) | 2.10 | 70.00 | 1986S | (2,411,180) | 11.00 | 3.00 |
| 1955, Flat pack | * | 2.10 | 90.00 | 1986S, Prestige set (Statue | | | |
| 1956 | (669,384) | 2.10 | 28.00 | of Liberty half, dollar) | (599,317) | 48.50 | 24.00 |
| 1957 | (1,247,952) | 2.10 | 18.00 | 1987S | (3,792,233) | 11.00 | 3.00 |
| 1958 | (875,652) | 2.10 | 25.00 | 1987S, Prestige set | | | |
| 1959 | (1,149,291) | 2.10 | 18.00 | (Constitution dollar) | (435,495) | 45.00 | 24.00 |
| 1960, With Lg Date cent | (1,691,602) | 2.10 | 17.00 | 1988S | (3,031,287) | 11.00 | 3.00 |
| 1960, With Sm Date cent | * | 2.10 | 20.00 | 1988S, Prestige set | | | |
| 1961 | (3,028,244) | 2.10 | 17.00 | (Olympic dollar) | (231,661) | 45.00 | 24.00 |
| 1962 | (3,218,019) | 2.10 | 17.00 | 1989S | (3,009,107) | 11.00 | 4.00 |
| 1963 | (3,075,645) | 2.10 | 17.00 | 1989S, Prestige set | | | |
| 1964 | (3,950,762) | 2.10 | 17.00 | (Congressional half, | | | |
| 1968S | (3,041,506) | 5.00 | 4.00 | dollar) | (211,807) | 45.00 | 28.00 |
| 1969S | (2,934,631) | 5.00 | 4.50 | 1990S | (2,793,433) | 11.00 | 3.00 |
| 1970S | (2,632,810) | 5.00 | 5.00 | 1990S, With No S cent | (3,555) | 11.00 | 4,200.00 |
| 1970S, With Sm Date cent | * | 5.00 | 60.00 | 1990S, With No S cent | | | |
| 1971S | (3,220,733) | 5.00 | 3.00 | (Prestige set) | * | 45.00 | 4,100.00 |
| 1972S | (3,260,996) | 5.00 | 3.00 | 1990S, Prestige set | | | |
| 1973S | (2,760,339) | 7.00 | 3.50 | (Eisenhower dollar) | (506,126) | 45.00 | 24.00 |
| 1974S | (2,612,568) | 7.00 | 5.00 | 1991S | (2,610,833) | 11.00 | 6.00 |
| 1975S, With 1976 quarter, | | | | 1991S, Prestige set (Mt. | | | |
| half, and dollar | (2,845,450) | 7.00 | 5.00 | Rushmore half, dollar) | (256,954) | 59.00 | 35.00 |
| 1976S | (4,149,730) | 7.00 | 5.00 | 1992S | (2,675,618) | 11.00 | 3.00 |
| 1976S, 3-piece set | (3,998,621) | 15.00 | 14.00 | 1992S, Prestige set | | | |
| 1977S | (3,251,152) | 9.00 | 4.00 | (Olympic half, dollar) | (183,293) | 56.00 | 36.00 |

* Included in number above.

# PROOF AND MINT SETS

| Year | Mintage | Issue Price | Current Value |
|---|---|---|---|
| 1992S, Silver . . . . . . . . . . .(1,009,586) | $21.00 | $17.00 |
| 1992S, Silver Premier set . . .(308,055) | 37.00 | 18.00 |
| 1993S . . . . . . . . . . . . . . . .(2,409,394) | 12.50 | 5.00 |
| 1993S, Prestige set (Bill of | | |
| Rights half, dollar) . . . .(224,045) | 57.00 | 30.00 |
| 1993S, Silver . . . . . . . . . . .(570,213) | 21.00 | 17.00 |
| 1993S, Silver Premier set . . .(191,140) | 37.50 | 17.00 |
| 1994S . . . . . . . . . . . . . . . .(2,308,701) | 12.50 | 6.00 |
| 1994S, Prestige set (World | | |
| Cup half, dollar) . . . . . .(175,893) | 57.00 | 30.00 |
| 1994S, Silver . . . . . . . . . . .(636,009) | 21.00 | 18.00 |
| 1994S Silver Premier set . . .(149,320) | 37.50 | 18.00 |
| 1995S . . . . . . . . . . . . . . .(2,010,384) | 12.50 | 14.00 |
| 1995S, Prestige set (Civil | | |
| War half, dollar) . . . . . .(107,112) | 57.00 | 70.00 |
| 1995S, Silver . . . . . . . . . . .(549,878) | 21.00 | 50.00 |
| 1995S, Silver Premier set . . .(130,107) | 37.50 | 55.00 |
| 1996S . . . . . . . . . . . . . . . .(1,695,244) | 12.50 | 8.00 |
| 1996S, Prestige set | | |
| (Olympic half, dollar) . . .(55,000) | 57.00 | 225.00 |
| 1996S, Silver . . . . . . . . . . .(623,655) | 21.00 | 20.00 |
| 1996S, Silver Premier set . . .(151,366) | 37.50 | 21.00 |
| 1997S . . . . . . . . . . . . . . . .(1,975,000) | 12.50 | 13.00 |
| 1997S, Prestige set | | |
| (Botanic dollar) . . . . . . .(80,000) | 48.00 | 68.00 |
| 1997S, Silver . . . . . . . . . . .(605,473) | 21.00 | 31.00 |
| 1997S, Silver Premier set . . .(136,205) | 37.50 | 32.00 |
| 1998S . . . . . . . . . . . . . . . .(2,086,507) | 12.50 | 7.00 |
| 1998S, Silver . . . . . . . . . . .(638,134) | 21.00 | 17.00 |
| 1998S, Silver Premier set . . .(240,658) | 37.50 | 18.00 |
| 1999S, 9-piece set . . . . . .(2,543,401) | 19.95 | 15.00 |
| 1999S, 5-piece quarter set (1,169,958) | 13.95 | 12.00 |
| 1999S, Silver 9-piece set . .(804,565) | 31.95 | 110.00 |
| 2000S, 10-piece set . . . . .(3,082,572) | 19.95 | 5.00 |
| 2000S, 5-piece quarter set . .(937,600) | 13.95 | 3.00 |
| 2000S, Silver 10-piece set . .(965,421) | 31.95 | 30.00 |
| 2001S, 10-piece set . . . . .(2,294,909) | 19.95 | 25.00 |
| 2001S, 5-piece quarter set . .(799,231) | 13.95 | 20.00 |
| 2001S, Silver 10-piece set . .(889,697) | 31.95 | 45.00 |
| 2002S, 10-piece set . . . . .(2,319,766) | 19.95 | 10.00 |
| 2002S, 5-piece quarter set . .(764,479) | 13.95 | 8.00 |
| 2002S, Silver 10-piece set . .(892,229) | 31.95 | 35.00 |
| 2003S, 10-piece set . . . . .(2,172,684) | 19.95 | 7.00 |
| 2003S, 5-piece quarter set (1,235,832) | 13.95 | 4.00 |
| 2003S, Silver 10-piece set (1,125,755) | 31.95 | 32.00 |

| Year | Mintage | Issue Price | Current Value |
|---|---|---|---|
| 2004S, 11-piece set . . . . .(1,789,488) | $22.95 | $10.00 |
| 2004S, 5-piece quarter set . .(951,196) | 15.95 | 5.00 |
| 2004S, Silver 11-piece set (1,175,934) | 37.95 | 32.00 |
| 2004S, Silver 5-piece | | |
| quarter set . . . . . . . . .(593,852) | 23.95 | 25.00 |
| 2005S, 11-piece set . . . . .(2,275,000) | 22.95 | 5.00 |
| 2005S, 5-piece quarter set . .(987,960) | 15.95 | 3.50 |
| 2005S, Silver 11-piece set (1,069,679) | 37.95 | 32.00 |
| 2005S, Silver 5-piece | | |
| quarter set . . . . . . . . .(608,970) | 23.95 | 25.00 |
| 2006S, 10-piece set . . . . .(2,000,428) | 22.95 | 11.00 |
| 2006S, 5-piece quarter set . .(882,000) | 15.95 | 6.50 |
| 2006S, Silver 10-piece set (1,054,008) | 37.95 | 32.00 |
| 2006S, Silver 5-piece | | |
| quarter set . . . . . . . . .(531,000) | 23.95 | 25.00 |
| 2007S, 14-piece set . . . . .(1,702,116) | 26.95 | 18.00 |
| 2007S, 5-piece quarter set . .(672,662) | 13.95 | 7.50 |
| 2007S, 4-piece | | |
| Presidential set . . . . .(1,285,972) | 14.95 | 9.00 |
| 2007S, Silver 14-piece set . .(875,050) | 44.95 | 35.00 |
| 2007S, Silver 5-piece | | |
| quarter set . . . . . . . . .(672,662) | 25.95 | 25.00 |
| 2008S, 14-piece set . . . . .(1,405,674) | 26.95 | 45.00 |
| 2008S, 5-piece quarter set . .(672,438) | 13.95 | 25.00 |
| 2008S, 4-piece | | |
| Presidential set . . . . . .(869,202) | 14.95 | 14.00 |
| 2008S, Silver 14-piece set . .(763,887) | 44.95 | 48.00 |
| 2008S, Silver 5-piece | | |
| quarter set . . . . . . . . .(429,021) | 25.95 | 25.00 |
| 2009S, 18-piece set . . . . .(1,296,853) | 29.95 | 25.00 |
| 2009S, 6-piece quarter set . .(630,976) | 14.95 | 20.00 |
| 2009S, 4-piece | | |
| Presidential set . . . . . .(627,925) | 14.95 | 6.00 |
| 2009S, Silver 18-piece set . .(694,406) | 52.95 | 50.00 |
| 2009S, Silver 6-piece | | |
| quarter set . . . . . . . . .(299,183) | 29.95 | 24.00 |
| 2009S, 4-piece Lincoln | | |
| Bicentennial set . . . . . . . . . . . . . | 7.95 | 6.00 |
| 2010S, 14-piece set . . . . . .(978,016) | 31.95 | 35.00 |
| 2010S, 5-piece quarter set .(244,950) | 14.95 | 16.00 |
| 2010S, 4-piece | | |
| Presidential set . . . . . .(477,077) | 15.95 | 17.00 |
| 2010S, Silver 14-piece set .(476,999) | 56.95 | 50.00 |
| 2010S, Silver 5-piece | | |
| quarter set . . . . . . . . .(216,404) | 32.95 | 24.00 |

* Included in number above.

**219**

## UNCIRCULATED MINT SETS

Official Mint Sets are specially packaged by the government for sale to collectors. They contain uncirculated specimens of each year's coins for every denomination issued from each mint. Sets from 1947 through 1958 contain two examples of each regular-issue coin. No official sets were produced in 1950, 1982, or 1983. Privately assembled sets are valued according to individual coin prices. Only official sets are included in the following list. Unlike the Proof sets, these are normal coins intended for circulation and are not minted with any special consideration for quality.

| Year | Mintage | Issue Price | Current Value |
|---|---|---|---|
| 1947 P-D-S | 5,000 | $4.87 | $850.00 |
| 1948 P-D-S | 6,000 | 4.92 | 425.00 |
| 1949 P-D-S | 5,000 | 5.45 | 575.00 |
| 1951 P-D-S | 8,654 | 6.75 | 550.00 |
| 1952 P-D-S | 11,499 | 6.14 | 490.00 |
| 1953 P-D-S | 15,538 | 6.14 | 325.00 |
| 1954 P-D-S | 25,599 | 6.19 | 140.00 |
| 1955 P-D-S | 49,656 | 3.57 | 95.00 |
| 1956 P-D | 45,475 | 3.34 | 90.00 |
| 1957 P-D | 34,324 | 4.40 | 155.00 |
| 1958 P-D | 50,314 | 4.43 | 85.00 |
| 1959 P-D | 187,000 | 2.40 | 38.00 |
| 1960 P-D | 260,485 | 2.40 | 38.00 |
| 1961 P-D | 223,704 | 2.40 | 34.00 |
| 1962 P-D | 385,285 | 2.40 | 34.00 |
| 1963 P-D | 606,612 | 2.40 | 34.00 |
| 1964 P-D | 1,008,108 | 2.40 | 34.00 |
| 1965* | 2,360,000 | 4.00 | 4.50 |
| 1966* | 2,261,583 | 4.00 | 4.50 |
| 1967* | 1,863,344 | 4.00 | 5.00 |
| 1968 P-D-S | 2,105,128 | 2.50 | 4.00 |
| 1969 P-D-S | 1,817,392 | 2.50 | 4.00 |
| 1970 P-D-S | 2,038,134 | 2.50 | 9.00 |
| 1971 P-D-S | 2,193,396 | 3.50 | 2.00 |
| 1972 P-D-S | 2,750,000 | 3.50 | 2.00 |
| 1973 P-D-S | 1,767,691 | 6.00 | 9.00 |
| 1974 P-D-S | 1,975,981 | 6.00 | 4.00 |
| 1975 P-D | 1,921,488 | 6.00 | 4.00 |
| 1776–1976, 3-piece set | 4,908,319 | 9.00 | 14.00 |
| 1976 P-D | 1,892,513 | 6.00 | 4.00 |
| 1977 P-D | 2,006,869 | 7.00 | 5.00 |
| 1978 P-D | 2,162,609 | 7.00 | 4.00 |

| Year | Mintage | Issue Price | Current Value |
|---|---|---|---|
| 1979 P-D | 2,526,000 | $8.00 | $3.75 |
| 1980 P-D-S | 2,815,066 | 9.00 | 4.85 |
| 1981 P-D-S | 2,908,145 | 11.00 | 8.00 |
| 1984 P-D | 1,832,857 | 7.00 | 2.50 |
| 1985 P-D | 1,710,571 | 7.00 | 3.00 |
| 1986 P-D | 1,153,536 | 7.00 | 7.00 |
| 1987 P-D | 2,890,758 | 7.00 | 3.50 |
| 1988 P-D | 1,646,204 | 7.00 | 3.50 |
| 1989 P-D | 1,987,915 | 7.00 | 2.50 |
| 1990 P-D | 1,809,184 | 7.00 | 3.00 |
| 1991 P-D | 1,352,101 | 7.00 | 4.00 |
| 1992 P-D | 1,500,143 | 7.00 | 3.50 |
| 1993 P-D | 1,297,431 | 8.00 | 4.25 |
| 1994 P-D | 1,234,813 | 8.00 | 3.00 |
| 1995 P-D | 1,038,787 | 8.00 | 5.00 |
| 1996 P-D, Plus | | | |
| 1996W dime | 1,457,949 | 8.00 | 12.00 |
| 1997 P-D | 950,473 | 8.00 | 8.00 |
| 1998 P-D | 1,187,325 | 8.00 | 4.00 |
| 1999 P-D (18 pieces) | 1,243,867 | 14.95 | 7.00 |
| 2000 P-D (20 pieces) | 1,490,160 | 14.95 | 7.00 |
| 2001 P-D (20 pieces) | 1,116,915 | 14.95 | 11.00 |
| 2002 P-D (20 pieces) | 1,139,388 | 14.95 | 13.00 |
| 2003 P-D (20 pieces) | 1,001,532 | 14.95 | 11.00 |
| 2004 P-D (22 pieces) | 842,507 | 16.95 | 17.00 |
| 2005 P-D (22 pieces) | 1,160,000 | 16.95 | 7.00 |
| 2006 P-D (20 pieces) | 847,361 | 16.95 | 9.00 |
| 2007 P-D (28 pieces) | 895,628 | 22.95 | 17.00 |
| 2008 P-D (28 pieces) | 735,683 | 22.95 | 37.00 |
| 2009 P-D (36 pieces) | 643,897 | 27.95 | 20.00 |
| 2010 P-D (28 pieces) | 527,742 | 31.95 | 20.00 |

*Note:* Sets issued from 2005 to 2010 have a special Satin Finish that is somewhat different from the finish on Uncirculated coins made for general circulation. * Special Mint Set.

# $1 SILVER EAGLES

Values below are based on spot silver value of $30 per ounce.

| | Mintage | Unc. | PF | | Mintage | Unc. | PF |
|---|---|---|---|---|---|---|---|
| $1 1986 | 5,393,005 | $30 | | $1 1999P | (549,769) | | $45 |
| $1 1986S | (1,446,778) | | $45 | $1 2000(W) | 9,239,132 | $30 | |
| $1 1987 | 11,442,335 | 30 | | $1 2000P | (600,000) | | 45 |
| $1 1987S | (904,732) | | 45 | $1 2001(W) | 9,001,711 | 30 | |
| $1 1988 | 5,004,646 | 30 | | $1 2001W | (746,398) | | 45 |
| $1 1988S | (557,370) | | 45 | $1 2002(W) | 10,539,026 | 30 | |
| $1 1989 | 5,203,327 | 30 | | $1 2002W | (647,342) | | 45 |
| $1 1989S | (617,694) | | 45 | $1 2003(W) | 8,495,008 | 30 | |
| $1 1990 | 5,840,210 | 30 | | $1 2003W | (747,831) | | 45 |
| $1 1990S | (695,510) | | 45 | $1 2004(W) | 8,882,754 | 30 | |
| $1 1991 | 7,191,066 | 30 | | $1 2004W | (801,602) | | 45 |
| $1 1991S | (511,925) | | 45 | $1 2005(W) | 8,891,025 | 30 | |
| $1 1992 | 5,540,068 | 30 | | $1 2005W | (816,663) | | 45 |
| $1 1992S | (498,654) | | 45 | $1 2006(W) | 10,676,522 | 30 | |
| $1 1993 | 6,763,762 | 30 | | $1 2006W, Burnished **(a)** | 468,020 | 60 | |
| $1 1993P | (405,913) | | 55 | $1 2006W | (1,092,477) | | 45 |
| $1 1994 | 4,227,319 | 30 | | $1 2006P, Reverse Proof | (248,875) | | 150 |
| $1 1994P | (372,168) | | 75 | $1 2007(W) | 9,028,036 | 30 | |
| $1 1995 | 4,672,051 | 32 | | $1 2007 W, Burnished **(a)** | 621,333 | 31 | |
| $1 1995P | (438,511) | | 65 | $1 2007W | (821,759) | | 45 |
| $1 1995W | (30,125) | | 2,200 | $1 2008(W) | 20,583,000 | 30 | |
| $1 1996 | 3,603,386 | 35 | | $1 2008W, Burnished **(a)** | 533,757 | 35 | |
| $1 1996P | (500,000) | | 55 | $1 2008W | (700,979) | | 45 |
| $1 1997 | 4,295,004 | 32 | | $1 2009(W) **(b)** | 30,459,000 | 30 | |
| $1 1997P | (435,368) | | 55 | $1 2010(W) | 29,110,500 | 30 | |
| $1 1998 | 4,847,549 | 30 | | $1 2010 | (273,312) | | 45 |
| $1 1998P | (450,000) | | 45 | $1 2011(W) | | 30 | |
| $1 1999 | 7,408,640 | 30 | | $1 2011 | | | 45 |

*Note:* Starting in 2010, the Mint is producing silver bullion coins in conjunction with the America the Beautiful™ quarter-dollar series. Designed to resemble their 25-cent counterparts, the bullion coins measure 3 inches in diameter and contain 5 ounces of .999-fine silver. The obverse is the same modified design as used for the U.S. Mint 50 State Quarters® Program; see page 114 for reverse designs. **a.** "Burnished" refers to special American Eagle Uncirculated coins in silver, gold, and platinum sold directly by the U.S. Mint. Similar in appearance to ordinary Uncirculated American Eagle bullion coins, these coins can be distinguished by the presence of a mintmark and the use of burnished coin blanks. (Proof coins also have a mintmark but have highly reflective, mirrorlike surfaces.) **b.** No Proof dollars were made in 2009. Beware of alterations made privately outside the Mint.

## AMERICAN EAGLE GOLD COINS

Bullion values are based on spot gold at $1,400 per ounce.

### $5 Tenth-Ounce Gold

| | Mintage | Unc. | PF | | Mintage | Unc. | PF |
|---|---|---|---|---|---|---|---|
| $5 MCMLXXXVI (1986) | .912,609 | $140 | | $5 1999W | .(48,428) | | $170 |
| $5 MCMLXXXVII (1987) | .580,266 | 140 | | $5 2000 | .569,153 | $140 | |
| $5 MCMLXXXVIII (1988) | .159,500 | 150 | | $5 2000W | .(49,971) | | 170 |
| $5 MCMLXXXVIII (1988)P | .(143,881) | | $170 | $5 2001 | .269,147 | 140 | |
| $5 MCMLXXXIX (1989) | .264,790 | 140 | | $5 2001W | .(37,530) | | 170 |
| $5 MCMLXXXIX (1989)P | .(84,647) | | 170 | $5 2002 | .230,027 | 140 | |
| $5 MCMXC (1990) | .210,210 | 140 | | $5 2002W | .(40,864) | | 170 |
| $5 MCMXC (1990)P | .(99,349) | | 170 | $5 2003 | .245,029 | 140 | |
| $5 MCMXCI (1991) | .165,200 | 140 | | $5 2003W | .(40,027) | | 170 |
| $5 MCMXCI (1991)P | .(70,334) | | 170 | $5 2004 | .250,016 | 140 | |
| $5 1992 | .209,300 | 140 | | $5 2004W | .(35,131) | | 170 |
| $5 1992P | .(64,874) | | 170 | $5 2005 | .300,043 | 140 | |
| $5 1993 | .210,709 | 140 | | $5 2005W | .(49,265) | | 170 |
| $5 1993P | .(58,649) | | 170 | $5 2006 | .285,006 | 140 | |
| $5 1994 | .206,380 | 140 | | $5 2006W, Burnished | .20,643 | 150 | |
| $5 1994W | .(62,849) | | 170 | $5 2006W | .(47,277) | | 170 |
| $5 1995 | .223,025 | 140 | | $5 2007 | .190,010 | 140 | |
| $5 1995W | .(62,667) | | 170 | $5 2007W, Burnished | .22,501 | 150 | |
| $5 1996 | .401,964 | 140 | | $5 2007W | .(58,553) | | 170 |
| $5 1996W | .(57,047) | | 170 | $5 2008 | .305,000 | 140 | |
| $5 1997 | .528,266 | 140 | | $5 2008W, Burnished | .12,657 | 150 | |
| $5 1997W | .(34,977) | | 170 | $5 2008W | .(28,116) | | 170 |
| $5 1998 | .1,344,520 | 140 | | $5 2009 | .270,000 | 140 | |
| $5 1998W | .(39,395) | | 170 | $5 2010 | .380,000 | 140 | |
| $5 1999 | .2,750,338 | 140 | | $5 2010W | .(10,411) | | 170 |

### $10 Quarter-Ounce Gold

| | Mintage | Unc. | PF | | Mintage | Unc. | PF |
|---|---|---|---|---|---|---|---|
| $10 MCMLXXXVI (1986) | .726,031 | $350 | | $10 MCMXCI (1991)P | .(50,839) | | $375 |
| $10 MCMLXXXVII (1987) | .269,255 | 350 | | $10 1992 | .59,546 | $350 | |
| $10 MCMLXXXVIII (1988) | .49,000 | 350 | | $10 1992P | .(46,269) | | 375 |
| $10 MCMLXXXVIII (1988)P | .(98,028) | | $375 | $10 1993 | .71,864 | 350 | |
| $10 MCMLXXXIX (1989) | .81,789 | 350 | | $10 1993P | .(46,464) | | 375 |
| $10 MCMLXXXIX (1989)P | .(54,170) | | 375 | $10 1994 | .72,650 | 350 | |
| $10 MCMXC (1990) | .41,000 | 350 | | $10 1994W | .(48,172) | | 375 |
| $10 MCMXC (1990)P | .(62,674) | | 375 | $10 1995 | .83,752 | 350 | |
| $10 MCMXCI (1991) | .36,100 | 360 | | $10 1995W | .(47,526) | | 375 |

| | Mintage | Unc. | PF |
|---|---|---|---|
| $10 1996 | 60,318 | $350 | |
| $10 1996W | (38,219) | | $375 |
| $10 1997 | 108,805 | 350 | |
| $10 1997W | (29,805) | | 375 |
| $10 1998 | 309,829 | 350 | |
| $10 1998W | (29,503) | | 375 |
| $10 1999 | 564,232 | 350 | |
| $10 1999W | (34,417) | | 375 |
| $10 2000 | 128,964 | 350 | |
| $10 2000W | (36,036) | | 375 |
| $10 2001 | 71,280 | 350 | |
| $10 2001W | (25,613) | | 375 |
| $10 2002 | 62,027 | 350 | |
| $10 2002W | (29,242) | | 375 |
| $10 2003 | 74,029 | 350 | |
| $10 2003W | (30,292) | | 375 |

| | Mintage | Unc. | PF |
|---|---|---|---|
| $10 2004 | 72,014 | $350 | |
| $10 2004W | (28,839) | | $375 |
| $10 2005 | 72,015 | 350 | |
| $10 2005W | (37,207) | | 375 |
| $10 2006 | 60,004 | 350 | |
| $10 2006W, Burnished | 15,188 | 550 | |
| $10 2006W | (36,127) | | 375 |
| $10 2007 | 34,004 | 350 | |
| $10 2007W, Burnished | 12,766 | 550 | |
| $10 2007W | (46,189) | | 375 |
| $10 2008 | 70,000 | 350 | |
| $10 2008W, Burnished | 8,883 | 650 | |
| $10 2008W | (18,877) | | 375 |
| $10 2009 | 110,000 | 350 | |
| $10 2010 | 58,000 | 350 | |
| $10 2010W | (4,413) | | 375 |

## $25 Half-Ounce Gold

| | Mintage | Unc. | PF |
|---|---|---|---|
| $25 MCMLXXXVI (1986) | 599,566 | $700 | |
| $25 MCMLXXXVII (1987) | 131,255 | 700 | |
| $25 MCMLXXXVII (1987)P | (143,398) | | $825 |
| $25 MCMLXXXVIII (1988) | 45,000 | 700 | |
| $25 MCMLXXXVIII (1988)P | (76,528) | | 825 |
| $25 MCMLXXXIX (1989) | 44,829 | 700 | |
| $25 MCMLXXXIX (1989)P | (44,798) | | 825 |
| $25 MCMXC (1990) | 31,000 | 700 | |
| $25 MCMXC (1990)P | (51,636) | | 825 |
| $25 MCMXCI (1991) | 24,100 | 1,200 | |
| $25 MCMXCI (1991)P | (53,125) | | 825 |
| $25 1992 | 54,404 | 750 | |
| $25 1992P | (40,976) | | 825 |
| $25 1993 | 73,324 | 700 | |
| $25 1993P | (43,819) | | 825 |
| $25 1994 | 62,400 | 700 | |
| $25 1994W | (44,584) | | 825 |
| $25 1995 | 53,474 | 700 | |
| $25 1995W | (45,388) | | 825 |
| $25 1996 | 39,287 | 700 | |
| $25 1996W | (35,058) | | 825 |
| $25 1997 | 79,605 | 700 | |
| $25 1997W | (26,344) | | 825 |
| $25 1998 | 169,029 | 700 | |
| $25 1998W | (25,374) | | 825 |
| $25 1999 | 263,013 | 700 | |

| | Mintage | Unc. | PF |
|---|---|---|---|
| $25 1999W | (30,427) | | $825 |
| $25 2000 | 79,287 | $700 | |
| $25 2000W | (32,028) | | 825 |
| $25 2001 | 48,047 | 700 | |
| $25 2001W | (23,240) | | 825 |
| $25 2002 | 70,027 | 700 | |
| $25 2002W | (26,646) | | 825 |
| $25 2003 | 79,029 | 700 | |
| $25 2003W | (28,270) | | 825 |
| $25 2004 | 98,040 | 700 | |
| $25 2004W | (27,330) | | 825 |
| $25 2005 | 80,023 | 700 | |
| $25 2005W | (34,311) | | 825 |
| $25 2006 | 66,005 | 700 | |
| $25 2006W, Burnished | 15,164 | 800 | |
| $25 2006W | (34,322) | | 825 |
| $25 2007 | 47,002 | 700 | |
| $25 2007W, Burnished | 11,455 | 800 | |
| $25 2007W | (44,025) | | 825 |
| $25 2008 | 61,000 | 700 | |
| $25 2008W, Burnished | 15,682 | 800 | |
| $25 2008W | (22,602) | | 825 |
| $25 2009 | 110,000 | 700 | |
| $25 2010 | 40,000 | 700 | |
| $25 2010W | (4,002) | | 825 |

## $50 One-Ounce Gold

| | Mintage | Unc. | PF |
|---|---|---|---|
| $50 MCMLXXXVI (1986) | 1,362,650 | $1,400 | |
| $50 MCMLXXXVI (1986)W | (446,290) | | $1,600 |
| $50 MCMLXXXVII (1987) | 1,045,500 | 1,400 | |

| | Mintage | Unc. | PF |
|---|---|---|---|
| $50 MCMLXXXVII (1987)W | (147,498) | | $1,600 |
| $50 MCMLXXXVIII (1988) | 465,000 | $1,400 | |
| $50 MCMLXXXVIII (1988)W | (87,133) | | 1,600 |

*Chart continued on next page.*

| | Mintage | Unc. | PF |
|---|---|---|---|
| $50 MCMLXXXIX (1989) | .415,790 | $1,400 | |
| $50 MCMLXXXIX (1989)W | .(54,570) | | $1,600 |
| $50 MCMXC (1990) | .373,210 | 1,400 | |
| $50 MCMXC (1990)W | .(62,401) | | 1,600 |
| $50 MCMXCI (1991) | .243,100 | 1,400 | |
| $50 MCMXCI (1991)W | .(50,411) | | 1,600 |
| $50 1992 | .275,000 | 1,400 | |
| $50 1992W | .(44,826) | | 1,600 |
| $50 1993 | .480,192 | 1,400 | |
| $50 1993W | .(34,369) | | 1,600 |
| $50 1994 | .221,633 | 1,400 | |
| $50 1994W | .(46,674) | | 1,600 |
| $50 1995 | .200,636 | 1,400 | |
| $50 1995W | .(46,368) | | 1,600 |
| $50 1996 | .189,148 | 1,400 | |
| $50 1996W | .(36,153) | | 1,600 |
| $50 1997 | .664,508 | 1,400 | |
| $50 1997W | .(32,999) | | 1,600 |
| $50 1998 | .1,468,530 | 1,400 | |
| $50 1998W | .(25,886) | | 1,600 |
| $50 1999 | .1,505,026 | 1,400 | |
| $50 1999W | .(31,427) | | 1,600 |
| $50 2000 | .433,319 | 1,400 | |
| $50 2000W | .(33,007) | | 1,600 |

| | Mintage | Unc. | PF |
|---|---|---|---|
| $50 2001 | .143,605 | $1,400 | |
| $50 2001W | .(24,555) | | $1,600 |
| $50 2002 | .222,029 | 1,400 | |
| $50 2002W | .(27,499) | | 1,600 |
| $50 2003 | .416,032 | 1,400 | |
| $50 2003W | .(28,344) | | 1,600 |
| $50 2004 | .417,019 | 1,400 | |
| $50 2004W | .(28,215) | | 1,600 |
| $50 2005 | .356,555 | 1,400 | |
| $50 2005W | .(35,246) | | 1,600 |
| $50 2006 | .237,510 | 1,400 | |
| $50 2006W, Burnished | .45,053 | 1,500 | |
| $50 2006W | .(47,092) | | 1,600 |
| $50 2006W, Reverse Proof | .(9,996) | | 2,000 |
| $50 2007 | .140,016 | 1,400 | |
| $50 2007W, Burnished | .18,066 | 1,500 | |
| $50 2007W | .(51,810) | | 1,600 |
| $50 2008 | .710,000 | 1,400 | |
| $50 2008W, Burnished | .11,908 | 1,500 | |
| $50 2008W | .(30,237) | | 1,600 |
| $50 2009 | .1,493,000 | 1,400 | |
| $50 2010 | .988,500 | 1,400 | |
| $50 2010W | .(25,000) | | 1,600 |

## Gold Bullion Sets

| | PF |
|---|---|
| 1987 Gold Set. $50, $25 | $2,425 |
| 1988 Gold Set. $50, $25, $10, $5 | 2,970 |
| 1989 Gold Set. $50, $25, $10, $5 | 2,970 |
| 1990 Gold Set. $50, $25, $10, $5 | 2,970 |
| 1991 Gold Set. $50, $25, $10, $5 | 2,970 |
| 1992 Gold Set. $50, $25, $10, $5 | 2,970 |
| 1993 Gold Set. $50, $25, $10, $5 | 2,970 |
| 1993 Bicentennial Gold Set. $25, $10, $5, $1 silver eagle, and medal | 1,425 |
| 1994 Gold Set. $50, $25, $10, $5 | 2,970 |
| 1995 Gold Set. $50, $25, $10, $5 | 2,970 |
| 1995 Anniversary Gold Set. $50, $25, $10, $5, and $1 silver eagle | 5,175 |
| 1996 Gold Set. $50, $25, $10, $5 | 2,970 |
| 1997 Gold Set. $50, $25, $10, $5 | 2,970 |

| | PF |
|---|---|
| 1997 Impressions of Liberty Set. $100 platinum, $50 gold, $1 silver | $3,385 |
| 1998 Gold Set. $50, $25, $10, $5 | 2,970 |
| 1999 Gold Set. $50, $25, $10, $5 | 2,970 |
| 2000 Gold Set. $50, $25, $10, $5 | 2,970 |
| 2001 Gold Set. $50, $25, $10, $5 | 2,970 |
| 2002 Gold Set. $50, $25, $10, $5 | 2,970 |
| 2003 Gold Set. $50, $25, $10, $5 | 2,970 |
| 2004 Gold Set. $50, $25, $10, $5 | 2,970 |
| 2005 Gold Set. $50, $25, $10, $5 | 2,970 |
| 2006 Gold Set. $50, $25, $10, $5 | 2,970 |
| 2007 Gold Set. $50, $25, $10, $5 | 2,970 |
| 2008 Gold Set. $50, $25, $10, $5 | 2,970 |
| 2010 Gold Set. $50, $25, $10, $5 | 2,970 |

a. The U.S. Mint did not issue a 2009 gold set.

## 2006 20th Anniversary Sets

| | |
|---|---|
| 2006W $50 Gold Set. Uncirculated, Proof, Reverse Proof | $5,000 |
| 2006 Silver Dollars. Uncirculated, Proof, Reverse Proof | 225 |

| | |
|---|---|
| 2006W 1-oz. Gold- and Silver-Dollar Set. Uncirculated | $1,530 |

## Gold Bullion Burnished Sets 2006–2008

| | Unc. |
|---|---|
| 2006W Burnished Gold Set. $50, $25, $10, $5 . . . . . . . . . . . . . . . . . . . . . . . . . . . . . . . . . . . . . . . . . . . . . . . . . . . | $3,000 |
| 2007W Burnished Gold Set. $50, $25, $10, $5 . . . . . . . . . . . . . . . . . . . . . . . . . . . . . . . . . . . . . . . . . . . . . . . . . . . | 3,000 |
| 2008W Burnished Gold Set. $50, $25, $10, $5 . . . . . . . . . . . . . . . . . . . . . . . . . . . . . . . . . . . . . . . . . . . . . . . . . . . | 3,100 |

# AMERICAN BUFFALO .9999 FINE GOLD BULLION COINS

| | Mintage | Unc. | PF |
|---|---|---|---|
| $5 2008W, Burnished . . . . . . | 17,429 | $375 | |
| $5 2008W . . . . . . . . . . . . | (18,884) | | $400 |
| $10 2008W, Burnished . . . . . . | 9,949 | 750 | |
| $10 2008W . . . . . . . . . . . . | (13,125) | | 800 |
| $25 2008W, Burnished . . . . . | 16,908 | 1,200 | |
| $25 2008W . . . . . . . . . . . . | (12,169) | | 1,300 |
| $50 2006 . . . . . . . . . . . . | 337,012 | 1,400 | |
| $50 2006W . . . . . . . . . . . . | (246,267) | | 1,500 |
| $50 2007 . . . . . . . . . . . . | 136,503 | 1,400 | |
| $50 2007W . . . . . . . . . . . . | (58,998) | | 1,500 |
| $50 2008 . . . . . . . . . . . . | 189,500 | 1,400 | |

| | Mintage | Unc. | PF |
|---|---|---|---|
| $50 2008W . . . . . . . . . . . . | (18,863) | | $2,600 |
| $50 2008W, Burnished . . . . . . | 9,074 | $2,200 | |
| $50 2009 . . . . . . . . . . . . | 200,000 | 1,400 | |
| $50 2009W . . . . . . . . . . . . | (49,388) | | 1,500 |
| $50 2010 . . . . . . . . . . . . | 209,000 | 1,400 | |
| $50 2010W . . . . . . . . . . . . | (38,895) | | 1,500 |
| | | | |
| 2008W Four-coin set . . . . . . . . . . . . | | 5,000 | 6,000 |
| 2008W Double Prosperity set. Uncirculated $25 Buffalo gold and $25 American Eagle coins | | 2,700 | |

# FIRST SPOUSE $10 GOLD BULLION COINS
## Half-Ounce 24-Karat Gold

**Martha Washington**     **Abigail Adams**     **Jefferson's Liberty**     **Dolley Madison**

*See next page for chart.*

| | Mintage | Unc. | PF |
|---|---|---|---|
| $10 2007W, Martha Washington | (19,169) ....17,661 | $750 | $800 |
| $10 2007W, Abigail Adams | (17,149) ....17,142 | 750 | 800 |
| $10 2007W, Thomas Jefferson's Liberty | (19,815) ....19,823 | 750 | 800 |
| $10 2007W, Dolley Madison | (17,661) ....11,813 | 750 | 800 |

**Elizabeth Monroe**    **Louisa Adams**    **Jackson's Liberty**    **Van Buren's Liberty**

| | Mintage | Unc. | PF |
|---|---|---|---|
| $10 2008W, Elizabeth Monroe | (7,933) ....4,519 | $750 | $800 |
| $10 2008W, Louisa Adams | (7,454) ....4,223 | 750 | 800 |
| $10 2008W, Andrew Jackson's Liberty | (7,454) ....4,281 | 750 | 800 |
| $10 2008W, Martin Van Buren's Liberty | (6,187) ....3,443 | 750 | 800 |

**Anna Harrison**

**Letitia Tyler**

**Julia Tyler**

**Sarah Polk**

**Margaret Taylor**

| | Mintage | Unc. | PF |
|---|---|---|---|
| $10 2009W, Anna Harrison | (5,801) ......2,993 | $750 | $775 |
| $10 2009W, Letitia Tyler | (4,341) ......2,381 | 750 | 775 |
| $10 2009W, Julia Tyler | (3,878) ......2,188 | 750 | 775 |
| $10 2009W, Sarah Polk | (3,512) ......1,893 | 750 | 775 |
| $10 2009W, Margaret Taylor | | 750 | 775 |

**Abigail Fillmore**   **Jane Pierce**   **Buchanan's Liberty**   **Mary Lincoln**

| | Mintage | Unc. | PF |
|---|---|---|---|
| $10 2010W, Abigail Fillmore | | $750 | $775 |
| $10 2010W, Jane Pierce | | 750 | 775 |
| $10 2010W, James Buchanan's Liberty | | 750 | 775 |
| $10 2010W, Mary Lincoln | | 750 | 775 |

**Eliza Johnson**   **Julia Grant**   **Lucy Hayes**   **Lucretia Garfield**

*U.S. Mint artist renderings.*

| | Mintage | Unc. | PF |
|---|---|---|---|
| $10 2011W, Eliza Johnson | | $750 | $775 |
| $10 2011W, Julia Grant | | 750 | 775 |
| $10 2011W, Lucy Hayes | | 750 | 775 |
| $10 2011W, Lucretia Garfield | | 750 | 775 |

## MMIX ULTRA HIGH RELIEF GOLD COIN

A modern version of the famous United States 1907 Ultra High Relief double eagle gold pattern was produced in 2009 at the Philadelphia Mint. It was made as a tour de force to demonstrate how technical advances in minting techniques can now accommodate manufacturing such a coin. The original design was never made for commercial use because it was at that time impossible to make it in sufficient quantities.

The design used on these coins was the artistry of Augustus Saint-Gaudens. A version of it in much lower relief was used on double eagle coins minted from 1907 to 1933. In recreating the artist's attempt to mint a stunning coin in ultra high relief, the 2009 version was made in a slightly smaller diameter, and composed of 24-karat gold, thus making it easier to strike and maintain the fidelity of the design. Through 21st-century technology the original Saint-Gaudens plasters were digitally mapped by the Mint and used in the die-making process. The date was changed to 2009, and four additional stars were added to represent the current 50 states. The inscription "In God We Trust" was not used on the 1907 version.

The MMIX Ultra High Relief gold coins are 4 mm thick and contain one ounce of .999 fine gold. All are Uncirculated (business strikes). All are made at the West Point Mint, and packaged by the Mint in a special mahogany box.

**MMIX Ultra High Relief Gold Coin**
*Photographed at an angle to show the edge, lettered E PLURIBUS UNUM, and the depth of relief.*

|  | Mintage | Unc. |
|---|---|---|
| MMIX Ultra High Relief $20 Gold Coin | 115,178 | $1,500 |

## AMERICAN EAGLE PLATINUM COINS

The one-ounce American Eagle platinum coin is designated $100 and contains one ounce of pure platinum. Fractional denominations containing 1/2 ounce, 1/4 ounce, or 1/10 ounce are called $50, $25, and $10, respectively.

Bullion values are based on spot platinum at $1,800 per ounce.

**Obverse for
Bullion and
Proof, All Years**

**Reverse for
Bullion, All Years;
for Proof in 1997**

### *Vistas of Liberty Reverse Designs*

**1998, Eagle Over
New England**

**1999, Eagle Above
Southeastern Wetlands**

**2000, Eagle Above
America's Heartland**

**2001,
Eagle Above
America's
Southwest**

**2002,
Eagle Fishing
in America's
Northwest**

## $10 Tenth-Ounce Platinum

| | Mintage | Unc. | PF | | Mintage | Unc. | PF |
|---|---|---|---|---|---|---|---|
| $10 1997 | 70,250 | $180 | | $10 2001W | (12,174) | | $200 |
| $10 1997W | (36,993) | | $200 | $10 2002 | 23,005 | $180 | |
| $10 1998 | 39,525 | 180 | | $10 2002W | (12,365) | | 200 |
| $10 1998W | (19,847) | | 200 | $10 2003 | 22,007 | 180 | |
| $10 1999 | 55,955 | 180 | | $10 2003W | (9,534) | | 200 |
| $10 1999W | (19,133) | | 200 | $10 2004 | 15,010 | 180 | |
| $10 2000 | 34,027 | 180 | | $10 2004W | (7,161) | | 350 |
| $10 2000W | (15,651) | | 200 | $10 2005 | 14,013 | 180 | |
| $10 2001 | 52,017 | 180 | | $10 2005W | (8,104) | | 200 |

*Chart continued on next page.*

| | Mintage | Unc. | PF |
|---|---|---|---|
| $10 2006 | 11,001 | $180 | |
| $10 2006W, Burnished | 3,544 | 225 | |
| $10 2006W | (10,205) | | $200 |
| $10 2007 | 13,003 | 180 | |
| $10 2007W, Burnished | 5,556 | 200 | |

| | Mintage | Unc. | PF |
|---|---|---|---|
| $10 2007W | (8,176) | | $200 |
| $10 2008 | 17,000 | $180 | |
| $10 2008W, Burnished | 3,706 | 190 | |
| $10 2008W | (5,138) | | 225 |

## $25 Quarter-Ounce Platinum

| | Mintage | Unc. | PF |
|---|---|---|---|
| $25 1997 | 27,100 | $450 | |
| $25 1997W | (18,628) | | $500 |
| $25 1998 | 38,887 | 450 | |
| $25 1998W | (14,873) | | 500 |
| $25 1999 | 39,734 | 450 | |
| $25 1999W | (13,507) | | 500 |
| $25 2000 | 20,054 | 450 | |
| $25 2000W | (11,995) | | 500 |
| $25 2001 | 21,815 | 450 | |
| $25 2001W | (8,847) | | 500 |
| $25 2002 | 27,405 | 450 | |
| $25 2002W | (9,282) | | 500 |
| $25 2003 | 25,207 | 450 | |
| $25 2003W | (7,044) | | 500 |

| | Mintage | Unc. | PF |
|---|---|---|---|
| $25 2004 | 18,010 | $450 | |
| $25 2004W | (5,193) | | $850 |
| $25 2005 | 12,013 | 450 | |
| $25 2005W | (6,592) | | 525 |
| $25 2006 | 12,001 | 450 | |
| $25 2006W, Burnished | 2,676 | 500 | |
| $25 2006W | (7,813) | | 500 |
| $25 2007 | 8,402 | 450 | |
| $25 2007W, Burnished | 3,690 | 500 | |
| $25 2007W | (6,017) | | 500 |
| $25 2008 | 22,800 | 450 | |
| $25 2008W, Burnished | 2,481 | 500 | |
| $25 2008W | (4,153) | | 600 |

## $50 Half-Ounce Platinum

| | Mintage | Unc. | PF |
|---|---|---|---|
| $50 1997 | 20,500 | $900 | |
| $50 1997W | (15,431) | | $1,000 |
| $50 1998 | 32,415 | 900 | |
| $50 1998W | (13,836) | | 1,000 |
| $50 1999 | 32,309 | 900 | |
| $50 1999W | (11,103) | | 1,000 |
| $50 2000 | 18,892 | 900 | |
| $50 2000W | (11,049) | | 1,000 |
| $50 2001 | 12,815 | 900 | |
| $50 2001W | (8,254) | | 1,000 |
| $50 2002 | 24,005 | 900 | |
| $50 2002W | (8,772) | | 1,000 |
| $50 2003 | 17,409 | 900 | |
| $50 2003W | (7,131) | | 1,000 |

| | Mintage | Unc. | PF |
|---|---|---|---|
| $50 2004 | 13,236 | $900 | |
| $50 2004W | (5,063) | | $1,400 |
| $50 2005 | 9,013 | 900 | |
| $50 2005W | (5,942) | | 1,000 |
| $50 2006 | 9,602 | 900 | |
| $50 2006W, Burnished | 2,577 | 900 | |
| $50 2006W | (7,649) | | 1,000 |
| $50 2007 | 7,001 | 900 | |
| $50 2007W, Burnished | 3,635 | 900 | |
| $50 2007W | (25,519) | | 1,000 |
| $50 2008 | 14,000 | 900 | |
| $50 2008W, Burnished | 2,253 | 900 | |
| $50 2008W | (4,020) | | 1,000 |

## $100 One-Ounce Platinum

| | Mintage | Unc. | PF | | Mintage | Unc. | PF |
|---|---|---|---|---|---|---|---|
| $100 1997 | 56,000 | $1,800 | | $100 2004W | (6,007) | | $1,900 |
| $100 1997W | (20,851) | | $1,900 | $100 2005 | 6,310 | $1,800 | |
| $100 1998 | 133,002 | 1,800 | | $100 2005W | (6,602) | | 1,900 |
| $100 1998W | (14,912) | | 1,900 | $100 2006 | 6,000 | 1,800 | |
| $100 1999 | 56,707 | 1,800 | | $100 2006W, Burnished | 3,068 | 1,800 | |
| $100 1999W | (12,363) | | 1,900 | $100 2006W | (9,152) | | 1,900 |
| $100 2000 | 10,003 | 1,800 | | $100 2007 | 7,202 | 1,800 | |
| $100 2000W | (12,453) | | 1,900 | $100 2007W, Burnished | 4,177 | 1,800 | |
| $100 2001 | 14,070 | 1,800 | | $100 2007W | (8,363) | | 1,900 |
| $100 2001W | (8,969) | | 1,900 | $100 2008 | 21,800 | 1,800 | |
| $100 2002 | 11,502 | 1,800 | | $100 2008W, Burnished | 2,876 | 1,800 | |
| $100 2002W | (9,834) | | 1,900 | $100 2008W | (4,769) | | 2,000 |
| $100 2003 | 8,007 | 1,800 | | $100 2009W | (8,000) | | 2,000 |
| $100 2003W | (8,246) | | 1,900 | $100 2010W | | | 1,900 |
| $100 2004 | 7,009 | 1,800 | | | | | |

## Platinum Bullion Sets

| | |
|---|---|
| 1997 Platinum Set. $100, $50, $25, $10 | $3,350 |
| 1998 Platinum Set. $100, $50, $25, $10 | 3,350 |
| 1999 Platinum Set. $100, $50, $25, $10 | 3,350 |
| 2000 Platinum Set. $100, $50, $25, $10 | 3,350 |
| 2001 Platinum Set. $100, $50, $25, $10 | 3,350 |
| 2002 Platinum Set. $100, $50, $25, $10 | 3,350 |
| 2003 Platinum Set. $100, $50, $25, $10 | 3,350 |
| 2004W Platinum Set. $100, $50, $25, $10 | 3,350 |
| 2005W Platinum Set. $100, $50, $25, $10 | 4,500 |
| 2006W Platinum Set. $100, $50, $25, $10 | 3,600 |
| 2007W Platinum Set. $100, $50, $25, $10 | 3,600 |
| 2008W Platinum Burnished Set. $100, $50, $25, $10 | 3,400 |

Prices are for original Uncirculated or Proof pieces with box and papers.

Private coins were circulated in most instances because of a shortage of regular coinage. Some numismatists use the general term *private gold* to refer to coins struck outside of the United States Mint. In the sense that no state or territory had authority to coin money, *private gold* simply refers to those interesting necessity pieces of various shapes, denominations, and degrees of intrinsic worth which were circulated in isolated areas of our country by individuals, assayers, bankers, etc. Some numismatists use the words *territorial* and *state* to cover certain issues because they were coined and circulated in a territory or state. While the state of California properly sanctioned the ingots stamped by F.D. Kohler as state assayer, in no instance were any of the gold pieces struck by authority of any of the territorial governments.

The stamped ingots put out by Augustus Humbert, the United States assayer of gold, were not recognized at the United States Mint as an official issue of coins, but simply as ingots, though Humbert placed the value and fineness on the pieces as an official agent of the federal government.

## TEMPLETON REID
### Georgia Gold 1830

The first private gold coinage in the 19th century was struck by Templeton Reid, a jeweler and gunsmith, in Milledgeville, Georgia, in July 1830. To be closer to the mines, he moved to Gainesville, where most of his coins were made. Although weights were accurate, Reid's assays were not, and his coins were slightly short of claimed value. Accordingly, he was severely attacked in the newspapers and soon lost the public's confidence. His mint closed before the end of that October.

|  | VG | VF |
|---|---|---|
| 1830, $2.50 | $30,000 | $50,000 |
| 1830, $5 | 75,000 | 125,000 |
| 1830, TEN DOLLARS | 135,000 | 225,000 |
| (No Date) TEN DOLLARS | 120,000 | 180,000 |

## California Gold 1849

1849 TEN DOLLAR CALIFORNIA GOLD *(unique, in Smithsonian collection)* ..........................

## THE BECHTLERS
## RUTHERFORD COUNTY, NC, 1831–1852

Two skilled German metallurgists, Christopher Bechtler and his son August, and later Christopher Bechtler, Junior, a nephew of Christopher the elder, operated a private mint at Rutherfordton, North Carolina. Rutherford County, in which Rutherfordton is located, was a principal source of the nation's gold supply from 1790 to 1848.

### Christopher Bechtler

| | VF | EF | AU | Unc. |
|---|---|---|---|---|
| ONE DOLLAR CAROLINA, 28.G, N Reversed | $1,000 | $1,800 | $2,500 | $5,000 |
| ONE GOLD DOLLAR N. CAROLINA, 28.G, No Star | 2,200 | 3,250 | 4,500 | 9,000 |
| ONE GOLD DOLLAR N. CAROLINA, 30.G. | 1,350 | 2,000 | 3,000 | 7,500 |
| 2.50 CAROLINA, 67.G., 21 CARATS | 3,000 | 5,000 | 6,000 | 11,000 |
| 2.50 CAROLINA, 70.G, 20 CARATS | 3,200 | 5,500 | 6,500 | 13,000 |
| 2.50 GEORGIA, 64.G, 22 CARATS | 3,500 | 6,000 | 6,750 | 15,000 |
| 2.50 NORTH CAROLINA, 75.G., 20 C., RUTHERFORD in a Circle. Border of Large Beads | 9,000 | 12,000 | 19,000 | 30,000 |
| 2.50 NORTH CAROLINA, 20 C. Without 75.G. | 9,000 | 13,000 | 20,000 | 35,000 |

Without 150.G.

| | VF | EF | AU | Unc. |
|---|---|---|---|---|
| 5 DOLLARS NORTH CAROLINA GOLD, 150.G., 20.CARATS | $9,000 | $13,000 | $20,000 | $35,000 |
| Similar, Without 150.G. | | — | — | |
| 5 DOLLARS CAROLINA, RUTHERFORD, 140.G., 20 CARATS | | | | |
|   Plain Edge | 3,250 | 5,000 | 6,500 | 11,000 |
|   Reeded Edge | 8,000 | 14,000 | 19,000 | 29,000 |
| 5 DOLLARS CAROLINA GOLD, RUTHERF., 140.G., 20 CARATS, | | | | |
|   AUGUST 1, 1834 | 4,000 | 6,000 | 10,000 | 20,000 |
| Similar, but "20" Distant From CARATS | 3,250 | 5,500 | 6,500 | 13,000 |
| 5 DOLLARS CAROLINA GOLD, 134.G., 21 CARATS, With Star | 3,000 | 4,000 | 5,000 | 8,500 |
| 5 DOLLARS GEORGIA GOLD, RUTHERFORD, 128.G., 22 CARATS | 3,250 | 4,500 | 7,000 | 13,000 |
| 5 DOLLARS GEORGIA GOLD, RUTHERF, 128.G., 22 CARATS | 3,250 | 4,500 | 7,000 | 13,000 |

## August Bechtler

| | VF | EF | AU | Unc. |
|---|---|---|---|---|
| 1 DOL:, CAROLINA GOLD, 27.G., 21.C. | $800 | $1,200 | $1,600 | $2,500 |
| 5 DOLLARS, CAROLINA GOLD, 134.G:, 21 CARATS | 2,700 | 4,000 | 5,750 | 16,000 |

| | VF | EF | AU | Unc. |
|---|---|---|---|---|
| 5 DOLLARS, CAROLINA GOLD, 128.G., 22 CARATS .................. | $6,000 | $8,000 | $12,000 | $18,000 |
| 5 DOLLARS, CAROLINA GOLD, 141.G., 20 CARATS .................. | 5,100 | 7,500 | 11,500 | 19,000 |

## NORRIS, GREGG & NORRIS
## SAN FRANCISCO 1849

Numismatists consider these pieces the first of the California private gold coins. A newspaper account dated May 31, 1849, described a five-dollar gold coin struck at Benicia City, though with the imprint San Francisco, and the private stamp of Norris, Gregg & Norris.

| | F | VF | EF | AU | Unc. |
|---|---|---|---|---|---|
| 1849 Half Eagle, Plain Edge ......................... | $2,500 | $3,500 | $5,500 | $8,000 | $16,500 |
| 1849 Half Eagle, Reeded Edge ....................... | 2,500 | 3,500 | 5,500 | 8,000 | 16,500 |
| 1850 Half Eagle, With STOCKTON Beneath Date *(unique, in Smithsonian collection)* | | | | | |

## MOFFAT & CO.
## SAN FRANCISCO 1849–1853

The firm of Moffat & Co. was perhaps the most important of the California private coiners. The assay office they conducted was semi-official in character, and successors to this firm later sold its facilities to the Treasury Department, which used them to create the San Francisco Mint.

In June or July, 1849, Moffat & Co. began to issue small rectangular pieces of gold in values from $9.43 to $264. The $9.43, $14.25, and $16.00 varieties are the only types known today.

| | EF |
|---|---|
| $9.43 Ingot *(unique, in Smithsonian collection)* ............................................... | — |
| $14.25 Ingot *(unique, in Smithsonian collection)* ............................................. | — |
| $16.00 Ingot ............................................................................. | $60,000 |

The dies for the ten-dollar piece were cut by Albert Kuner. The words MOFFAT & CO. appear on Liberty's coronet instead of the word LIBERTY as in regular United States issues.

|  | F | VF | EF | AU | Unc. |
|---|---|---|---|---|---|
| 1849 FIVE DOL. *(all varieties)* | $900 | $1,400 | $1,900 | $2,500 | $6,000 |
| 1850 FIVE DOL. *(all varieties)* | 900 | 1,500 | 2,000 | 2,750 | 6,500 |
| 1849 TEN DOL. | 1,800 | 2,750 | 5,500 | 9,000 | 18,000 |
| 1849 TEN D. | 1,900 | 2,900 | 6,000 | 10,000 | 20,000 |

## UNITED STATES ASSAY OFFICE

### Augustus Humbert

### United States Assayer of Gold, 1851

When Augustus Humbert was appointed United States assayer, he placed his name and the government imprint on the ingots of gold issued by Moffat & Co. The assay office, a provisional government mint, was a temporary expedient to accommodate the Californians until the establishment of a permanent branch mint. The fifty-dollar gold piece was accepted as legal tender on a par with standard U.S. gold coins.

### *Lettered Edge Varieties*

|  | F | VF | EF | AU | Unc. |
|---|---|---|---|---|---|
| 1851 50 D C 880 THOUS., No 50 on Reverse. Sunk in Edge: AUGUSTUS HUMBERT UNITED STATES ASSAYER OF GOLD CALIFORNIA 1851 | $10,500 | $16,000 | $25,000 | $32,000 | $65,000 |

**50 on Reverse**

| | F | VF | EF | AU | Unc. |
|---|---|---|---|---|---|
| 1851 50 D C 880 THOUS, Similar to Last Variety, but 50 on Reverse | $11,000 | $20,000 | $27,000 | $50,000 | $85,000 |
| 1851 50 D C, 887 THOUS., With 50 on Reverse | 10,000 | 18,000 | 25,000 | 40,000 | 70,000 |

## *Reeded Edge Varieties*

| | F | VF | EF | AU | Unc. |
|---|---|---|---|---|---|
| 1851 FIFTY DOLLS, 880 THOUS., "Target" Reverse | $7,000 | $9,000 | $13,000 | $21,000 | $35,000 |
| 1851 FIFTY DOLLS, 887 THOUS., "Target" Reverse | 7,000 | 9,000 | 13,000 | 21,000 | 35,000 |
| 1852 FIFTY DOLLS, 887 THOUS., "Target" Reverse | 7,000 | 9,000 | 13,000 | 22,000 | 37,500 |

Moffat & Co. proceeded in January 1852 to issue a new ten-dollar piece bearing the stamp MOFFAT & CO.

| | F | VF | EF | AU | Unc. |
|---|---|---|---|---|---|
| 1852 TEN D. MOFFAT & CO. (Close Date) | $1,900 | $3,200 | $6,500 | $15,000 | $35,000 |

| | F | VF | EF | AU | Unc. |
|---|---|---|---|---|---|
| 1852 TEN DOLS. 1852, 2 Over 1 | $1,650 | $2,750 | $4,200 | $7,000 | $14,500 |
| 1852 TEN DOLS. | 1,350 | 2,000 | 2,750 | 5,000 | 12,500 |

| | F | VF | EF | AU | Unc. |
|---|---|---|---|---|---|
| 1852 TWENTY DOLS., 1852, 2 Over 1 | $3,500 | $5,200 | $10,000 | $19,500 | $46,000 |

## United States Assay Office of Gold – 1852

The firm of Moffat & Co. was reorganized by Curtis, Perry, and Ward, who assumed the government contract to conduct the United States Assay Office of Gold.

| | F | VF | EF | AU | Unc. |
|---|---|---|---|---|---|
| 1852 FIFTY DOLLS., 887 THOUS. | $7,200 | $9,500 | $15,000 | $21,000 | $38,000 |
| 1852 FIFTY DOLLS., 900 THOUS. | 7,500 | 10,000 | 16,500 | 23,000 | 45,000 |

| | F | VF | EF | AU | Unc. |
|---|---|---|---|---|---|
| 1852 TEN DOLS., 884 THOUS. | $1,000 | $1,650 | $2,500 | $4,000 | $9,000 |
| 1853 TEN D., 884 THOUS. | 3,500 | 7,000 | 13,500 | 18,000 | 35,000 |
| 1853 TEN D., 900 THOUS. | 2,000 | 3,000 | 4,500 | 8,000 | 12,000 |
| 1853 TWENTY D., 884 THOUS. | 3,500 | 5,000 | 9,000 | 14,000 | 25,000 |
| 1853 TWENTY D., 900 THOUS. | 1,250 | 1,650 | 2,500 | 3,500 | 6,500 |

## Moffat & Company Gold

The last Moffat issue was an 1853 twenty-dollar piece that is very similar to the U.S. double eagle of that period. It was struck after the retirement of John L. Moffat from Moffat & Company.

| | F | VF | EF | AU | Unc. |
|---|---|---|---|---|---|
| 1853, TWENTY D. | $2,000 | $2,600 | $3,900 | $6,750 | $16,000 |

# CINCINNATI MINING & TRADING CO. (1849)

The origin and location of this company are unknown. It might have been organized in Ohio, and conducted business in California.

| | EF | Unc. |
|---|---|---|
| 1849 FIVE DOLLARS | — | — |
| 1849 TEN DOLLARS | $350,000 | — |

## MASSACHUSETTS AND CALIFORNIA COMPANY

This company was believed to have been organized in Northampton, Massachusetts, in May 1849. Pieces with 5D are not genuine.

| | F | VF | EF |
|---|---|---|---|
| 1849 FIVE D. | $65,000 | $95,000 | $150,000 |

## MINERS' BANK
### SAN FRANCISCO 1849

The institution of Wright & Co., exchange brokers located in Portsmouth Square, San Francisco, was known as the Miners' Bank.

A ten-dollar piece was issued in the autumn of 1849, but the coins were not readily accepted because they were worth less than face value.

| | VF | EF | AU | Unc. |
|---|---|---|---|---|
| (1849) TEN D. | $9,000 | $16,500 | $25,000 | $45,000 |

## J.S. ORMSBY
### SACRAMENTO 1849

The initials J.S.O., which appear on certain issues of California privately coined gold pieces, represent the firm of J.S. Ormsby & Co. The firm struck both five- and ten-dollar denominations, all undated.

| | VF |
|---|---|
| (1849) 5 DOLLS *(unique)* | — |
| (1849) 10 DOLLS *(4 known)* | $175,000 |

## PACIFIC COMPANY, SAN FRANCISCO 1849

The origin of the Pacific Company is uncertain. All data regarding the firm are based on conjecture.

Edgar H. Adams wrote that he believed that the coins bearing the stamp of the Pacific Company were produced by the coining firm of Broderick and Kohler. The coins were probably hand struck with the aid of a sledgehammer.

| | EF |
|---|---|
| 1849, 1 DOLLAR *(2 known)* | — |
| 1849, 5 DOLLARS *(4 known)* | $200,000 |
| 1849, 10 DOLLARS *(4 known)* | 300,000 |

## F.D. KOHLER
## CALIFORNIA STATE ASSAYER 1850

The State Assay Office was authorized on April 12, 1850. That year, Governor Peter Burnett appointed F.D. Kohler, who thereupon sold his assaying business to Baldwin & Co. Kohler served at both the San Francisco and Sacramento offices. The State Assay Offices were discontinued when the U.S. Assay Office was established, on February 1, 1851. Ingots ranged from $36.55 to $150.00.

| | EF |
|---|---|
| $36.55 Sacramento | — |
| $37.31 San Francisco | — |
| $40.07 San Francisco | — |
| $45.34 San Francisco | — |
| $50.00 San Francisco | — |
| $54.09 San Francisco | — |

## DUBOSQ & COMPANY
## SAN FRANCISCO 1850

Theodore Dubosq, a Philadelphia jeweler, took melting and coining machinery to San Francisco in 1849.

|  | VF |
|---|---|
| 1850, FIVE D. | $100,000 |
| 1850, TEN D. | 100,000 |

## BALDWIN & CO.
## SAN FRANCISCO 1850

George C. Baldwin and Thomas S. Holman were in the jewelry business in San Francisco and were known as Baldwin & Co. They were the successors to F.D. Kohler & Co., taking over its machinery and other equipment in May 1850.

|  | F | VF | EF | AU | Unc. |
|---|---|---|---|---|---|
| 1850, FIVE DOL. | $3,750 | $6,200 | $12,000 | $18,000 | $25,000 |
| 1850, TEN DOLLARS, Horseman Type | 19,000 | 35,000 | 50,000 | 70,000 | 110,000 |

|  | F | VF | EF | AU | Unc. |
|---|---|---|---|---|---|
| 1851, TEN D. | $5,000 | $12,500 | $18,000 | $29,000 | $67,500 |

| | VF | EF | AU | Unc. |
|---|---|---|---|---|
| 1851 TWENTY D. . . . . . . . . . . . . . . . . . . . . . . . . . . . . . . . . . . . . . . . . . . . | $100,000 | $170,000 | — | — |

## SHULTZ & COMPANY
## SAN FRANCISCO 1851

The firm, located in back of Baldwin's establishment, operated a brass foundry beginning in 1851. Judge G.W. Shultz and William T. Garratt were partners in the enterprise.

| | F | VF |
|---|---|---|
| 1851, FIVE D. . . . . . . . . . . . . . . . . . . . . . . . . . . . . . . . . . . . . . . . . . . . . . . . . . . . . . . . | $16,000 | $33,000 |

## DUNBAR & COMPANY
## SAN FRANCISCO 1851

Edward E. Dunbar operated the California Bank in San Francisco. Dunbar later returned to New York City and organized the famous Continental Bank Note Co.

| | EF |
|---|---|
| 1851, FIVE D. . . . . . . . . . . . . . . . . . . . . . . . . . . . . . . . . . . . . . . . . . . . . . . . . . . . . . . . . . | $160,000 |

## WASS, MOLITOR & CO.
## SAN FRANCISCO 1852–1855

The gold-smelting and assaying plant of Wass, Molitor & Co. was operated by two Hungarian patriots, Count S.C. Wass and A.P. Molitor. They maintained an excellent laboratory and complete apparatus for analysis and coinage of gold.

| | F | VF | EF | AU | Unc. |
|---|---|---|---|---|---|
| 1852, FIVE DOLLARS .................................... | $2,100 | $4,100 | $8,500 | $15,000 | $29,000 |

**Large Head**                    **Small Head**

| | F | VF | EF | AU | Unc. |
|---|---|---|---|---|---|
| 1852, TEN D., Large Head .......................... | $1,400 | $2,200 | $3,750 | $7,000 | $12,500 |
| 1852, TEN D., Small Head .......................... | 3,200 | 4,250 | 10,000 | 16,000 | 37,000 |
| 1855, TEN D. ....................................... | 6,100 | 9,100 | 12,500 | 15,000 | 30,000 |

**Large Head**                    **Small Head**

| | F | VF | EF | AU | Unc. |
|---|---|---|---|---|---|
| 1855, TWENTY DOL., Large Head ...................... | — | — | $175,000 | — | — |
| 1855, TWENTY DOL., Small Head ...................... | $6,500 | $16,000 | 20,000 | $40,000 | $75,000 |

| | F | VF | EF | AU | Unc. |
|---|---|---|---|---|---|
| 1855, 50 DOLLARS | $12,500 | $17,000 | $20,000 | $40,000 | $85,000 |

## KELLOGG & CO.
## SAN FRANCISCO 1854–1855

When the U.S. Assay Office ceased operations, a period ensued during which no private firm was striking gold. The new San Francisco branch mint did not produce coins for some months after Curtis & Perry took the government contract. The lack of coin was again keenly felt by businessmen, who petitioned Kellogg & Richter to "supply the vacuum" by issuing private coin. Their plea was soon answered, for on February 9, 1854, Kellogg & Co. placed their first twenty-dollar piece in circulation.

| | F | VF | EF | AU | Unc. | PF |
|---|---|---|---|---|---|---|
| 1854, TWENTY D. | $1,500 | $2,000 | $2,750 | $4,500 | $11,000 | |
| 1855, TWENTY D. | 1,500 | 2,000 | 3,200 | 5,000 | 13,500 | |
| 1855, FIFTY DOLLS. | | | | | | $200,000 |

## OREGON EXCHANGE COMPANY
## OREGON CITY 1849
### The Beaver Coins of Oregon

On February 16, 1849, the territorial legislature passed an act providing for a mint and specified five- and ten-dollar gold coins without alloy. Oregon City, the largest city in the territory with a population of about 1,000, was designated as the location for the mint. However, Oregon was then brought into the United States as a territory. When the new governor arrived on March 2, he declared the coinage act unconstitutional. Still, a local company coined these private pieces.

|  | F | VF | EF | AU | Unc. |
|---|---|---|---|---|---|
| 1849 5 D. | $15,000 | $23,000 | $31,000 | $66,000 | — |
| 1849 TEN.D | 37,000 | 68,000 | 120,000 | 175,000 | — |

## MORMON GOLD PIECES
## SALT LAKE CITY, UTAH, 1849–1860

Brigham Young was the instigator of the coinage system and personally supervised the mint, which was housed in a little adobe building in Salt Lake City. The mint was inaugurated late in 1848 as a public convenience.

|  | F | VF | EF | AU | Unc. |
|---|---|---|---|---|---|
| 1849, TWO.AND.HALF.DO. | $5,500 | $9,000 | $15,000 | $26,000 | $40,000 |
| 1849, FIVE.DOLLARS | 4,000 | 8,000 | 14,000 | 16,500 | 31,000 |

|  | F | VF | EF |
|---|---|---|---|
| 1849, TEN.DOLLARS | $100,000 | $150,000 | $185,000 |
| 1849, TWENTY.DOLLARS | 40,000 | 77,500 | 100,000 |

|  | F | VF | EF | AU | Unc. |
|---|---|---|---|---|---|
| 1850, FIVE DOLLARS | $4,750 | $8,500 | $13,000 | $23,000 | $45,000 |
| 1860, 5.D. | 9,000 | 16,500 | 22,000 | 32,500 | 45,000 |

## COLORADO GOLD PIECES
### Clark, Gruber & Co.
### Denver 1860–1861

Clark, Gruber & Co. was a well-known private minting firm in Denver, Colorado, in the early 1860s.

|  | F | VF | EF | AU | Unc. |
|---|---|---|---|---|---|
| 1860, 2 1/2 D | $850 | $1,250 | $2,000 | $3,200 | $6,750 |
| 1860, FIVE D | 950 | 1,500 | 2,100 | 3,750 | 7,000 |

|  | F | VF | EF | AU | Unc. |
|---|---|---|---|---|---|
| 1860, TEN D | $4,000 | $6,000 | $9,000 | $16,000 | $27,000 |
| 1860, TWENTY D | 25,000 | 42,500 | 80,000 | 120,000 | 250,000 |

|  | F | VF | EF | AU | Unc. |
|---|---|---|---|---|---|
| 1861, 2 1/2 D | $900 | $1,400 | $2,100 | $3,500 | $8,000 |
| 1861, FIVE D | 1,200 | 1,700 | 2,600 | 4,700 | 17,000 |
| 1861, TEN D | 1,200 | 1,800 | 2,750 | 4,750 | 15,000 |

|                        | F      | VF      | EF      | AU      |
|------------------------|--------|---------|---------|---------|
| 1861, TWENTY D.        | $7,000 | $16,000 | $26,000 | $50,000 |

### John Parsons & Company
### Tarryall Mines – Colorado, 1861

Very little is known regarding the mint of John Parsons and Co., although it is reasonably certain that it operated in the South Park section of Park County, Colorado, near the original town of Tarryall, in the summer of 1861.

|                              | VF      |
|------------------------------|---------|
| (1861) Undated 2 1/2 D.      | $95,000 |
| (1861) Undated FIVE D.       | 125,000 |

### J.J. Conway & Co.
### Georgia Gulch, Colorado, 1861

Records show that the Conway mint operated for a short while in 1861. As in all gold mining areas, the value of gold dust caused disagreement among the merchants and the miners. The firm of J.J. Conway & Co. solved this difficulty by bringing out its gold pieces in August 1861.

|                                 | VF      |
|---------------------------------|---------|
| (1861) Undated 2 1/2 DOLL'S     | $75,000 |
| (1861) Undated FIVE DOLLARS     | 100,000 |
| (1861) Undated TEN DOLLARS      | —       |

## CALIFORNIA SMALL-DENOMINATION GOLD

There was a scarcity of small coins during the California Gold Rush and, starting in 1852, quarter, half, and dollar pieces were privately minted from native gold to alleviate the shortage. The need and acceptability of these pieces declined after 1856 and they then became popular as souvenirs. Authentic pieces all have CENTS, DOLLAR, or an abbreviation thereof on the reverse. The tokens are much less valuable. Modern restrikes and replicas (often having a bear in the design) have no numismatic value.

The values in the following charts are only for coins made before 1883 with the denomination on the reverse expressed as CENTS, DOL., DOLL., or DOLLAR.

### Quarter Dollar – Octagonal

|  | EF-40 | AU-50 | MS-60 |
|---|---|---|---|
| Liberty Head | $75 | $100 | $170 |
| Indian Head | 90 | 125 | 175 |
| Washington Head | 350 | 550 | 850 |

### Quarter Dollar – Round

|  | EF-40 | AU-50 | MS-60 |
|---|---|---|---|
| Liberty Head | $75 | $100 | $170 |
| Indian Head | 80 | 110 | 200 |
| Washington Head | 350 | 550 | 750 |

### Half Dollar – Octagonal

|  | EF-40 | AU-50 | MS-60 |
|---|---|---|---|
| Liberty Head | $75 | $100 | $175 |
| Liberty Head / Eagle | 400 | 600 | 1,000 |
| Indian Head | 85 | 125 | 270 |

### Half Dollar – Round

|  | EF-40 | AU-50 | MS-60 |
|---|---|---|---|
| Liberty Head | $85 | $125 | $225 |
| Indian Head | 75 | 110 | 185 |

### Dollar – Octagonal

|  | EF-40 | AU-50 | MS-60 |
|---|---|---|---|
| Liberty Head | $200 | $300 | $650 |
| Liberty Head / Eagle | 800 | 1,500 | 2,000 |
| Indian Head | 250 | 400 | 700 |

### Dollar – Round

|  | EF-40 | AU-50 | MS-60 |
|---|---|---|---|
| Liberty Head | $900 | $1,350 | $2,000 |
| Indian Head | 900 | 1,350 | 2,250 |

## HARD TIMES TOKENS (1832–1844)

During the financial crises of 1832 to 1844 many government coins were hoarded, and privately made tokens were used out of necessity. The so-called Hard Times tokens of this period were slightly smaller and lighter than normal large cents. They were made of copper or brass and are of two general groups: political tokens whose theme centered on President Andrew Jackson's fight against the Bank of the United States, and tradesmen's cards, issued by merchants. Many different designs and varieties exist.

| | VF | EF |
|---|---|---|
| Hard Times Tokens, 1832–1844, most common pieces ............................... | $12 | $25 |

## CIVIL WAR TOKENS (1860s)

Civil War tokens are generally divided into two groups: tradesmen's tokens, and anonymously issued pieces with political or patriotic themes. They came into existence only because of the scarcity of government coins and disappeared as soon as the bronze coins of 1864 met the public demand for small copper change.

These tokens vary greatly in composition and design. A number were more or less faithful imitations of the copper-nickel cent. A few of this type have the word NOT in very small letters above the words ONE CENT.

| | F | VF | EF | Unc. |
|---|---|---|---|---|
| Copper or Brass Tokens ......................................... | $7 | $12 | $15 | $25 |
| Nickel or German Silver Tokens .................................. | 18 | 25 | 55 | 100 |
| White-Metal Tokens ............................................. | 25 | 30 | 45 | 80 |
| Copper-Nickel Tokens ........................................... | 30 | 50 | 80 | 125 |
| Silver Tokens .................................................. | 75 | 150 | 225 | 400 |

Values shown are for the most common tokens in each composition.

# BULLION VALUES

These charts show the bullion values of common-date circulation-strike silver and gold coins. These are intrinsic values and do not reflect any numismatic premium a coin might have. The weight listed under each denomination is its actual silver weight (ASW) or actual gold weight (AGW). Dealers generally purchase common silver coins at around 15% below bullion value, and sell them at around 15% above bullion value. Nearly all U.S. gold coins have an additional numismatic premium beyond their bullion content. Gold bullion values here are based on AGW only; consult a coin dealer to ascertain current buy and sell prices.

## Bullion Values of Silver Coins

| Silver Price Per Ounce | Wartime Nickel .05626 oz. | Dime .07234 oz. | Quarter .18084 oz. | Half Dollar .36169 oz. | Silver Clad Half Dollar .14792 oz. | Silver Dollar .77344 oz. |
|---|---|---|---|---|---|---|
| $17.50 | $0.98 | $1.27 | $3.16 | $6.33 | $2.59 | $13.54 |
| 20.00 | 1.13 | 1.45 | 3.62 | 7.23 | 2.96 | 15.47 |
| 22.50 | 1.27 | 1.63 | 4.07 | 8.14 | 3.33 | 17.40 |
| 25.00 | 1.41 | 1.81 | 4.52 | 9.04 | 3.70 | 19.34 |
| 27.50 | 1.55 | 1.99 | 4.97 | 9.95 | 4.07 | 21.27 |
| 30.00 | 1.69 | 2.17 | 5.43 | 10.85 | 4.44 | 23.20 |
| 32.50 | 1.83 | 2.35 | 5.88 | 11.75 | 4.81 | 25.14 |
| 35.00 | 1.97 | 2.53 | 6.33 | 12.66 | 5.18 | 27.07 |
| 37.50 | 2.11 | 2.71 | 6.78 | 13.56 | 5.55 | 29.00 |
| 40.00 | 2.25 | 2.89 | 7.23 | 14.47 | 5.92 | 30.94 |
| 42.50 | 2.39 | 3.07 | 7.69 | 15.37 | 6.29 | 32.87 |
| 45.00 | 2.53 | 3.26 | 8.14 | 16.28 | 6.66 | 34.80 |
| 47.50 | 2.67 | 3.44 | 8.59 | 17.18 | 7.03 | 36.74 |
| 50.00 | 2.81 | 3.62 | 9.04 | 18.08 | 7.40 | 38.67 |

## Bullion Values of Gold Coins

| Gold Price Per Ounce | $5.00 Liberty Head 1839–1908 Indian Head 1908–1929 .24187 oz. | $10.00 Liberty Head 1838–1907 Indian Head 1907–1933 .48375 oz. | $20.00 1849–1933 .96750 oz. |
|---|---|---|---|
| $900 | $217.68 | $435.38 | $870.75 |
| 950 | 229.78 | 459.56 | 919.13 |
| 1,000 | 241.87 | 483.75 | 967.50 |
| 1,050 | 253.96 | 507.94 | 1,015.88 |
| 1,100 | 266.06 | 532.13 | 1,064.25 |
| 1,150 | 278.15 | 556.31 | 1,112.63 |
| 1,200 | 290.24 | 580.50 | 1,161.00 |
| 1,250 | 302.34 | 604.69 | 1,209.38 |
| 1,300 | 314.43 | 628.88 | 1,257.75 |
| 1,350 | 326.52 | 653.06 | 1,306.13 |
| 1,400 | 338.62 | 677.25 | 1,354.50 |
| 1,450 | 350.71 | 701.44 | 1,402.88 |
| 1,500 | 362.81 | 725.63 | 1,451.25 |
| 1,550 | 374.90 | 749.81 | 1,499.63 |
| 1,600 | 386.99 | 774.00 | 1,548.00 |
| 1,650 | 399.09 | 798.19 | 1,596.38 |
| 1,700 | 411.18 | 822.38 | 1,644.75 |
| 1,750 | 423.27 | 846.56 | 1,693.13 |
| 1,800 | 435.37 | 870.75 | 1,741.50 |
| 1,850 | 447.46 | 894.94 | 1,789.88 |
| 1,900 | 459.55 | 919.13 | 1,838.25 |

Note: The U.S. bullion coins first issued in 1986 are unlike the older regular issues. They contain the following amounts of pure metal: silver $1, 1 oz.; gold $50, 1 oz.; gold $25, 1/2 oz.; gold $10, 1/4 oz.; gold $5, 1/10 oz.

Is it time to sell your coins? Perhaps you've inherited some of them; or maybe you've collected for years, and you want to explore a new pastime or you need to cash in on your investment. In any case, you have some decisions to make. Will you sell your collection privately, or at a public auction—or perhaps sell it yourself on the Internet? Will you sell locally or to dealers nationwide? What are the benefits of each path, and which will bring the greatest profits? To get started, ask yourself:

## WHAT AM I SELLING?

**Rolls of Modern Coins; Proof Sets; Modern Commemoratives; Bullion; Etc.** This includes bulk investment coins, such as American Eagle bullion pieces, bags of common circulated coins, and so on. It also includes modern commemoratives and coin sets, not all of which have increased in value in the secondary market. Such accumulations are best sold privately to a coin dealer or to another collector. Auctioning them yourself, on the Internet, is another route. Consigning them to an auction house is not likely to be your best option; this venue is typically reserved for scarcer coins.

**Coins With Sentimental—but Not Necessarily High-Dollar—Value.** You might have inherited an accumulation (as opposed to a studiously compiled collection) of coins—for example, a coffee can full of wheat cents. Your local coin dealer can make you an offer, either buying the entire lot or searching through them to "cherrypick" the better pieces. If you have the time, you might sell them yourself, through an Internet auction site. Also, you might donate them to a local Boy Scout troop or similar organization (this may be tax-deductible).

**Rare and/or Significant Coins.** For rare, valuable, and historically significant coins, public consigned auctions are often the best way to sell—dedicated collectors know they're good sources for scarce coins. A coin consigned to a well-established auction house with numismatic experience will be carefully studied, cataloged, and presented to a serious audience. You save the time and effort of searching for potential buyers. The auction firm makes money by collecting a commission on each sale.

Another option for selling your rare and significant coins is to approach a dealer nationally recognized as an expert in the field—for example, a specialist who focuses on colonial coins. You can also receive tax benefits from donating your coins to the American Numismatic Association (ANA), the American Numismatic Society, or a museum.

## SELLING TO A COIN SHOP

Your local coin shop has the advantage of the personal touch. Good coin-shop proprietors are happy to educate and advise their customers. An active coin dealer stays up to date on the hobby and the market, knows about tax and estate laws that might affect your sale, and can study your collection and make educated decisions. Many dealers have a wide audience for selling coins—which provides the leverage to offer you a good price.

A coin shop can be a venue for selling numismatic items of any value. The owner can often make you an offer and write you a check on the spot. Of course, very rare or specialized coins will likely fetch a higher price at public auction.

You should feel comfortable with the integrity of the shop's proprietor and staff. Talk to coin-collector friends, inquire at the local coin club, and check with the Better Business Bureau. Look at the shop's Web site, advertisements, and flyers or publications—do they project fairness and professionalism?

Coin shops can be found in a phone book or online business directory. Call to make sure the owner or a qualified assistant will be there to examine your coins. A busy dealer can schedule a convenient time to meet with you. Solicit at least two quotes before you decide to sell.

## SELLING THROUGH THE MAIL

You can ship your coins to a dealer for their offer; again, trust is important. Does the dealer belong to the ANA or the Professional Numismatists Guild? Does he advertise in hobby newspapers such as *Coin World* and *Numismatic News?* Search the dealer's name on the Internet: do you find satisfied customers, or complaints and concerns?

Inquire by mail, email, or phone before shipping any coins. The dealer might request a list beforehand, and should be able to give you a general idea of value without seeing the coins in person. Once you're comfortable and have decided to sell, ask the dealer for advice on shipping and insurance. Keep in mind that the dealer will need to examine your coins before making a firm offer.

Even if you live near a coin shop, you can broaden the playing field if you're open to selling your coins through the mail to established, respected dealers. This is a good option if you have the time. The entire transaction (finding dealers; packing and shipping; waiting for the check) will likely take longer than getting a local offer.

## SELLING TO A DEALER AT A COIN SHOW

Between the national coin shows and the hundreds of coin clubs that sponsor city and regional shows, chances are a show is held somewhere near you at least once a year. With dozens or even hundreds of dealers in one venue, you can shop your coins around before you sell; and, as at coin shop, payment is immediate.

Remember, a coin show is a public venue. Be alert; use common sense. Outside the show, do not publicize the fact that you're carrying valuable coins.

Most shows list participating dealers in their programs. Decide in advance the ones you want to approach (e.g., the silver-dollar specialists, if you have Morgan dollars to sell). Or simply stroll the aisles and introduce yourself to dealers who sell items similar to those in your collection. This is all part of the fun of a coin show.

## CONSIGNING AT A PUBLIC AUCTION

Numismatic auction firms are often connected to larger retailers that also sell through the mail, online, etc. As always, reputation is important. Study a potential auctioneer's Web site; learn about their staff, past sales results, any media coverage they might receive. Look at their catalogs: are they professionally made? The effort and experience an auction firm brings to its work will affect how much your coins sell for.

## SELLING ONLINE

Selling your coins yourself online can be fun, but it requires time and (usually) some skill with scanning or photography. Each auction site has its own rules, policies, and rates; read them carefully. Be security-conscious (e.g., rent a Post Office box instead of using your home address, and insist on full, guaranteed payment before you ship any coins). You can also use the Internet to sell your coins at a fixed price, through a bulletin-board posting or other announcement. Any online sale to the public requires you to take on responsibilities similar to those of a coin shop or auction firm. There is work involved, but the experience can be enjoyable and profitable.

---

You now have a good, basic understanding of how to sell your coins. For more information, visit your local library or bookstore. *The Expert's Guide to Collecting and Investing in Rare Coins* (Bowers) and the *Whitman Guide to Coin Collecting* (Bressett) are two recommended resources. Best wishes for a successful sale!